THE STUDENT'S
COMPLETE
VOCABULARY GUIDE
TO THE
GREEK
NEW TESTAMENT

THE STUDENT'S
COMPLETE
VOCABULARY GUIDE
TO THE
GREEK
NEW TESTAMENT

*Complete Frequency Lists,
Cognate Groupings & Principal Parts*

WARREN C. TRENCHARD

ZondervanPublishingHouse
Academic and Professional Books
Grand Rapids, Michigan
A Division of HarperCollinsPublishers

The Student's Complete Vocabulary Guide to the Greek New Testament
Copyright © 1992 by Warren C. Trenchard

Requests for information should be addressed to:
Zondervan Publishing House
Academic and Professional Books
Grand Rapids, Michigan 49530

Library of Congress Cataloging-in-Publication Data

Trenchard, Warren C. (Warren Charles)
    The student's complete vocabulary guide to the Greek New Testament /
Warren Trenchard.
        p.   cm.
    Includes bibliographical references and index.
    ISBN 0-310-53341-4
    1. Greek language, Biblical–Vocabulary   2. Bible. N.T.–Language, style.
    I. Title.
PA863.T74   1992
487'.4–dc20   92-33255
                                                                                CIP

Cover design by Art Jacobs

Printed in the United States of America

92 93 94 95 96 /   / 10 9 8 7 6 5 4 3 2 1

τοῖς μαθηταῖς μου τῆς Ἑλληνικῆς γλώσσης

Contents

Preface

The idea for this book came to me several years ago, while teaching intermediate NT Greek. One of the textbooks I used was *Lexical Aids for Students of New Testament Greek* by Bruce M. Metzger, first published in 1946. I had students learn part of the vocabulary of the NT according to his frequency lists, which included only the common words that occur ten or more times, i.e., 1066 words. However, I was especially intrigued by the possibilities of more efficient learning through the use of his second part, "Words Classified According to Their Root." Unfortunately, this section of Metzger's book was more illustrative than complete. I decided to prepare a volume that would build on this model by including all the common words of the NT vocabulary that have a cognate relationship with at least one other word.

I also felt that such a volume should include the complete vocabulary of 5425 words, listed according to frequency of use. It should also have a complete list of all the verbs of the NT with their principal parts that are found in the NT, a list of all the proper words of the NT, and a variety of other lists.

In the meantime, two other similar books were published: Robert E. Van Voorst's *Building Your New Testament Greek Vocabulary* (1990) and Thomas A. Robinson's *Mastering Greek Vocabulary* (1990). Each has extended the cognate root approach of Metzger's second section. While these volumes have many commendable characteristics and qualities, neither has attempted to include the entire NT vocabulary.

I have used the following main sources in the preparation of this volume:

Abbott-Smith, G. *A Manual Greek Lexicon of the New Testament.* 3d ed. New York: Charles Schribner's Sons, 1937.

Aland, Kurt; Black, Matthew; Martini, Carlo M.; Metzger, Bruce M.; and Wikgren, Allen; eds. *The Greek New Testament.* 3d ed. (corrected). [New York]: United Bible Societies, 1983.

Bauer, Walter. *A Greek-English Lexicon of the New Testament and Other Early Christian Literature.* Edited by William F. Arndt and F. Wilbur Gingrich. 2d ed. by F. Wilbur Gingrich and Frederick W. Danker. Chicago: The University of Chicago Press, 1979.

Blass, F., and Debrunner, A. *A Greek Grammar of the New Testament and Other Early Christian Literature.* Translated and revised by Robert W. Funk. Chicago: The University of Chicago Press, 1961.

Concordance to the Novum Testamentum Graece of Nestle-Aland, 26th Edition, and to the Greek New Testament, 3rd Edition. 3d ed. Edited by the Institute for New Testament Textual Research and the Computer Center of Münster University. Berlin: Walter de Gruyter, 1987.

GRAMCORD. Version 4.05b. [A computerized grammatical concordance of the Greek NT.]

Greenlee, J. Harold. *A New Testament Greek Morpheme Lexicon*. Grand Rapids, Michigan: Zondervan Publishing House, 1983.

Liddell, Henry George, and Scott, Robert. *A Greek-English Lexicon*. New ed. by Henry Stuart Jones. Oxford: Clarendon Press, 1940.

Louw, Johannes P., and Nida, Eugene A., eds. *Greek-English Lexicon of the New Testament Based on Semantic Domains*. 2 vols. 2d ed. New York: United Bible Societies, 1989.

Marinone, N. *All the Greek Verbs*. London: Duckworth, 1985.

Moule, C. F. D. *An Idiom Book of New Testament Greek*. 2d ed. Cambridge: Cambridge University Press, 1959.

Moulton, James Hope. *A Grammar of New Testament Greek*. 4 vols. Vol. 2 edited by Wilbert Francis Howard. Vols. 3 and 4 by Nigel Turner. Edinburgh: T. & T. Clark, 1906-76.

Moulton, James Hope, and Milligan, George. *The Vocabulary of the Greek Testament Illustrated from the Papyri and Other Non-Literary Sources*. London: Hodder and Stoughton, 1930.

Newman, Jr., Barclay M. *A Concise Greek-English Dictionary of the New Testament*. London: United Bible Societies, 1971.

Robertson, A. T. *A Grammar of the Greek New Testament in the Light of Historical Research*. Nashville, Tennessee: Broadman Press, 1934.

I am pleased to acknowledge my deep debt and to express my sincere gratitude to many people, without whose assistance this book would not likely have been published. My student Liisa Hawes did all the initial data collection. My son Mark Trenchard entered the data into the computer database and assisted with editing. My colleague Randy Chenowith prepared the desktop publishing models and provided general counsel on computer-related matters. My colleague Kay Nelson provided access to special computer equipment. My student Craig Newitt did the final formatting and entered many of the corrections. My colleagues Ed Rice and Dianne Straub assisted with the final production. My editor at Zondervan, Ed van der Maas, believed in this project from the beginning and provided invaluable guidance and numerous suggestions for improvement. Of course, I take responsibity for the work, including its errors and mistakes. I am also very grateful to Canadian Union College and Parkland ColorPress Ltd. for the use of computer, printer, and typesetting equipment.

Finally, I thank my wife, Marilyn, and my sons, Mark, David, and Kevin, for their understanding and patience during the thousands of hours that I spent on this project. However, such an acknowledgment is small consolation for what we could have been doing together.

Warren C. Trenchard
Canadian Union College
20 August 1992

Abbreviations

acc.	accusative	neut.	neuter
act.	active	nom.	nominative
adj.	adjective	NT	New Testament
adv.	adverb	opp.	opposite
aor.	aorist	part.	particle
comp.	comparative	partic.	participle
conj.	conjunction	pass.	passive
contr.	contraction	perf.	perfect
dat.	dative	pers.	personified
dep.	deponent	pl.	plural
esp.	especially	plup.	pluperfect
fem.	feminine	pos.	positive
fig.	figurative	poss.	possible/possibly
form.	formula	prep.	preposition
fut.	future	pres.	present
gen.	genitive	prn.	pronoun
gener.	generally	prob.	probably
imper.	imperative	prop.	properly
impers.	impersonal	sing.	singular
impf.	imperfect	subst.	substantive
impr.	improper	superl.	superlative
interrog.	interrogative	trans.	transitive
intrans.	intransitive	UBS³	United Bible Societies, *The Greek New Testament*, Third Edition (Corrected)
lit.	literal		
masc.	masculine		
met.	metaphorical		
mid.	middle	untrans.	untranslatable
neg.	negative	w.	with

Section One

Cognate Word Groups

The most efficient way to learn a large portion of the vocabulary of the Greek NT is to study the words in cognate groups. This section, consisting of almost 4,900 entries, lists all the common words of the NT (i.e., all words other than proper words) which have a cognate relationship with at least one other word.

Greek words potentially consist of several components. All words have a basic element, or stem, which conveys the general meaning. Verbs, nouns, adjectives, and adverbs use a wide variety of suffixes to convey particular nuances of meaning. In addition, there are several prefixes, which may be used with any part of speech to form compounds, that have particular meanings. Several lists of these prefixes and suffixes with their general meaning are given below.

Other compounds are formed by the combination of two or more words. In this section, compound words are listed in each group that represents their component parts.

The most common such compounds are those formed by the addition of a preposition to another word. However, because of their high frequency, compounds that involve prepositions are listed only under their nonprepositional parts. The only exceptions are the words which derive solely from prepositions.

Compounding a preposition with another word has various effects. Often, the preposition adds its basic spatial meaning to the word, e.g., βαίνω means "I come," and καταβαίνω means "I come down." Sometimes, the preposition intensifies the meaning of the word or gives it a completely new meaning, e.g., γινώσκω means "I know," but ἀναγινώσκω means "I read." At other times, the preposition has no apparent effect on the word.

The form εὐ- is not actually a prefix. It is the word εὖ, which is itself found in the NT. However, because of its frequent use in compounds, it is treated here as a prefix and not as a key word .

Prefixes

ἀ- (ἀν-)	negative indicator: not, a-, dis-, un-
ἀ-	intensive indicator
δυσ-	negative indicator: bad, mis-, ill-
εὐ-	positive indicator: well, good
νη-	negative indicator: not

Verb Suffixes

-αζω	to do, be, cause
-αινω	to cause, do, be
-αιρω	to do
-ανω	to do
-αω	to do
-ευω	to do, be
-εω	to do, be
-ζω	to do, be
-ιζω	to do, be
-ιρω	to do
-μι	to do
-οω	to cause, do
-σκω	to do, be
-σσω	to do
-υνω	to cause, do
-ω	to do

Noun Suffixes

-αδιον	diminutive, small
-αριδιον	diminutive, small
-αριον	diminutive, small
-εια	quality
-ειον	place
-ευς	agent
-ή, ἡ	product of verb action, other
-ης, ὁ	agent
-ια	quality
-ιά	object, result of action
-ιδιον	diminutive, small
-ιον	diminutive, small, related to
-ιος	related to
-ισκη	diminutive, small
-ισκος	diminutive, small
-ισσα	fem. indicator
-ις	diminutive, small, fem. indicator, object
-λος	characterized by
-μα	object, result of action
-μονη	action, state
-μος	process, state
-ον	object, other
-ος, τό	object, concept
-οτης, ἡ	quality

-σις	action
-συνη	quality
-τηριον	place of action
-της, ὁ	agent, one who does
-τον	object
-τρια	fem. indicator
-τρον	instrument
-τωρ	agent, one who does
-ων	object, quality

Adjective Suffixes

-ην	quality
-ης	quality
-ικος	having characteristics of
-ιμος	fitness, ability
-ινος	made of
-ιος	related to
-ιστος	superl. indicator
-ιων	comp. indicator
-κοντα	multiples of ten
-κοσιοι	multiples of one hundred
-μος	quality
-μων	quality
-νος	pertaining to
-ος	quality
-ους	made of
-πλασιων	multiples indicator, times
-πλους	multiples indicator, times
-ρος	quality
-τατος	superl. indicator, most, -est
-τεος	obligation, intention, must do
-τερος	comp. indicator, more, -er
-τηρος	quality
-τος	possibility, -able
-υς	quality
-ωλος	quality
-ων	comp. indicator, -er, quality
-ως	quality

Adverb Suffixes

-η	manner, location
-θα	reference to place

-θαδε	to or at a place
-θεν	from a place
-ι	of time or place
-ιστα	superl. indicator
-κις	multiples indicator, times
-σε	to a place
-σι	related to time
-τερον	comp. indicator
-τερω	comp. indicator
-τος	related to place
-ω	from
-ως	manner, -ly

The word groups have a particular organization. Each group is headed by a word that is characteristic of the group and that serves as the key word. The words within the groups are listed according to the main parts of speech. For each represented part of speech, the simple forms come before the compound forms. The order of parts of speech within the groups and how to recognize them is as follows:

verbs	generally indicated by the endings *-ω*, *-μαι*, or *-μι*
nouns	indicated by an article, ὁ, ἡ, or τό
adjectives	indicted by two or three gender endings, e.g., *-ος*, *-η*, *-ον*
adverbs	single forms, with the ending *-ως* or one of the adverb suffixes
other words	other single forms

The determination of cognate word groups largely follows those identified by J. Harold Greenlee in *A New Testament Greek Morpheme Lexicon*. In a few instances, the groups depart from Greenlee if both the forms of the words and their meanings differ significantly from each other. One example is Greenlee's group headed by ἄγω. Greenlee is technically right to trace all the words in the group to the root word ἄγω. However, because the group contains several diversely formed word sets with widely different meanings, they are listed in this section as separate groups. These groups are headed by ἀγανακτέω, ἄγγελος, ἀγοράζω, ἄγω, and ἄξιος. This is the most radical departure from Greenlee in the section.

Rarely, a word group in this section combines two of Greenlee's groups. This is done when the words in both groups have clearly related meanings and similar forms.

Where possible, the key words in this section are those identified by Greenlee as root words. However, since Greenlee includes many root words not found in the NT, one cannot always use his root words as the key words. In these cases, key words are selected on the basis of such factors as frequency, similarity to the root word, and meaning.

Where only a set of related compound words occurs in the NT, the words form a group, with one of the compounds serving as the key word. Note, e.g., the groups headed by ἀκολουθέω, ἀνατολή, and καθίζω.

Seventeen groups of words are included whose key words are not used in the NT, because they are compounds whose only link resides in the key word itself. The most important example is the group headed by βαίνω.

The only proper word that serves as a key word is Ζεύς (gen. Διός). This is because it is the basis of the common words διοπετής and εὐδία.

ἀγαθός

ἀγαθοεργέω	(1)	I do good
ἀγαθοποιέω	(9)	I do good, what is right
ἀγαθουργέω	(1)	I do good (contr. of ἀγαθοεργέω)
ἀγαθωσύνη, ης, ἡ	(4)	goodness, uprightness, generosity
ἀγαθοποιΐα, ας, ἡ	(1)	doing good, doing right
ἀγαθός, ή, όν	(102)	good, useful, fit; good, possessions, good things (subst.)
ἀγαθοποιός, όν	(1)	doing good, upright; one who does good (subst. in NT)
ἀφιλάγαθος, ον	(1)	not loving the good
φιλάγαθος, ον	(1)	loving what is good

ἀγαλλιάω

ἀγαλλιάω	(11)	I exult, am glad, overjoyed
ἀγαλλίασις, εως, ἡ	(5)	exultation, extreme joy

ἀγανακτέω

ἀγανακτέω	(7)	I am aroused, indignant, angry
ἀγανάκτησις, εως, ἡ	(1)	indignation

ἀγαπάω

ἀγαπάω	(143)	I love, cherish, show love, long for
ἀγάπη, ης, ἡ	(116)	love, love feast
ἀγαπητός, ή, όν	(61)	beloved, dear

ἄγγελος

ἀγγέλλω	(1)	I announce
ἀναγγέλλω	(14)	I report, disclose, announce, proclaim
ἀπαγγέλλω	(45)	I report, announce, tell, proclaim
διαγγέλλω	(3)	I proclaim far and wide, give notice of
ἐξαγγέλλω	(2)	I proclaim, report, tell
ἐπαγγέλλομαι	(15)	I announce, proclaim, promise, offer, profess
εὐαγγελίζω	(54)	I bring or preach good news, proclaim, preach (act.-mid.)
καταγγέλλω	(18)	I proclaim, make known
παραγγέλλω	(32)	I give orders, command, instruct, direct
προεπαγγέλλω	(2)	I promise beforehand or previously (mid.-pass. in NT)
προευαγγελίζομαι	(1)	I proclaim good news in advance
προκαταγγέλλω	(2)	I announce beforehand, foretell
ἀγγελία, ας, ἡ	(2)	message, command
ἄγγελος, ου, ὁ	(175)	messenger, angel
ἀρχάγγελος, ου, ὁ	(2)	archangel
ἐπαγγελία, ας, ἡ	(52)	promise, pledge, offer, what is promised
ἐπάγγελμα, ατος, τό	(2)	promise
εὐαγγέλιον, ου, τό	(76)	good news, gospel
εὐαγγελιστής, οῦ, ὁ	(3)	one who proclaims good news, evangelist
καταγγελεύς, έως, ὁ	(1)	proclaimer, preacher, herald
παραγγελία, ας, ἡ	(5)	order, command, precept, advice, instruction
ἰσάγγελος, ον	(1)	like a angel

ἄγγος

ἀγγεῖον, ου, τό	(1)	vessel, flask, container
ἄγγος, ους, τό	(1)	vessel, container

ἅγιος

ἁγιάζω	(28)	I make holy, consecrate, sanctify, dedicate, reverence
ἁγνίζω	(7)	I purify, cleanse
ἁγιασμός, οῦ, ὁ	(10)	holiness, consecration, sanctification
ἁγιότης, ητος, ἡ	(1)	holiness
ἁγιωσύνη, ης, ἡ	(3)	holiness
ἁγνεία, ας, ἡ	(2)	purity, chastity
ἁγνισμός, οῦ, ὁ	(1)	purification
ἁγνότης, ητος, ἡ	(2)	purity, sincerity
ἅγιος, α, ον	(233)	dedicated to God, holy, pure; saints, sanctuary (subst.)
ἁγνός, ή, όν	(8)	pure, holy, innocent, chaste
ἁγνῶς	(1)	purely, sincerely

ἀγκάλη

ἐναγκαλίζομαι	(2)	I take in my arms, embrace
ἀγκάλη, ης, ἡ	(1)	arm

ἄγκυρα

ἄγκιστρον, ου, τό	(1)	fishhook
ἄγκυρα, ας, ἡ	(4)	anchor

ἀγοράζω

ἀγοράζω	(30)	I buy, purchase
ἀλληγορέω	(1)	I speak allegorically
δημηγορέω	(1)	I deliver a public address, make a speech
ἐξαγοράζω	(4)	I buy, redeem; make the most of (mid.)
ἀγορά, ᾶς, ἡ	(11)	market place
ἀγοραῖος, ον	(2)	pertaining to a market; loafer, court session (subst.)

ἄγρα

ἀγρεύω	(1)	I catch
ἀγρυπνέω	(4)	I am awake, keep watch, guard
ζωγρέω	(2)	I capture alive, catch
ἄγρα, ας, ἡ	(2)	catching, catch
ἀγρυπνία, ας, ἡ	(2)	wakefulness

ἀγρός

ἀγραυλέω	(1)	I live outdoors
ἀγρός, οῦ, ὁ	(36)	field, country; farms (pl.)
ἀγριέλαιος, ου, ἡ	(2)	wild olive tree
ἄγριος, α, ον	(3)	found in the open field, wild, stormy

ἄγω

ἄγω	(67)	I lead, bring, arrest, guide, spend time, celebrate, go
ἡγεμονεύω	(2)	I am governor, command, rule
ἡγέομαι	(28)	I lead, guide, rule, think, consider
ἀνάγω	(23)	I lead up, bring up, restore; put out to sea (mid. or pass.)
ἀπάγω	(15)	I lead away, bring before, lead; am misled (pass.)

διάγω	(2)	I spend my life, live
διηγέομαι	(8)	I tell, relate, describe
δουλαγωγέω	(1)	I enslave, bring into subjection
εἰσάγω	(11)	I bring in, lead in
ἐκδιηγέομαι	(2)	I tell (in detail)
ἐξάγω	(12)	I lead out, bring out
ἐξηγέομαι	(6)	I explain, interpret, tell, report, describe, make known
ἐπάγω	(3)	I bring upon
ἐπανάγω	(3)	I put out (so sea), go out, return
ἐπισυνάγω	(8)	I gather together
κατάγω	(9)	I lead or bring down; put in (pass.)
κατηγορέω	(23)	I accuse, bring charges against
μετάγω	(2)	I guide, steer, control
ὁδηγέω	(5)	I lead, guide
παράγω	(10)	I pass by or away, go away; pass away, disappear (pass.)
παρεισάγω	(1)	I bring in secretly or maliciously
περιάγω	(6)	I lead around, take about, go around or about
προάγω	(20)	I lead forward or out; go or come before (intrans.)
προηγέομαι	(1)	I outdo, lead the way, consider better
προσαγορεύω	(1)	I call, name, designate
προσάγω	(4)	I bring forward or to
συλαγωγέω	(1)	I carry off as a captive
συνάγω	(59)	I gather, bring together, invite as a guest
συναπάγω	(3)	I am led or carried away (pass. in NT)
ὑπάγω	(79)	I go away, go home, go
χαλιναγωγέω	(2)	I guide with bit and bridle, hold in check, control
χειραγωγέω	(2)	I take or lead by the hand
χορηγέω	(2)	I provide, supply
ἀγέλη, ης, ἡ	(7)	herd
ἀγωγή, ῆς, ἡ	(1)	way of life, conduct
ἡγεμονία, ας, ἡ	(1)	chief command, rule, government
ἡγεμών, όνος, ὁ	(20)	prince, governor, ruler
ἀρχηγός, οῦ, ὁ	(4)	leader, ruler, prince, originator, founder
ἀρχισυνάγωγος, ου, ὁ	(9)	leader or president of a synagogue
διήγησις, εως, ἡ	(1)	narrative, account
ἐπεισαγωγή, ῆς, ἡ	(1)	introduction
ἐπισυναγωγή, ῆς, ἡ	(2)	assembling, meeting
καθηγητής, οῦ, ὁ	(2)	teacher
κατηγορία, ας, ἡ	(3)	accusation, charge
κατήγορος, ου, ὁ	(4)	accuser
κατήγωρ, ορος, ὁ	(1)	accuser
ὁδηγός, οῦ, ὁ	(5)	leader, guide
παιδαγωγός, οῦ, ὁ	(3)	attendant, custodian, guide
πανήγυρις, εως, ἡ	(1)	festal gathering
παρηγορία, ας, ἡ	(1)	comfort
προσαγωγή, ῆς, ἡ	(3)	approach, access
στρατηγός, οῦ, ὁ	(10)	chief magistrate, captain
συναγωγή, ῆς, ἡ	(56)	synagogue, assembly, meeting (for worship)
χειραγωγός, οῦ, ὁ	(1)	one who leads another by the hand, leader
ἀνεκδιήγητος, ον	(1)	indescribable
ἀποσυνάγωγος, ον	(3)	expelled from the synagogue, excommunicated
παρείσακτος, ον	(1)	smuggled or sneaked in
ἄγε	(2)	come! (pres. imper. of ἄγω)

ἀγών

ἀγωνίζομαι	(8)	I engage in a contest, fight, struggle
ἀνταγωνίζομαι	(1)	I struggle
ἐπαγωνίζομαι	(1)	I fight, contend
καταγωνίζομαι	(1)	I conquer, defeat, overcome
συναγωνίζομαι	(1)	I help, assist
ἀγών, ῶνος, ὁ	(6)	contest, struggle, fight
ἀγωνία, ας, ἡ	(1)	agony, anxiety

ἀδελφός

ἀδελφή, ῆς, ἡ	(26)	sister, fellow believer
ἀδελφός, οῦ, ὁ	(343)	brother, fellow believer, fellow countryman, neighbor
ἀδελφότης, ητος, ἡ	(2)	brotherhood
φιλαδελφία, ας, ἡ	(6)	brotherly love, love of brother or sister
ψευδάδελφος, ου, ὁ	(2)	false brother
φιλάδελφος, ον	(1)	loving one's brother or sister

ἀεί

ἀΐδιος, ον	(2)	eternal
ἀεί	(7)	always, continually, from the beginning

ἀθλέω

ἀθλέω	(2)	I compete in a contest
συναθλέω	(2)	I fight or work together with
ἄθλησις, εως, ἡ	(1)	contest, hard struggle

αἰδώς

αἰδώς, οῦς, ἡ	(1)	modesty
ἀναίδεια, ας, ἡ	(1)	shamelessness, persistence, impudence

αἷμα

αἱμορροέω	(1)	I suffer with hemorrhage, bleed
αἷμα, ατος, τό	(97)	blood, death, murder
αἱματεκχυσία, ας, ἡ	(1)	shedding of blood

αἶνος

αἰνέω	(8)	I praise
ἐπαινέω	(6)	I praise, commend
παραινέω	(2)	I advise, recommend, urge
αἴνεσις, εως, ἡ	(1)	praise
αἴνιγμα, ατος, τό	(1)	riddle, obscure image
αἶνος, ου, ὁ	(2)	praise
ἔπαινος, ου, ὁ	(11)	praise, approval, thing worthy of praise

αἱρέω

αἱρετίζω	(1)	I choose
αἱρέω	(3)	I choose, prefer
ἀναιρέω	(24)	I take away, do away with, destroy, kill; take up (mid.)
ἀφαιρέω	(10)	I take away, cut off
διαιρέω	(2)	I distribute, divide
ἐξαιρέω	(8)	I take out; set free, rescue, select, choose (mid.)
καθαιρέω	(9)	I take or bring down, conquer, destroy

περιαιρέω	(5)	I take away, remove; am abandoned (pass.)
προαιρέω	(1)	I bring out; decide, make up my mind (mid. in NT)
αἵρεσις, εως, ἡ	(9)	sect, party, school, dissension, faction, opinion
ἀναίρεσις, εως, ἡ	(1)	murder, killing
διαίρεσις, εως, ἡ	(3)	apportionment, division, difference
καθαίρεσις, εως, ἡ	(3)	tearing down, destruction
αἱρετικός, ή, όν	(1)	factious, causing divisions
αὐθαίρετος, ον	(2)	of one's own accord

αἴρω

αἴρω	(101)	I take, take up, take away, remove, raise; arise (pass.)
ἀπαίρω	(3)	I take away (pass. in NT)
ἐξαίρω	(1)	I remove, drive away
ἐπαίρω	(19)	I lift up; am in opposition, am presumptuous (pass.)
μεταίρω	(2)	I go away, leave
συναίρω	(3)	I settle
τιμωρέω	(2)	I punish
ὑπεραίρω	(3)	I exalt myself, am puffed up with pride (mid. in NT)
τιμωρία, ας, ἡ	(1)	punishment

αἰσθάνομαι

αἰσθάνομαι	(1)	I understand
αἴσθησις, εως, ἡ	(1)	insight, experience
αἰσθητήριον, ου, τό	(1)	sense, faculty

αἰσχρός

αἰσχύνω	(5)	I am ashamed, disgraced (pass. in NT)
ἐπαισχύνομαι	(11)	I am ashamed
καταισχύνω	(13)	I dishonor, put to shame; am disappointed (pass.)
αἰσχρότης, ητος, ἡ	(1)	ugliness, wickedness
αἰσχύνη, ης, ἡ	(6)	modesty, shame, disgrace, shameful deed
αἰσχρολογία, ας, ἡ	(1)	evil speech, obscene speech
αἰσχρός, ά, όν	(4)	ugly, shameful, disgraceful
αἰσχροκερδής, ές	(2)	fond of dishonest gain, greedy for money
ἀνεπαίσχυντος, ον	(1)	unashamed
αἰσχροκερδῶς	(1)	greedily

αἰτέω

αἰτέω	(70)	I ask, ask for, demand
ἀπαιτέω	(2)	I ask for, demand
ἐξαιτέω	(1)	I ask for, demand (mid. in NT)
ἐπαιτέω	(2)	I beg
παραιτέομαι	(12)	I ask for, excuse, decline, reject, refuse, dismiss, avoid
προσαιτέω	(1)	I beg
αἴτημα, ατος, τό	(3)	request
προσαίτης, ου, ὁ	(2)	beggar

αἰτία

προαιτιάομαι	(1)	I accuse beforehand
αἰτία, ας, ἡ	(20)	cause, reason, relationship, charge, accusation
αἰτίωμα, ατος, τό	(1)	charge, complaint
αἴτιος, α, ον	(5)	responsible, guilty; cause, guilt (subst. in NT)
ἀναίτιος, ον	(2)	innocent

αἰών

αἰών, ῶνος, ὁ	(122)	very long time, eternity, age, world
αἰώνιος, α, ον	(71)	eternal

ἀκολουθέω

ἀκολουθέω	(90)	I follow, accompany, am a disciple
ἐξακολουθέω	(3)	I follow, obey
ἐπακολουθέω	(4)	I follow, come after, devote myself to
κατακολουθέω	(2)	I follow
παρακολουθέω	(4)	I follow, accompany, follow closely, investigate
συνακολουθέω	(3)	I follow, accompany

ἀκούω

ἀκούω	(428)	I hear, listen to, learn, obey, understand
διακούω	(1)	I give a hearing
εἰσακούω	(5)	I listen to, obey, hear
ἐπακούω	(1)	I hear, listen to
παρακούω	(3)	I overhear, ignore, disobey
προακούω	(1)	I hear before
ὑπακούω	(21)	I obey, follow, am subject to, answer (the door)
ἀκοή, ῆς, ἡ	(24)	hearing, listening, ear, fame, report, account
παρακοή, ῆς, ἡ	(3)	disobedience, disloyalty
ὑπακοή, ῆς, ἡ	(15)	obedience
ὑπήκοος, ον	(3)	obedient

ἀκριβής

ἀκριβόω	(2)	I ascertain, inquire with exactness
ἀκρίβεια, ας, ἡ	(1)	exactness, precision
ἀκριβής, ές	(1)	exact, strict
ἀκριβῶς	(9)	accurately, carefully, well

ἀκροατής

ἐπακροάομαι	(1)	I listen to
ἀκροατήριον, ου, τό	(1)	audience room, auditorium
ἀκροατής, οῦ, ὁ	(4)	hearer

ἄκρον

ἀκμάζω	(1)	I am ripe
ἄκανθα, ης, ἡ	(14)	thorn plant, thorn
ἄκρον, ου, τό	(6)	high point, top, tip, end
ἀκροβυστία, ας, ἡ	(20)	foreskin, uncircumcision, Gentile(s)
ἀκροθίνιον, ου τό	(1)	first fruits, booty, spoils (pl. in NT)
ἀκάνθινος, η, ον	(2)	thorny
ἀκρογωνιαῖος, α, ον	(2)	lying at the extreme corner; cornerstone (subst.)
ὑπέρακμος, ον	(1)	past one's prime
ἀκμήν	(1)	even yet, still
ἄχρι	(49)	until, to, as far as (impr. prep.); until (conj.)

ἀλαζών

ἀλαζονεία, ας, ἡ	(2)	pretension, arrogance, pride
ἀλαζών, όνος, ὁ	(2)	boaster, braggart

ἅλας

ἁλιεύω	(1)	I fish
ἁλίζω	(2)	I salt
συναλίζω	(1)	I eat with, assemble
ἅλας, ατος, τό	(8)	salt
ἁλιεύς, έως, ὁ	(5)	fisherman
θάλασσα, ης, ἡ	(91)	sea, lake
αἰγιαλός, οῦ, ὁ	(6)	shore, beach
ἁλυκός, ή, όν	(1)	salty
ἄναλος, ον	(1)	without salt, saltless
διθάλασσος, ον	(1)	with the sea on both sides, between the seas
ἐνάλιος, ον	(1)	belong to the sea; sea creature (subst. in NT)
παραθαλάσσιος, α, ον	(1)	by the sea or lake
παράλιος, ον	(1)	by the seacoast; seacoast district (subst. in NT)

ἀλείφω

ἀλείφω	(9)	I anoint
ἐξαλείφω	(5)	I wipe away, wipe out, remove, destroy

ἀλέκτωρ

ἀλέκτωρ, ορος, ὁ	(12)	cock, rooster
ἀλεκτοροφωνία, ας, ἡ	(1)	crowing of a cock, cockcrow, before dawn

ἀλήθω

ἀλήθω	(2)	I grind
ἄλευρον, ου, τό	(2)	wheat flour

ἅλλομαι

ἅλλομαι	(3)	I leap, spring up, well up, bubble up
σαλεύω	(15)	I shake, cause to move to and fro, incite
ἐξάλλομαι	(1)	I jump up
ἐφάλλομαι	(1)	I leap upon
σάλος, ου, ὁ	(1)	waves (of a rough sea)
ἀσάλευτος, ον	(2)	immovable, unshaken

ἄλλος

ἀλλάσσω	(6)	I change, alter, exchange
ἀλληγορέω	(1)	I speak allegorically
ἀπαλλάσσω	(3)	I free, release; am cured, leave, depart (pass.)
ἀπαλλοτριόω	(3)	I estrange; am estranged (pass. in NT)
ἀποκαταλλάσσω	(3)	I reconcile
διαλλάσσομαι	(1)	I become reconciled
καταλλάσσω	(6)	I reconcile
μεταλλάσσω	(2)	I exchange
συναλλάσσω	(1)	I reconcile
ἀλλοτριεπίσκοπος, ου, ὁ	(1)	one who meddles in the affairs of others, busybody
ἀντάλλαγμα, ατος, τό	(2)	something given in exchange
καταλλαγή, ῆς, ἡ	(4)	reconciliation
παραλλαγή, ῆς, ἡ	(1)	change, variation
ἄλλος, η, ο	(155)	other, another, different, more
ἀλλότριος, α, ον	(14)	belonging to another, strange, hostile; stranger (subst.)
ἀλλογενής, ές	(1)	foreign; foreigner (subst. in NT)
ἀλλόφυλος, ον	(1)	foreign; a heathen, Gentile (subst. in NT)

ἀλλαχόθεν	(1)	from another place
ἀλλαχοῦ	(1)	elsewhere, in another direction
ἄλλως	(1)	otherwise, in another way
ἀλλά	(638)	but, yet, rather, nevertheless, at least
ἀλλήλων	(100)	each other, one another, mutually

ἀλοάω

ἀλοάω	(3)	I thresh
ἅλων, ωνος, ἡ	(2)	threshing floor, threshed grain
μητρολῴας, ου, ὁ	(1)	one who murders one's mother
πατρολῴας, ου, ὁ	(1)	one who murders one's father

ἅλωσις

αἰχμαλωτεύω	(1)	I capture, take captive
αἰχμαλωτίζω	(4)	I capture, make captive, mislead, deceive
ἀναλίσκω	(2)	I consume
καταναλίσκω	(1)	I consume
προσαναλίσκω	(1)	I spend lavishly, spend
ἅλωσις, εως, ἡ	(1)	capture, catching
αἰχμαλωσία, ας, ἡ	(3)	captivity, prisoners of war
αἰχμάλωτος, ου, ὁ	(1)	captive
συναιχμάλωτος, ου, ὁ	(3)	fellow prisoner

ἁμαρτάνω

ἁμαρτάνω	(43)	I do wrong, sin
προαμαρτάνω	(2)	I sin before
ἁμάρτημα, ατος, τό	(4)	sin, transgression
ἁμαρτία, ας, ἡ	(173)	sin, sinfulness
ἁμαρτωλός, όν	(47)	sinful; sinner (subst.)
ἀναμάρτητος, ον	(1)	without sin

ἄμπελος

ἄμπελος, ου, ἡ	(9)	vine, grapevine
ἀμπελών, ῶνος, ὁ	(23)	vineyard
ἀμπελουργός, οῦ, ὁ	(1)	vine dresser, gardener

ἄν

ἄν	(167)	conditional part., part. of contingency (untrans.)
ἐάν	(351)	if, when
ἐάνπερ	(3)	if indeed, if only, supposing that
ἐπάν	(3)	when, as soon as
κἄν	(17)	and if, even if, if only (= καὶ ἐάν)
ὅταν	(123)	at the time that, whenever, when

ἀνά

διανύω	(1)	I complete, continue, arrive, travel
ἀνωτερικός, ή, όν	(1)	upper, inland
ἀνώτερος, α, ον	(2)	higher, above, earlier (neut. as adv. in NT)
ἄνω	(9)	above, up, upwards
ἄνωθεν	(13)	from above, from heaven, for a long time, again, anew
ἐπάνω	(19)	above, over, more than; over, above, on (impr. prep.)
ὑπεράνω	(3)	(high) above (impr. prep. in NT)
ἀνά	(13)	upwards, up, each; among, between (w. μέσον)

ἀνάγκη

ἀναγκάζω	(9)	I compel, force, invite, strongly urge
ἀνάγκη, ης, ἡ	(17)	necessity, compulsion, distress, calamity
ἀναγκαῖος, α, ον	(8)	necessary
ἀναγκαστῶς	(1)	by compulsion
ἐπάναγκες	(1)	by compulsion, necessarily

ἀνατολή

ἀνατέλλω	(9)	I cause to spring up, rise, spring up, am descended
ἐξανατέλλω	(2)	I spring up, sprout
ἀνατολή, ῆς, ἡ	(11)	rising, east; east (pl.)

ἄνεμος

ἀνεμίζω	(1)	I am moved by the wind (pass. in NT)
ἄνεμος, ου, ὁ	(31)	wind

ἀνήρ

ἀνδρίζομαι	(1)	I act like a man, act courageously
ἀνήρ, ἀνδρός, ὁ	(216)	man (male), husband, grown man, someone
ἀνδραποδιστής, οῦ, ὁ	(1)	slave dealer, kidnapper
ἀνδροφόνος, ου, ὁ	(1)	murderer
ὕπανδρος, ον	(1)	married (of a woman)
φίλανδρος, ον	(1)	loving one's husband

ἄνθραξ

ἀνθρακιά, ᾶς, ἡ	(2)	charcoal fire
ἄνθραξ, ακος, ὁ	(1)	charcoal

ἄνθρωπος

ἄνθρωπος, ου, ὁ	(550)	human being, man, adult male, husband
ἀνθρωποκτόνος, ου, ὁ	(3)	murderer
φιλανθρωπία, ας, ἡ	(2)	love for people, kindness, hospitality
ἀνθρώπινος, η, ον	(7)	human
ἀνθρωπάρεσκος, ον	(2)	trying to please people
φιλανθρώπως	(1)	benevolently, kindly

ἀνοίγω

ἀνοίγω	(77)	I open
διανοίγω	(8)	I open, explain, interpret
ἄνοιξις, εως, ἡ	(1)	opening

ἀντί

ἀπαντάω	(?)	I meet
καταντάω	(13)	I come, arrive, attain
συναντάω	(6)	I meet, happen
ὑπαντάω	(10)	I meet, oppose
ἀπάντησις, εως, ἡ	(3)	meeting; to meet (w. εἰς in NT)
ὑπάντησις, εως, ἡ	(3)	meeting
ἐναντίος, α, ον	(8)	opposite, against, contrary, hostile
ὑπεναντίος, α, ον	(2)	opposed, contrary, hostile; opponent (subst.)
ἄντικρυς	(1)	opposite (impr. prep. in NT)
ἀπέναντι	(5)	opposite, against, contrary to (impr. prep. in NT)

ἔναντι	(2)	opposite, before, in the judgment of (impr. prep. in NT)
ἐναντίον	(8)	before, in the judgment of (impr. prep. in NT)
κατέναντι	(8)	opposite; opposite, in the sight of, before (impr. prep.)
τοὐναντίον	(3)	on the other hand, rather (= τὸ ἐναντίον)
ἀντί	(22)	instead of, for, in behalf of

ἀντλέω

ἀντλέω	(4)	I draw (water)
ἄντλημα, ατος, τό	(1)	bucket

ἀξίνη

κατάγνυμι	(4)	I break
ναυαγέω	(2)	I suffer shipwreck
ἀξίνη, ης, ἡ	(2)	ax

ἄξιος

ἀξιόω	(7)	I consider worthy, make worthy, consider suitable
καταξιόω	(3)	I consider worthy
ἄξιος, α, ον	(41)	comparable, worthy, proper, fit, deserving
ἀνάξιος, ον	(1)	unworthy
ἀξίως	(6)	worthily, suitably, properly
ἀναξίως	(1)	in an unworthy manner, unworthily, improperly

ἅπαξ

ἅπαξ	(14)	once, once for all
ἐφάπαξ	(5)	at once, once for all

ἀπάτη

ἀπατάω	(3)	I deceive, cheat, mislead
ἐξαπατάω	(6)	I deceive
φρεναπατάω	(1)	I deceive
ἀπάτη, ης, ἡ	(7)	deception, deceitfulness, pleasure
φρεναπάτης, ου, ὁ	(1)	deceiver, one who misleads

ἀπειλή

ἀπειλέω	(2)	I threaten, warn
προσαπειλέω	(1)	I threaten further or in addition (mid. in NT)
ἀπειλή, ῆς, ἡ	(3)	threat

ἁπλότης

ἁπλότης, ητος, ἡ	(8)	simplicity, sincerity, generosity
ἁπλοῦς, ῆ, οῦν	(2)	single, simple, sincere, healthy, generous
ἁπλῶς	(1)	generously

ἀπό

ποταπός, ή, όν	(7)	of what sort or kind, how great or glorious
ἀπάντησις, εως, ἡ	(3)	meeting; to meet (w. εἰς in NT)
ἀπέναντι	(5)	opposite, against, contrary to (impr. prep. in NT)
ἀπό	(646)	from, away from, because of, with, for, of, by

ἅπτω

ἅπτω	(39)	I kindle; touch, take hold, injure (mid.)

ἀνάπτω	(2)	I kindle, set fire
καθάπτω	(1)	I take hold of, seize, fasten on
περιάπτω	(1)	I kindle
ἀφή, ῆς, ἡ	(2)	ligament

ἀρά

καταράομαι	(5)	I curse
ἀρά, ᾶς, ἡ	(1)	curse
κατάρα, ας, ἡ	(6)	curse, something accursed
ἐπάρατος, ον	(1)	accursed
ἐπικατάρατος, ον	(2)	cursed

ἄργυρος

ἀργύριον, ου, τό	(20)	silver, money
ἄργυρος, ου, ὁ	(5)	silver, money
ἀργυροκόπος, ου, ὁ	(1)	silversmith
φιλαργυρία, ας, ἡ	(1)	love of money, miserliness, avarice
ἀργυροῦς, ᾶ, οῦν	(3)	made of silver
ἀφιλάργυρος, ον	(2)	not loving money, not greedy
φιλάργυρος, ον	(2)	fond of money, avaricious

ἀρέσκω

ἀρέσκω	(17)	I strive to please, please
εὐαρεστέω	(3)	I please, am pleasing
ἀρεσκεία, ας, ἡ	(1)	desire to please
ἀρετή, ῆς, ἡ	(5)	virtue, miracle
ἀρεστός, ή, όν	(4)	pleasing
ἀνθρωπάρεσκος, ον	(2)	trying to please people
εὐάρεστος, ον	(9)	pleasing, acceptable
εὐαρέστως	(1)	acceptably, pleasingly

ἀρήν

| ἀρήν, ἀρνός, ὁ | (1) | lamb |
| ἀρνίον, ου, τό | (30) | lamb, sheep |

ἀριθμός

ἀριθμέω	(3)	I count
καταριθμέω	(1)	I count, count among; belong to (pass. in NT)
ἀριθμός, οῦ, ὁ	(18)	number, total
ἀναρίθμητος, ον	(1)	innumerable, countless

ἄριστον

| ἀριστάω | (3) | I eat breakfast, eat a meal, dine |
| ἄριστον, ου, τό | (3) | breakfast, noon meal, meal |

ἀρκέω

ἀρκέω	(8)	I am enough, am sufficient; am satisfied (pass.)
ἐπαρκέω	(3)	I help, aid
αὐτάρκεια, ας, ἡ	(2)	sufficiency, contentment
ἀρκετός, ή, όν	(3)	enough, sufficient, adequate
αὐτάρκης, ες	(1)	content, self-sufficient

ἁρμόζω

ἁρμόζω	(1)	I betroth, join in marriage (mid. in NT)
συναρμολογέω	(2)	I join together; am joined or fit together (pass. in NT)
ἁρμός, οῦ, ὁ	(1)	joint

ἀρνέομαι

| ἀρνέομαι | (33) | I refuse, deny, repudiate, disown, reject |
| ἀπαρνέομαι | (11) | I deny, reject |

ἄροτρον

| ἀροτριάω | (3) | I plow |
| ἄροτρον, ου, τό | (1) | plow |

ἁρπάζω

ἁρπάζω	(14)	I snatch, seize, steal
διαρπάζω	(3)	I plunder thoroughly, rob
συναρπάζω	(4)	I seize, drag away
ἁρπαγή, ῆς, ἡ	(3)	robbery, what has been stolen, plunder
ἁρπαγμός, οῦ, ὁ	(1)	something to hold, prize
ἅρπαξ, αγος	(5)	ravenous; swindler, robber (subst.)

ἄρσην

| ἀρσενοκοίτης, ου, ὁ | (2) | male homosexual |
| ἄρσην, εν | (9) | male |

ἄρτι

ἐξαρτίζω	(2)	I complete, equip
καταρτίζω	(13)	I restore, make complete, prepare, make
προκαταρτίζω	(1)	I prepare in advance
ἀπαρτισμός, οῦ, ὁ	(1)	completion
κατάρτισις, εως, ἡ	(1)	being made complete
καταρτισμός, οῦ, ὁ	(1)	equipment, equipping, training
ἄρτιος, α, ον	(1)	complete, capable, proficient
ἀρτιγέννητος, ον	(1)	new born
ἄρτι	(36)	now, just, at once, immediately

ἄρχω

ἄρχω	(86)	I rule; begin (mid.)
ἐνάρχομαι	(2)	I begin, make a beginning
πειθαρχέω	(4)	I obey, follow
προενάρχομαι	(2)	I begin (beforehand)
προϋπάρχω	(2)	I exist before
τετρααρχέω	(3)	I am tetrarch or ruler
ὑπάρχω	(60)	I am, exist, am present, am at one's disposal
ἀρχή, ῆς, ἡ	(55)	beginning, origin, first cause, ruler, authority, domain
ἄρχων, οντος, ὁ	(37)	ruler, lord, prince, authority, official, judge
ἀπαρχή, ῆς, ἡ	(9)	first fruits, first portion, first, birth certificate
ἀρχάγγελος, ου, ὁ	(2)	archangel
ἀρχηγός, οῦ, ὁ	(4)	leader, ruler, prince, originator, founder
ἀρχιερεύς, έως, ὁ	(122)	high priest; chief priests, ruling priests (pl.)
ἀρχιποίμην, ενος, ὁ	(1)	chief shepherd
ἀρχισυνάγωγος, ου, ὁ	(9)	leader or president of a synagogue

ἀρχιτέκτων, ονος, ὁ	(1)	master builder
ἀρχιτελώνης, ου, ὁ	(1)	chief tax collector
ἀρχιτρίκλινος, ου, ὁ	(3)	head waiter, butler, master of a feast
ἐθνάρχης, ου, ὁ	(1)	ethnarch, governor, official
ἑκατοντάρχης, ου, ὁ	(20)	centurion, captain, officer
ἐπαρχεία, ας, ἡ	(2)	province
πατριάρχης, ου, ὁ	(4)	patriarch, father of a nation
πολιτάρχης, ου, ὁ	(2)	civic magistrate, politarch
τετραάρχης, ου, ὁ	(4)	tetrarch
ὕπαρξις, εως, ἡ	(2)	property, possession
χιλίαρχος, ου, ὁ	(21)	military tribune, high ranking officer
ἀρχαῖος, α, ον	(11)	ancient, old
ἀρχιερατικός, όν	(1)	high-priestly

ἀσπάζομαι

ἀσπάζομαι	(59)	I greet, welcome, take leave, cherish, hail, pay respects
ἀπασπάζομαι	(1)	I take leave of, say farewell to
ἀσπασμός, οῦ, ὁ	(10)	greeting

ἀστήρ

ἀστήρ, έρος, ὁ	(24)	star
ἄστρον, ου, τό	(4)	star, constellation

ἀστραπή

ἀστράπτω	(2)	I flash, gleam
ἐξαστράπτω	(1)	I flash, gleam
περιαστράπτω	(2)	I shine around
ἀστραπή, ῆς, ἡ	(9)	lightning, light

αὐγή

αὐγάζω	(1)	I see, shine forth
διαυγάζω	(1)	I shine through, dawn
αὐγή, ῆς, ἡ	(1)	dawn
ἀπαύγασμα, ατος, τό	(1)	radiance, reflection
διαυγής, ές	(1)	transparent, pure
τηλαυγῶς	(1)	plainly, clearly

αὐλέω

αὐλέω	(3)	I play the flute
αὐλητής, οῦ, ὁ	(2)	flute player
αὐλός, οῦ, ὁ	(1)	flute

αὐλή

αὐλίζομαι	(2)	I spend the night, find lodging
αὐλή, ῆς, ἡ	(12)	courtyard, palace, farm, house
ἔπαυλις, εως, ἡ	(1)	farm, homestead, residence
προαύλιον, ου, τό	(1)	porch, gateway

αὐξάνω

αὐξάνω	(23)	I grow, increase
συναυξάνω	(1)	I grew together, grow side by side (pass. in NT)
ὑπεραυξάνω	(1)	I grow wonderfully, increase abundantly

αὔξησις, εως, ἡ	(2)	growth, increase

αὔριον

αὔριον	(14)	tomorrow, next day, soon
ἐπαύριον	(17)	tomorrow, the next day

αὐστηρός

αὐστηρός, ά, όν	(2)	severe, austere, exacting, strict
αὐχμηρός, ά, όν	(1)	dry, dirty, dark

αὐτός

αὐθεντέω	(1)	I have authority, domineer, control
αὐτάρκεια, ας, ἡ	(2)	sufficiency, contentment
αὐτόπτης, ου, ὁ	(1)	eyewitness
ἐνιαυτός, οῦ, ὁ	(14)	year, era
αὐτός, ή, ὁ	(5595)	self, even, same (adj.); he, she, it (prn.)
αὐθάδης, ες	(2)	self-willed, stubborn, arrogant
αὐθαίρετος, ον	(2)	of one's own accord
αὐτάρκης, ες	(1)	content, self-sufficient
αὐτοκατάκριτος, ον	(1)	self-condemned
αὐτόματος, η, ον	(2)	by itself
αὐτόφωρος, ον	(1)	in the act
αὐτόχειρ, ρος	(1)	with one's own hand
φίλαυτος, ον	(1)	loving oneself, selfish
αὐτοῦ	(4)	here, there
ἐξαυτῆς	(6)	at once, immediately
παραυτίκα	(1)	on the spot; momentary (adj. in NT)
ὡσαύτως	(17)	similarly, likewise
ἑαυτοῦ, ῆς, οῦ	(319)	(of) himself, herself, itself
ἐμαυτοῦ, ῆς	(37)	(of) myself
σεαυτοῦ, ῆς	(43)	(of) yourself

ἄφνω

αἰφνίδιος, ον	(2)	sudden
ἄφνω	(3)	suddenly, immediately
ἐξαίφνης	(5)	suddenly, unexpectedly
ἐξάπινα	(1)	suddenly

ἀφρός

ἀφρίζω	(2)	I foam at the mouth
ἐπαφρίζω	(1)	I cause to foam up
ἀφρός, οῦ, ὁ	(1)	foam

βαθύς

βαθύνω	(1)	I make deep, go down deep
βάθος, ους, τό	(8)	depth
βαθύς, εῖα, ύ	(4)	deep

[βαίνω]

βεβαιόω	(8)	I make firm, establish, confirm, strengthen
βεβηλόω	(2)	I desecrate, profane
ἀναβαίνω	(82)	I go up, ascend, embark, come up, grow up

ἀναβιβάζω	(1)	I bring up, pull up
ἀποβαίνω	(4)	I go away, get out, turn out, lead
διαβαίνω	(3)	I go through, cross, come over
διαβεβαιόομαι	(2)	I speak confidently, insist
ἐκβαίνω	(1)	I go out, come from
ἐμβαίνω	(16)	I go in, step in, embark
ἐμβατεύω	(1)	I enter, possess, go into detail, take my stand on
ἐμβιβάζω	(1)	I put in, aboard
ἐπιβαίνω	(6)	I go up or upon, mount, board, embark, arrive
ἐπιβιβάζω	(3)	I cause to mount
καταβαίνω	(81)	I come down, go down, climb down, fall down
μεταβαίνω	(12)	I go or pass over, move
παραβαίνω	(3)	I turn aside; transgress, break (trans.)
προβαίνω	(5)	I go on, advance
προβιβάζω	(1)	I put forward, prompt, instruct
προσαναβαίνω	(1)	I go or move up
συγκαταβαίνω	(1)	I go come down with
συμβαίνω	(8)	I happen, come about
συμβιβάζω	(7)	I unite, conclude, demonstrate, teach
συναναβαίνω	(2)	I come or go up with
ὑπερβαίνω	(1)	I overstep, transgress, sin
βαθμός, οῦ, ὁ	(1)	step, rank
βάσις, εως, ἡ	(1)	foot
βεβαίωσις, εως, ἡ	(2)	confirmation, establishment, verification
βῆμα, ατος, τό	(12)	step, judicial bench, speaker's platform,
βωμός, ου, ὁ	(1)	altar
ἀναβαθμός, οῦ, ὁ	(2)	step; flight of stairs (pl.)
ἔκβασις, εως, ἡ	(2)	way out, end, outcome
κατάβασις, εως, ἡ	(1)	descent, road leading down, slope
παράβασις, εως, ἡ	(7)	overstepping, transgression, violation
παραβάτης, ου, ὁ	(5)	transgressor, sinner
πρόβατον, ου, τό	(39)	sheep
βέβαιος, α, ον	(8)	firm, permanent, secure, reliable, certain, valid
βέβηλος, ον	(5)	profane, godless, irreligious
ἀπαράβατος, ον	(1)	permanent, unchangeable
προβατικός, ή, όν	(1)	pertaining to sheep

βάλλω

βάλλω	(122)	I throw, cast, pour, let fall, put, bring, sweep down
βολίζω	(2)	I take a sounding, heave the lead
ἀμφιβάλλω	(1)	I cast a fishnet
ἀναβάλλω	(1)	I postpone, adjourn
ἀντιβάλλω	(1)	I put against, place against, exchange
ἀποβάλλω	(2)	I throw away, take off, lose
διαβάλλω	(1)	I bring charges
ἐκβάλλω	(81)	I drive out, send out, lead out, take out
ἐμβάλλω	(1)	I throw in
ἐπιβάλλω	(18)	I throw over, lay on, put on, sew on, beat upon, belong to
καταβάλλω	(2)	I throw down, strike down; lay (mid.)
λιθοβολέω	(7)	I throw stones, stone (to death)
μεταβάλλω	(1)	I change my mind (mid. in NT)
παραβάλλω	(1)	I approach, come near, arrive
παραβολεύομαι	(1)	I risk
παρεμβάλλω	(1)	I set up, throw up
περιβάλλω	(23)	I put on, clothe, dress

προβάλλω	(2)	I put forward, put out (leaves)
συμβάλλω	(6)	I converse, consider, meet, engage; help (mid.)
ὑπερβάλλω	(5)	I go beyond, surpass, outdo
ὑποβάλλω	(1)	I instigate (secretly)
βελόνη, ης, ἡ	(1)	needle
βέλος, ους, τό	(1)	arrow
βολή, ῆς, ἡ	(1)	throw
ἀμφίβληστρον, ου, τό	(1)	casting-net
ἀναβολή, ῆς, ἡ	(1)	delay, postponement
ἀποβολή, ῆς, ἡ	(2)	rejection, loss
ἐκβολή, ῆς, ἡ	(1)	throwing out, jettisoning
ἐπίβλημα, ατος, τό	(4)	patch
καταβολή, ῆς, ἡ	(11)	foundation, beginning
παραβολή, ῆς, ἡ	(50)	parable, comparison, type, symbol, figure
παρεμβολή, ῆς, ἡ	(10)	camp, barracks, headquarters, army, battle line
περιβόλαιον, ου, τό	(2)	covering, cloak, robe
τρίβολος, ου, ὁ	(2)	thorn plant, thistle
ὑπερβολή, ῆς, ἡ	(8)	excess, extraordinary quality or character
βλητέος, α, ον	(1)	must be put
ἀπόβλητος, ον	(1)	rejected
διάβολος, ον	(37)	slanderous; the devil (subst.)
ὑπερβαλλόντως	(1)	exceedingly, immeasurably

βάπτω

βαπτίζω	(77)	I dip, immerse, baptize
βάπτω	(4)	I dip
ἐμβάπτω	(2)	I dip in
βάπτισμα, ατος, τό	(19)	baptism
βαπτισμός, οῦ, ὁ	(4)	dipping, washing, baptism
βαπτιστής, οῦ, ὁ	(12)	Baptist, Baptizer

βάρος

βαρέω	(6)	I weigh down, burden
ἐπιβαρέω	(3)	I weigh down, burden
καταβαρέω	(1)	I burden, am a burden
καταβαρύνω	(1)	I weigh down; am heavy (pass. in NT)
βάρος, ους, τό	(6)	weight, burden, fullness
βαρύς, εῖα, ύ	(6)	heavy, burdensome, severe, weighty, important, fierce
ἀβαρής, ές	(1)	light weight, not burdensome
βαρύτιμος, ον	(1)	very expensive, very precious
βαρέως	(2)	with difficulty

βάσανος

βασανίζω	(12)	I torture, torment, harass
βασανισμός, οῦ, ὁ	(6)	tormenting, torment
βασανιστής, οῦ, ὁ	(1)	torturer, jailer
βάσανος, ου, ἡ	(3)	torture, torment, severe pain

βασιλεύς

βασιλεύω	(21)	I am king, rule, become king
συμβασιλεύω	(2)	I rule (as king) or reign with
βασιλεία, ας, ἡ	(162)	kingdom, kingship, royal rule, royal power, reign
βασιλεύς, έως, ὁ	(115)	king
βασίλισσα, ης, ἡ	(4)	queen

βασίλειος, ον	(2)	royal
βασιλικός, ή, όν	(5)	royal

βαστάζω

βαστάζω	(27)	I take up, carry, bear, endure, remove, steal
δυσβάστακτος, ον	(2)	difficult to carry, hard to bear

βδελύσσομαι

βδελύσσομαι	(2)	I abhor, detest
βδέλυγμα, ατος, τό	(6)	abomination, detestable thing
βδελυκτός, ή, όν	(1)	abominable, detestable

βία

βιάζομαι	(2)	I use force, violence (mid. dep.); suffer violence (pass.)
παραβιάζομαι	(2)	I use force, urge strongly
βία, ας, ή	(3)	force, use of force, violence
βιαστής, οῦ, ὁ	(1)	violent person
βίαιος, α, ον	(1)	violent, forcible, strong

βίβλος

βιβλαρίδιον, ου, τό	(3)	little book, little scroll
βιβλίον, ου, τό	(34)	book, scroll, document, record
βίβλος, ου, ή	(10)	book, sacred book, record

βιβρώσκω

βιβρώσκω	(1)	I eat
βρῶμα, ατος, τό	(17)	food
βρῶσις, εως, ή	(11)	eating, food, corrosion, rust
βρώσιμος, ον	(1)	eatable
σητόβρωτος, ον	(1)	moth-eaten
σκωληκόβρωτος, ον	(1)	eaten by worms

βίος

βιόω	(1)	I live
βίος, ου, ὁ	(10)	life, conduct, property
βίωσις, εως, ή	(1)	manner of life
βιωτικός, ή, όν	(3)	belonging to life

βλάπτω

βλάπτω	(2)	I harm, injure
βλαβερός, ά, όν	(1)	harmful

βλέπω

βλέπω	(133)	I see, look at, am able to see, take care, watch, perceive
ἀναβλέπω	(25)	I look up, see again, receive sight
ἀποβλέπω	(1)	I look, pay attention
διαβλέπω	(3)	I look intently, see clearly
ἐμβλέπω	(12)	I look at, consider
ἐπιβλέπω	(3)	I look at, consider, care about
περιβλέπω	(7)	I look around (mid. in NT)
προβλέπω	(1)	I see beforehand; select, provide (mid. in NT)
βλέμμα, ατος, τό	(1)	glance, look

ἀνάβλεψις, εως, ἡ   (1)   recovery of sight

βοή

βοάω   (12)   I call, shout, cry out
ἀναβοάω   (1)   I cry out, shout
βοηθέω   (8)   I help
βοή, ῆς, ἡ   (1)   cry, shout
βοήθεια, ας, ἡ   (2)   help, support
βοηθός, όν   (1)   helpful; helper (subst. in NT)

βόσκω

βόσκω   (9)   I feed, tend; graze (pass.)
βοτάνη, ης, ἡ   (1)   fodder, herb, plant

βούλομαι

βουλεύω   (6)   I deliberate, resolve, decide (mid. in NT)
βούλομαι   (37)   I wish, want, desire
συμβουλεύω   (4)   I advise; consult, plot (mid.)
βουλευτής, οῦ, ὁ   (2)   council member
βουλή, ῆς, ἡ   (12)   purpose, counsel, resolution, decision
βούλημα, ατος, τό   (3)   intention, purpose
ἐπιβουλή, ῆς, ἡ   (4)   plot
συμβούλιον, ου, τό   (8)   plan, purpose, council
σύμβουλος, ου, ὁ   (1)   advisor, counselor

βραβεύω

βραβεύω   (1)   I rule, control
καταβραβεύω   (1)   I decide against, rob of a prize, cheat, condemn
βραβεῖον, ου, τό   (2)   prize

βραδύς

βραδύνω   (2)   I hesitate, delay, hold back
βραδυπλοέω   (1)   I sail slowly
βραδύτης, ητος, ἡ   (1)   slowness
βραδύς, εῖα, ύ   (3)   slow

βρέχω

βρέχω   (7)   I wet, send rain; it rains (impers.)
βροχή, ῆς, ἡ   (2)   rain

βρύχω

βρύχω   (1)   I gnash
βρυγμός, οῦ, ὁ   (7)   gnashing, chattering

βυθός

βυθίζω   (2)   I sink, plunge
βυθός, οῦ, ὁ   (1)   depth, open sea
ἄβυσσος, ου, ἡ   (9)   abyss, depth, underworld

βύσσος

βύσσος, ου, ἡ   (1)   fine linen

| βύσσινος, η, ον | (5) | made of fine linen; fine linen (subst.) |

γάζα

| γάζα, ης, ἡ | (1) | treasury, treasure |
| γαζοφυλάκιον, ου, τό | (5) | treasure room, treasury, contribution box |

γάμος

γαμέω	(28)	I marry
γαμίζω	(7)	I give in marriage, marry
γαμίσκω	(1)	I give in marriage
ἐπιγαμβρεύω	(1)	I marry as next of kin
γάμος, ου, ὁ	(16)	wedding, wedding banquet, marriage, wedding hall
ἄγαμος, ον	(4)	unmarried; unmarried man or woman (subst. in NT)

γάρ

| γάρ | (1041) | for, so, then |
| τοιγαροῦν | (2) | then, therefore, for that very reason |

γέ

εὖγε	(1)	well done! excellent!
γέ	(25)	indeed, even, at least
καίτοιγε	(1)	and yet, although
μενοῦνγε	(3)	rather, on the contrary, indeed
μήτιγε	(1)	not to speak of, let alone

γελάω

γελάω	(2)	I laugh
καταγελάω	(3)	I laugh at, ridicule
γέλως, ωτος, ὁ	(1)	laughter

γέμω

γεμίζω	(8)	I fill
γέμω	(11)	I am full
γόμος, ου, ὁ	(3)	load, cargo

γῆ

γεωργέω	(1)	I cultivate, till
γῆ, γῆς, ἡ	(250)	earth, soil, ground, land, region, humankind
ἀνάγαιον, ου, τό	(2)	room upstairs
γεώργιον, ου, τό	(1)	cultivated land, field
γεωργός, οῦ, ὁ	(19)	farmer, vine dresser, tenant farmer
ἐπίγειος, ον	(7)	earthly, human

γῆρας

γηράσκω	(2)	I grow old
γερουσία, ας, ἡ	(1)	council of elders (Sanhedrin)
γέρων, οντος, ὁ	(1)	old man
γῆρας, ως, τό	(1)	old age

γίνομαι

| γεννάω | (97) | I beget, become the father of, bear, give birth, produce |

γίνομαι	(669)	I become, am born, happen, come, go, am, exist
ἀναγεννάω	(2)	I beget again, cause to be born again
ἀπογίνομαι	(1)	I die
γενεαλογέω	(1)	I trace descent; am descended from (pass. in NT)
διαγίνομαι	(3)	I pass, elapse
ἐπιγίνομαι	(1)	I come up or on, happen
ζωογονέω	(3)	I give life to, make alive, keep alive
παραγίνομαι	(37)	I come, arrive, appear, stand by, come to the aid of
προγίνομαι	(1)	I happen before
συμπαραγίνομαι	(1)	I come together
τεκνογονέω	(1)	I bear children
γενεά, ᾶς, ἡ	(43)	family, descent, clan, race, generation, age
γενέσια, ων, τά	(2)	birthday celebration (pl. from subst. adj.)
γένεσις, εως, ἡ	(5)	beginning, origin, descent, birth, existence
γενετή, ῆς, ἡ	(1)	birth
γένημα, ατος, τό	(4)	produce, fruit, yield
γέννημα, ατος, τό	(4)	child, offspring
γένος, ους, τό	(20)	race, descendant(s), family, nation, class
γονεύς, έως, ὁ	(20)	parent; parents (pl. in NT)
γενεαλογία, ας, ἡ	(2)	genealogy
παλιγγενεσία, ας, ἡ	(2)	rebirth, regeneration, new age
συγγένεια, ας, ἡ	(3)	relationship, kinship, relatives
συγγενίς, ίδος, ἡ	(1)	female relative, kinswoman
τεκνογονία, ας, ἡ	(1)	bearing of children
γεννητός, ή, όν	(2)	born, begotten
γνήσιος, α ον	(4)	born in wedlock, legitimate, genuine
ἀγενεαλόγητος, ον	(1)	without genealogy
ἀγενής, ές	(1)	base, low, insignificant
ἀλλογενής, ές	(1)	foreign; foreigner (subst. in NT)
ἀρτιγέννητος, ον	(1)	new born
ἔκγονος, ον	(1)	born of; descendants, grandchildren (subst. pl. in NT)
εὐγενής, ές	(3)	well-born, noble-minded, open-minded
μονογενής, ές	(9)	only, unique
πρόγονος, ον	(2)	born before; forefathers, ancestors (pl. subst. in NT)
συγγενής, ές	(11)	related; relative, fellow countryman (subst. in NT)
γνησίως	(1)	sincerely, genuinely

γινώσκω

γινώσκω	(222)	I know, learn, understand, perceive, acknowledge
γνωρίζω	(25)	I make known, reveal, know
ἀγνοέω	(22)	I do not know, am ignorant, do not understand
ἀναγινώσκω	(32)	I read, read aloud
ἀναγνωρίζω	(1)	I learn to know again
διαγινώσκω	(2)	I decide, determine
ἐπιγινώσκω	(44)	I know, understand, recognize, learn, notice, know well
καταγινώσκω	(3)	I condemn, convict
προγινώσκω	(5)	I know before or in advance, choose beforehand
γνώμη, ης, ἡ	(9)	purpose, opinion, consent, decision
γνῶσις, εως, ἡ	(29)	knowledge, Gnosis
γνώστης, ου, ὁ	(1)	one acquainted, expert
ἀγνόημα, ατος, τό	(1)	sin committed in ignorance
ἄγνοια, ας, ἡ	(4)	ignorance
ἀγνωσία, ας, ἡ	(2)	ignorance, lack of spiritual discernment
ἀνάγνωσις, εως, ἡ	(3)	reading, public reading
διάγνωσις, εως, ἡ	(1)	decision

ἐπίγνωσις, εως, ἡ	(20)	knowledge, recognition
καρδιογνώστης, ου, ὁ	(2)	knower of hearts
πρόγνωσις, εως, ἡ	(2)	foreknowledge
συγγνώμη, ης, ἡ	(1)	concession, indulgence, pardon
γνωστός, ή, όν	(15)	known, notable, intelligible; acquaintance, (subst.)
ἄγνωστος, ον	(1)	unknown
ἀκατάγνωστος, ον	(1)	beyond reproach, above criticism

γλυκύς

γλεῦκος, ους, τό	(1)	sweet new wine
γλυκύς, εῖα, ύ	(4)	sweet

γλῶσσα

γλῶσσα, ης, ἡ	(50)	tongue, language
γλωσσόκομον, ου, τό	(2)	money box
ἑτερόγλωσσος, ον	(1)	speaking a foreign or strange language

γναφεύς

κνήθω	(1)	I itch; feel an itching (pass. in NT)
γναφεύς, έως, ὁ	(1)	bleacher, fuller
ἄγναφος, ον	(2)	unbleached, unshrunken, new

γογγύζω

γογγύζω	(8)	I grumble, murmur, speak secretly, whisper
διαγογγύζω	(2)	I complain, grumble
γογγυσμός, οῦ, ὁ	(4)	complaint, displeasure, secret talk, whispering
γογγυστής, οῦ, ὁ	(1)	grumbler

γόνυ

γονυπετέω	(4)	I kneel down
γόνυ, ατος, τό	(12)	knee

γράφω

γράφω	(191)	I write, record, compose
ἀπογράφω	(4)	I register, record
ἐγγράφω	(3)	I write in, record
ἐπιγράφω	(5)	I write on or in
καταγράφω	(1)	I write
προγράφω	(4)	I write before, mark out, portray publicly
γράμμα, ατος, τό	(14)	letter (of alphabet); document, epistle, book (mostly pl.)
γραμματεύς, έως, ὁ	(63)	secretary, clerk, expert in the law, scribe, scholar
γραφή, ῆς, ἡ	(50)	writing, scripture; scriptures (pl.)
ἀπογραφή, ῆς, ἡ	(2)	list, census, registration
ἐπιγραφή, ῆς, ἡ	(5)	inscription, superscription
ὑπογραμμός, οῦ, ὁ	(1)	example
χειρόγραφον, ου, τό	(1)	handwritten document, document of indebtedness, bond
γραπτός, ή, όν	(1)	written
ἀγράμματος, ον	(1)	unable to write, illiterate, uneducated

γυμνός

γυμνάζω	(4)	I exercise naked, train
γυμνιτεύω	(1)	I am poorly clothed

γυμνασία, ας, ἡ	(1)	training
γυμνότης, ητος, ἡ	(3)	nakedness, destitution, lack of sufficient clothing
γυμνός, ή, όν	(15)	naked, without an outer garment, poorly dressed

γυνή

γυναικάριον, ου, τό	(1)	idle or silly woman
γυνή, αικός, ἡ	(215)	woman, wife, bride
γυναικεῖος, α, ον	(1)	feminine, female

γωνία

γωνία, ας, ἡ	(9)	corner
ἀκρογωνιαῖος, α, ον	(2)	lying at the extreme corner; cornerstone (subst.)
τετράγωνος, ον	(1)	square

δαιμόνιον

δαιμονίζομαι	(13)	I am possessed by a demon
δαιμόνιον, ου, τό	(63)	demon, evil spirit, deity
δαίμων, ονος, ὁ	(1)	demon, evil spirit
δεισιδαιμονία, ας, ἡ	(1)	religion
δαιμονιώδης, ες	(1)	demonic
δεισιδαίμων, ον	(1)	religious

δάκρυον

δακρύω	(1)	I weep
δάκρυον, ου, τό	(10)	tear; weeping (pl.)

δαμάζω

δαμάζω	(4)	I subdue, tame, control
δάμαλις, εως, ἡ	(1)	heifer, young cow

δανίζω

δανίζω	(4)	I lend (money); borrow (mid.)
δάνειον, ου, τό	(1)	loan, debt
δανιστής, οῦ, ὁ	(1)	money lender, creditor

δαπάνη

δαπανάω	(5)	I spend, spend freely, waste
ἐκδαπανάω	(1)	I spend, exhaust
προσδαπανάω	(1)	I spend in addition
δαπάνη, ης, ἡ	(1)	cost, expense
ἀδάπανος, ον	(1)	free of charge

δέ

μηδείς, μηδεμία, μηδέν	(90)	no; no one, nobody, nothing (subst.); in no way (adv.)
οὐδείς, οὐδεμία, οὐδέν	(234)	no; no one, nothing (subst.); in no way (neut. acc.)
μηδαμῶς	(2)	by no means, certainly not, no
μηδέποτε	(1)	never
μηδέπω	(1)	not yet
οὐδαμῶς	(1)	by no means
οὐδέποτε	(16)	never
οὐδέπω	(4)	not yet
δέ	(2792)	but, and, rather, now, then, so

μηδέ	(56)	and not, but not, nor, not even
οὐδέ	(143)	and not, neither, nor, not even

δείκνυμι

δειγματίζω	(2)	I expose, make an example of, disgrace
δείκνυμι	(33)	I point out, show, explain, prove
ἀναδείκνυμι	(2)	I show forth, show clearly, appoint, commission
ἀποδείκνυμι	(4)	I make, proclaim, appoint, display, prove
ἐνδείκνυμι	(11)	I show, demonstrate, do (mid. in NT)
ἐπιδείκνυμι	(7)	I show, demonstrate, give proof
παραδειγματίζω	(1)	I expose, make an example of, hold up to contempt
ὑποδείκνυμι	(6)	I show, give direction, prove, warn
δακτύλιος, ου, ὁ	(1)	ring
δάκτυλος, ου, ὁ	(8)	finger
δεῖγμα, ατος, τό	(1)	example
ἀνάδειξις, εως, ἡ	(1)	commissioning, installation, revelation
ἀπόδειξις, εως, ἡ	(1)	proof
ἔνδειγμα, ατος, τό	(1)	evidence, plain indication, proof
ἔνδειξις, εως, ἡ	(4)	sign, proof
ὑπόδειγμα, ατος, τό	(6)	example, model, pattern, copy, imitation
χρυσοδακτύλιος, ον	(1)	wearing a gold ring

δεῖπνον

δειπνέω	(4)	I eat, dine
δεῖπνον, ου, τό	(16)	dinner, supper, main meal, banquet

δέκα

δεκατόω	(2)	I collect or receive tithes; pay tithes (pass.)
ἀποδεκατόω	(4)	I tithe, give one tenth, collect a tithe
δωδεκάφυλον, ου, τό	(1)	the twelve tribes
δέκα	(25)	ten
δέκατος, η, ον	(7)	tenth; tithe, tenth part, tithe (subst.)
δεκαοκτώ	(2)	eighteen
δεκαπέντε	(3)	fifteen
δεκατέσσαρες	(5)	fourteen
δώδεκα	(75)	twelve
δωδέκατος, η, ον	(1)	twelfth
ἕνδεκα	(6)	eleven
ἑνδέκατος, η, ον	(3)	eleventh
πεντεκαιδέκατος, η, ον	(1)	fifteenth
τεσσαρεσκαιδέκατος, η, ον	(2)	fourteenth

δεξιός

δεξιολάβος, ου, ὁ	(1)	spearman or slinger
δεξιός, ά, όν	(54)	right; right hand, right side (subst.)

δέομαι

δέομαι	(22)	I ask, beg, pray
προσδέομαι	(1)	I need in addition, have need
δέησις, εως, ἡ	(18)	prayer, entreaty, petition
ἐνδεής, ές	(1)	poor, impoverished

δέος

δειλιάω	(1)	I am cowardly, timid
δειλία, ας, ἡ	(1)	cowardice
δέος, ους, τό	(1)	fear, awe, reverence
δειλός, ή, όν	(3)	cowardly, timid
δεινῶς	(2)	fearfully, terribly

δέρω

δέρω	(15)	I skin; beat (fig. in NT)
δέρμα, ατος, τό	(1)	skin
δερμάτινος, η, ον	(2)	(made of) leather

δεῦρο

δεῦρο	(9)	come, until now
δεῦτε	(12)	come (serves as pl. of δεῦρο)

δέχομαι

δέχομαι	(56)	I take, receive, welcome, grasp, tolerate, accept
δοκιμάζω	(22)	I put to the test, examine, prove by testing, approve
ἀναδέχομαι	(2)	I accept, receive, welcome
ἀπεκδέχομαι	(8)	I await eagerly, wait
ἀποδέχομαι	(7)	I welcome, accept, recognize, praise
ἀποδοκιμάζω	(9)	I reject, declare useless
διαδέχομαι	(1)	I receive possession of
εἰσδέχομαι	(1)	I take in, receive, welcome
ἐκδέχομαι	(6)	I expect, wait
ἐνδέχομαι	(1)	it is possible (impers. in NT)
ἐπιδέχομαι	(2)	I receive as a guest, welcome, accept, recognize
ξενοδοχέω	(1)	I show hospitality
παραδέχομαι	(6)	I accept, receive, acknowledge, welcome
προσδέχομαι	(14)	I receive, welcome, expect, wait for
ὑποδέχομαι	(4)	I receive, welcome
δοκιμασία, ας, ἡ	(1)	testing, examination
δοκιμή, ῆς, ἡ	(7)	character, test, ordeal, proof
δοκίμιον, ου, τό	(2)	testing, means of testing; genuineness (subst. neut. adj.)
δοχή, ῆς, ἡ	(2)	reception, banquet
ἀποδοχή, ῆς, ἡ	(2)	acceptance, approval
ἀποκαραδοκία, ας, ἡ	(2)	eager expectation
διάδοχος, ου, ὁ	(1)	successor
ἐκδοχή, ῆς, ἡ	(1)	expectation
πανδοχεῖον, ου, τό	(1)	inn
πανδοχεύς, έως, ὁ	(1)	innkeeper
δεκτός, ή, όν	(5)	acceptable, welcome, favorable
δόκιμος, ον	(7)	approved, genuine, tried and true, respected
ἀδόκιμος, ον	(8)	not standing the test, unqualified, worthless
ἀνένδεκτος, ον	(1)	impossible
ἀπόδεκτος, ον	(2)	pleasing, acceptable
εὐπρόσδεκτος, ον	(5)	acceptable, pleasant, welcome

δέω

δεῖ	(101)	it is necessary, one must, one should (impers.)
δεσμεύω	(3)	I bind, tie up
δέω	(43)	I bind, tie

καταδέω	(1)	I bind up, bandage
οἰκοδεσποτέω	(1)	I manage my household, keep house
περιδέω	(1)	I bind, wrap
συνδέω	(1)	I bind with; am in prison with (pass. in NT)
ὑποδέω	(3)	I tie or bind beneath, put on shoes (mid. in NT)
δέσμη, ης, ἡ	(1)	bundle
δέσμιος, ου, ὁ	(16)	prisoner
δεσμός, οῦ, ὁ	(18)	bond, fetter; bonds, imprisonment, prison (pl.)
δεσμωτήριον, ου, τό	(4)	prison, jail
δεσμώτης, ου, ὁ	(2)	prisoner
δεσπότης, ου, ὁ	(10)	lord, master, owner
δεσμοφύλαξ, ακος, ὁ	(3)	jailer, keeper of the prison
διάδημα, ατος, τό	(3)	diadem, crown
οἰκοδεσπότης, ου, ὁ	(12)	master of the house
σύνδεσμος, ου, ὁ	(4)	that which binds together, bond, fetter
ὑπόδημα, ατος, τό	(10)	sandal, footwear

δή

δήπου	(1)	of course, surely
δή	(5)	indeed, now, then, therefore
ἐπειδή	(10)	when, after, since, since then, because
ἐπειδήπερ	(1)	inasmuch as, since

δῆλος

δηλόω	(7)	I reveal, make clear, show
ἀδηλότης, ητος, ἡ	(1)	uncertainty
δῆλος, η, ον	(3)	clear, plain, evident
ἄδηλος, ον	(2)	not clear, unseen, indistinct
ἔκδηλος, ον	(1)	quite evident, plain
κατάδηλος, ον	(1)	very clear or evident
πρόδηλος, ον	(3)	clear, evident, known to all
ἀδήλως	(1)	uncertainly

δῆμος

ἀποδημέω	(6)	I go on a journey, am away, am absent
δημηγορέω	(1)	I deliver a public address, make a speech
ἐκδημέω	(3)	I leave my country or home, am away from home
ἐνδημέω	(3)	I am at home
ἐπιδημέω	(2)	I stay in a place as a stranger, visit, live in a place
δῆμος, ου, ὁ	(4)	people, populace, crowd, popular assembly
δημιουργός, οῦ, ὁ	(1)	craftsman, maker, creator, builder
συνέκδημος, ου, ὁ	(2)	traveling companion
δημόσιος, α, ον	(4)	public; publicly (used as adv.)
ἀπόδημος, ον	(1)	away on a journey
παρεπίδημος, ον	(3)	sojourning; stranger, exile, alien (subst. in NT)

διά

διανύω	(1)	I complete, continue, arrive, travel
διά	(667)	through, during, with, at, by (gen.); because of (acc.)
διό	(53)	therefore, for this reason
διόπερ	(2)	therefore, for this very reason
διότι	(23)	because, therefore, for, that

διάκονος

διακονέω	(37)	I wait at table, serve, care for, help, serve as deacon
διακονία, ας, ἡ	(34)	service, office, ministry, aid, office of deacon
διάκονος, ου, ὁ, ἡ	(29)	servant, helper, deacon (masc.); helper, deaconess (fem.)

διδάσκω

διδάσκω	(97)	I teach
ἑτεροδιδασκαλέω	(2)	I teach a different doctrine
διδασκαλία, ας, ἡ	(21)	teaching (both act and content), instruction
διδάσκαλος, ου, ὁ	(59)	teacher
διδαχή, ῆς, ἡ	(30)	teaching (both act and content), instruction
νομοδιδάσκαλος, ου, ὁ	(3)	teacher of the law
ψευδοδιδάσκαλος, ου, ὁ	(1)	false teacher, one who teaches falsehoods
διδακτικός, ή, όν	(2)	able to teach
διδακτός, ή, όν	(3)	instructed, imparted, taught
θεοδίδακτος, ον	(1)	taught by God
καλοδιδάσκαλος, ον	(1)	teaching what is good

δίδωμι

δίδωμι	(415)	I give, grant, give out, entrust, give back, put, give up
δωρέομαι	(3)	I give, present, bestow
ἀναδίδωμι	(1)	I deliver, hand over
ἀνταποδίδωμι	(7)	I give back, repay, return
ἀποδίδωμι	(48)	I give away, give up, pay, return, reward; sell (mid.)
διαδίδωμι	(4)	I distribute
ἐκδίδωμι	(4)	I let out for hire, lease, rent (mid. in NT)
ἐπιδίδωμι	(9)	I give, hand over, deliver, give up or over, surrender
μεταδίδωμι	(5)	I give, impart, share
παραδίδωμι	(119)	I entrust, give up, hand over (into custody), hand down
προδίδωμι	(1)	I give in advance
δόμα, ατος, τό	(4)	gift
δόσις, εως, ἡ	(2)	gift, giving
δότης, ου, ὁ	(1)	giver
δωρεά, ᾶς, ἡ	(11)	gift, bounty
δώρημα, ατος, τό	(2)	gift, present
δῶρον, ου, τό	(19)	gift, present, offering, offering
ἀνταπόδομα, ατος, τό	(2)	repayment, retribution
ἀνταπόδοσις, εως, ἡ	(1)	repaying, reward
μισθαποδοσία, ας, ἡ	(3)	reward, punishment, retribution
μισθαποδότης, ου, ὁ	(1)	rewarder
παράδοσις, εως, ἡ	(13)	tradition
προδότης, ου, ὁ	(3)	traitor, betrayer
ἔκδοτος, ον	(1)	given up, delivered up, handed over
εὐμετάδοτος, ον	(1)	generous
πατροπαράδοτος, ον	(1)	inherited, handed down from one's father
δωρεάν	(9)	as a gift, without payment, undeservedly, in vain

δίκη

δικαιόω	(39)	I justify, vindicate, treat as just, acquit, make free
ἀδικέω	(28)	I do wrong, am in the wrong, treat unjustly, injure
ἐκδικέω	(6)	I avenge, procure justice, punish
καταδικάζω	(5)	I condemn, find or pronounce guilty
δικαιοσύνη, ης, ἡ	(92)	righteousness, uprightness, justice
δικαίωμα, ατος, τό	(10)	regulation, requirement, righteous deed

δικαίωσις, εως, ἡ	(2)	justification, vindication, acquittal
δικαστής, οῦ, ὁ	(2)	judge
δίκη, ης, ἡ	(3)	penalty, punishment; Justice (pers.)
ἀδίκημα, ατος, τό	(3)	wrong, crime, misdeed
ἀδικία, ας, ἡ	(25)	wrongdoing, unrighteousness, wickedness, injustice
ἀντίδικος, ου, ὁ	(5)	opponent, enemy
δικαιοκρισία, ας, ἡ	(1)	righteous judgment, just verdict
ἐκδίκησις, εως, ἡ	(9)	vengeance, punishment
καταδίκη, ης, ἡ	(1)	condemnation, sentence
δίκαιος, α, ον	(79)	upright, just, righteous, honest, good, innocent, right
ἄδικος, ον	(12)	unjust, dishonest, untrustworthy
ἔκδικος, ον	(2)	avenging; avenger, one who punishes (subst. in NT)
ἔνδικος, ον	(2)	just, deserved
ὑπόδικος, ον	(1)	liable to judgment or punishment, accountable
δικαίως	(5)	justly, uprightly
ἀδίκως	(1)	unjustly

δίψος

διψάω	(16)	I am thirsty, thirst, long for
δίψος, ους, τό	(1)	thirst

διώκω

διώκω	(45)	I hasten, persecute, drive away, pursue, seek after
ἐκδιώκω	(1)	I persecute severely
καταδιώκω	(1)	I search for, hunt for
διωγμός, οῦ, ὁ	(10)	persecution
διώκτης, ου, ὁ	(1)	persecutor

δοκέω

δογματίζω	(1)	I submit to rules and regulations (pass. in NT)
δοκέω	(62)	I think, suppose, seem, have a reputation
δοξάζω	(61)	I praise, honor, glorify
ἐνδοξάζομαι	(2)	I am glorified, honored
εὐδοκέω	(21)	I am well pleased, consent, resolve, like, approve
προσδοκάω	(16)	I wait for, look for, expect
συνδοξάζω	(1)	I am glorified with, share in the glory (pass. in NT)
συνευδοκέω	(6)	I agree with, approve of, sympathize with
δόγμα, ατος, τό	(5)	decree, ordinance, decision, command
δόξα, ης, ἡ	(166)	brightness, splendor, glory, majesty, reflection, fame
εὐδοκία, ας, ἡ	(9)	good will, favor, good pleasure, wish, desire
κενοδοξία, ας, ἡ	(1)	vanity, conceit, excessive ambition
προσδοκία, ας, ἡ	(2)	expectation
ἔνδοξος, ον	(4)	honored, distinguished, glorious, splendid
κενόδοξος, ον	(1)	conceited, boastful
παράδοξος, ον	(1)	strange, wonderful, remarkable, unusual

δόλος

δελεάζω	(3)	I lure, entice
δολιόω	(1)	I deceive
δολόω	(1)	I falsify, adulterate
δόλος, ου, ὁ	(11)	deceit, treachery, cunning
δόλιος, α, ον	(1)	deceitful, treacherous
ἄδολος, ον	(1)	without deceit, unadulterated, pure

δοῦλος

δουλεύω	(25)	I am a slave, serve, obey
δουλόω	(8)	I enslave, subject, bring into bondage
δουλαγωγέω	(1)	I enslave, bring into subjection
καταδουλόω	(2)	I enslave, reduce to slavery, take advantage of
δουλεία, ας, ἡ	(5)	slavery
δούλη, ης, ἡ	(3)	female slave, bondmaid
δοῦλος, ου, ὁ	(124)	slave, minister
ὀφθαλμοδουλία, ας, ἡ	(2)	eyeservice, service to attract attention
σύνδουλος, ου, ὁ	(10)	fellow slave
δοῦλος, η, ον	(2)	slavish, servile, subject

δράσσομαι

δράσσομαι	(1)	I catch, seize
δραχμή, ῆς, ἡ	(3)	drachma (Greek silver coin)
δίδραχμον, ου, τό	(2)	two-drachma piece (Greek silver coin)

δύναμαι

δύναμαι	(210)	I can, am able
δυναμόω	(2)	I strengthen
δυνατέω	(3)	I am strong, able
ἀδυνατέω	(2)	I am powerless; it is impossible (impers. in NT)
ἐνδυναμόω	(7)	I strengthen; become or grow strong (pass.)
καταδυναστεύω	(2)	I oppress, exploit, dominate
δύναμις, εως, ἡ	(119)	power, ability, miracle, army, power (supernatural)
δυνάστης, ου, ὁ	(3)	ruler, sovereign, court official
δυνατός, ή, όν	(32)	powerful, strong, mighty, able
ἀδύνατος, ον	(10)	powerless, impotent, impossible

δύνω

δύνω	(2)	I go down, set (of the sun)
ἀπεκδύομαι	(2)	I take off, strip off, disarm
ἐκδύω	(6)	I strip, take off; undress myself (mid.)
ἐνδιδύσκω	(2)	I dress, put on
ἐνδύνω	(1)	I go in, enter, creep in, worm into
ἐνδύω	(27)	I dress, clothe; put on, wear (mid.)
ἐπενδύομαι	(2)	I put on (in addition)
ἐπιδύω	(1)	I set (of the sun)
παρεισδύω	(1)	I slip in stealthily, sneak in
δύσις, εως, ἡ	(1)	setting (of the sun), west
δυσμή, ῆς, ἡ	(5)	going down, setting (of the sun), west (pl. in NT)
ἀπέκδυσις, εως, ἡ	(1)	removal, stripping off
ἔνδυμα, ατος, τό	(8)	garment, clothing
ἔνδυσις, εως, ἡ	(1)	putting on, wearing
ἐπενδύτης, ου, ὁ	(1)	outer garment, coat

δύο

διπλόω	(1)	I double, pay back double
διστάζω	(2)	I doubt
διχάζω	(1)	I separate, turn against
διχοτομέω	(2)	I cut in two, punish severely
δίδραχμον, ου, τό	(2)	two-drachma piece (Greek silver coin)
διετία, ας, ἡ	(2)	period of two years

διομυριάς, άδος, ή	(1)	double myriad, twenty thousand
διχοστασία, ας, ή	(2)	dissension
δωδεκάφυλον, ου, τό	(1)	the twelve tribes
δευτεραῖος, α, ον	(1)	on the second day
δεύτερος, α, ον	(43)	second, secondly; second time (subst.)
διακόσιοι, αι, α	(8)	two hundred
διπλοῦς, ῆ, οῦν	(4)	double, two-fold
δύο	(135)	two
διετής, ές	(1)	two years old
διθάλασσος, ον	(1)	with the sea on both sides, between the seas
δίλογος, ον	(1)	double-tongued, insincere
δίστομος, ον	(3)	double-edged
διοχίλιοι, αι, α	(1)	two thousand
δίψυχος, ον	(2)	double-minded, doubting, hesitating
δώδεκα	(75)	twelve
δωδέκατος, η, ον	(1)	twelfth
δίς	(6)	twice

δῶμα

ἀνοικοδομέω	(2)	I build up again, rebuild
ἐποικοδομέω	(7)	I build upon
οἰκοδομέω	(40)	I build, erect, restore, rebuild, build up, edify, benefit
συνοικοδομέω	(1)	I build together; am built up together (pass. in NT)
δῶμα, ατος, τό	(7)	roof, housetop
ἐνδώμησις, εως, ή	(1)	interior structure, material, foundation
οἰκοδομή, ῆς, ή	(18)	building up, edification, building, edifice
οἰκοδόμος, ου, ὁ	(1)	builder

ἐάω

ἐάω	(11)	I let, permit, let go, leave alone
προσεάω	(1)	I permit to go farther
ἔα	(1)	ah! ha! (poss. pres. imper. of ἐάω)

ἐγγύς

ἐγγίζω	(42)	I approach, come near
ἐγγύς	(31)	near, close to;near, close to (impr. prep.)

ἐγείρω

γρηγορέω	(22)	I am awake, keep awake, am alert, am watchful
ἐγείρω	(144)	I raise up, restore, wake; rise, awaken, appear (pass.)
διαγρηγορέω	(1)	I keep awake
διεγείρω	(6)	I wake up, arouse, stir up; awaken (pass.)
ἐξεγείρω	(2)	I awaken, raise, cause to appear, bring into being
ἐπεγείρω	(2)	I awaken, arouse, excite
συνεγείρω	(3)	I raise together with
ἔγερσις, εως, ή	(1)	resurrection

ἐγώ

ἐμός, ή, όν	(76)	my, mine; my property (subst.)
ἡμέτερος, α, ον	(7)	our
μηδαμῶς	(2)	by no means, certainly not, no
ἐγώ, ἐμοῦ; ἡμεῖς, ἡμῶν	(2666)	I; we
ἐμαυτοῦ, ῆς	(37)	(of) myself

κἀγώ (84) and I, but I, I also, I myself, I in turn (= καὶ ἐγώ)

ἔδαφος

ἐδαφίζω (1) I dash or raze to the ground, completely destroy
ἔδαφος, ους, τό (1) ground

ἑδραῖος

ἐνεδρεύω (2) I lie in wait, plot
καθέζομαι (7) I sit, sit down, am situated
κάθημαι (91) I sit, sit down, stay, live, reside
παρακαθέζομαι (1) I sit beside; have seated myself beside (pass. in NT)
παρεδρεύω (1) I wait upon, serve
συγκάθημαι (2) I sit with
ἑδραίωμα, ατος, τό (1) foundation, support
ἀφεδρών, ῶνος, ὁ (2) latrine, toilet
ἐνέδρα, ας, ἡ (2) plot, ambush
καθέδρα, ας, ἡ (3) chair, seat
πρωτοκαθεδία, ας, ἡ (4) place of honor, best seat
συνέδριον, ου, τό (22) Sanhedrin, council
ἑδραῖος, α, ον (3) seated; firm, steadfast (met. in NT)
εὐπάρεδρος, ον (1) constant; devotion (subst. in NT)

ἔθνος

ἔθνος, ους, τό (162) nation, people; Gentiles, heathen (pl.)
ἐθνάρχης, ου, ὁ (1) ethnarch, governor, official
ἐθνικός, ή, όν (4) Gentile, heathen; the Gentile (subst. in NT)
ἐθνικῶς (1) in Gentile fashion, like the heathen

ἔθος

ἐθίζω (1) I accustom
ἔθος, ους, τό (12) habit, usage, custom, law
ἦθος, ους, τό (1) custom, habit
κακοήθεια, ας, ἡ (1) malice, malignity
συνήθεια, ας, ἡ (3) being accustomed, custom, habit

εἰ

εἰ (503) if, that, whether
ἐάν (351) if, when
ἐάνπερ (3) if indeed, if only, supposing that
εἴπερ (6) if indeed, if after all, since
εἴτε (65) if, whether
κἄν (17) and if, even if, if only (= καὶ ἐάν)
ὡσεί (21) as, like, about
ὡσπερεί (1) like, as though, as it were

εἶδος

εἰδέα, ας, ἡ (1) appearance
εἶδος, ους, τό (5) form, outward appearance, kind, sight
εἰδωλεῖον, ου, τό (1) idol's temple
εἴδωλον, ου, τό (11) image, idol
εἰδωλολάτρης, ου, ὁ (7) idolater
εἰδωλολατρία, ας, ἡ (4) idolatry
συνείδησις, εως, ἡ (30) conscience, consciousness

γραώδης, ες	(1)	characteristic of old women
δαιμονιώδης, ες	(1)	demonic
εἰδωλόθυτος, ον	(9)	meat offered to an idol (subst. in NT)
κατείδωλος, ον	(1)	full of idols
πετρώδης, ες	(4)	rocky; rocky ground (subst. in NT)
ἴδε	(29)	look, see, behold, here is, here (imper. of εἶδον)
ἰδού	(200)	look, see, behold, consider, here is (imper. of εἶδον)

εἴκω

εἴκω	(1)	I yield
ὑπείκω	(1)	I yield, submit

εἰκών

ἔοικα	(2)	I am like, resemble
εἰκών, όνος, ἡ	(23)	image, likeness, form, appearance
ἐπιείκεια, ας, ἡ	(2)	clemency, gentleness, graciousness
ἐπιεικής, ές	(5)	yielding, gentle, kind

[εἴλω]

ἐνειλέω	(1)	I wrap, confine
ὁμιλέω	(4)	I speak, talk, converse
συνομιλέω	(1)	I talk or converse with
ὁμιλία, ας, ἡ	(1)	association, company

εἰμί

εἰμί	(2460)	I am, exist, occur, mean, live, stay, am present
ἄπειμι	(7)	I am absent, am away
ἔνειμι	(1)	I am in or inside
ἔνι	(6)	there is (= ἔνεστιν; impers. and with neg. in NT)
ἔξεστι	(31)	it is permitted, it is possible, it is proper (impers.)
ἐξουσιάζω	(4)	I have the right or power over
κατεξουσιάζω	(2)	I exercise authority, tyrannize
πάρειμι	(24)	I am present or here, have come
συμπάρειμι	(1)	I am present with
σύνειμι	(2)	I am with
οὐσία, ας, ἡ	(2)	property, wealth
ἀπουσία, ας, ἡ	(1)	absence
ἐξουσία, ας, ἡ	(102)	authority, right, ability, power, official, jurisdiction
παρουσία, ας, ἡ	(24)	presence, coming, advent, arrival
ἐπιούσιος, ον	(2)	for today, for tomorrow, necessary for existence
περιούσιος, ον	(1)	chosen, special
ὄντως	(10)	really, certainly, in truth; real (adj.)

[εἶμι]

ἄπειμι	(1)	I go, come
εἴσειμι	(4)	I go in, go into
ἔξειμι	(4)	I go out or away, go on a journey
ἔπειμι	(5)	I come after; next, next day (partic. in NT)
καθίημι	(4)	I let down
σύνειμι	(1)	I come together
ἀπρόσιτος, ον	(1)	unapproachable

εἰρήνη

εἰρηνεύω	(4)	I keep the peace, live at peace
εἰρηνοποιέω	(1)	I make peace
εἰρήνη, ης, ἡ	(92)	peace, harmony, order, health
εἰρηνικός, ή, όν	(2)	peaceable, peaceful
εἰρηνοποιός, ον	(1)	making peace; peacemaker (subst. in NT)

εἰς

ἐσώτερος, α, ον	(2)	inner; inside (adv. as impr. prep.)
ἔσω	(9)	in, inside; inside, into (impr. prep.); insider (subst.)
ἔσωθεν	(12)	from inside, within; inside, inner nature (subst.)
εἰς	(1768)	into, in, toward, to, among, near, on, for, against, as, at

εἷς

ἐξουδενέω	(1)	I treat with contempt
ἐξουθενέω	(11)	I despise, reject, treat with contempt
ἑνότης, ητος, ἡ	(2)	unity
εἷς, μία, ἕν	(344)	one, a, single, someone, anyone
ἕνδεκα	(6)	eleven
ἑνδέκατος, η, ον	(3)	eleventh
μηδείς, μηδεμία, μηδέν	(90)	no; no one, nobody, nothing (subst.); in no way (adv.)
οὐδείς, οὐδεμία, οὐδέν	(234)	no; no one, nothing (subst.); in no way (neut. acc.)

εἶτα

εἶτα	(15)	then, next, furthermore
ἔπειτα	(16)	then, thereupon, next
μετέπειτα	(1)	afterwards

ἐκ

ἔσχατος, η, ον	(52)	last, least; end (subst.); finally (neut. acc.)
ἐξώτερος, α, ον	(3)	farthest, extreme
ἐκτός	(8)	outside; outside, except (impr. prep.)
ἔξω	(63)	outside, outer, out; outside, out of (impr. prep.)
ἔξωθεν	(13)	from the outside, outside; (from) outside (impr. prep)
ἐσχάτως	(1)	finally
ἐκπερισσῶς	(1)	excessively
παρεκτός	(3)	besides, outside; apart from, except for (impr. prep.)
ὑπερεκπερισσοῦ	(3)	beyond all measure; infinitely more than (impr. prep.)
ἐκ	(914)	from, out of, away from, by, of, because of

ἕκαστος

ἕκαστος, η, ον	(82)	each, every; each one, every one (subst.)
ἑκάστοτε	(1)	at any time, always

ἑκατόν

ἑκατοντάρχης, ου, ὁ	(20)	centurion, captain, officer
ἑκατόν	(17)	one hundred
ἑκατονταετής, ές	(1)	a hundred years old
ἑκατονταπλασίων, ον	(3)	a hundred fold

ἐκεῖ

ἐκεῖνος, η, ο	(265)	that; that person or thing, he, she, it (subst.)
ἐκεῖ	(105)	there, in that place, to that place
ἐκεῖθεν	(37)	from there
ἐκεῖσε	(2)	there, at that place
ἐπέκεινα	(1)	farther on, beyond (impr. prep. in NT)
κἀκεῖ	(10)	and there, there also (= καὶ ἐκεῖ)
κἀκεῖθεν	(10)	and from there, and then (= καὶ ἐκεῖθεν)
ὑπερέκεινα	(1)	beyond (impr. prep. in NT)
κἀκεῖνος, η, ο	(22)	and that one or he, that one or he also (= καὶ ἐκεῖνος)

ἐκών

ἑκούσιος, α, ον	(1)	voluntary, willing
ἑκών, οῦσα, όν	(2)	willing, of one's own free will
ἄκων, ουσα, ον	(1)	unwilling; unwillingly (adv.)
ἑκουσίως	(2)	willingly, intentionally

ἐλαία

ἐλαία, ας, ἡ	(13)	olive tree, olive
ἔλαιον, ου, τό	(11)	olive oil, oil
ἐλαιών, ῶνος, ὁ	(3)	olive grove, olive orchard
ἀγριέλαιος, ου, ἡ	(2)	wild olive tree
καλλιέλαιος, ου, ἡ	(1)	cultivated olive tree

ἐλάσσων

ἐλαττονέω	(1)	I have less, too little
ἐλαττόω	(3)	I make lower, inferior; diminish (pass.)
ἐλάσσων, ον	(4)	smaller, younger, inferior, lesser
ἐλάχιστος, η, ον	(14)	smallest, least, very small, insignificant, very few

ἐλαύνω

ἐλαύνω	(5)	I drive, advance, row
ἀπελαύνω	(1)	I drive away

ἐλαφρός

ἐλαφρία, ας, ἡ	(1)	vacillation, levity
ἐλαφρός, ά, όν	(2)	light, insignificant

ἐλέγχω

ἐλέγχω	(17)	I bring to light, expose, convince, reprove, punish
διακατελέγχομαι	(1)	I refute
ἐλεγμός, οῦ, ὁ	(1)	conviction, reproof, punishment
ἔλεγξις, εως, ἡ	(1)	conviction, rebuke, reproof
ελεγχος, ου, ὁ	(1)	proof, proving, inner conviction
ἀπελεγμός, οῦ, ὁ	(1)	refutation, exposure, discredit

ἔλεος

ἐλεάω	(3)	I have mercy on, show kindness
ἐλεέω	(29)	I have mercy, am merciful; find mercy (pass.)
ἔλεος, ους, τό	(27)	mercy, compassion, pity
ἐλεημοσύνη, ης, ἡ	(13)	kind deed, alms, charitable giving
ἐλεεινός, ή, όν	(2)	miserable, pitiable

ἐλεήμων, ον	(2)	merciful, sympathetic
ἀνελεήμων, ον	(1)	unmerciful
ἀνέλεος, ον	(1)	merciless

ἐλεύθερος

ἐλευθερόω	(7)	I free, set free
ἐλευθερία, ας, ἡ	(11)	freedom, liberty
ἀπελεύθερος, ου, ὁ	(1)	freed person
ἐλεύθερος, α, ον	(23)	free, independent; free person (subst.)

ἕλκος

ἑλκόω	(1)	I cause sores; am covered with sores (pass. in NT)
ἕλκος, ους, τό	(3)	sore, abscess, ulcer

ἕλκω

ἕλκω	(8)	I drag, draw
ἐξέλκω	(1)	I drag away, lure away

ἐλπίς

ἐλπίζω	(31)	I hope, expect
ἀπελπίζω	(1)	I despair, expect in return
προελπίζω	(1)	I hope before, am the first to hope
ἐλπίς, ίδος, ἡ	(53)	hope, expectation, something hoped for

ἐν

δυσεντέριον, ου, τό	(1)	dysentery
ἐναντίος, α, ον	(8)	opposite, against, contrary, hostile
ὑπεναντίος, α, ον	(2)	opposed, contrary, hostile; opponent (subst.)
ἔνθεν	(2)	from here
ἐντός	(2)	inside, within, among (impr. prep. in NT)
ἀπέναντι	(5)	opposite, against, contrary to (impr. prep. in NT)
ἔμπροσθεν	(48)	in front, ahead; in front of, before (impr. prep.)
ἔναντι	(2)	opposite, before, in the judgment of (impr. prep. in NT)
ἐναντίον	(8)	before, in the judgment of (impr. prep. in NT)
ἐνθάδε	(8)	here, in or to this place
ἐντεῦθεν	(10)	from here, from this
κατέναντι	(8)	opposite; opposite, in the sight of, before (impr. prep.)
τοὐναντίον	(3)	on the other hand, rather (= τὸ ἐναντίον)
ἐν	(2752)	in, on, at, near, to, by, before, among, with, within, when

ἐννέα

ἔνατος, η, ον	(10)	ninth
ἐνενήκοντα	(4)	ninety
ἐννέα	(5)	nine

ἐντολή

ἐντέλλομαι	(15)	I command
ἔνταλμα, ατος, τό	(3)	commandment
ἐντολή, ῆς, ἡ	(67)	commandment, command, order, law

ἕξ

ἕκτος, η, ον	(14)	sixth

ἕξ	(13)	six
ἑξακόσιοι, αι, α	(2)	six hundred
ἑξήκοντα	(9)	sixty

ἑορτή

ἑορτάζω	(1)	I celebrate
ἑορτή, ῆς, ἡ	(25)	festival

ἐπί

ἐπάνω	(19)	above, over, more than; over, above, on (impr. prep.)
ἐπεί	(26)	because, since, for, for otherwise
ἐπί	(890)	on, over, when (gen.); on, at, in (dat.); on, to, for (acc.)

ἐπιποθέω

ἐπιποθέω	(9)	I long for, desire, yearn over
ἐπιπόθησις, εως, ἡ	(2)	longing
ἐπιποθία, ας, ἡ	(1)	longing, desire
ἐπιπόθητος, ον	(1)	longed for, desired

ἑπτά

ἑβδομήκοντα	(5)	seventy
ἕβδομος, η, ον	(9)	seventh; the seventh (subst.)
ἑπτά	(88)	seven
ἑπτακισχίλιοι, αι, α	(1)	seven thousand
ἑβδομηκοντάκις	(1)	seventy times
ἑπτάκις	(4)	seven times

ἔργον

ἐργάζομαι	(41)	I work, do, perform, bring about
ἀγαθοεργέω	(1)	I do good
ἀγαθουργέω	(1)	I do good (contr. of ἀγαθοεργέω)
ἀργέω	(1)	I am idle, grow weary
γεωργέω	(1)	I cultivate, till
ἐνεργέω	(21)	I work, am at work, produce
εὐεργετέω	(1)	I do good
ἱερουργέω	(1)	I serve as a priest
καταργέω	(27)	I make ineffective, nullify, abolish; cease (pass.)
κατεργάζομαι	(22)	I do, achieve, accomplish, produce, prepare, conquer
λειτουργέω	(3)	I perform a service, serve
περιεργάζομαι	(1)	I am a busybody
προσεργάζομαι	(1)	I make more, earn in addition
συνεργέω	(5)	I work together with, cooperate with, help
συνυπουργέω	(1)	I join in helping, cooperate with
ἐργασία, ας, ἡ	(6)	practice, pursuit, trade, profit, gain, effort
ἐργάτης, ου, ὁ	(16)	workman, laborer, doer
ἔργον, ου, τό	(169)	work, deed, action, manifestation, occupation, thing
ἀμπελουργός, οῦ, ὁ	(1)	vine dresser, gardener
γεώργιον, ου, τό	(1)	cultivated land, field
γεωργός, οῦ, ὁ	(19)	farmer, vine dresser, tenant farmer
δημιουργός, οῦ, ὁ	(1)	craftsman, maker, creator, builder
ἐνέργεια, ας, ἡ	(8)	working, operation, action
ἐνέργημα, ατος, τό	(2)	working, activity
εὐεργεσία, ας, ἡ	(2)	doing good, service, good deed, kindness

εὐεργέτης, ου, ὁ	(1)	benefactor
λειτουργία, ας, ἡ	(6)	service, ceremonial duty, ministry
λειτουργός, οῦ, ὁ	(5)	servant, minister
πανουργία, ας, ἡ	(5)	cunning, craftiness, trickery
ῥαδιούργημα, ατος, τό	(1)	crime, villainy
ῥαδιουργία, ας, ἡ	(1)	wickedness, villainy, unscrupulousness
ἀργός, ή, όν	(8)	unemployed, idle, lazy, careless, useless
ἐνεργής, ές	(3)	effective, active, powerful
κακοῦργος, ον	(4)	evil doing; criminal, evildoer (subst. in NT)
λειτουργικός, ή, όν	(1)	engaged in holy service, serving, ministering
οἰκουργός, όν	(1)	working at home, domestic
πανοῦργος, ον	(1)	clever, crafty, sly
περίεργος, ον	(2)	meddlesome; busybody, magic (subst. in NT)
συνεργός, όν	(13)	working together; helper, fellow worker (subst. in NT)

ἔρημος

ἐρημόω	(5)	I am laid waste, depopulated (pass. in NT)
ἐρημία, ας, ἡ	(4)	uninhabited region, desert
ἐρήμωσις, εως, ἡ	(3)	devastation, destruction, depopulation
ἔρημος, ον	(48)	abandoned, desolate; desert, wilderness (fem. subst.)

ἔρις

ἐρίζω	(1)	I quarrel, wrangle
ἔρις, ιδος, ἡ	(9)	strife, discord, contention

ἔριφος

ἐρίφιον, ου, τό	(1)	kid, goat
ἔριφος, ου, ὁ	(2)	kid, goat

ἑρμηνεύω

ἑρμηνεύω	(3)	I explain, interpret, translate
διερμηνεύω	(6)	I translate, explain, interpret
μεθερμηνεύω	(8)	I translate
ἑρμηνεία, ας, ἡ	(2)	translation, interpretation
διερμηνευτής, οῦ, ὁ	(1)	interpreter, translator
δυσερμήνευτος, ον	(1)	hard to explain

ἔρχομαι

ἔρχομαι	(634)	I come, appear, go
ἀνέρχομαι	(3)	I go up, come up
ἀντιπαρέρχομαι	(2)	I pass by on the opposite side
ἀπέρχομαι	(117)	I go away, depart, pass away, go, go after
διέρχομαι	(43)	I go through, cross over, come, go about, spread
εἰσέρχομαι	(194)	I come in or into, go in or into, enter, share in, fall into
ἐξέρχομαι	(218)	I go out or away, come out, disembark, leave
ἐπανέρχομαι	(2)	I return
ἐπεισέρχομαι	(1)	I come upon, rush in suddenly and forcibly
ἐπέρχομαι	(9)	I come, come along, appear, approach, come upon, attack
κατέρχομαι	(16)	I come down, arrive, put in
παρεισέρχομαι	(2)	I slip in, come in
παρέρχομαι	(29)	I go or pass by, pass, pass away, neglect, disobey, come
περιέρχομαι	(3)	I go around, wander
προέρχομαι	(9)	I go forward, go before, come out

προσέρχομαι	(86)	I come or go to, approach, agree with
συνεισέρχομαι	(2)	I enter or go in with
συνέρχομαι	(30)	I come together, come or go with, have sexual relations
ἔλευσις, εως, ἡ	(1)	coming, advent
προσήλυτος, ου, ὁ	(4)	proselyte, convert

ἐρωτάω

ἐραυνάω	(6)	I search, examine, investigate
ἐρωτάω	(63)	I ask, ask a question, request
διερωτάω	(1)	I learn by inquiry
ἐξεραυνάω	(1)	I inquire carefully
ἐπερωτάω	(56)	I ask, ask for
ἐπερώτημα, ατος, τό	(1)	question, request, appeal
ἀνεξεραύνητος, ον	(1)	unfathomable, unsearchable

ἐσθίω

ἐσθίω	(158)	I eat, consume
κατεσθίω	(14)	I eat up, consume, devour, destroy
νηστεύω	(20)	I fast, go without food
συνεσθίω	(5)	I eat with
νηστεία, ας, ἡ	(5)	fasting, abstention from food, hunger
νῆστις, ιδος, ὁ, ἡ	(2)	not eating, hungry

[ἐτάζω]

| ἀνετάζω | (2) | I give a hearing |
| ἐξετάζω | (3) | I examine, inquire |

ἕτερος

ἑτεροδιδασκαλέω	(2)	I teach a different doctrine
ἑτεροζυγέω	(1)	I am unevenly yoked, mismated
ἕτερος, α, ον	(98)	other, another, different; next day, neighbor (subst.)
ἑτερόγλωσσος, ον	(1)	speaking a foreign or strange language
ἑτέρως	(1)	differently, otherwise
πότερον	(1)	whether

ἔτι

ἔτι	(93)	still, yet, more
μηκέτι	(22)	no longer, not from now on
οὐκέτι	(47)	no longer, no more, then not

ἕτοιμος

ἑτοιμάζω	(40)	I prepare, put or keep in readiness
προετοιμάζω	(2)	I prepare beforehand
ἑτοιμασία, ας, ἡ	(1)	readiness, preparation
ἕτοιμος, η, ον	(17)	ready, prepared
ἑτοίμως	(3)	readily

ἔτος

ἔτος, ους, τό	(49)	year
διετία, ας, ἡ	(2)	period of two years
τριετία, ας, ἡ	(1)	period of three years
διετής, ές	(1)	two years old

ἑκατονταετής, ές	(1)	a hundred years old
τεσσερακονταετής, ές	(2)	forty years

εὐθύς

εὐθύνω	(2)	I straighten, guide straight
εὐθυδρομέω	(2)	I sail a straight course
κατευθύνω	(3)	I make straight, lead, direct
εὐθύτης, ητος, ἡ	(1)	straightness; uprightness (fig. in NT)
εὐθύς, εῖα, ύ	(51)	straight, right, upright
εὐθέως	(36)	immediately, at once
εὐθύς	(8)	immediately, at once, then, so then

εὑρίσκω

εὑρίσκω	(176)	I find, discover; obtain (mid.)
ἀνευρίσκω	(2)	I find by searching
ἐφευρετής, οῦ, ὁ	(1)	inventor, contriver

εὔχομαι

εὔχομαι	(7)	I pray, wish
προσεύχομαι	(85)	I pray
εὐχή, ῆς, ἡ	(3)	prayer, oath, vow
προσευχή, ῆς, ἡ	(36)	prayer, place of prayer

ἐχθρός

ἔχθρα, ας, ἡ	(6)	enmity, hatred, hostility
ἐχθρός, ά, όν	(32)	hostile, hated, hating; enemy (subst.)

ἔχω

ἔχω	(708)	I have, hold, wear, keep, cause, consider; am (intrans.)
ἀνέχω	(15)	I endure, bear with, put up with, accept (mid. in NT)
ἀντέχω	(4)	I cling to, hold fast to, help (mid. in NT)
ἀπέχω	(19)	I receive in full, am enough, am distant; abstain (mid.)
ἀσχημονέω	(2)	I behave disgracefully, behave indecently
ἐνέχω	(3)	I have a grudge against; am subject to (pass.)
ἐπέχω	(5)	I hold fast, notice, fix my attention on, stop, stay
εὐνουχίζω	(2)	I castrate, emasculate, make a eunuch of myself
κακουχέω	(2)	I mistreat, torment
κατέχω	(17)	I hold back, suppress, restrain, hold fast, possess
μετασχηματίζω	(5)	I change, transform, apply
μετέχω	(8)	I share, participate, belong, eat, drink, enjoy
παρέχω	(16)	I offer, grant, cause; show myself, grant, get (mid.)
περιέχω	(2)	I seize; stand, say (intrans.)
πλεονεκτέω	(5)	I take advantage of, outwit, defraud
προέχω	(1)	I excel; am better off, protect myself (prob. mid. in NT)
προσέχω	(24)	I pay attention to, care for, devote myself to, officiate
συγκακουχέομαι	(1)	I suffer with
συνευωχέομαι	(2)	I feast together
συνέχω	(12)	I torment, stop, press hard, hold prisoner, embrace, rule
συσχηματίζω	(2)	I form; am formed like, conformed to (pass. in NT)
ὑπερέχω	(5)	I have power over, surpass, excel
ὑπέχω	(1)	I undergo or suffer (punishment)
ἕξις, εως, ἡ	(1)	exercise, practice
ὀχύρωμα, ατος, τό	(1)	stronghold, fortress, prison

σχῆμα, ατος, τό	(2)	outward appearance, form, shape, present form
ἀνοχή, ῆς, ἡ	(2)	forbearance, clemency, tolerance
ἀσχημοσύνη, ης, ἡ	(2)	shameless deed, shame (= genitals)
ἐξοχή, ῆς, ἡ	(1)	prominence
εὐνοῦχος, ου, ὁ	(8)	eunuch, castrated man
εὐσχημοσύνη, ης, ἡ	(1)	propriety, presentability, decorum
κατάσχεσις, εως, ἡ	(2)	possession, taking possession
μετοχή, ῆς, ἡ	(1)	sharing, participation
περιοχή, ῆς, ἡ	(1)	portion, section, passage
πλεονέκτης, ου, ὁ	(4)	greedy or covetous person
πλεονεξία, ας, ἡ	(10)	greediness, avarice, covetousness, something forced
ῥαβδοῦχος, ου, ὁ	(2)	constable, policeman
συνοχή, ῆς, ἡ	(2)	distress, dismay, anguish
ὑπεροχή, ῆς, ἡ	(2)	abundance, superiority, place of prominence or authority
ἀνεκτός, όν	(5)	bearable, endurable
ἀνεξίκακος, ον	(1)	bearing evil without resentment, patient
ἀσχήμων, ον	(1)	shameful, unpresentable; genitals (subst. in NT)
ἔνοχος, ον	(10)	caught in, subject to, liable, guilty, deserving
εὐσχήμων, ον	(5)	proper, presentable, prominent, noble
μέτοχος, ον	(6)	sharing or participating in; partner, companion (subst.)
συμμέτοχος, ον	(2)	sharing with; sharer (subst. in NT)
ἑξῆς	(5)	next (day), soon after
σχεδόν	(3)	nearly, almost
εὐσχημόνως	(3)	decently, becomingly
καθεξῆς	(5)	in order, one after the other; successor (subst.)
νουνεχῶς	(1)	wisely, thoughtfully

ζάω

ζάω	(140)	I live, become alive again, recover, remain alive
ἀναζάω	(2)	I come to life again, spring into life
ἀναζωπυρέω	(1)	I rekindle, kindle, inflame
ζωγρέω	(2)	I capture alive, catch
ζωογονέω	(3)	I give life to, make alive, keep alive
ζωοποιέω	(11)	I make alive, give life to
συζάω	(3)	I live with or together
συζωοποιέω	(2)	I make alive together with
ζωή, ῆς, ἡ	(135)	life
ζῷον, ου, τό	(23)	living thing or being, animal

Ζεύς

Ζεύς, Διός, ὁ	(2)	Zeus
εὐδία, ας, ἡ	(1)	fair weather
διοπετής, ές	(1)	fallen from heaven

ζέω

ζέω	(2)	I boil (fig. in NT)
ζηλεύω	(1)	I am eager, earnest
ζηλόω	(11)	I strive, desire, show zeal, am filled with jealousy
ζυμόω	(4)	I ferment, leaven, cause to rise
παραζηλόω	(4)	I make jealous
ζῆλος, ου, ὁ	(16)	zeal, ardor, jealousy
ζηλωτής, οῦ, ὁ	(8)	zealot, enthusiast, fanatic
ζύμη, ης, ἡ	(13)	yeast, leaven
ζεστός, ή, όν	(3)	hot

| ἄζυμος, ον | (9) | unleavened; festival of unleavened bread (subst.) |

ζημία

| ζημιόω | (6) | I suffer damage or loss, lose, am punished (pass. in NT) |
| ζημία, ας, ἡ | (4) | damage, loss |

ζητέω

ζητέω	(117)	I seek, look for, investigate, try to obtain, wish, request
ἀναζητέω	(3)	I look, search
ἐκζητέω	(7)	I seek out, search for, charge with
ἐπιζητέω	(13)	I search, wish for, demand
συζητέω	(10)	I discuss, dispute, debate, argue
ζήτημα, ατος, τό	(5)	controversial question or issue
ζήτησις, εως, ἡ	(7)	investigation, controversy, debate
ἐκζήτησις, εως, ἡ	(1)	useless speculation
συζητητής, οῦ, ὁ	(1)	disputant, debater

ζυγός

ἑτεροζυγέω	(1)	I am unevenly yoked, mismated
συζεύγνυμι	(2)	I yoke together, join together
ζεῦγος, ους, τό	(2)	yoke, pair
ζευκτηρία, ας, ἡ	(1)	bands, ropes
ζυγός, οῦ, ὁ	(6)	yoke, balance scales
σύζυγος, ου, ὁ	(1)	yoke fellow, fellow worker
ὑποζύγιον, ου, τό	(2)	pack animal, donkey

ζώννυμι

ζώννυμι	(3)	I gird, dress
ἀναζώννυμι	(1)	I bind up, gird up
διαζώννυμι	(3)	I tie around
περιζώννυμι	(6)	I gird about, wrap around; dress myself (mid.)
ὑποζώννυμι	(1)	I undergird, brace
ζώνη, ης, ἡ	(8)	belt, girdle

ἤ

ἤ	(343)	or, either, nor, what, than
ἤπερ	(1)	than
ἤτοι	(1)	or, either

ἡδονή

συνήδομαι	(1)	I rejoice in
ἡδονή, ῆς, ἡ	(5)	pleasure, enjoyment, lust, passion
ἡδύοσμον, ου, τό	(2)	mint (plant)
αὐθάδης, ες	(2)	self-willed, stubborn, arrogant
φιλήδονος, ον	(1)	loving pleasure, given over to pleasure
ἀσμένως	(1)	gladly
ἡδέως	(5)	gladly; very gladly (superl. ἥδιστα)

ἥκω

ἥκω	(26)	I have come, am present, come
ἀνήκω	(3)	it is proper, fitting (impers. in NT)
καθήκω	(2)	it is proper (impers. in NT)

ἡλικία

ἡλικία, ας, ἡ	(8)	age, time of life, years, maturity, stature
συνηλικιώτης, ου, ὁ	(1)	contemporary person
ἡλίκος, η, ον	(3)	how great, how large, how small
πηλίκος, η, ον	(2)	how large, how great
τηλικοῦτος, αύτη, οὗτο	(4)	so great, so large, so important

ἥλιος

ἥλιος, ου, ὁ	(32)	sun
εἰλικρίνεια, ας, ἡ	(3)	sincerity, purity of motive
εἰλικρινής, ές	(2)	pure, sincere

ἧλος

προσηλόω	(1)	I nail securely
ἧλος, ου, ὁ	(2)	nail

ἡμέρα

ἡμέρα, ας, ἡ	(389)	day (opp. night), daylight, day (24 hours), time
ἐφημερία, ας, ἡ	(2)	class or division (of priests)
μεσημβρία, ας, ἡ	(2)	midday, noon, south
νυχθήμερον, ου, τό	(1)	a day and a night
ἐφήμερος, ον	(1)	for the day, daily
καθημερινός, ή, όν	(1)	daily
ὀκταήμερος, ον	(1)	on the eighth day
σήμερον	(41)	today; today (subst.)

ἥμισυς

ἡμίωρον, ου, τό	(1)	half hour
ἥμισυς, εια, υ	(5)	half; one half (neut. subst.)
ἡμιθανής, ές	(1)	half dead

ἥσσων

ἑσσόομαι	(1)	I am defeated, inferior, treated worse
ἡττάομαι	(2)	I am defeated, succumb
ἥττημα, ατος, τό	(2)	defeat, failure
ἥσσων, ον	(2)	worse (subst.); less (neut. as adv.)

ἡσύχιος

ἡσυχάζω	(5)	I am quiet, rest
ἡσυχία, ας, ἡ	(4)	quietness, rest, silence
ἡσύχιος, ον	(2)	quiet, peaceful

ἦχος

ἠχέω	(1)	I sound, ring out
ἐξηχέω	(1)	I ring out, sound forth (pass. in NT)
κατηχέω	(8)	I make myself understood, inform, teach, instruct
ἦχος, ου, ὁ	(3)	sound, tone, noise, report, news
ἦχος, ους, τό	(1)	sound, tone, noise, roar

θάμβος

θαμβέω	(3)	I am astounded, amazed (pass. in NT)

ἐκθαμβέω	(4)	I am amazed, alarmed (pass. in NT)
θάμβος, ους, τό	(3)	astonishment, fear
ἔκθαμβος, ον	(1)	utterly astonished

θάπτω

θάπτω	(11)	I bury
ἐνταφιάζω	(2)	I prepare for burial, bury
συνθάπτω	(2)	I bury with; am buried with (pass. in NT)
ταφή, ῆς, ἡ	(1)	burial place
τάφος, ου, ὁ	(7)	grave, tomb
ἐνταφιασμός, οῦ, ὁ	(2)	preparation for burial, burial

θάρσος

θαρρέω	(6)	I am confident, courageous
θαρσέω	(7)	I am courageous; have courage! (imper. in NT)
θάρσος, ους, τό	(1)	courage

θαυμάζω

θαυμάζω	(43)	I wonder, marvel, am amazed; admire (trans.)
ἐκθαυμάζω	(1)	I wonder greatly
θαῦμα, ατος, τό	(2)	wonder, marvel, amazement
θαυμάσιος, α, ον	(1)	wonderful
θαυμαστός, ή, όν	(6)	wonderful, marvelous, remarkable

θεάομαι

θεάομαι	(22)	I see, look at, behold, visit
θεατρίζω	(1)	I put to shame, expose publicly
ἀναθεωρέω	(2)	I examine, observe carefully
θεωρέω	(58)	I look at, perceive, see, notice, observe, experience
παραθεωρέω	(1)	I overlook, neglect
θέατρον, ου, τό	(3)	theater, play, spectacle
θεωρία, ας, ἡ	(1)	spectacle, sight

θεῖον

| θεῖον, ου, τό | (7) | sulfur |
| θειώδης, ες | (1) | sulfurous yellow |

θέλω

θέλω	(208)	I wish, desire, want, will, like, enjoy, maintain
θέλημα, ατος, τό	(62)	will, wish, desire
θέλησις, εως, ἡ	(1)	will
ἐθελοθρησκία, ας, ἡ	(1)	self-made or would-be religion

θεός

θεά, ᾶς, ἡ	(1)	goddess
θειότης, ητος, ἡ	(1)	divinity, divine nature
θεός, οῦ, ὁ, ἡ	(1317)	God, god; goddess (fem.)
θεότης, ητος, ἡ	(1)	deity, divinity
θεοσέβεια, ας, ἡ	(1)	reverence for God, piety, religion
θεῖος, α, ον	(3)	divine; divine being, divinity (neut. subst.)
ἄθεος, ον	(1)	without God, godless
θεοδίδακτος, ον	(1)	taught by God

θεομάχος, ον	(1)	fighting against or opposing God
θεόπνευστος, ον	(1)	inspired by God
θεοσεβής, ές	(1)	god-fearing, devout, religious, pious
θεοστυγής, ές	(1)	hating god
φιλόθεος, ον	(1)	loving God, devout

θεράπων

θεραπεύω	(43)	I serve, am a servant, heal, restore
θεραπεία, ας, ή	(3)	serving, service, care, healing, servants
θεράπων, οντος, ὁ	(1)	servant

θέρμη

θερίζω	(21)	I reap, harvest
θερμαίνω	(6)	I warm myself (mid. in NT)
θερισμός, οῦ, ὁ	(13)	reaping, harvest, crop
θεριστής, οῦ, ὁ	(2)	reaper, harvester
θέρμη, ης, ή	(1)	heat
θέρος, ους, τό	(3)	summer

θηλάζω

θηλάζω	(5)	I give suck, suck, nurse
ἀναθάλλω	(1)	I cause to grow again, revive
θῆλυς, εια, υ	(5)	female; woman (subst.)

θηρίον

θηρεύω	(1)	I catch, hunt
θηριομαχέω	(1)	I fight wild animals
θήρα, ας, ή	(1)	net, trap
θηρίον, ου, τό	(46)	animal, beast, snake; monster (fig.)

θλίβω

θλίβω	(10)	I press upon, oppress; am narrow, afflicted (pass.)
ἀποθλίβω	(1)	I press upon, crowd
συνθλίβω	(2)	I press together or upon
θλῖψις, εως, ή	(45)	oppression, affliction, tribulation, trouble

θνῄσκω

θανατόω	(11)	I put to death, kill
θνῄσκω	(9)	I die; have died, am dead (perf. in NT)
ἀποθνῄσκω	(111)	I die, decay, face death, am mortal
συναποθνῄσκω	(3)	I die with
θάνατος, ου, ὁ	(120)	death
ἀθανασία, ας, ή	(3)	immortality
θανάσιμος, ον	(1)	deadly; deadly poison or thing (subst. in NT)
θνητός, ή, όν	(6)	mortal
ἐπιθανάτιος, ον	(1)	condemned to death
ἡμιθανής, ές	(1)	half dead
θανατηφόρος, ον	(1)	death-bringing, deadly

θόρυβος

θορυβάζω	(1)	I cause trouble; am troubled, distracted (pass. in NT)
θορυβέω	(4)	I throw into disorder; am troubled, distressed (pass.)

| θόρυβος, ου, ὁ | (7) | noise, turmoil, excitement, uproar, disturbance, riot |

θρησκός

θρησκεία, ας, ἡ	(4)	religion, worship
ἐθελοθρησκία, ας, ἡ	(1)	self-made or would-be religion
θρησκός, όν	(1)	religious

θρίξ

| θρίξ, τριχός, ἡ | (15) | hair |
| τρίχινος, η, ον | (1) | made of hair |

θροέω

θρηνέω	(4)	I mourn, lament, sing a dirge; mourn for (trans.)
θροέω	(3)	I am disturbed, frightened (pass. in NT)
ἀθροίζω	(1)	I collect, gather
ἐπαθροίζω	(1)	I collect in addition, gather more (pass. in NT)
συναθροίζω	(2)	I gather, bring together; am gathered, meet (pass.)

θυγάτηρ

| θυγάτηρ, τρός, ἡ | (28) | daughter, girl, female descendant, female inhabitant |
| θυγάτριον, ου, τό | (2) | little daughter |

θυμός

θυμόω	(1)	I make angry; become angry (pass. in NT)
ἀθυμέω	(1)	I am discouraged, lose heart
διενθυμέομαι	(1)	I consider, reflect, ponder
ἐνθυμέομαι	(2)	I consider, think
ἐπιθυμέω	(16)	I desire, long for, lust for
εὐθυμέω	(3)	I am cheerful, keep up my courage
θυμομαχέω	(1)	I am very angry
μακροθυμέω	(10)	I have patience, wait patiently, am patient
θύελλα, ης, ἡ	(1)	windstorm, whirlwind
θυμός, οῦ, ὁ	(18)	passion, anger, rage, wrath
ἐνθύμησις, εως, ἡ	(4)	thought, reflection, idea
ἐπιθυμητής, οῦ, ὁ	(1)	one who desires
ἐπιθυμία, ας, ἡ	(38)	desire, longing, craving, lust
μακροθυμία, ας, ἡ	(14)	patience, steadfastness, endurance, forbearance
προθυμία, ας, ἡ	(5)	willingness, readiness, goodwill, zeal
εὔθυμος, ον	(1)	cheerful, encouraged
πρόθυμος, ον	(3)	ready, willing, eager; eagerness, desire (subst.)
εὐθύμως	(1)	cheerfully
μακροθύμως	(1)	patiently
ὁμοθυμαδόν	(11)	with one mind, by common consent, together
προθύμως	(1)	willingly, eagerly, freely

θύρα

θύρα, ας, ἡ	(39)	door, gate, entrance
θυρεός, οῦ, ὁ	(1)	shield
θυρίς, ίδος, ἡ	(2)	window
θυρωρός, οῦ, ὁ, ἡ	(4)	doorkeeper

θύω

θυμιάω	(1)	I make an incense offering
θύω	(14)	I sacrifice, slaughter, kill, celebrate
θυμίαμα, ατος, τό	(6)	incense, incense offering
θυμιατήριον, ου, τό	(1)	altar of incense
θυσία, ας, ἡ	(28)	act of offering, sacrifice, offering
θυσιαστήριον, ου, τό	(23)	altar
θύϊνος, η, ον	(1)	from the citron tree, scented
εἰδωλόθυτος, ον	(9)	meat offered to an idol (subst. in NT)
ἱερόθυτος, ον	(1)	offered in sacrifice

ἰάομαι

ἰάομαι	(26)	I heal, cure, restore
ἴαμα, ατος, τό	(3)	healing
ἴασις, εως, ἡ	(3)	healing
ἰατρός, οῦ, ὁ	(7)	physician

ἴδιος

ἰδιώτης, ου, ὁ	(5)	layman, amateur, untrained, ungifted
ἴδιος, α, ον	(114)	one's own; home, property (subst.); individually (adv.)

ἱερός

ἱερατεύω	(1)	I am a priest, perform the service of a priest
ἱεροσυλέω	(1)	I rob temples, commit sacrilege
ἱερουργέω	(1)	I serve as a priest
ἱερατεία, ας, ἡ	(2)	priestly office or service
ἱεράτευμα, ατος, τό	(2)	priesthood
ἱερεύς, έως, ὁ	(31)	priest
ἱερόν, οῦ, τό	(71)	temple, sanctuary
ἱερωσύνη, ης, ἡ	(3)	priestly office, priesthood
ἀρχιερεύς, έως, ὁ	(122)	high priest; chief priests, ruling priests (pl.)
ἱερός, ά, όν	(3)	holy; the holy things (neut. subst.)
ἀρχιερατικός, όν	(1)	high-priestly
ἱερόθυτος, ον	(1)	offered in sacrifice
ἱεροπρεπής, ές	(1)	holy, worthy of reverence
ἱερόσυλος, ον	(1)	temple robber, sacrilegious person (subst. in NT)

[ἵημι]

ἀνίημι	(4)	I loosen, unfasten, abandon, give up
ἀφίημι	(143)	I let go, give up, divorce, cancel, forgive, leave, tolerate
παρίημι	(2)	I neglect; am weakened, listless, drooping (pass.)
συνίημι	(26)	I understand, comprehend
ἄνεσις, εως, ἡ	(5)	relaxing, rest, relaxation, relief
ἄφεσις, εως, ἡ	(17)	release, pardon, forgiveness
πάρεσις, εως, ἡ	(1)	passing over, letting go unpunished, overlooking
σύνεσις, εως, ἡ	(7)	intelligence, insight, understanding
ἀσύνετος, ον	(5)	senseless, foolish, without understanding
ἐγκάθετος, ον	(1)	hired to lie in wait; spy (subst. in NT)
συνετός, ή, όν	(4)	intelligent, wise

ἱκανός

ἱκανόω	(2)	I make sufficient, qualify, empower, authorize
ἀφικνέομαι	(1)	I reach, become known
διϊκνέομαι	(1)	I pierce, penetrate
ἐφικνέομαι	(2)	I come to, reach
ἱκανότης, ητος, ἡ	(1)	fitness, capability, qualification
ἱκετηρία, ας, ἡ	(1)	supplication, request
ἄφιξις, εως, ἡ	(1)	departure
ἱκανός, ή, όν	(39)	sufficient, large, many, able, fit; bond (subst.)

ἵλεως

ἱλάσκομαι	(2)	I expiate, make atonement for; am merciful (pass.)
ἱλαρότης, ητος, ἡ	(1)	cheerfulness
ἱλασμός, οῦ, ὁ	(2)	expiation, propitiation, means of forgiveness
ἱλαστήριον, ου, τό	(2)	means of expiation or forgiveness, mercy seat
ἱλαρός, ά, όν	(1)	cheerful, glad
ἵλεως, ων	(2)	gracious, merciful

ἱμάτιον

ἱματίζω	(2)	I dress, clothe
ἀμφιέζω	(1)	I clothe
ἀμφιέννυμι	(3)	I clothe, dress, adorn
ἐσθής, ῆτος, ἡ	(8)	clothing
ἱμάτιον, ου, τό	(60)	garment, cloak, coat, robe; clothing (pl.)
ἱματισμός, οῦ, ὁ	(5)	clothing, apparel

ἵνα

ἵνα	(663)	in order that, that, so that
ἱνατί	(6)	why? for what reason?

ἰός

κατιόω	(1)	I rust over; become rusty, tarnished (pass. in NT)
ἰός, οῦ, ὁ	(3)	poison, rust

ἵππος

ἱππεύς, έως, ὁ	(2)	horseman, cavalryman
ἵππος, ου, ὁ	(17)	horse, steed
ἱππικός, ή, όν	(1)	pertaining to a horseman; cavalry (subst. in NT)

ἴσος

ἰσότης, ητος, ἡ	(3)	equality, fairness
ἴσος, η, ον	(8)	equal, same, consistent; equally (neut. pl. as adv.)
ἰσάγγελος, ον	(1)	like a angel
ἰσότιμος, ον	(1)	equal in value, of the same kind
ἰσόψυχος, ον	(1)	of like soul or mind
ἴσως	(1)	perhaps, probably

ἵστημι

ἵστημι	(154)	I set, make stand; stand, stop, stand firm (intrans.)
στήκω	(10)	I stand, stand firm, am steadfast
ἀναστατόω	(3)	I disturb, trouble, upset
ἀνθίστημι	(14)	I set myself against, oppose, resist, withstand

ἀνίστημι	(108)	I raise, erect, bring to life, rise, stand up, arise, appear
ἀντικαθίστημι	(1)	I place against, oppose, resist
ἀποκαθίστημι	(8)	I restore, reestablish, cure, give back, restore
ἀστατέω	(1)	I am unsettled, homeless
ἀφίστημι	(14)	I mislead, go away, fall away, keep away
διΐστημι	(3)	I go away, part, pass
ἐνίστημι	(7)	I am present, impending, imminent
ἐξανίστημι	(3)	I raise up, beget, stand up
ἐξίστημι	(17)	I confuse, amaze, lose my mind, am astonished
ἐπανίστημι	(2)	I set up, rise up, rise in rebellion
ἐπίσταμαι	(14)	I understand, know
ἐφίστημι	(21)	I stand by, appear, attack; am present, imminent (perf.)
καθίστημι	(21)	I bring, appoint, ordain, make
κατεφίσταμαι	(1)	I rise up against, attack
μεθίστημι	(5)	I remove, transfer, turn away, mislead
παρίστημι	(41)	I place beside, present, render, approach, stand by
περιΐστημι	(4)	I stand around; avoid, shun (mid.)
προΐστημι	(8)	I rule, manage, am concerned about, care for
συνεφίστημι	(1)	I rise up together, join in an attack
συνίστημι	(16)	I recommend, commend, show, stand by, hold together
στάμνος, ου, ἡ	(1)	jar
στασιαστής, οῦ, ὁ	(1)	rebel, revolutionary, insurrectionist
στάσις, εως, ἡ	(9)	existence, standing, dissension, revolt, rebellion
στατήρ, ῆρος, ὁ	(1)	stater (Greek silver coin)
στοά, ᾶς, ἡ	(4)	colonnade, portico, porch
ἀκαταστασία, ας, ἡ	(5)	disturbance, disorder, unruliness, insurrection
ἀνάστασις, εως, ἡ	(42)	rise, resurrection
ἀποκατάστασις, εως, ἡ	(1)	restoration
ἀποστασία, ας, ἡ	(2)	rebellion, apostasy
ἀποστάσιον, ου, τό	(3)	notice of divorce
διάστημα, ατος, τό	(1)	interval
διχοστασία, ας, ἡ	(2)	dissension
ἔκστασις, εως, ἡ	(7)	astonishment, terror, trance, ecstasy
ἐξανάστασις, εως, ἡ	(1)	resurrection
ἐπίστασις, εως, ἡ	(2)	attack, pressure, attention, care, superintendence, delay
ἐπιστάτης, ου, ὁ	(7)	master
κατάστημα, ατος, τό	(1)	behavior, demeanor
προστάτις, ιδος, ἡ	(1)	patroness, helper
πρωτοστάτης, ου, ὁ	(1)	leader, ringleader
ὑπόστασις, εως, ἡ	(5)	essence, substance, reality, situation, realization
ἀκατάστατος, ον	(2)	unstable, restless
ἐπιστήμων, ον	(1)	expert, learned, understanding
εὐπερίστατος, ον	(1)	easily ensnaring
συστατικός, ή, όν	(1)	commendatory

ἰσχύς

ἰσχύω	(28)	I am strong, powerful, healthy, able, valid
διϊσχυρίζομαι	(2)	I insist, maintain firmly
ἐνισχύω	(2)	I grow strong, strengthen
ἐξισχύω	(1)	I am able, strong
ἐπισχύω	(1)	I grow strong, insist
κατισχύω	(3)	I am strong, prevail, am able, am victorious over
ἰσχύς, ύος, ἡ	(10)	strength, might, power
ἰσχυρός, ά, όν	(29)	strong, mighty, powerful, loud, severe, weighty

ἰχθύς

ἰχθύδιον, ου, τό	(2)	little fish
ἰχθύς, ύος, ὁ	(20)	fish

ἴχνος

ἴχνος, ους, τό	(3)	footprint
ἀνεξιχνίαστος, ον	(2)	inscrutable, incomprehensible

καθαρός

καθαίρω	(1)	I make clean, prune
καθαρίζω	(31)	I make or declare clean, cleanse, purity
διακαθαίρω	(1)	I clean out
διακαθαρίζω	(1)	I clean out
ἐκκαθαίρω	(2)	I clean out, cleanse
καθαρισμός, οῦ, ὁ	(7)	purification
καθαρότης, ητος, ἡ	(1)	purity, purification
ἀκαθαρσία, ας, ἡ	(10)	impurity, dirt, refuse, immorality, viciousness
περικάθαρμα, ατος, τό	(1)	dirt, refuse, off-scouring
καθαρός, ά, όν	(27)	clean, pure, ritually pure, guiltless
ἀκάθαρτος, ον	(32)	impure, unclean; vicious

καθίζω

καθίζω	(46)	I cause to sit down, appoint; stay, live (intrans.)
ἀνακαθίζω	(2)	I sit up
ἐπικαθίζω	(1)	I sit, sit on
συγκαθίζω	(2)	I cause to sit down with, sit down with

καί

πεντεκαιδέκατος, η, ον	(1)	fifteenth
τεσσαρεσκαιδέκατος, η, ον	(2)	fourteenth
κἀκεῖ	(10)	and there, there also (= καὶ ἐκεῖ)
κἀκεῖθεν	(10)	and from there, and then (= καὶ ἐκεῖθεν)
καί	(9153)	and, even, also, but, and then, and yet, namely, both
κἀγώ	(84)	and I, but I, I also, I myself, I in turn (= καὶ ἐγώ)
καίπερ	(5)	though, although
καίτοι	(2)	and yet, although
καίτοιγε	(1)	and yet, although
κἀκεῖνος, η, ο	(22)	and that one or he, that one or he also (= καὶ ἐκεῖνος)
κἄν	(17)	and if, even if, if only (= καὶ ἐάν)

καινός

ἀνακαινίζω	(1)	I renew, restore
ἀνακαινόω	(2)	I renew
ἐγκαινίζω	(2)	I renew, inaugurate, dedicate
καινότης, ητος, ἡ	(2)	newness
ἀνακαίνωσις, εως, ἡ	(2)	renewal
ἐγκαίνια, ων, τά	(1)	Festival of Rededication, Feast of Lights, Hanukkah
καινός, ή, όν	(42)	new, unused, unknown

καιρός

ἀκαιρέομαι	(1)	I have no time, no opportunity
εὐκαιρέω	(3)	I have time or opportunity, spend time

καιρός, οῦ, ὁ	(85)	time, point or period of time, season, age, right time
εὐκαιρία, ας, ἡ	(2)	favorable opportunity, right moment
εὔκαιρος, ον	(2)	well-timed, suitable
πρόσκαιρος, ον	(4)	lasting only for a time, temporary
ἀκαίρως	(1)	out of season, unseasonably
εὐκαίρως	(2)	conveniently

καίω

καίω	(12)	I light, burn, keep burning
καυματίζω	(4)	I burn, scorch
καυσόω	(2)	I am consumed by heat, burn up (pass. in NT)
καυστηριάζω	(1)	I brand with a hot iron, sear
ἐκκαίω	(1)	I kindle; am inflamed (pass. in NT)
κατακαίω	(12)	I burn down, burn up, consume
κάμινος, ου, ἡ	(4)	oven, furnace
καῦμα, ατος, τό	(2)	burning, heat
καῦσις, εως, ἡ	(1)	burning
καύσων, ωνος, ὁ	(3)	heat, burning
ὁλοκαύτωμα, ατος, τό	(3)	whole burnt offering

κακός

κακόω	(6)	I harm, mistreat, make angry, embitter
ἐγκακέω	(6)	I become tired, despondent, afraid
κακολογέω	(4)	I speak evil of, revile, insult
κακοπαθέω	(3)	I suffer misfortune, bear hardship patiently
κακοποιέω	(4)	I do wrong, harm, injure
κακουχέω	(2)	I mistreat, torment
συγκακοπαθέω	(2)	I suffer together with, share in hardship with
συγκακουχέομαι	(1)	I suffer with
κακία, ας, ἡ	(11)	badness, wickedness, malice, trouble
κάκωσις, εως, ἡ	(1)	mistreatment, oppression
κακοήθεια, ας, ἡ	(1)	malice, malignity
κακοπαθία, ας, ἡ	(1)	suffering, misfortune, misery, strenuous effort
κακός, ή, όν	(50)	bad, evil, dangerous; evil, misfortune, harm (subst.)
ἄκακος, ον	(2)	innocent, guileless, unsuspecting
ἀνεξίκακος, ον	(1)	bearing evil without resentment, patient
κακοποιός, όν	(3)	doing evil; evildoer, criminal, sorcerer (subst. in NT)
κακοῦργος, ον	(4)	evil doing; criminal, evildoer (subst. in NT)
κακῶς	(16)	badly, wrongly, wickedly

καλάμη

καλάμη, ης, ἡ	(1)	stalk, straw, stubble
κάλαμος, ου, ὁ	(12)	reed, measuring rod, reed pen

καλέω

καλέω	(148)	I call, address as, name, invite, summon, call in
ἀντικαλέω	(1)	I invite in return
ἐγκαλέω	(7)	I accuse, bring charges against
εἰσκαλέομαι	(1)	I invite in
ἐπικαλέω	(30)	I call, name; call upon, appeal (mid.)
μετακαλέω	(4)	I call to myself, summon, invite (mid. in NT)
παρακαλέω	(109)	I call, invite, urge, implore, request, comfort, cheer up
προκαλέω	(1)	I provoke, challenge (mid. in NT)
προσκαλέω	(29)	I summon, call to myself, invite, call (mid. in NT)

συγκαλέω	(8)	I call together; call to myself, summon (mid.)
συμπαρακαλέω	(1)	I receive encouragement together (pass. in NT)
κλῆσις, εως, ἡ	(11)	call, calling, invitation, position, vocation
ἔγκλημα, ατος, τό	(2)	charge, accusation
ἐκκλησία, ας, ἡ	(114)	assembly, church, congregation
παράκλησις, εως, ἡ	(29)	encouragement, appeal, comfort, consolation
παράκλητος, ου, ὁ	(5)	helper, intercessor
κλητός, ή, όν	(10)	called, invited
ἀνέγκλητος, ον	(5)	blameless, irreproachable

καλός

καλοποιέω	(1)	I do what is right or good
καλλιέλαιος, ου, ἡ	(1)	cultivated olive tree
καλός, ή, όν	(100)	beautiful, good, useful, fine, noble, blameless, better
καλοδιδάσκαλος, ον	(1)	teaching what is good
καλῶς	(37)	well, beautifully, fitly, commendably, rightly

καλύπτω

καλύπτω	(8)	I cover, hide, conceal
ἀνακαλύπτω	(2)	I uncover, unveil
ἀποκαλύπτω	(26)	I uncover, reveal, disclose
ἐπικαλύπτω	(1)	I cover
κατακαλύπτω	(3)	I cover, veil; cover myself (mid. in NT)
παρακαλύπτω	(1)	I hide, conceal; am hidden (pass. in NT)
περικαλύπτω	(3)	I cover, conceal
συγκαλύπτω	(1)	I cover up, conceal
κάλυμμα, ατος, τό	(4)	covering, veil
ἀποκάλυψις, εως, ἡ	(18)	revelation, disclosure
ἐπικάλυμμα, ατος, τό	(1)	cover, veil, pretext
ἀκατακάλυπτος, ον	(2)	uncovered

κάμπτω

κάμπτω	(4)	I bend, bow
ἀνακάμπτω	(4)	I return
συγκάμπτω	(1)	I (cause to) bend

καρδία

καρδία, ας, ἡ	(156)	heart, inner self, mind, interior
καρδιογνώστης, ου, ὁ	(2)	knower of hearts
σκληροκαρδία, ας, ἡ	(3)	hardness of heart, stubbornness

καρπός

καρποφορέω	(8)	I bear fruit, am productive
καρπός, οῦ, ὁ	(66)	fruit, crop, result, advantage
ἄκαρπος, ον	(7)	unfruitful, fruitless, useless, unproductive
καρποφόρος, ον	(1)	fruitful

κατά

κατώτερος, α, ον	(1)	lower
κάτω	(9)	below, downwards, down
κατέναντι	(8)	opposite; opposite, in the sight of, before (impr. prep.)
κατωτέρω	(1)	lower, below, under
ὑποκάτω	(11)	under, below (impr. prep. in NT)

κατά	(473)	down from, against (gen.); along, to, according to (acc.)

καυχάομαι

καυχάομαι	(37)	I boast, glory, pride myself; boast about (trans.)
ἐγκαυχάομαι	(1)	I boast
κατακαυχάομαι	(4)	I boast against, brag, exult over, triumph over
καύχημα, ατος, τό	(11)	boast, object of boasting, pride, boasting
καύχησις, εως, ἡ	(11)	boasting, pride, object of boasting

κεῖμαι

κεῖμαι	(24)	I lie, recline, stand, am laid, am appointed, exist, am
κοιμάω	(18)	I sleep, fall asleep, die (pass. in NT)
ἀνάκειμαι	(14)	I lie, recline, am at table
ἀντίκειμαι	(8)	I am opposed
ἀπόκειμαι	(4)	I am put away, am stored up; it is destined (impers.)
ἐπίκειμαι	(7)	I lie upon, press upon, am imposed
κατάκειμαι	(12)	I lie down, recline, dine
παράκειμαι	(2)	I am ready, at hand
περίκειμαι	(5)	I am placed around, surrounded, bound, subject to
πρόκειμαι	(5)	I am set before, am present, publicly exhibited
συνανάκειμαι	(7)	I eat with, recline at table with
κοίμησις, εως, ἡ	(1)	sleep, rest
κοίτη, ης, ἡ	(4)	bed, marriage bed, sexual intercourse, semen
κοιτών, ῶνος, ὁ	(1)	bedroom
ἀρσενοκοίτης, ου, ὁ	(2)	male homosexual

κείρω

κείρω	(4)	I shear; have my hair cut (mid.)
κειρία, ας, ἡ	(1)	bandage, grave clothes
κέρμα, ατος, τό	(1)	piece of money, coin
κοράσιον, ου, τό	(8)	girl
ἐπικουρία, ας, ἡ	(1)	help
κερματιστής, οῦ, ὁ	(1)	money-changer

κελεύω

κελεύω	(25)	I command, order, urge
ἐπικέλλω	(1)	I bring to shore, run aground
κέλευσμα, ατος, τό	(1)	signal, shout of command

κενός

κενόω	(5)	I make empty, destroy, render void
κενοδοξία, ας, ἡ	(1)	vanity, conceit, excessive ambition
κενοφωνία, ας, ἡ	(2)	empty talk, chatter
κενός, ή, όν	(18)	empty, empty-handed, without content or result, vain
κενόδοξος, όν	(1)	conceited, boastful
κενῶς	(1)	in an empty manner, idly, in vain

κέντρον

ἐγκεντρίζω	(6)	I graft
ἐκκεντέω	(2)	I pierce
κέντρον, ου, τό	(4)	sting, goad

κέραμος

κεραμεύς, έως, ὁ	(3)	potter
κεράμιον, ου, τό	(2)	earthenware vessel, jar
κέραμος, ου, ὁ	(1)	roof tile
κεραμικός, ή, όν	(1)	belonging to the potter, made of clay

κεράννυμι

κεράννυμι	(3)	I mix, pour
συγκεράννυμι	(2)	I blend, unite, arrange
ἀκέραιος, ον	(3)	pure, innocent
ἄκρατος, ον	(1)	unmixed, pure

κέρας

κεραία, ας, ἡ	(2)	projection, serif, stroke (part of a letter)
κέρας, ατος, τό	(11)	horn, corner, end
κεράτιον, ου, τό	(1)	carob pod

κέρδος

κερδαίνω	(17)	I gain, profit, spare myself
κέρδος, ους, τό	(3)	gain
αἰσχροκερδής, ές	(2)	fond of dishonest gain, greedy for money
αἰσχροκερδῶς	(1)	greedily

κεφαλή

κεφαλιόω	(1)	I strike on the head
ἀνακεφαλαιόω	(2)	I sum up, recapitulate
ἀποκεφαλίζω	(4)	I behead
κεφαλή, ῆς, ἡ	(75)	head, extremity, point
κεφαλίς, ίδος, ἡ	(1)	roll
κεφάλαιον, ου, τό	(2)	main point, sum of money
περικεφαλαία, ας, ἡ	(2)	helmet
προσκεφάλαιον, ου, τό	(1)	pillow, cushion

κῆπος

κῆπος, ου, ὁ	(5)	garden
κηπουρός, οῦ, ὁ	(1)	gardener

κηρύσσω

κηρύσσω	(61)	I proclaim, announce, preach
προκηρύσσω	(1)	I proclaim or preach beforehand
κήρυγμα, ατος, τό	(9)	proclamation, preaching, message
κῆρυξ, υκος, ὁ	(3)	herald, preacher

κιθάρα

κιθαρίζω	(2)	I play the lyre or harp
κιθάρα, ας, ἡ	(4)	lyre, harp
κιθαρῳδός, οῦ, ὁ	(2)	lyre player, harpist

κίνδυνος

κινδυνεύω	(4)	I am in danger, run a risk
κίνδυνος, ου, ὁ	(9)	danger, risk

κινέω

κινέω	(8)	I move, remove, shake, arouse, cause
μετακινέω	(1)	I shift, remove
συγκινέω	(1)	I set in motion, arouse
ἀμετακίνητος, ον	(1)	immovable, firm

κλαίω

κλαίω	(40)	I weep, cry; week for (trans.)
κλαυθμός, οῦ, ὁ	(9)	weeping, crying

κλάω

κλάω	(14)	I break (bread)
ἐκκλάω	(3)	I break off
κατακλάω	(2)	I break in pieces
κλάδυς, ου, ὁ	(11)	branch
κλάσις, εως, ἡ	(2)	breaking
κλάσμα, ατος, τό	(9)	fragment, piece, crumb
κλῆμα, ατος, τό	(4)	branch

κλείω

κλείω	(16)	I shut, lock, bar, close
ἀποκλείω	(1)	I close, shut
ἐκκλείω	(2)	I shut out, exclude
κατακλείω	(2)	I shut up, lock up
συγκλείω	(4)	I enclose, confine, imprison, catch
κλείς, κλειδός, ἡ	(6)	key

κλέπτω

κλέπτω	(13)	I steal
κλέμμα, ατος, τό	(1)	stealing, theft
κλέπτης, ου, ὁ	(16)	thief
κλοπή, ῆς, ἡ	(2)	theft, stealing

κλῆρος

κληρόω	(1)	I appoint by lot, choose
κατακληρονομέω	(1)	I give as an inheritance
κληρονομέω	(18)	I inherit, acquire, obtain, receive
προσκληρόω	(1)	I allot; am attached to, join (pass. in NT)
κλῆρος, ου, ὁ	(11)	lot, portion, share, place
κληρονομία, ας, ἡ	(14)	inheritance, possession, property, salvation
κληρονόμος, ου, ὁ	(15)	heir
ναύκληρος, ου, ὁ	(1)	ship owner, captain
ὁλοκληρία, ας, ἡ	(1)	wholeness, soundness, perfect health
ὁλόκληρος, ον	(?)	whole, complete, sound, blameless
συγκληρονόμος, ον	(4)	inheriting together with; fellow heir (subst. in NT)

κλίνω

κλίνω	(7)	I incline, bow, lay down, draw to a close; rout (pass.)
ἀνακλίνω	(6)	I lay (down), put to bed; recline to eat, lie down (pass.)
ἐκκλίνω	(3)	I turn away, turn aside, shun
κατακλίνω	(5)	I cause to lie or sit down; recline at table, dine (pass.)
προσκλίνω	(1)	I incline toward, attach myself to, join (pass. in NT)

κλίμα, ατος, τό	(3)	district, region
κλινάριον, ου, τό	(1)	bed, cot
κλίνη, ης, ἡ	(9)	bed, couch, pallet, stretcher, sickbed
κλινίδιον, ου, τό	(2)	bed, pallet, stretcher
κλισία, ας, ἡ	(1)	group (of people eating)
ἀρχιτρίκλινος, ου, ὁ	(3)	head waiter, butler, master of a feast
πρόσκλισις, εως, ἡ	(1)	partiality
πρωτοκλισία, ας, ἡ	(5)	place of honor
ἀκλινής, ές	(1)	without wavering, firmly

κλύδων

κλυδωνίζομαι	(1)	I am tossed by waves
κατακλύζω	(1)	I flood, inundate
κλύδων, ωνος, ὁ	(2)	rough water, waves
κατακλυσμός, οῦ, ὁ	(4)	flood, deluge

κοινός

κοινόω	(14)	I make common, defile, desecrate, consider unclean
κοινωνέω	(8)	I share, participate, give a share
συγκοινωνέω	(3)	I participate in
κοινωνία, ας, ἡ	(19)	fellowship, close relationship, participation, gift
κοινωνός, οῦ, ὁ, ἡ	(10)	companion, partner, sharer
συγκοινωνός, οῦ, ὁ	(4)	participant, partner, sharer
κοινός, ή, όν	(14)	common, ordinary, profane, unclean
κοινωνικός, ή, όν	(1)	liberal, generous

κόκκος

κόκκος, ου, ὁ	(7)	seed, grain
κόκκινος, η, ον	(6)	red, scarlet; scarlet cloth (neut. subst.)

κολλάω

κολλάω	(12)	I unite; cling to, join, join myself to (pass. in NT)
προσκολλάω	(2)	I am faithfully devoted to, join (pass. in NT)

κολυμβάω

κολυμβάω	(1)	I swim
ἐκκολυμβάω	(1)	I swim away
κολυμβήθρα, ας, ἡ	(3)	pool, swimming pool

κόμη

κομάω	(2)	I wear long hair
κόμη, ης, ἡ	(1)	hair

κονιάω

κονιάω	(2)	I whitewash
κονιορτός, οῦ, ὁ	(5)	dust

κόπριον

κοπρία, ας, ἡ	(1)	dung heap, garbage pile
κόπριον, ου, τό	(1)	dung, manure

κόπτω

κοπάζω	(3)	I stop, abate, rest
κοπιάω	(23)	I become tired or weary, work hard, labor, struggle
κόπτω	(8)	I cut off; mourn (mid.)
ἀποκόπτω	(6)	I cut off, make a eunuch of, castrate
ἐγκόπτω	(5)	I hinder, thwart, prevent
ἐκκόπτω	(10)	I cut off or down, remove
κατακόπτω	(1)	I beat, bruise
προκόπτω	(6)	I go forward, progress, advance, am far gone
προσκόπτω	(8)	I strike or beat against, stumble, take offense at, reject
κοπετός, οῦ, ὁ	(1)	mourning, lamentation
κοπή, ῆς, ἡ	(1)	cutting down, slaughter, defeat
κόπος, ου, ὁ	(18)	trouble, work, labor
ἀργυροκόπος, ου, ὁ	(1)	silversmith
ἐγκοπή, ῆς, ἡ	(1)	hindrance, obstacle
προκοπή, ῆς, ἡ	(3)	progress, advancement
πρόσκομμα, ατος, τό	(6)	stumbling, offense, obstacle
προσκοπή, ῆς, ἡ	(1)	cause for offense
κωφός, ή, όν	(14)	dull, dumb, mute, deaf
ἀπρόσκοπος, ον	(3)	undamaged, blameless, giving no offense
εὔκοπος, ον	(7)	easy; easier (comp. in NT)

κορβᾶν

κορβᾶν	(1)	corban, gift
κορβανᾶς, ᾶ, ὁ	(1)	temple treasury

κόσμος

κομίζω	(10)	I bring; receive, obtain, recover (mid.)
κοσμέω	(10)	I put in order, trim, adorn, decorate, do credit to
ἐκκομίζω	(1)	I carry out
συγκομίζω	(1)	I bury
κόσμος, ου, ὁ	(186)	world, universe, earth, humankind, totality, adornment
γλωσσόκομον, ου, τό	(2)	money box
κοσμοκράτωρ, ορος, ὁ	(1)	world ruler
κοσμικός, ή, όν	(2)	earthly, worldly
κόσμιος, ον	(2)	respectable, honorable, modest
κομψότερον	(1)	better

κράζω

κράζω	(56)	I cry out, call out
κραυγάζω	(9)	I cry out, scream
ἀνακράζω	(5)	I cry out, shout
κραυγή, ῆς, ἡ	(6)	shouting, clamor, loud cry, crying

κρανίον

κρανίον, ου, τό	(4)	skull
ἀποκαραδοκία, ας, ἡ	(2)	eager expectation

κράτος

καρτερέω	(1)	I endure, persevere, am strong
κραταιόω	(4)	I strengthen; become strong, grow strong (pass. in NT)
κρατέω	(47)	I grasp, attain, hold, hold fast or back, arrest, retain
ἐγκρατεύομαι	(2)	I control myself

προσκαρτερέω	(10)	I attach or devote myself to, continue in, am ready
κράτος, ους, τό	(12)	power, might, mighty deed, sovereignty, rule
ἀκρασία, ας, ἡ	(2)	lack of self-control, self-indulgence
ἐγκράτεια, ας, ἡ	(4)	self-control
κοσμοκράτωρ, ορος, ὁ	(1)	world ruler
παντοκράτωρ, ορος, ὁ	(10)	Almighty, Omnipotent One
προσκαρτέρησις, εως, ἡ	(1)	perseverance, patience
κραταιός, ά, όν	(1)	powerful, mighty
κράτιστος, η, ον	(4)	most noble, most excellent
κρείττων, ον	(19)	better, higher in rank, more useful; better (adv.)
ἀκρατής, ές	(1)	without self-control, dissolute
ἐγκρατής, ές	(1)	self-controlled, disciplined
περικρατής, ές	(1)	having power, being in command or control

κρεμάννυμι

κρεμάννυμι	(7)	I hang, crucify; hang, depend (mid.)
ἐκκρεμάννυμι	(1)	I hang out; hang on (mid. in NT)
κατακρημνίζω	(1)	I throw down from a cliff
κρημνός, οῦ, ὁ	(3)	steep slope or bank, cliff

κριθή

κριθή, ῆς, ἡ	(1)	barley
κρίθινος, η, ον	(2)	made of barley flour

κρίνω

κρίνω	(114)	I judge, prefer, consider, decide, condemn
ἀνακρίνω	(16)	I question, examine, judge, call to account
ἀνταποκρίνομαι	(2)	I answer in turn, answer back
ἀποκρίνομαι	(231)	I answer, reply, continue, begin
διακρίνω	(19)	I differentiate, judge; dispute, waver (mid.)
ἐγκρίνω	(1)	I class
ἐπικρίνω	(1)	I decide, determine
κατακρίνω	(18)	I condemn, pass judgment on
συγκρίνω	(3)	I compare, explain, interpret, combine
συνυποκρίνομαι	(1)	I join in pretending, join in playing the hypocrite
ὑποκρίνομαι	(1)	I pretend
κρίμα, ατος, τό	(27)	judgment, decision, lawsuit, verdict, condemnation
κρίσις, εως, ἡ	(47)	judging, judgment, condemnation, punishment, court
κριτήριον, ου, τό	(3)	court, tribunal, lawsuit
κριτής, οῦ, ὁ	(19)	judge
ἀνάκρισις, εως, ἡ	(1)	investigation, hearing
ἀπόκριμα, ατος, τό	(1)	official report, decision, verdict
ἀπόκρισις, εως, ἡ	(4)	answer
διάκρισις, εως, ἡ	(3)	distinguishing, ability to discriminate, quarrel
εἰλικρίνεια, ας, ἡ	(3)	sincerity, purity of motive
κατάκριμα, ατος, τό	(3)	punishment, doom
κατάκρισις, εως, ἡ	(2)	condemnation
πρόκριμα, ατος, τό	(1)	prejudice, discrimination
ὑπόκρισις, εως, ἡ	(6)	hypocrisy, pretense, outward show
ὑποκριτής, οῦ, ὁ	(17)	hypocrite, pretender
κριτικός, ή, όν	(1)	able to discern or judge
ἀδιάκριτος, ον	(1)	unwavering, impartial
ἀκατάκριτος, ον	(2)	uncondemned, without a proper trial
ἀνυπόκριτος, ον	(6)	genuine, sincere

| αὐτοκατάκριτος, ον | (1) | self-condemned |
| εἰλικρινής, ές | (2) | pure, sincere |

κρύπτω

κρύπτω	(18)	I hide, conceal, cover, keep secret
ἀποκρύπτω	(4)	I hide, conceal, keep secret
ἐγκρύπτω	(2)	I hide, conceal in, put into
περικρύβω	(1)	I hide, conceal
κρύπτη, ης, ἡ	(1)	dark and hidden place, cellar
κρυπτός, ή, όν	(17)	hidden, secret; hidden thing or place (subst.)
κρυφαῖος, α, ον	(2)	hidden, secret
ἀπόκρυφος, ον	(3)	hidden, secret
κρυφῇ	(1)	in secret, secretly

κρύσταλλος

| κρυσταλλίζω | (1) | I shine like crystal, am as transparent as crystal |
| κρύσταλλος, ου, ὁ | (2) | crystal, ice |

κτάομαι

κτάομαι	(7)	I get, acquire, take
κτῆμα, ατος, τό	(4)	property, possession, piece of land
κτῆνος, ους, τό	(4)	domesticated animal, animal used for riding; cattle (pl.)
κτήτωρ, ορος, ὁ	(1)	owner

[κτείνω]

| ἀποκτείνω | (74) | I kill, put to death |
| ἀνθρωποκτόνος, ου, ὁ | (3) | murderer |

κτίζω

κτίζω	(15)	I create, make; Creator (partic.)
κτίσις, εως, ἡ	(19)	creation, creature, world, act of creation
κτίσμα, ατος, τό	(4)	creature, what is created
κτίστης, ου, ὁ	(1)	Creator

κυβέρνησις

| κυβέρνησις, εως, ἡ | (1) | administration, ability to lead |
| κυβερνήτης, ου, ὁ | (2) | captain, steersman, pilot |

κυκλόω

κυκλεύω	(1)	I surround
κυκλόω	(4)	I surround, encircle, go around
περικυκλόω	(1)	I surround, encircle
κυκλόθεν	(3)	all around, from all sides; around (impr. prep.)
κύκλῳ	(8)	around, all around; nearby (adj.); around (impr. prep.)

κυλίω

κυλίω	(1)	I roll; roll myself, roll about (pass. in NT)
ἀποκυλίω	(4)	I roll away
προσκυλίω	(2)	I roll against or to
κυλισμός, οῦ, ὁ	(1)	rolling, wallowing

κῦμα

ἀποκυέω	(2)	I give birth to, bear, bring into being
κῦμα, ατος, τό	(5)	wave
ἔγκυος, ον	(1)	pregnant

κύπτω

κύπτω	(2)	I bend down
ἀνακύπτω	(4)	I raise myself up, stand erect
κατακύπτω	(1)	I bend down
παρακύπτω	(5)	I bend over, stoop, look, steal a glance
συγκύπτω	(1)	I am bent over, bent double

κύριος

κυριεύω	(7)	I am lord or master, rule, control, lord it over
κυρόω	(2)	I confirm, ratify, decide in favor of
ἀκυρόω	(3)	I make void
κατακυριεύω	(4)	I subdue, gain power over, rule over
προκυρόω	(1)	I ratify previously
κυρία, ας, ἡ	(2)	lady, mistress
κύριος, ου, ὁ	(717)	lord, Lord, master, owner, sir
κυριότης, ητος, ἡ	(4)	lordship, dominion, ruling power
κυριακός, ή, όν	(2)	belonging to the Lord, Lord's

κύων

κυνάριον, ου, τό	(4)	little dog, dog
κύων, κυνός, ὁ	(5)	dog

κωλύω

κολάζω	(2)	I punish
κολοβόω	(4)	I curtail, shorten
κωλύω	(23)	I hinder, prevent, forbid. restrain, withhold
διακωλύω	(1)	I prevent
κόλασις, εως, ἡ	(2)	punishment
δύσκολος, ον	(1)	hard, difficult
ἀκωλύτως	(1)	without hindrance, freely
δυσκόλως	(3)	hardly, with difficulty

κώμη

κώμη, ης, ἡ	(27)	village, small town, inhabitants of a village
κῶμος, ου, ὁ	(3)	excessive feasting, carousing, revelry
κωμόπολις, εως, ἡ	(1)	market town, country town, town

λαλέω

λαλέω	(296)	I speak, say, proclaim, whisper, sound
διαλαλέω	(2)	I discuss
ἐκλαλέω	(1)	I tell
καταλαλέω	(5)	I speak against, defame, slander
προσλαλέω	(2)	I speak to or with, address
συλλαλέω	(6)	I talk or discuss with
λαλιά, ᾶς, ἡ	(3)	speech, speaking, accent, way of speaking
καταλαλιά, ᾶς, ἡ	(2)	evil speech, slander, insult
ἀλάλητος, ον	(1)	unexpressed, wordless

ἄλαλος, ον	(3)	mute, dumb; mute person (subst.)
ἀνεκλάλητος, ον	(1)	inexpressible
κατάλαλος, ον	(1)	speaking evil of others; slanderer (subst. in NT)
μογιλάλος, ον	(1)	speaking with difficulty, having a speech impediment

λαμβάνω

λαμβάνω	(258)	I take, remove, seize, collect, receive, obtain, put on
ἀναλαμβάνω	(13)	I take up, take along
ἀντιλαμβάνω	(3)	I help, take part in, practice, benefit by (mid. in NT)
ἀπολαμβάνω	(10)	I receive, recover, take aside
ἐπιλαμβάνομαι	(19)	I take hold of, catch, arrest, am concerned with, help
εὐλαβέομαι	(1)	I am afraid, concerned
καταλαμβάνω	(15)	I seize, win, attain, overtake, catch; grasp (mid.)
μεταλαμβάνω	(7)	I receive my share, share in, receive
παραλαμβάνω	(49)	I take, take along, receive, accept
προλαμβάνω	(3)	I do before, anticipate, take, detect
προσλαμβάνω	(12)	I take aside, accept, receive, take along (mid. in NT)
προσωπολημπτέω	(1)	I show partiality
συλλαμβάνω	(16)	I arrest, catch, become pregnant; seize, help (mid.)
συμπαραλαμβάνω	(4)	I take along with
συμπεριλαμβάνω	(1)	I embrace, throw my arms around
συναντιλαμβάνομαι	(2)	I help, come to the aid of
ὑπολαμβάνω	(5)	I take up, support, reply, suppose
λῆμψις, εως, ἡ	(1)	receiving
ἀνάλημψις, εως, ἡ	(1)	ascension
ἀντίλημψις, εως, ἡ	(1)	help
δεξιολάβος, ου, ὁ	(1)	spearman or slinger
εὐλάβεια, ας, ἡ	(2)	fear (of God), reverence, awe, anxiety
μετάλημψις, εως, ἡ	(1)	sharing, taking, receiving
πρόσλημψις, εως, ἡ	(1)	acceptance
προσωπολήμπτης, ου, ὁ	(1)	one who shows partiality
προσωπολημψία, ας, ἡ	(4)	partiality
ἀνεπίλημπτος, ον	(3)	irreproachable
εὐλαβής, ές	(4)	devout, God-fearing
ἀπροσωπολήμπτως	(1)	impartially

λάμπω

λάμπω	(7)	I shine, flash, shine forth
ἐκλάμπω	(1)	I shine (out)
περιλάμπω	(2)	I shine around
λαμπάς, άδος, ἡ	(9)	torch, lamp
λαμπρότης, ητος, ἡ	(1)	brilliance, splendor, brightness
λαμπρός, ά, όν	(9)	bright, shining, radiant, clear; splendor (subst.)
λαμπρῶς	(1)	splendidly

λανθάνω

λανθάνω	(6)	I escape notice, am hidden, am unaware
ἀλητεύω	(2)	I am truthful, tell the truth
ἐκλανθάνομαι	(1)	I forget (altogether)
ἐπιλανθάνομαι	(8)	I forget, overlook
λήθη, ης, ἡ	(1)	forgetfulness
ἀλήθεια, ας, ἡ	(109)	truth, truthfulness, reality
ἐπιλησμονή, ῆς, ἡ	(1)	forgetfulness
ἀληθής, ές	(26)	true, righteous, honest, truthful, real, genuine

ἀληθινός, ή, όს	(28)	true, dependable, real, genuine
λάθρα	(4)	secretly
ἀληθῶς	(18)	truly, in truth, really, actually

λαός

λειτουργέω	(3)	I perform a service, serve
λαός, οῦ, ὁ	(142)	people, crowd, populace
λειτουργία, ας, ἡ	(6)	service, ceremonial duty, ministry
λειτουργός, οῦ, ὁ	(5)	servant, minister
λειτουργικός, ή, όν	(1)	engaged in holy service, serving, ministering

[λᾶς]

| λατομέω | (2) | I hew, cut, shape |
| λαξευτός, ή, όν | (1) | hewn in the rock |

λατρεύω

λατρεύω	(21)	I serve, worship
λατρεία, ας, ἡ	(5)	service, worship, rite
εἰδωλολάτρης, ου, ὁ	(7)	idolater
εἰδωλολατρία, ας, ἡ	(4)	idolatry

λέγω

λέγω	(2354)	I say, speak, tell, mean, ask, answer, declare, call, name
λογίζομαι	(40)	I calculate, count, credit, evaluate, consider, think
ἀναλογίζομαι	(1)	I consider carefully
ἀνθομολογέομαι	(1)	I praise, thank
ἀντιλέγω	(11)	I speak against, contradict, oppose, refuse
ἀπολέγω	(1)	I disown, renounce (mid. in NT)
ἀπολογέομαι	(10)	I speak in my own defense, defend myself
βατταλογέω	(1)	I babble, use many words
γενεαλογέω	(1)	I trace descent; am descended from (pass. in NT)
διαλέγομαι	(13)	I discuss, speak, preach
διαλογίζομαι	(16)	I consider, ponder, reason, argue
ἐκλέγομαι	(22)	I choose, select
ἐλλογέω	(2)	I charge to someone's account
ἐνευλογέω	(2)	I bless
ἐξομολογέω	(10)	I promise, consent; confess, admit, praise
ἐπιλέγω	(2)	I call, name; choose, select (mid.)
εὐλογέω	(42)	I speak well of, praise, bless, consecrate
κακολογέω	(4)	I speak evil of, revile, insult
καταλέγω	(1)	I select, enlist, enroll
κατευλογέω	(1)	I bless
λογομαχέω	(1)	I dispute about words, split hairs
ὁμολογέω	(26)	I confess, promise, admit, declare, acknowledge, praise
παραλέγομαι	(2)	I sail past, coast along
παραλογίζομαι	(2)	I deceive, delude
προλέγω	(15)	I tell beforehand or in advance, say before or already
στρατολογέω	(1)	I gather an army, enlist soldiers, enlist
συλλέγω	(8)	I collect, gather
συλλογίζομαι	(1)	I reason, discuss, debate
συναρμολογέω	(2)	I join together; am joined or fit together (pass. in NT)
λογεία, ας, ἡ	(2)	collection
λόγιον, ου, τό	(4)	saying; oracles, sayings (pl. in NT)
λογισμός, οῦ, ὁ	(2)	thought, reasoning

λόγος, ου, ὁ	(330)	word, statement, message, subject, account, Word
αἰσχρολογία, ας, ἡ	(1)	evil speech, obscene speech
ἀναλογία, ας, ἡ	(1)	right relationship, proportion
ἀντιλογία, ας, ἡ	(4)	contradiction, dispute, hostility, rebellion
ἀπολογία, ας, ἡ	(8)	defense, reply
γενεαλογία, ας, ἡ	(2)	genealogy
διάλεκτος, ου, ἡ	(6)	language
διαλογισμός, οῦ, ὁ	(14)	thought, opinion, reasoning, doubt, dispute
ἐκλογή, ῆς, ἡ	(7)	selection, election, choosing, that which is selected
εὐλογία, ας, ἡ	(16)	praise, flattery, blessing, consecration, bounty
λογομαχία, ας, ἡ	(1)	word battle, dispute about words
ματαιολογία, ας, ἡ	(1)	empty or fruitless talk
μωρολογία, ας, ἡ	(1)	foolish or silly talk
ὁμολογία, ας, ἡ	(6)	confession, confessing, acknowledgment, profession
πιθανολογία, ας, ἡ	(1)	persuasive speech, plausible argument
πολυλογία, ας, ἡ	(1)	wordiness, many words
χρηστολογία, ας, ἡ	(1)	smooth talk, plausible speech
λογικός, ή, όν	(2)	rational, spiritual
λόγιος, α, ον	(1)	learned, cultured
ἀγενεαλόγητος, ον	(1)	without genealogy
ἄλογος, ον	(3)	without reason, contrary to reason
ἀναπολόγητος, ον	(2)	without excuse, inexcusable
δίλογος, ον	(1)	double-tongued, insincere
ἐκλεκτός, ή, όν	(22)	chosen, select, choice, excellent
εὐλογητός, ή, όν	(8)	blessed, praised
ματαιολόγος, ον	(1)	talking idly; idle or empty talker (subst. in NT)
σπερμολόγος, ον	(1)	picking up seeds; babbler (subst. in NT)
συνεκλεκτός, ή, όν	(1)	chosen together with; one also chosen (fem. subst. in NT)
ψευδολόγος, ον	(1)	speaking falsely; liar (subst. in NT)
ὁμολογουμένως	(1)	confessedly, undeniably

λείπω

λείπω	(6)	I leave, fall short, lack
ἀπολείπω	(7)	I leave behind, desert; remain (pass.)
διαλείπω	(1)	I stop, cease
ἐγκαταλείπω	(10)	I leave behind, abandon, leave
ἐκλείπω	(4)	I fail, die out, cease, grow dark
ἐπιλείπω	(1)	I fail
καταλείπω	(24)	I leave, leave behind, abandon, neglect; remain (pass.)
περιλείπομαι	(2)	I remain, am left behind
ὑπολείπω	(1)	I leave remaining; am left behind (pass. in NT)
ὑπολιμπάνω	(1)	I leave (behind)
λεῖμμα, ατος, τό	(1)	remnant
ὑπόλειμμα, ατος, τό	(1)	remnant
λοιπός, ή, όν	(55)	remaining, other, rest; finally, henceforth (neut. as adv.)
ἀδιάλειπτος, ον	(2)	unceasing, constant
ἀνέκλειπτος, ον	(1)	unfailing, inexhaustible
ἐπίλοιπος, ον	(1)	left, remaining
κατάλοιπος, ον	(1)	left, remaining
ἀδιαλείπτως	(4)	constantly, unceasingly

λεπίς

λεπίς, ίδος, ἡ	(1)	fish scale; scale (fig. in NT)
λέπρα, ας, ἡ	(4)	leprosy, skin disease

λεπρός, ά, όν	(9)	leprous; leper, person with a skin disease (subst.)
λεπτός, ή, όν	(3)	small; lepton, small copper coin (subst. in NT)

λευκός

λευκαίνω	(2)	I make white
λευκός, ή, όν	(25)	white, bright, shining

ληνός

ληνός, οῦ, ἡ	(5)	wine press
ὑπολήνιον, ου, τό	(1)	wine trough

λίαν

λίαν	(12)	very much, exceedingly, very, quite
ὑπερλίαν	(2)	exceedingly; special (adj. in NT)

λίβανος

λίβανος, ου, ὁ	(2)	frankincense
λιβανωτός, οῦ, ὁ	(2)	censer

λίθος

λιθάζω	(9)	I stone
καταλιθάζω	(1)	I stone to death
λιθοβολέω	(7)	I throw stones, stone (to death)
λίθος, ου, ὁ	(59)	stone
χρυσόλιθος, ου, ὁ	(1)	chrysolite
λίθινος, η, ον	(3)	(made of) stone
λιθόστρωτος, ον	(1)	paved with stones; stone pavement (neut. subst. in NT)

λοίδορος

λοιδορέω	(4)	I revile, insult
ἀντιλοιδορέω	(1)	I revile or insult in return
λοιδορία, ας, ἡ	(3)	abuse (verbal), reproach, reviling
λοίδορος, ου, ὁ	(2)	reviler, slanderer

λούω

λούω	(5)	I wash, bathe
ἀπολούω	(2)	I wash away; wash myself (mid. in NT)
λουτρόν, οῦ, τό	(2)	bath, washing

λύπη

λυπέω	(26)	I grieve, pain, offend; become sad, grieve (pass.)
συλλυπέω	(1)	I grieve with; am deeply grieved (pass. in NT)
λύπη, ης, ἡ	(16)	grief, sorrow, pain, affliction
ἄλυπος, ον	(1)	free from anxiety
περίλυπος, ον	(5)	very sad, deeply grieved

λύχνος

λυχνία, ας, ἡ	(12)	lampstand
λύχνος, ου, ὁ	(14)	lamp

λύω

λυτρόω	(3)	I set free, redeem, rescue (mid.); am ransomed (pass.)
λύω	(42)	I loose, untie, set free, destroy, abolish, allow
ἀναλύω	(2)	I depart, return, die
ἀπολύω	(66)	I set free, release, divorce, dismiss; go away (mid.)
διαλύω	(1)	I break up, dissolve, scatter
ἐκλύω	(5)	I become weary, give out (pass. in NT)
ἐπιλύω	(2)	I set free, explain, interpret, settle, resolve
καταλύω	(17)	I throw down, tear down, destroy, abolish, find lodging
λυσιτελέω	(1)	I am advantageous or better; it is better (impers. in NT)
παραλύω	(5)	I weaken; am weakened, paralyzed (pass. in NT)
λύσις, εως, ἡ	(1)	release, separation, divorce
λύτρον, ου, τό	(2)	price of release, ransom
λύτρωσις, εως, ἡ	(3)	redemption, ransoming, releasing
λυτρωτής, οῦ, ὁ	(1)	redeemer
ἀνάλυσις, εως, ἡ	(1)	departure, death
ἀντίλυτρον, ου, τό	(1)	ransom
ἀπολύτρωσις, εως, ἡ	(10)	release, redemption
ἐπίλυσις, εως, ἡ	(1)	explanation, interpretation
κατάλυμα, ατος, τό	(3)	inn, lodging, guest room, dining room
ἀκατάλυτος, ον	(1)	indestructible, endless
ἀλυσιτελής, ές	(1)	unprofitable
παραλυτικός, ή, όν	(10)	lame; lame person, paralytic (subst. in NT)

μάγος

μαγεύω	(1)	I practice magic
μαγεία, ας, ἡ	(1)	magic
μάγος, ου, ὁ	(6)	wise man, Magus, magician

μαίνομαι

μαίνομαι	(5)	I am mad, out of my mind, insane
μαντεύομαι	(1)	I prophesy, give an oracle
ἐμμαίνομαι	(1)	I am enraged
μανία, ας, ἡ	(1)	madness, insanity, frenzy

μακάριος

μακαρίζω	(2)	I call or consider blessed, happy, fortunate
μακαρισμός, οῦ, ὁ	(3)	blessing, happiness
μακάριος, α, ον	(50)	blessed, happy, fortunate

μαλακός

μαλακία, ας, ἡ	(3)	weakness, sickness
μαλακός, ή, όν	(4)	soft, homosexual

μᾶλλον

μάλιστα	(12)	most of all, above all, especially, particularly
μᾶλλον	(81)	more, more than ever, rather, more surely

μανθάνω

μαθητεύω	(4)	I make a disciple of; become a disciple (pass.)
μανθάνω	(25)	I learn, find out
καταμανθάνω	(1)	I observe, notice
μαθητής, οῦ, ὁ	(261)	disciple, learner, pupil, follower

μαθήτρια, ας, ἡ	(1)	woman disciple
συμμαθητής, οῦ, ὁ	(1)	fellow pupil, fellow disciple
ἀμαθής, ές	(1)	ignorant

μαραίνω

μαραίνω	(1)	I destroy; die out, fade, wither (pass. in NT)
ἀμαράντινος, η, ον	(1)	unfading
ἀμάραντος, ον	(1)	unfading

μάρτυς

μαρτυρέω	(76)	I bear witness, testify, am a witness, confirm, approve
μαρτύρομαι	(5)	I testify, bear witness, insist, implore
διαμαρτύρομαι	(15)	I charge, warn, testify, bear witness
ἐπιμαρτυρέω	(1)	I bear witness, testify
καταμαρτυρέω	(3)	I bear witness against, testify against
προμαρτύρομαι	(1)	I bear witness to beforehand, predict
συμμαρτυρέω	(3)	I testify with, confirm, testify in support of
συνεπιμαρτυρέω	(1)	I testify at the same time
ψευδομαρτυρέω	(5)	I bear false witness, give false testimony
μαρτυρία, ας, ἡ	(37)	testimony, witness, reputation
μαρτύριον, ου, τό	(19)	testimony, proof
μάρτυς, υρος, ὁ	(35)	witness, martyr
ψευδομαρτυρία, ας, ἡ	(2)	false testimony
ψευδόμαρτυς, υρος, ὁ	(2)	one who gives false testimony, false witness
ἀμάρτυρος, ον	(1)	without witness

μαστιγόω

μασάομαι	(1)	I bite
μαστιγόω	(7)	I whip, flog, scourge, punish
μαστίζω	(1)	I strike with a whip, scourge
ἀπομάσσω	(1)	I wipe off (mid. in NT)
ἐκμάσσω	(5)	I wipe, dry
μάστιξ, ιγος, ἡ	(6)	whip, lash, suffering; lashing (pl.)

μάταιος

ματαιόω	(1)	I think about worthless things, am foolish (pass. in NT)
ματαιότης, ητος, ἡ	(3)	emptiness, futility, purposelessness, worthlessness
ματαιολογία, ας, ἡ	(1)	empty or fruitless talk
μάταιος, α, ον	(6)	empty, idle, fruitless, useless, powerless, worthless
ματαιολόγος, ον	(1)	talking idly; idle or empty talker (subst. in NT)
μάτην	(2)	in vain, to no end

μάχη

μάχομαι	(4)	I fight, quarrel, dispute
διαμάχομαι	(1)	I contend sharply
θηριομαχέω	(1)	I fight wild animals
θυμομαχέω	(1)	I am very angry
λογομαχέω	(1)	I dispute about words, split hairs
μάχαιρα, ης, ἡ	(29)	sword, saber
μάχη, ης, ἡ	(4)	battle; fighting, quarrels, strife (pl. in NT)
λογομαχία, ας, ἡ	(1)	word battle, dispute about words
ἄμαχος, ον	(2)	peaceable
θεομάχος, ον	(1)	fighting against or opposing God

μέγας

μεγαλύνω	(8)	I make large or long, magnify, praise, extol
μεγαλειότης, ητος, ἡ	(3)	grandeur, greatness, majesty
μεγαλωσύνη, ης, ἡ	(3)	majesty, greatness, Majesty
μέγεθος, ους, τό	(1)	greatness
μεγιστάν, ᾶνος, ὁ	(3)	great person, courtier
μεγαλεῖος, α, ον	(1)	magnificent; mighty deed (neut. subst. in NT)
μέγας, μεγάλη, μέγα	(243)	large, great, loud, important, strong, high
μεγαλοπρεπής, ές	(1)	magnificent, sublime, majestic
μεγάλως	(1)	greatly, very much

μεθύω

μεθύσκω	(5)	I get drunk, become intoxicated (pass. in NT)
μεθύω	(5)	I am drunk
μέθη, ης, ἡ	(3)	drunkenness
μέθυσος, ου, ὁ	(2)	drunkard
ἀμέθυστος, ου, ἡ	(1)	amethyst

μέλει

μέλει	(10)	it is a concern (impers.)
μελετάω	(2)	I practice, think about
ἀμελέω	(4)	I neglect, am unconcerned, disregard
ἐπιμελέομαι	(3)	I care for, take care of
μεταμέλομαι	(6)	I regret, repent, change my mind
προμελετάω	(1)	I prepare
ἐπιμέλεια, ας, ἡ	(1)	care, attention
ἀμεταμέλητος, ον	(2)	not to be regretted, without regret, irrevocable
ἐπιμελῶς	(1)	carefully

μέμφομαι

μέμφομαι	(2)	I find fault, blame
μωμάομαι	(2)	I find fault with, censure, blame
μομφή, ῆς, ἡ	(1)	blame, cause for complaint, complaint
μῶμος, ου, ὁ	(1)	blemish, defect
ἄμεμπτος, ον	(5)	blameless, faultless
ἀμώμητος, ον	(1)	blameless, unblemished
ἄμωμος, ον	(8)	unblemished, blameless
μεμψίμοιρος, ον	(1)	faultfinding, complaining
ἀμέμπτως	(2)	blamelessly, blameless

μέν

μέν	(179)	on the one hand, to be sure, indeed
μήν	(18)	indeed, surely
μενοῦν	(1)	rather, on the contrary, indeed
μενοῦνγε	(3)	rather, on the contrary, indeed
μέντοι	(8)	really, actually, though, to be sure, indeed, but

μένω

μένω	(118)	I remain, stay, abide, live, dwell, last; wait for (trans.)
ἀναμένω	(1)	I wait for, expect
διαμένω	(5)	I remain, continue
ἐμμένω	(4)	I stay, remain, stand by, remain true
ἐπιμένω	(16)	I stay, remain, continue, persist, persevere

καταμένω	(1)	I stay, live
παραμένω	(4)	I remain, stay, serve, continue in office
περιμένω	(1)	I wait for
προσμένω	(7)	I remain or stay with, continue in, remain longer
ὑπομένω	(17)	I remain, hold out, endure
μονή, ῆς, ἡ	(2)	staying, room, abode
ὑπομονή, ῆς, ἡ	(32)	patience, endurance, perseverance

μεριμνάω

μεριμνάω	(19)	I have anxiety, am anxious, care for
προμεριμνάω	(1)	I am anxious beforehand, worry in advance
μέριμνα, ης, ἡ	(6)	anxiety, worry, care
ἀμέριμνος, ον	(2)	free from care, without worry

μέρος

μερίζω	(14)	I divide, separate, distribute, apportion; share (mid.)
διαμερίζω	(11)	I divide, separate, distribute, share
συμμερίζω	(1)	I share with (mid. in NT)
μερίς, ίδος, ἡ	(5)	part, share, portion, district
μερισμός, οῦ, ὁ	(2)	separation, distribution, apportionment
μεριστής, οῦ, ὁ	(1)	divider, arbitrator
μέρος, ους, τό	(42)	part, piece, party, matter, share; district, side (pl.)
διαμερισμός, οῦ, ὁ	(1)	dissension, disunity
πολυμερῶς	(1)	in many ways

μέσος

μεσιτεύω	(1)	I guarantee, mediate, act as surety
μεσόω	(1)	I am in or at the middle, am half over
μεσίτης, ου, ὁ	(6)	mediator, arbitrator, intermediary
μεσημβρία, ας, ἡ	(2)	midday, noon, south
μεσονύκτιον, ου, τό	(4)	midnight
μεσότοιχον, ου, τό	(1)	dividing wall
μεσουράνημα, ατος, τό	(3)	midheaven, zenith
μέσος, η, ον	(58)	middle; the middle (subst.); in the middle of (impr. prep.)

μεστός

μεστόω	(1)	I fill; am full (pass. in NT)
μεστός, ή, όν	(9)	full

μετά

μεταξύ	(9)	meanwhile, after; between, in the middle (impr. prep.)
μετά	(469)	with, among, against (gen.); after, behind (acc.)

μέτρον

μετρέω	(11)	I measure, give out, apportion
ἀντιμετρέω	(1)	I measure in return, repay
μετριοπαθέω	(1)	I deal gently
μετρητής, οῦ, ὁ	(1)	measure (liquid)
μέτρον, ου, τό	(14)	measure, quantity, number
σιτομέτριον, ου, τό	(1)	grain or food allowance, ration
ἄμετρος, ον	(2)	immeasurable
μετρίως	(1)	moderately

μή

μηδείς, μηδεμία, μηδέν	(90)	no; no one, nobody, nothing (subst.); in no way (adv.)
μηδαμῶς	(2)	by no means, certainly not, no
μηδέποτε	(1)	never
μηδέπω	(1)	not yet
μηκέτι	(22)	no longer, not from now on
μήπω	(2)	not yet
μή	(1042)	not (used w. non-ind. verbs and neg. answer questions)
μηδέ	(56)	and not, but not, nor, not even
μήποτε	(25)	never, lest, that . . . not, whether perhaps, perhaps
μήτε	(34)	and not, nor
μήτι	(17)	(used in questions expecting a neg. answer)
μήτιγε	(1)	not to speak of, let alone

μῆκος

μηκύνω	(1)	I make long; become long, grow (mid. in NT)
μακροθυμέω	(10)	I have patience, wait patiently, am patient
μῆκος, ους, τό	(3)	length
μακροθυμία, ας, ἡ	(14)	patience, steadfastness, endurance, forbearance
μακρός, ά, όν	(4)	long, far away, distant
μακροχρόνιος, ον	(1)	long-lived
μακράν	(10)	far, far away
μακρόθεν	(14)	from far away, from a distance, far off
μακροθύμως	(1)	patiently

μήν

μήν, μηνός, ὁ	(1)	month, new moon
νεομηνία, ας, ἡ	(1)	new moon (festival)
τετράμηνος, ον	(1)	lasting four months; period of four months (subst. in NT)
τρίμηνος, ον	(1)	of three months; three months (subst. in NT)

μήτηρ

μήτηρ, τρός, ἡ	(83)	mother
μήτρα, ας, ἡ	(2)	womb
μητρολῴας, ου, ὁ	(1)	one who murders one's mother
ἀμήτωρ, ορος	(1)	without a mother

μιαίνω

μιαίνω	(5)	I stain, defile, contaminate
μίασμα, ατος, τό	(1)	defilement, corruption
μιασμός, οῦ, ὁ	(1)	defilement, corruption
ἀμίαντος, ον	(4)	undefiled, pure

μίγνυμι

μίγνυμι	(4)	I mingle, mix
συναναμίγνυμι	(3)	I mix up together; mingle or associate with (pass. in NT)
μίγμα, ατος, τό	(1)	mixture, compound

μιμέομαι

μιμέομαι	(4)	I imitate, follow
μιμητής, οῦ, ὁ	(6)	imitator
συμμιμητής, οῦ, ὁ	(1)	fellow imitator

μιμνῄσκομαι

μιμνῄσκομαι	(23)	I remember, keep in mind, think of
μνημονεύω	(21)	I remember, keep in mind, think of, mention
ἀναμιμνῄσκω	(6)	I remind; remember (pass.)
ἐπαναμιμνῄσκω	(1)	I remind
ὑπομιμνῄσκω	(7)	I remind, call to mind; remember (pass.)
μνεία, ας, ἡ	(7)	memory, remembrance, mention
μνῆμα, ατος, τό	(8)	grave, tomb
μνημεῖον, ου, τό	(40)	monument, grave, tomb
μνήμη, ης, ἡ	(1)	remembrance, memory
μνημόσυνον, ου, τό	(3)	memory, memorial offering
ἀνάμνησις, εως, ἡ	(4)	reminder, remembrance
ὑπόμνησις, εως, ἡ	(3)	remembering, reminding, remembrance

μισθός

μισθόω	(2)	I hire (mid. in NT)
μίσθιος, ου, ὁ	(2)	day laborer, hired worker
μισθός, οῦ, ὁ	(29)	pay, wages, reward, punishment
μίσθωμα, ατος, τό	(1)	rent, rented house
μισθωτός, οῦ, ὁ	(3)	hired worker
ἀντιμισθία, ας, ἡ	(2)	reward, penalty, exchange
μισθαποδοσία, ας, ἡ	(3)	reward, punishment, retribution
μισθαποδότης, ου, ὁ	(1)	rewarder

μόγις

μόχθος, ου, ὁ	(3)	labor, exertion, hardship
μογιλάλος, ον	(1)	speaking with difficulty, having a speech impediment
μόγις	(1)	scarcely, with difficulty
μόλις	(6)	scarcely, with difficulty, only rarely

μοιχός

μοιχάω	(4)	I commit adultery (pass. in NT)
μοιχεύω	(15)	I commit adultery
μοιχαλίς, ίδος, ἡ	(7)	adulteress; adulterous (adj.)
μοιχεία, ας, ἡ	(3)	adultery
μοιχός, οῦ, ὁ	(3)	adulterer

μολύνω

μολύνω	(3)	I stain, defile, make unclean
μολυσμός, οῦ, ὁ	(1)	defilement

μόνος

μονόω	(1)	I make solitary; am left alone (pass. in NT)
μόνος, η, ον	(114)	only, alone, deserted, isolated; only, alone (neut as adv.)
μονογενής, ές	(9)	only, unique
μονόφθαλμος, ον	(2)	one-eyed

μορφή

μορφόω	(1)	I form, shape
μεταμορφόω	(4)	I am transformed, changed
συμμορφίζω	(1)	I take on the same form, am conformed to (pass in NT)
μορφή, ῆς, ἡ	(3)	form, outward appearance, shape

| μόρφωσις, εως, ἡ | (2) | embodiment, formulation, outward form, appearance |
| σύμμορφος, ον | (2) | having the same form, similar in form |

μόσχος

| μοσχοποιέω | (1) | I make a calf |
| μόσχος, ου, ὁ | (6) | calf, young bull or ox |

μῦθος

παραμυθέομαι	(4)	I encourage, cheer up, console, comfort
μῦθος, ου, ὁ	(5)	tale, story, legend, myth, fable
παραμυθία, ας, ἡ	(1)	encouragement, comfort, consolation
παραμύθιον, ου, τό	(1)	encouragement, consolation

μυκτηρίζω

| μυκτηρίζω | (1) | I treat with contempt, mock |
| ἐκμυκτηρίζω | (2) | I ridicule, sneer |

μύλος

μύλος, ου, ὁ	(4)	mill, millstone
μυλικός, ή, όν	(1)	belonging to a mill
μύλινος, η, ον	(1)	belonging to a mill; millstone (subst. in NT)

μυρίος

μυριάς, άδος, ἡ	(8)	myriad, ten thousand
δισμυριάς, άδος, ἡ	(1)	double myriad, twenty thousand
μύριοι, αι, α	(2)	ten thousand
μυρίος, α, ον	(1)	innumerable, countless

μύρον

| μυρίζω | (1) | I anoint |
| μύρον, ου, τό | (14) | ointment, perfume |

[μύω]

καμμύω	(2)	I close
μυέω	(1)	I initiate; learn the secret of (pass. in NT)
μυωπάζω	(1)	I am shortsighted
μυστήριον, ου, τό	(28)	secret, mystery

μωρός

μωραίνω	(4)	I make foolish; become foolish or tasteless (pass.)
μωρία, ας, ἡ	(5)	foolishness
μωρολογία, ας, ἡ	(1)	foolish or silly talk
μωρός, ά, όν	(12)	foolish, stupid, fool; foolishness (subst.)

ναός

| ναός, οῦ, ὁ | (45) | temple, sanctuary, shrine |
| νεωκόρος, ου, ὁ | (1) | temple keeper |

ναῦς

| ναυαγέω | (2) | I suffer shipwreck |
| ναῦς, ὁ | (1) | ship |

| ναύτης, ου, ὁ | (3) | sailor |
| ναύκληρος, ου, ὁ | (1) | ship owner, captain |

νεκρός

νεκρόω	(3)	I put to death; am as good as dead (pass.)
νέκρωσις, εως, ἡ	(2)	death, putting to death, deadness, deadening
νεκρός, ά, όν	(128)	dead, useless; dead person (subst.)

νέος

ἀνανεόω	(1)	I renew
νεανίας, ου, ὁ	(3)	youth, young man, servant
νεανίσκος, ου, ὁ	(11)	youth, young man, servant
νεότης, ητος, ἡ	(4)	youth
νοσσιά, ᾶς, ἡ	(1)	brood
νοσσίον, ου, τό	(1)	young bird
νοσσός, οῦ, ὁ	(1)	young bird
νεομηνία, ας, ἡ	(1)	new moon (festival)
νέος, α, ον	(23)	new, fresh, young
νεωτερικός, ή, όν	(1)	youthful
νεόφυτος, ον	(1)	newly converted

νεύω

νεύω	(2)	I nod, motion
διανεύω	(1)	I nod, beckon
ἐκνεύω	(1)	I turn, withdrew
ἐννεύω	(1)	I nod, make signals, gesture
ἐπινεύω	(1)	I consent, agree
κατανεύω	(1)	I signal, motion to

νέφος

| νεφέλη, ης, ἡ | (25) | cloud |
| νέφος, ους, τό | (1) | cloud, host |

νήπιος

| νηπιάζω | (1) | I am a child |
| νήπιος, α, ον | (15) | infant, minor, immature, innocent; child (subst.) |

νῆσος

| νησίον, ου, τό | (1) | island, small island |
| νῆσος, ου, ἡ | (9) | island |

νήφω

νήφω	(6)	I am well-balanced, self-controlled, sober
ἀνανήφω	(1)	I become sober again, return to my senses
ἐκνήφω	(1)	I became sober
νηφάλιος, α, ον	(3)	temperate, sober, clear-headed, self-controlled

νίκη

νικάω	(28)	I conquer, prevail, win (a verdict), overcome
ὑπερνικάω	(1)	I am completely victorious
νίκη, ης, ἡ	(1)	victory
νῖκος, ους, τό	(4)	victory

νίπτω

νίπτω	(17)	I wash
ἀπονίπτω	(1)	I wash off
νιπτήρ, ῆρος, ὁ	(1)	washbasin
ἄνιπτος, ον	(2)	unwashed

νόμος

νομίζω	(15)	I think, believe, suppose; am the custom (pass.)
ἀπονέμω	(1)	I show (honor)
διανέμω	(1)	I distribute
κατακληρονομέω	(1)	I give as an inheritance
κληρονομέω	(18)	I inherit, acquire, obtain, receive
νομοθετέω	(2)	I receive the law, enact by law
οἰκονομέω	(1)	I am manager
παρανομέω	(1)	I break or act contrary to the law
νόμισμα, ατος, τό	(1)	coin, money
νόμος, ου, ὁ	(194)	law, rule, principle, norm, (Jewish) religion
ἀνομία, ας, ἡ	(15)	lawlessness, lawless deed
κληρονομία, ας, ἡ	(14)	inheritance, possession, property, salvation
κληρονόμος, ου, ὁ	(15)	heir
νομοδιδάσκαλος, ου, ὁ	(3)	teacher of the law
νομοθεσία, ας, ἡ	(1)	giving of the law
νομοθέτης, ου, ὁ	(1)	lawgiver
οἰκονομία, ας, ἡ	(9)	management, commission, plan, training, office
οἰκονόμος, ου, ὁ	(10)	steward, manager, administrator, treasurer
παρανομία, ας, ἡ	(1)	lawlessness, evil-doing
νομικός, ή, όν	(9)	pertaining to the law; legal expert, lawyer (subst.)
ἄνομος, ον	(9)	lawless, wicked, Gentile; criminal, lawless one (subst.)
ἔννομος, ον	(2)	legal, lawful, subject to law, regular
συγκληρονόμος, ον	(4)	inheriting together with; fellow heir (subst. in NT)
νομίμως	(2)	in accordance with the rules, lawfully
ἀνόμως	(2)	without the law

νόσος

νοσέω	(1)	I have an unhealthy craving
νόσος, ου, ἡ	(11)	disease, illness

νοῦς

νοέω	(14)	I perceive, understand, comprehend, consider, think
εὐνοέω	(1)	I make friends
κατανοέω	(14)	I notice, look, consider, contemplate
μετανοέω	(34)	I repent, change my mind, feel remorse, am converted
νουθετέω	(8)	I admonish, warn, instruct
προνοέω	(3)	I think of beforehand, care for, have regard for
ὑπονοέω	(3)	I suspect, suppose
νόημα, ατος, τό	(6)	thought, mind, purpose, design, plot
νοῦς, νοός ὁ	(24)	mind, understanding, intellect, attitude, thought, opinion
ἄνοια, ας, ἡ	(2)	folly, foolishness, fury
διανόημα, ατος, τό	(1)	thought
διάνοια, ας, ἡ	(12)	understanding, mind, insight, thought
ἔννοια, ας, ἡ	(2)	thought, knowledge, insight, intention
ἐπίνοια, ας, ἡ	(1)	thought, conception, intent
εὔνοια, ας, ἡ	(1)	good will, zeal, enthusiasm
μετάνοια, ας, ἡ	(22)	repentance, change of mind, remorse, conversion

νουθεσία, ας, ἡ	(3)	admonition, instruction, warning
πρόνοια, ας, ἡ	(2)	foresight, care, provision
ὑπόνοια, ας, ἡ	(1)	suspicion, conjecture
ἀμετανόητος, ον	(1)	unrepentant
ἀνόητος, ον	(6)	unintelligent, foolish
δυσνόητος, ον	(1)	hard to understand
νουνεχῶς	(1)	wisely, thoughtfully

νύμφη

νύμφη, ης, ἡ	(8)	bride, daughter-in-law
νυμφίος, ου, ὁ	(16)	bridegroom
νυμφών, ῶνος, ὁ	(3)	wedding hall, bridal chamber

νῦν

νῦν	(147)	now, as things now stand; the present, now (subst.)
νυνί	(20)	now
τοίνυν	(3)	hence, so, indeed, therefore, then

νύξ

διανυκτερεύω	(1)	I spend the night
νύξ, νυκτός, ἡ	(61)	night
μεσονύκτιον, ου, τό	(4)	midnight
νυχθήμερον, ου, τό	(1)	a day and a night
ἔννυχος, ον	(1)	at night (acc. neut. pl. as adv. in NT)

νύσσω

νύσσω	(1)	I prick, stab, pierce
κατανύσσομαι	(1)	I am pierced, stabbed
κατάνυξις, εως, ἡ	(1)	stupor, numbness

ξένος

ξενίζω	(10)	I entertain, surprise, astonish; stay (pass.)
ξενοδοχέω	(1)	I show hospitality
ξενία, ας, ἡ	(2)	hospitality, guest room, place of lodging
φιλοξενία, ας, ἡ	(2)	hospitality
ξένος, η, ον	(14)	strange, foreign, unusual; stranger, alien, host (subst.)
φιλόξενος, ον	(3)	hospitable

ξηρός

ξηραίνω	(15)	I dry; dry up, wither, stop, become stiff
ξηρός, ά, όν	(8)	dry, dried up; dry land, withered (subst.)

ξύλον

ξυράω	(3)	I have myself shaved (mid.); am shaved (pass.)
ξύλον, ου, τό	(20)	wood, stocks, pole, club, cross, tree
ξύλινος, η, ον	(2)	wooden

ὁ

τοιόσδε, άδε, όνδε	(1)	such as this, of this kind
τοιοῦτος, αύτη, οῦτον	(57)	of such a kind, such; such a person or thing (subst.)
ὧδε	(61)	here, hither, to this place, in this case
ὁ, ἡ, τό	(19870)	the

| ὅδε, ἥδε, τόδε | (10) | this, such and such |
| οἷος, α, ον | (14) | of what sort, as, such as |

ὄγκος

| ὄγκος, ου, ὁ | (1) | weight, burden, impediment |
| ὑπέρογκος, ον | (2) | puffed up, haughty, bombastic, boastful |

ὁδός

ὁδεύω	(1)	I go, travel, am on a journey
διοδεύω	(2)	I go, travel through, go about
εὐοδόω	(4)	I prosper, succeed (pass. in NT)
ὁδηγέω	(5)	I lead, guide
ὁδοιπορέω	(1)	I travel, am on my way
συνοδεύω	(1)	I travel with
ὁδός, οῦ, ἡ	(101)	way, road, journey, way of life, conduct, Way, teaching
ἄμφοδον, ου, τό	(1)	street
διέξοδος, ου, ἡ	(1)	outlet (used of streets)
εἴσοδος, ου, ἡ	(5)	entrance, access, coming
ἔξοδος, ου, ἡ	(3)	the Exodus, departure, death
μεθοδεία, ας, ἡ	(2)	scheming, craftiness
ὁδηγός, οῦ, ὁ	(5)	leader, guide
ὁδοιπορία, ας, ἡ	(2)	walking, journey
πάροδος, ου, ἡ	(1)	passage, passing by
συνοδία, ας, ἡ	(1)	caravan, group of travelers

ὀδύνη

| ὀδυνάω | (4) | I suffer pain, am deeply distressed (pass. in NT) |
| ὀδύνη, ης, ἡ | (2) | pain, woe, sorrow |

ὄζω

ὄζω	(1)	I smell, stink, give off an odor
ὀσμή, ῆς, ἡ	(6)	fragrance, odor
ὄσφρησις, εως, ἡ	(1)	sense of smell, nose
εὐωδία, ας, ἡ	(3)	fragrance, aroma

ὀθόνη

| ὀθόνη, ης, ἡ | (2) | linen cloth, sheet |
| ὀθόνιον, ου, τό | (5) | linen cloth, bandage |

οἶδα

| οἶδα | (318) | I know, am acquainted with, know how, understand |
| σύνοιδα | (2) | I share knowledge with, am aware of |

οἶκος

οἰκέω	(9)	I live, dwell; inhabit (trans.)
ἀνοικοδομέω	(2)	I build up again, rebuild
ἐγκατοικέω	(1)	I live, dwell
ἐνοικέω	(5)	I live, dwell in
ἐποικοδομέω	(7)	I build upon
κατοικέω	(44)	I live, dwell, reside; inhabit (trans.)
κατοικίζω	(1)	I cause to dwell
μετοικίζω	(2)	I cause to migrate, resettle, remove, deport

οἰκοδεσποτέω	(1)	I manage my household, keep house
οἰκοδομέω	(40)	I build, erect, restore, rebuild, build up, edify, benefit
οἰκονομέω	(1)	I am manager
παροικέω	(2)	I inhabit or live as a stranger, migrate
περιοικέω	(1)	I live in the neighborhood of
συνοικέω	(1)	I live with
συνοικοδομέω	(1)	I build together; am built up together (pass. in NT)
οἰκετεία, ας, ἡ	(1)	slaves of a household
οἰκέτης, ου, ὁ	(4)	house slave, domestic, servant
οἴκημα, ατος, τό	(1)	room, prison
οἰκητήριον, ου, τό	(2)	dwelling, habitation
οἰκία, ας, ἡ	(93)	house, home, dwelling, household, family
οἰκιακός, οῦ, ὁ	(2)	member of a household
οἶκος, ου, ὁ	(114)	house, home, household, family, nation, property, temple
κατοίκησις, εως, ἡ	(1)	living quarters, dwelling
κατοικητήριον, ου, τό	(2)	dwelling place, house, home
κατοικία, ας, ἡ	(1)	dwelling place, habitation
μετοικεσία, ας, ἡ	(4)	deportation
οἰκοδεσπότης, ου, ὁ	(12)	master of the house
οἰκοδομή, ῆς, ἡ	(18)	building up, edification, building, edifice
οἰκοδόμος, ου, ὁ	(1)	builder
οἰκονομία, ας, ἡ	(9)	management, commission, plan, training, office
οἰκονόμος, ου, ὁ	(10)	steward, manager, administrator, treasurer
οἰκουμένη, ης, ἡ	(15)	world, inhabited earth, humankind, Roman Empire
παροικία, ας, ἡ	(2)	stay, sojourn, exile
οἰκεῖος, α, ον	(3)	member of the household (subst. in NT)
οἰκουργός, όν	(1)	working at home, domestic
πάροικος, ον	(4)	strange; stranger, alien (subst.)
περίοικος, ον	(1)	living around; neighbor (subst. in NT)
πανοικεί	(1)	with one's whole household

οἰκτίρω

οἰκτίρω	(2)	I have compassion
οἰκτιρμός, οῦ, ὁ	(5)	pity, mercy, compassion
οἰκτίρμων, ον	(3)	merciful, compassionate

οἶνος

οἶνος, ου, ὁ	(34)	wine, vineyard
οἰνοπότης, ου, ὁ	(2)	wine drinker, drunkard
οἰνοφλυγία, ας, ἡ	(1)	drunkenness
πάροινος, ον	(2)	drunken, addicted to wine; drunkard (subst. in NT)

ὀκνέω

| ὀκνέω | (1) | I hesitate, delay |
| ὀκνηρός, ά, όν | (3) | lazy, indolent, troublesome |

ὀκτώ

ὀγδοήκοντα	(2)	eighty
ὄγδοος, η, ον	(5)	eighth
ὀκτώ	(8)	eight
δεκαοκτώ	(2)	eighteen
ὀκταήμερος, ον	(1)	on the eighth day

ὄλεθρος

ὀλοθρεύω	(1)	I destroy, ruin
ἀπόλλυμι	(90)	I ruin, destroy, lose; am destroyed, die, am lost (mid.)
ἐξολεθρεύω	(1)	I destroy, root out
συναπόλλυμι	(1)	I am destroyed or perish with (mid. in NT)
ὄλεθρος, ου, ὁ	(4)	destruction, ruin, death
ὀλοθρευτής, οῦ, ὁ	(1)	destroyer (angel)
ἀπώλεια, ας, ἡ	(18)	destruction, waste, ruin

ὀλίγος

ὀλιγωρέω	(1)	I think lightly, make light
ὀλιγοπιστία, ας, ἡ	(1)	littleness of faith
ὀλίγος, η, ον	(40)	small, little, short; small amount (subst.); few (pl.)
ὀλιγόπιστος, ον	(5)	of little faith or trust
ὀλιγόψυχος, ον	(1)	fainthearted, discouraged
ὀλίγως	(1)	scarcely, barely

ὅλος

ὁλοκαύτωμα, ατος, τό	(3)	whole burnt offering
ὁλοκληρία, ας, ἡ	(1)	wholeness, soundness, perfect health
ὅλος, η, ον	(109)	whole, entire, complete, altogether
ὁλόκληρος, ον	(2)	whole, complete, sound, blameless
ὁλοτελής, ές	(1)	quite complete, wholly
ὅλως	(4)	generally speaking, actually, everywhere
καθόλου	(1)	entirely, completely

ὀμνύω

ὀμνύω	(26)	I swear, take an oath
ὁρκωμοσία, ας, ἡ	(4)	oath, taking an oath
συνωμοσία, ας, ἡ	(1)	conspiracy, plot

ὅμοιος

ὁμοιόω	(15)	I make like, compare; be like, resemble (pass.)
ἀνθομολογέομαι	(1)	I praise, thank
ἀφομοιόω	(1)	I make like, become like, resemble
ἐξομολογέω	(10)	I promise, consent; confess, admit, praise
ὁμιλέω	(4)	I speak, talk, converse
ὁμολογέω	(26)	I confess, promise, admit, declare, acknowledge, praise
παρομοιάζω	(1)	I am like, resemble
συνομιλέω	(1)	I talk or converse with
συνομορέω	(1)	I border on, am next door to
ὁμοιότης, ητος, ἡ	(2)	likeness, similarity
ὁμοίωμα, ατος, τό	(6)	likeness, image, appearance
ὁμοίωσις, εως, ἡ	(1)	likeness, resemblance
ὁμιλία, ας, ἡ	(1)	association, company
ὁμολογία, ας, ἡ	(6)	confession, confessing, acknowledgment, profession
ὅμοιος, α, ον	(45)	of the same nature, like, similar
ὁμοιοπαθής, ές	(2)	with the same nature, like in every way
ὁμότεχνος, ον	(1)	practicing the same trade
ὁμόφρων, ον	(1)	like-minded, united
παρόμοιος, ον	(1)	like, similar
ὁμοίως	(30)	likewise, so, similarly, in the same way
ὁμοῦ	(4)	together

ὅμως	(3)	nevertheless, yet, likewise, also
ὁμοθυμαδόν	(11)	with one mind, by common consent, together
ὁμολογουμένως	(1)	confessedly, undeniably

ὄνειδος

ὀνειδίζω	(9)	I reproach, revile, insult
ὀνειδισμός, οῦ, ὁ	(5)	reproach, reviling, disgrace, insult
ὄνειδος, ους, τό	(1)	disgrace, reproach, insult

ὄνομα

ὀνομάζω	(10)	I name, call, pronounce; am known (pass.)
ἐπονομάζω	(1)	I call, name; call myself (pass. in NT)
ὄνομα, ατος, τό	(231)	name, title, category, person, reputation, Name
τοὔνομα	(1)	named, by name (= τὸ ὄνομα)
εὐώνυμος, ον	(9)	left (as opposed to right)
ψευδώνυμος, ον	(1)	falsely called or named

ὄνος

ὀνάριον, ου, τό	(1)	little donkey, donkey
ὄνος, ου, ὁ, ἡ	(5)	donkey
ὀνικός, ή, όν	(2)	pertaining to a donkey

ὀξύς

παροξύνω	(2)	I irritate; become irritated or angry (pass. in NT)
ὄξος, ους, τό	(6)	sour wine, wine vinegar
παροξυσμός, οῦ, ὁ	(2)	provoking, encouragement, sharp disagreement
ὀξύς, εῖα, ύ	(8)	sharp, swift

ὀπίσω

ὄπισθεν	(7)	from behind, on the back; behind, after (impr. prep.)
ὀπίσω	(35)	behind, back; behind, after (impr. prep.)

ὅπλον

ὁπλίζω	(1)	I equip; arm myself (mid. in NT)
καθοπλίζω	(1)	I arm fully, equip
ὅπλον, ου, τό	(6)	tool, weapon
πανοπλία, ας, ἡ	(3)	full armor, panoply

ὀπώρα

ὀπώρα, ας, ἡ	(1)	fruit
φθινοπωρινός, ή, όν	(1)	belonging to late autumn

ὁράω

ὀπτάνομαι	(1)	I appear
ὁράω	(454)	I see, notice, experience, perceive, see to; appear (pass.)
φρουρέω	(4)	I guard, hold in custody, protect, keep
ἀντοφθαλμέω	(1)	I look directly at, face into
ἀφοράω	(2)	I look away, see
ἐποπτεύω	(2)	I observe, see
εὐπροσωπέω	(1)	I make a good showing
ἐφοράω	(2)	I gaze upon, look at, concern myself with
καθοράω	(1)	I perceive, notice

κατοπτρίζω	(1)	I look at (as in a mirror), contemplate (mid. in NT)
μυωπάζω	(1)	I am shortsighted
προοράω	(4)	I see previously, foresee; see before me (mid.)
προσωπολημπτέω	(1)	I show partiality
συνοράω	(2)	I perceive, realize
ὑπεροράω	(1)	I overlook, disregard
ὑπωπιάζω	(2)	I wear out, treat roughly, keep under control
ὄμμα, ατος, τό	(2)	eye
ὀπτασία, ας, ἡ	(4)	vision
ὅραμα, ατος, τό	(12)	vision
ὅρασις, εως, ἡ	(4)	appearance, vision
ὀφθαλμός, οῦ, ὁ	(100)	eye, sight
ὄψις, εως, ἡ	(3)	outward appearance, face
αὐτόπτης, ου, ὁ	(1)	eyewitness
ἐπόπτης, ου, ὁ	(1)	eyewitness
ἔσοπτρον, ου, τό	(2)	mirror
μέτωπον, ου, τό	(8)	forehead
ὀφθαλμοδουλία, ας, ἡ	(2)	eyeservice, service to attract attention
προσωπολήμπτης, ου, ὁ	(1)	one who shows partiality
προσωπολημψία, ας, ἡ	(4)	partiality
πρόσωπον, ου, τό	(76)	face, countenance, presence, appearance, surface, person
ὁρατος, ή, όν	(1)	visible
ἀόρατος, ον	(5)	unseen, invisible
μονόφθαλμος, ον	(2)	one-eyed
σκυθρωπός, ή, όν	(2)	sad, gloomy
ἀπροσωπολήμπτως	(1)	impartially
ἐνώπιον	(94)	before, in the presence of, in the opinion of (impr. prep.)
κατενώπιον	(3)	before, in the presence of (impr. prep. in NT)

ὀργή

ὀργίζω	(8)	I am angry (pass. in NT)
παροργίζω	(2)	I make angry
ὀργή, ῆς, ἡ	(36)	anger, indignation, wrath, punishment, judgment
παροργισμός, οῦ, ὁ	(1)	anger
ὀργίλος, η, ον	(1)	quick-tempered

ὀρέγω

ὀρέγω	(3)	I stretch myself, aspire to, desire, long for (mid. in NT)
ὀργυιά, ᾶς, ἡ	(2)	fathom (nautical measure)
ὄρεξις, εως, ἡ	(1)	longing, desire, passion

ὀρθός

ἀνορθόω	(3)	I rebuild, restore
ἐπιδιορθόω	(1)	I finish setting right, correct
ὀρθοποδέω	(1)	I am straightforward, progress (fig. in NT)
ὀρθοτομέω	(1)	I cut straight; use or interpret correctly (fig. in NT)
διόρθωμα, ατος, τό	(1)	reform
διόρθωσις, εως, ἡ	(1)	improvement, reformation, new order
ἐπανόρθωσις, εως, ἡ	(1)	correcting, restoration, improvement
ὀρθός, ή, όν	(2)	straight, upright
ὀρθῶς	(4)	rightly, correctly, properly

ὄρθρος

ὀρθρίζω	(1)	I get up early in the morning

ὄρθρος, ου, ὁ	(3)	dawn, early morning
ὀρθρινός, ή, όν	(1)	early in the morning

ὁρίζω

ὁρίζω	(8)	I appoint, determine, set, designate
ἀποδιορίζω	(1)	I divide, separate
ἀφορίζω	(10)	I separate, excommunicate, appoint
προορίζω	(6)	I decide beforehand, predestine
συνομορέω	(1)	I border on, am next door to
ὅριον, ου, τό	(12)	boundary; region, district (pl. in NT)
ὁροθεσία, ας, ἡ	(1)	boundary

ὅρκος

ὁρκίζω	(2)	I put under oath, implore, beg
ἐνορκίζω	(1)	I put under oath
ἐξορκίζω	(1)	I put under oath
ἐπιορκέω	(1)	I swear falsely, break my oath
ὅρκος, ου, ὁ	(10)	oath
ἐξορκιστής, οῦ, ὁ	(1)	exorcist
ὁρκωμοσία, ας, ἡ	(4)	oath, taking an oath
ἐπίορκος, ον	(1)	perjured; perjurer (subst. in NT)

ὁρμή

ὁρμάω	(5)	I rush
ὁρμή, ῆς, ἡ	(2)	impulse, inclination, desire, attempt
ὅρμημα, ατος, τό	(1)	violent rush, violence
ἀφορμή, ῆς, ἡ	(7)	occasion, pretext, opportunity, excuse
κονιορτός, οῦ, ὁ	(5)	dust

ὄρνις

ὄρνεον, ου, τό	(3)	bird
ὄρνις, ιθος, ὁ, ἡ	(2)	bird, cock or hen

ὄρος

ὄρος, ους, τό	(63)	mountain, hill, mount
ὀρεινός, ή, όν	(2)	mountainous; hill country (subst. in NT)

ὀρύσσω

ὀρύσσω	(3)	I dig
διορύσσω	(4)	I break through, break in
ἐξορύσσω	(2)	I dig out, tear out

ὀρφανός

ἀπορφανίζω	(1)	I make an orphan of, separate from
ὀρφανός, ή, όν	(2)	orphaned; orphan (subst.)

ὅς

ὅθεν	(15)	from where, where, whence, from which, therefore
οὗ	(24)	where, to which
πόθεν	(29)	from where? from which? whence?
ποσάκις	(3)	how many times? how often?
ἑκάστοτε	(1)	at any time, always

καθό	(4)	as, in so far as
πάντοτε	(41)	always, at all times
πώποτε	(6)	ever, at any time
τότε	(160)	then, thereafter
ὅς, ἥ, ὅ	(1365)	who, which, what, that, the one who, this one, he
πῶς	(103)	how? in what way? in what sense? how is it possible?
πώς	(15)	somehow, in some way, perhaps
διό	(53)	therefore, for this reason
διόπερ	(2)	therefore, for this very reason
διότι	(23)	because, therefore, for, that
καθά	(1)	just as
καθάπερ	(13)	just as
καθότι	(6)	as, to the degree, because
οἷος, α, ον	(14)	of what sort, as, such as
ὅστις, ἥτις, ὅ τι	(153)	whoever, everyone who, who
ὅταν	(123)	at the time that, whenever, when
ὅτε	(103)	when, while, as long as
ὅτι	(1296)	that, so that, because, for, (introduces direct discourse)

ὅσιος

ὁσιότης, ητος, ἡ	(2)	devoutness, piety, holiness
ὅσιος, α, ον	(8)	devout, pious, holy
ἀνόσιος, ον	(2)	unholy, wicked
ὁσίως	(1)	devoutly, in a holy manner

ὅσος

ὅσος, η, ον	(110)	as or how great, as or how much, as or how far
πόσος, η, ον	(27)	how great(?) how much(?) how many(?)
ὁσάκις	(3)	as often as, whenever

οὐ

ἐξουδενέω	(1)	I treat with contempt
ἐξουθενέω	(11)	I despise, reject, treat with contempt
οὐδείς, οὐδεμία, οὐδέν	(234)	no; no one, nothing (subst.); in no way (neut. acc.)
οὐ	(1606)	not (gener. used w. ind. verbs and pos. answer questions)
οὐχί	(54)	not, no (used with pos. answer questions)
οὐδαμῶς	(1)	by no means
οὐδέποτε	(16)	never
οὐδέπω	(4)	not yet
οὐκέτι	(47)	no longer, no more, then not
οὐκοῦν	(1)	so then, so
οὔπω	(26)	not yet
οὔτε	(87)	and not, neither, nor, no
οὔ	(17)	no
οὐδέ	(143)	and not, neither, nor, not even

οὖν

οὐκοῦν	(1)	so then, so
οὖν	(499)	so, therefore, consequently, accordingly, then
μενοῦν	(1)	rather, on the contrary, indeed
μενοῦνγε	(3)	rather, on the contrary, indeed
τοιγαροῦν	(2)	then, therefore, for that very reason

οὐρανός

οὐρανός, οῦ, ὁ	(273)	heaven, sky; God (fig.)
μεσουράνημα, ατος, τό	(3)	midheaven, zenith
οὐράνιος, ον	(9)	heavenly
ἐπουράνιος, ον	(19)	heavenly; heaven, heavenly places or things (pl. subst.)
οὐρανόθεν	(2)	from heaven

οὖς

ἐνωτίζομαι	(1)	I give ear, pay attention
οὖς, ὠτός, τό	(36)	ear, hearing
ὠτάριον, ου, τό	(2)	ear
ὠτίον, ου, τό	(3)	ear

οὗτος

οὗτος, αὕτη, τοῦτο	(1388)	this; this person or thing, he, she, it (subst.)
τηλικοῦτος, αύτη, οὗτο	(4)	so great, so large, so important
τοιοῦτος, αύτη, οὗτον	(57)	of such a kind, such; such a person or thing (subst.)
τοσοῦτος, αύτη, οὗτον	(20)	so great, so large, so many, so far, so much
οὕτως	(208)	in this manner, thus, so, as follows, just; such (adj.)

ὀφείλω

ὀφείλω	(35)	I owe, am indebted, ought, am obligated, commit a sin
προσοφείλω	(1)	I owe besides, owe
ὀφειλέτης, ου, ὁ	(7)	debtor, one who is obligated or guilty, sinner
ὀφειλή, ῆς, ἡ	(3)	debt, one's due, duty
ὀφείλημα, ατος, τό	(2)	debt, one's due, sin
χρεοφειλέτης, ου, ὁ	(2)	debtor
ὄφελον	(4)	O that, would that

ὄχλος

ὀχλέω	(1)	I trouble, disturb
ἐνοχλέω	(2)	I trouble
ὀχλοποιέω	(1)	I form a mob or crowd
παρενοχλέω	(1)	I cause difficulty, trouble, annoy
ὄχλος, ου, ὁ	(175)	crowd, throng, (common) people, multitude

ὀψάριον

ὀψάριον, ου, τό	(5)	fish
ὀψώνιον, ου, τό	(4)	pay, wages, support, compensation
παροψίς, ίδος, ἡ	(1)	dish

ὀψέ

ὄψιμος, ον	(1)	late; late or spring rain (subst. in NT)
ὄψιος, α, ον	(15)	late; evening (fem. subst.)
ὀψέ	(3)	late in the day, in the evening; after (impr. prep.)

παῖς

παιδεύω	(13)	I bring up, train, educate, discipline, correct, whip
παίζω	(1)	I play, amuse myself, dance
ἐμπαίζω	(13)	I ridicule, make fun of, mock, deceive, trick
παιδάριον, ου, τό	(1)	boy, youth, young slave
παιδεία, ας, ἡ	(6)	upbringing, training, instruction, discipline

παιδευτής, οῦ, ὁ	(2)	instructor, teacher, one who disciplines
παιδίον, ου, τό	(52)	child, infant
παιδίσκη, ης, ἡ	(13)	maid, servant girl, female slave
παῖς, παιδός, ὁ, ἡ	(24)	boy, son, child, servant, slave; girl, child (fem.)
ἐμπαιγμονή, ῆς, ἡ	(1)	mocking
ἐμπαιγμός, οῦ, ὁ	(1)	scorn, mocking, derisive torture
ἐμπαίκτης, ου, ὁ	(2)	mocker
παιδαγωγός, οῦ, ὁ	(3)	attendant, custodian, guide
ἀπαίδευτος, ον	(1)	uninstructed, uneducated, ignorant
παιδιόθεν	(1)	from childhood

πάλαι

παλαιόω	(4)	I make old, treat as obsolete; become old (pass.)
παλαιότης, ητος, ἡ	(1)	age, oldness, obsoleteness
παλαιός, ά, όν	(19)	old, former
πάλαι	(7)	long ago, formerly, for a long time, already
ἔκπαλαι	(2)	for a long time, long ago

πάλιν

παλιγγενεσία, ας, ἡ	(2)	rebirth, regeneration, new age
πάλιν	(141)	back, again, once more, furthermore, on the other hand

παρά

παρεκτός	(3)	besides, outside; apart from, except for (impr. prep.)
παρά	(194)	from (gen); beside, with (dat.); at, on, more than (acc.)

παρθένος

παρθενία, ας, ἡ	(1)	virginity
παρθένος, ου, ἡ, ὁ	(15)	virgin (female or male)

πᾶς

παρρησιάζομαι	(9)	I speak freely, have courage
πανδοχεῖον, ου, τό	(1)	inn
πανδοχεύς, έως, ὁ	(1)	innkeeper
πανήγυρις, εως, ἡ	(1)	festal gathering
πανοπλία, ας, ἡ	(3)	full armor, panoply
πανουργία, ας, ἡ	(5)	cunning, craftiness, trickery
παντοκράτωρ, ορος, ὁ	(10)	Almighty, Omnipotent One
παρρησία, ας, ἡ	(31)	outspokenness, openness, confidence, boldness
πᾶς, πᾶσα, πᾶν	(1244)	every, each, any, full, all; everyone, everything (subst.)
ἅπας, ασα, αν	(34)	all, whole; everybody, everything (pl.)
πανοῦργος, ον	(1)	clever, crafty, sly
παντελής, ές	(2)	complete; completely, fully, at all (w. εἰς τό in NT)
πανταχῇ	(1)	everywhere
πανταχοῦ	(7)	everywhere, in all directions
πάντῃ	(1)	in every way
πάντοθεν	(3)	from all directions, on all sides, entirely
πάντως	(8)	by all means, certainly, of course, perhaps, at least
παμπληθεί	(1)	all together
πανοικεί	(1)	with one's whole household
πάντοτε	(41)	always, at all times

πάσχω

πάσχω	(42)	I suffer, die, endure, experience
κακοπαθέω	(3)	I suffer misfortune, bear hardship patiently
μετριοπαθέω	(1)	I deal gently
προπάσχω	(1)	I suffer previously
συγκακοπαθέω	(2)	I suffer together with, share in hardship with
συμπαθέω	(2)	I sympathize with, have sympathy for
συμπάσχω	(2)	I suffer together with
πάθημα, ατος, τό	(16)	suffering, misfortune, passion
πάθος, ους, τό	(3)	passion
κακοπαθία, ας, ή	(1)	suffering, misfortune, misery, strenuous effort
πραϋπάθεια, ας, ή	(1)	gentleness
παθητός, ή, όν	(1)	subject to suffering
ὁμοιοπαθής, ές	(2)	with the same nature, like in every way
συμπαθής, ές	(1)	sympathetic

πατέω

πατέω	(5)	I tread, trample; walk (intrans.)
ἐμπεριπατέω	(1)	I walk about, move, live
καταπατέω	(5)	I trample, tread upon, treat with disdain
περιπατέω	(95)	I go (about), walk (around), live, conduct myself

πατήρ

πατήρ, πατρός, ὁ	(413)	father, ancestor, forefather, Father
πατριά, ᾶς, ἡ	(3)	family, clan, nation, people
πατρίς, ίδος, ἡ	(8)	fatherland, home town
πατριάρχης, ου, ὁ	(4)	patriarch, father of a nation
πατρολῴας, ου, ὁ	(1)	one who murders one's father
προπάτωρ, ορος, ὁ	(1)	forefather
πατρικός, ή, όν	(1)	handed down by one's father, paternal
πατρῷος, α, ον	(3)	paternal, belonging to one's ancestors
ἀπάτωρ, ορος	(1)	fatherless, without a father
πατροπαράδοτος, ον	(1)	inherited, handed down from one's father

παύω

παύω	(15)	I stop, keep; stop, cease (mid.)
ἀναπαύω	(12)	I cause to rest, give rest, refresh; rest (mid.)
ἐπαναπαύομαι	(2)	I rest, find rest of comfort
καταπαύω	(4)	I bring to rest, stop, rest
συναναπαύομαι	(1)	I rest with
ἀνάπαυσις, εως, ἡ	(5)	stopping, ceasing, rest, resting place
κατάπαυσις, εως, ἡ	(9)	rest, place of rest
ἀκατάπαυστος, ον	(1)	unceasing, restless

πεζεύω

πεζεύω	(1)	I travel by land
πέδη, ης, ἡ	(3)	fetter, shackle
στρατόπεδον, ου, τό	(1)	body of troops, army, legion
τράπεζα, ης, ἡ	(15)	table, meal, food, bank
τραπεζίτης, ου, ὁ	(1)	money changer, banker
πεδινός, ή, όν	(1)	flat, level
πεζῇ	(2)	by land

πείθω

πείθω	(52)	I convince, persuade, satisfy; trust (perf.); obey (pass.)
πιστεύω	(241)	I believe (in), have faith (in), trust, entrust
πιστόω	(1)	I feel confidence, am convinced (pass. in NT.)
ἀναπείθω	(1)	I persuade, incite
ἀπειθέω	(14)	I disobey, am disobedient, disbelieve
ἀπιστέω	(8)	I disbelieve, refuse to believe, am unfaithful
πειθαρχέω	(4)	I obey, follow
πεισμονή, ῆς, ἡ	(1)	persuasion
πίστις, εως, ἡ	(243)	faith, trust, faithfulness, belief, conviction, doctrine
ἀπείθεια, ας, ἡ	(7)	disobedience, disbelief
ἀπιστία, ας, ἡ	(11)	unfaithfulness, unbelief
ὀλιγοπιστία, ας, ἡ	(1)	littleness of faith
πεποίθησις, εως, ἡ	(6)	trust, confidence
πιθανολογία, ας, ἡ	(1)	persuasive speech, plausible argument
πειθός, ή, όν	(1)	persuasive
πιστικός, ή, όν	(2)	genuine, unadulterated
πιστός, ή, όν	(67)	faithful, reliable, believing, trusting; believer (subst.)
ἀπειθής, ές	(6)	disobedient
ἄπιστος, ον	(23)	unbelievable, faithless, unbelieving
εὐπειθής, ές	(1)	obedient, complaint
ὀλιγόπιστος, ον	(5)	of little faith or trust

πεινάω

πεινάω	(23)	I hunger, am hungry
πρόσπεινος, ον	(1)	hungry

πεῖρα

πειράζω	(38)	I try, attempt, test, tempt
πειράομαι	(1)	I try, attempt
ἐκπειράζω	(4)	I put to the test, try, tempt
πεῖρα, ας, ἡ	(2)	attempt, trial, experience
πειρασμός, οῦ, ὁ	(21)	test, trial, temptation, enticement, testing
ἀπείραστος, ον	(1)	without temptation, unable to be tempted
ἄπειρος, ον	(1)	unacquainted with, unaccustomed to

πέμπω

πέμπω	(79)	I send, instruct, commission, appoint
ἀναπέμπω	(5)	I send up, send back
ἐκπέμπω	(2)	I send out
μεταπέμπω	(9)	I send for, summon
προπέμπω	(9)	I accompany, escort, send or help on one's way
συμπέμπω	(2)	I send with

πενθερός

πενθερά, ᾶς, ἡ	(6)	mother-in-law
πενθερός, οῦ, ὁ	(1)	father-in-law

πένθος

πενθέω	(10)	I am sad, grieve, mourn; mourn over (trans.)
πένθος, ους, τό	(5)	grief, sadness, mourning, sorrow

πέντε

πεντηκοστή, ῆς, ἡ	(3)	Pentecost

πέμπτος, η, ον	(4)	fifth
πεντακόσιοι, αι, α	(2)	five hundred
πέντε	(38)	five
πεντήκοντα	(7)	fifty
δεκαπέντε	(3)	fifteen
πεντακισχίλιοι, αι, α	(6)	five thousand
πεντεκαιδέκατος, η, ον	(1)	fifteenth
πεντάκις	(1)	five times

[πέρ]

καθώσπερ	(1)	as, just as
διόπερ	(2)	therefore, for this very reason
ἐάνπερ	(3)	if indeed, if only, supposing that
εἴπερ	(6)	if indeed, if after all, since
ἐπειδήπερ	(1)	inasmuch as, since
ἤπερ	(1)	than
καθάπερ	(13)	just as
καίπερ	(5)	though, although
ὥσπερ	(36)	as, just as, even as
ὡσπερεί	(1)	like, as though, as it were

πέραν

διαπεράω	(6)	I cross over
πέρας, ατος, τό	(4)	end, limit, boundary; finally (adv.)
ἀπέραντος, ον	(1)	endless, limitless
περαιτέρω	(1)	further, beyond
πέραν	(23)	on the other side; other side (subst.); across (impr. prep.)
πέρυσι	(2)	last year, a year ago
ἀντιπέρα	(1)	opposite (impr. prep. in NT)

περί

περισσεύω	(39)	I am left over, exceed, overflow, abound, cause to abound
ὑπερπερισσεύω	(2)	I am present in abundance; overflow (pass.)
περισσεία, ας, ἡ	(4)	surplus, abundance
περίσσευμα, ατος, τό	(5)	abundance, fullness, what remains, scraps
περισσός, ή, όν	(6)	extraordinary, abundant, unnecessary; advantage (subst.)
περισσότερος, α, ον	(16)	greater, more, even more; more, even more (neut. adv.)
πέριξ	(1)	around, in the vicinity
περισσοτέρως	(12)	even more, far greater, so much more, especially
περισσῶς	(4)	exceedingly, beyond measure, very, even more
ἐκπερισσῶς	(1)	excessively
ὑπερεκπερισσοῦ	(3)	beyond all measure; infinitely more than (impr. prep.)
ὑπερπερισσῶς	(1)	beyond all measure
περί	(333)	about, concerning, for (gen.); around, near (acc.)

πέτομαι

πέτομαι	(5)	I fly
ἐκπετάννυμι	(1)	I spread, hold out
πετεινόν, οῦ, τό	(14)	bird
πτερύγιον, ου, τό	(2)	end, edge, pinnacle, summit
πτέρυξ, υγος, ἡ	(5)	wing
καταπέτασμα, ατος, τό	(6)	curtain, veil
πτηνός, ή, όν	(1)	winged; bird (subst. in NT)

πέτρα

| πέτρα, ας, ἡ | (15) | rock, stone, rocky grotto or ground |
| πετρώδης, ες | (4) | rocky; rocky ground (subst. in NT) |

πήγνυμι

παγιδεύω	(1)	I set a snare or trap, entrap
πήγνυμι	(1)	I set up
προσπήγνυμι	(1)	I fasten to, nail to (the cross), crucify
παγις, ίδος, ἡ	(5)	trap, snare
σκηνοπηγία, ας, ἡ	(1)	Feast of Tabernacles or Booths

[πηδάω]

ἀναπηδάω	(1)	I jump up, stand up
εἰσπηδάω	(1)	I leap in, rush in
ἐκπηδάω	(1)	I rush out

πιέζω

| πιάζω | (12) | I take hold of, seize, grasp, arrest, catch |
| πιέζω | (1) | I press down |

πικρός·

πικραίνω	(4)	I make bitter, embitter
παραπικραίνω	(1)	I am disobedient, rebellious
πικρία, ας, ἡ	(4)	bitterness, harshness
παραπικρασμός, οῦ, ὁ	(2)	revolt, rebellion
πικρός, ά, όν	(2)	bitter
πικρῶς	(2)	bitterly

πίμπλημι

πίμπλημι	(24)	I fill, fulfill, am fulfilled, come to an end (pass.)
πληθύνω	(12)	I increase, multiply; grow (pass.)
ἐμπίμπλημι	(5)	I fill, satisfy, enjoy
πλῆθος, ους, τό	(31)	number, large amount, crowd, people, community
πλήμμυρα, ης, ἡ	(1)	high water, flood
πλησμονή, ῆς, ἡ	(1)	satisfaction, gratification, indulgence
παμπληθεί	(1)	all together

πίμπρημι

| πίμπρημι | (1) | I burn with fever, swell up (pass. in NT) |
| ἐμπίμπρημι | (1) | I set on fire, burn |

πίναξ

| πινακίδιον, ου, τό | (1) | little writing tablet |
| πίναξ, ακος, ἡ | (5) | platter, dish |

πίνω

πίνω	(73)	I drink
ποτίζω	(15)	I give to drink, water
καταπίνω	(7)	I swallow, swallow up, devour; am drowned (pass.)
συμπίνω	(1)	I drink with
ὑδροποτέω	(1)	I drink water

πόμα, ατος, τό	(2)	drink
πόσις, εως, ἡ	(3)	drinking, drink
ποταμός, οῦ, ὁ	(17)	river, stream
ποτήριον, ου, τό	(31)	cup, drinking vessel
πότος, ου, ὁ	(1)	drinking, drinking party, carousal
οἰνοπότης, ου, ὁ	(2)	wine drinker, drunkard
συμπόσιον, ου, τό	(2)	group (eating together), party
ποταμοφόρητος, ον	(1)	swept away by a river or stream

πίπτω

πίπτω	(90)	I fall, fall down, fall to pieces, collapse, perish
ἀναπίπτω	(12)	I lie down, recline, lean, lean back
ἀντιπίπτω	(1)	I resist, oppose
ἀποπίπτω	(1)	I fall away
γονυπετέω	(4)	I kneel down
ἐκπίπτω	(10)	I fall off, fall from, lose, fail, run aground
ἐμπίπτω	(7)	I fall into, among
ἐπιπίπτω	(11)	I fall upon, approach eagerly, press close, come upon
καταπίπτω	(3)	I fall (down)
παραπίπτω	(1)	I fall away commit apostasy
περιπίπτω	(3)	I fall in with, encounter, fall into, strike
προσπίπτω	(8)	I fall down before, fall or beat upon, strike against
συμπίπτω	(1)	I fall in, collapse
πτῶμα, ατος, τό	(7)	corpse, (dead) body
πτῶσις, εως, ἡ	(2)	falling, fall
παράπτωμα, ατος, τό	(19)	false step, trespass, transgression, sin
διοπετής, ές	(1)	fallen from heaven
προπετής, ές	(2)	rash, reckless, thoughtless

πλάνη

πλανάω	(39)	I lead astray, mislead, deceive; go astray, wander (pass.)
ἀποπλανάω	(2)	I mislead; wander away (pass.)
πλάνη, ης, ἡ	(10)	wandering, error, delusion, deception
πλανήτης, ου, ὁ	(1)	wanderer, roamer; wandering (adj.)
πλάνος, ον	(5)	leading astray, deceitful; deceiver, impostor (subst.)

πλάσσω

πλάσσω	(2)	I form, mold
πλάσμα, ατος, τό	(1)	that which is formed or molded, image, figure
πλαστός, ή, όν	(1)	made up, fabricated, false

πλατύς

πλατύνω	(3)	I make broad, enlarge, open wide
πλατεῖα, ας, ἡ	(9)	wide road, street
πλάτος, ους, τό	(4)	breadth, width
πλατύς, εῖα, ύ	(1)	broad, wide

πλέκω

πλέκω	(3)	I weave, plait
ἐμπλέκω	(2)	I am entangled (pass. in NT)
πλέγμα, ατος, τό	(1)	woven, braided
ἐμπλοκή, ῆς, ἡ	(1)	braiding, braid

πλέω

πλέω	(6)	I travel by sea, sail
ἀποπλέω	(4)	I sail away
βραδυπλοέω	(1)	I sail slowly
διαπλέω	(1)	I sail through, sail across
ἐκπλέω	(3)	I sail away
καταπλέω	(1)	I sail, sail down
παραπλέω	(1)	I sail past
ὑποπλέω	(2)	I sail under the shelter of
πλοιάριον, ου, τό	(5)	small boat, boat
πλοῖον, ου, τό	(68)	ship, boat
πλοῦς, πλοός, ὁ	(3)	voyage, navigation

πληρόω

πλεονάζω	(9)	I grow, increase, have too much; cause to grow (trans.)
πληρόω	(86)	I fill, complete, finish, fulfill; pass, elapse (pass.)
ἀναπληρόω	(6)	I make complete, fulfill, replace
ἀνταναπληρόω	(1)	I fill up, complete
ἐκπληρόω	(1)	I fulfill
πλεονεκτέω	(5)	I take advantage of, outwit, defraud
πληροφορέω	(6)	I fill, fulfill, accomplish, convince, fully
προσαναπληρόω	(2)	I fill up, replenish, supply
συμπληρόω	(3)	I become full, approach, come (pass. in NT)
ὑπερπλεονάζω	(1)	I am present in great abundance
πλήρωμα, ατος, τό	(17)	fullness, fulfilling, fulfillment, contents, patch, total
ἐκπλήρωσις, εως, ἡ	(1)	completion
πλεονέκτης, ου, ὁ	(4)	greedy or covetous person
πλεονεξία, ας, ἡ	(10)	greediness, avarice, covetousness, something forced
πληροφορία, ας, ἡ	(4)	full assurance, certainty, conviction, fullness
πλήρης, ες	(16)	filled, full, complete, fully ripened, covered with
πλήν	(31)	but, yet, only, however (conj.); except (impr. prep.)

πλησίον

παραπλήσιος, α, ον	(1)	similar; nearly, almost (neut. as impr. prep.in NT)
πλησίον	(17)	neighbor, fellow (subst.); near, close to (impr. prep.)
παραπλησίως	(1)	similarly, likewise

πλήσσω

πλήσσω	(1)	I strike
ἐκπλήσσω	(13)	I am amazed, overwhelmed (pass. in NT)
ἐπιπλήσσω	(1)	I strike at, rebuke, reprove
πληγή, ῆς, ἡ	(22)	blow, stroke, plague, wound, bruise
πλήκτης, ου, ὁ	(2)	combative person, bully

πλοῦτος

πλουτέω	(12)	I am rich, become rich, am generous
πλουτίζω	(3)	I make rich
πλοῦτος, ου, ὁ, τό	(22)	wealth, riches, abundance
πλούσιος, α, ον	(28)	rich, wealthy
πλουσίως	(4)	richly, abundantly

πνέω

πνέω	(7)	I blow
ἐκπνέω	(3)	I breath out, expire, die

ἐμπνέω	(1)	I breathe
ὑποπνέω	(1)	I blow gently
πνεῦμα, ατος, τό	(379)	wind, breath, spirit, inner life, spirit (being), Spirit
πνοή, ῆς, ἡ	(2)	wind
πνευματικός, ή, όν	(26)	pertaining to the spirit, spiritual
θεόπνευστος, ον	(1)	inspired by God
πνευματικῶς	(2)	spiritually

πνίγω

πνίγω	(3)	I choke, strangle; drown (pass.)
ἀποπνίγω	(2)	I choke, drown
συμπνίγω	(5)	I choke, crowd around, crush
πνικτός, ή, όν	(3)	strangled, choked to death

ποιέω

ποιέω	(568)	I do, make
ἀγαθοποιέω	(9)	I do good, what is right
εἰρηνοποιέω	(1)	I make peace
ζωοποιέω	(11)	I make alive, give life to
κακοποιέω	(4)	I do wrong, harm, injure
καλοποιέω	(1)	I do what is right or good
μοσχοποιέω	(1)	I make a calf
ὀχλοποιέω	(1)	I form a mob or crowd
περιποιέω	(3)	I preserve, acquire, gain (mid. in NT)
προσποιέω	(1)	I act as if, pretend (mid. in NT)
συζωοποιέω	(2)	I make alive together with
ποίημα, ατος, τό	(2)	what is made, work, creation
ποίησις, εως, ἡ	(1)	doing, working
ποιητής, οῦ, ὁ	(6)	doer, maker
ἀγαθοποιΐα, ας, ἡ	(1)	doing good, doing right
εὐποιΐα, ας, ἡ	(1)	doing of good
περιποίησις, εως, ἡ	(5)	preserving, saving, gaining, possession
σκηνοποιός, οῦ, ὁ	(1)	tentmaker
ἀγαθοποιός, όν	(1)	doing good, upright; one who does good (subst. in NT)
ἀχειροποίητος, ον	(3)	not made by hand, spiritual
εἰρηνοποιός, ον	(1)	making peace; peacemaker (subst. in NT)
κακοποιός, όν	(3)	doing evil; evildoer, criminal, sorcerer (subst. in NT)
χειροποίητος, ον	(6)	made by human hands

ποικίλος

ποικίλος, η, ον	(10)	of various kinds, diverse
πολυποίκιλος, ον	(1)	many-sided

ποιμήν

ποιμαίνω	(11)	I tend (sheep); guide, protect, nurture (fig.)
ποιμήν, ένος, ὁ	(18)	shepherd
ποίμνη, ης, ἡ	(5)	flock (esp. of sheep)
ποίμνιον, ου, τό	(5)	flock (esp. of sheep)
ἀρχιποίμην, ενος, ὁ	(1)	chief shepherd

πόλεμος

πολεμέω	(7)	I make war, fight
πόλεμος, ου, ὁ	(18)	war, battle, fight, conflict, strife

πόλις

πολιτεύομαι	(2)	I live, conduct myself
πόλις, εως, ἡ	(162)	city, town, inhabitants (of a city)
πολιτεία, ας, ἡ	(2)	citizenship, commonwealth, state
πολίτευμα, ατος, τό	(1)	commonwealth, state
πολίτης, ου, ὁ	(4)	citizen, fellow citizen
κωμόπολις, εως, ἡ	(1)	market town, country town, town
πολιτάρχης, ου, ὁ	(2)	civic magistrate, politarch
συμπολίτης, ου, ὁ	(1)	fellow citizen

πολύς

πολυλογία, ας, ἡ	(1)	wordiness, many words
πολλαπλασίων, ον	(1)	many times as much, manifold
πολύς, πολλή, πολύ	(416)	much, many, large, great; often (adv.); many (subst.)
πολυποίκιλος, ον	(1)	many-sided
πολύσπλαγχνος, ον	(1)	very sympathetic or compassionate
πολυτελής, ές	(3)	very expensive, costly
πολύτιμος, ον	(3)	very precious, valuable
πολλάκις	(18)	many times, often, frequently
πολυμερῶς	(1)	in many ways
πολυτρόπως	(1)	in various ways

πόνος

διαπονέομαι	(2)	I am greatly disturbed, annoyed
καταπονέω	(2)	I subdue, oppress, torment, mistreat
πονηρία, ας, ἡ	(7)	wickedness, evil
πόνος, ου, ὁ	(4)	toil, pain, distress, affliction
πένης, ητος	(1)	poor; poor person (subst. in NT)
πενιχρός, ά, όν	(1)	poor, needy
πονηρός, ά, όν	(78)	evil, bad, wicked, sick; evil person, evil one, evil (subst.)

πορεύομαι

πορεύομαι	(153)	I go, proceed, travel, journey, live, die (mid.-pass. in NT)
ἀπορέω	(6)	I am at a loss, am uncertain
διαπορεύομαι	(5)	I go through, pass through, walk through
διαπορέω	(4)	I am greatly perplexed, at a loss
εἰσπορεύομαι	(18)	I go in, come in, enter
ἐκπορεύομαι	(33)	I go out, come out
ἐμπορεύομαι	(2)	I carry on business, buy and sell, exploit
ἐξαπορέομαι	(2)	I am in great difficulty, despair
ἐπιπορεύομαι	(1)	I come or go to
εὐπορέω	(1)	I have plenty, am well off
ὁδοιπορέω	(1)	I travel, am on my way
παραπορεύομαι	(5)	I go, pass by
προπορεύομαι	(2)	I go before
προσπορεύομαι	(1)	I come up to, approach
συμπορεύομαι	(4)	I go along with, come together, flock
πορεία, ας, ἡ	(2)	journey, trip, way, conduct
πορισμός, οῦ, ὁ	(2)	means of gain
ἀπορία, ας, ἡ	(1)	perplexity, anxiety
ἐμπορία, ας, ἡ	(1)	business, trade
ἐμπόριον, ου, τό	(1)	market
ἔμπορος, ου, ὁ	(5)	merchant, wholesale dealer
εὐπορία, ας, ἡ	(1)	prosperity

ὁδοιπορία, ας, ἡ	(2)	walking, journey

πόρνη

πορνεύω	(8)	I practice sexual immorality
ἐκπορνεύω	(1)	I engage in illicit sex, indulge in immorality
πορνεία, ας, ἡ	(25)	unlawful sexual intercourse, (sexual) immorality
πόρνη, ης, ἡ	(12)	prostitute, harlot
πόρνος, ου, ὁ	(10)	one who practices sexual immorality

πορφύρα

πορφύρα, ας, ἡ	(4)	purple cloth or garment
πορφυρόπωλις, ιδος, ἡ	(1)	(woman) dealer in purple cloth
πορφυροῦς, ᾶ, οῦν	(4)	purple; purple garment (subst.)

ποῦ

ποταπός, ή, όν	(7)	of what sort or kind, how great or glorious
ὅπου	(82)	where, in so far as, since
ὅπως	(53)	how, in what way, that, in order that
πότε	(19)	when?
ποῦ	(48)	where(?) at or to what place(?)
πού	(4)	somewhere, about, approximately
δήπου	(1)	of course, surely
μηδέποτε	(1)	never
οὐδέποτε	(16)	never
πότερον	(1)	whether
ὁποῖος, α, ον	(5)	of what sort
ποτέ	(29)	at some time, once, formerly, ever
μήποτε	(25)	never, lest, that . . . not, whether perhaps, perhaps

πούς

ὀρθοποδέω	(1)	I am straightforward, progress (fig. in NT)
πούς, ποδός, ὁ	(93)	foot
ἀνδραποδιστής, οῦ, ὁ	(1)	slave dealer, kidnapper
ὑποπόδιον, ου, τό	(7)	footstool
ποδήρης, ες	(1)	reaching the feet; robe reaching the feet (subst. in NT)
τετράπους, ουν	(3)	four-footed; four-footed animal (subst. in NT)

πρασιά

πρασιά, ᾶς, ἡ	(2)	garden plot (lit.); group (fig. in NT)
χρυσόπρασος, ου, ὁ	(1)	chrysoprase

πράσσω

πραγματεύομαι	(1)	I conduct business, am engaged in business
πράσσω	(39)	I do, accomplish, practice, collect; act, do, am (intrans.)
διαπραγματεύομαι	(1)	I gain by trading, earn
πρᾶγμα, ατος, τό	(11)	deed, thing, event, undertaking, matter, affair, lawsuit
πραγματεία, ας, ἡ	(1)	activity; undertakings, business, affairs (pl. in NT)
πράκτωρ, ορος, ὁ	(2)	officer (of a court)
πρᾶξις, εως, ἡ	(6)	activity, function, deed, evil deed

πραΰς

πραΰτης, ητος, ἡ	(11)	gentleness, humility, courtesy

πραϋπάθεια, ας, ἡ	(1)	gentleness
πραΰς, πραεῖα, πραΰ	(4)	gentle, humble, considerate

πρέπω

πρέπω	(7)	I am fitting; it is fitting or proper (impers. in NT)
εὐπρέπεια, ας, ἡ	(1)	fine appearance, beauty
ἱεροπρεπής, ές	(1)	holy, worthy of reverence
μεγαλοπρεπής, ές	(1)	magnificent, sublime, majestic

πρεσβύτης

πρεσβεύω	(2)	I am an ambassador or representative
πρεσβεία, ας, ἡ	(2)	embassy, delegation, ambassadors
πρεσβυτέριον, ου, τό	(3)	council of elders
πρεσβύτης, ου, ὁ	(3)	old or elderly man
πρεσβῦτις, ιδος, ἡ	(1)	old or elderly woman
συμπρεσβύτερος, ου, ὁ	(1)	fellow elder, fellow presbyter
πρεσβύτερος, α, ον	(66)	older; older person, ancestor, elder, presbyter (subst.)

πρίζω

πρίζω	(1)	I saw in two
διαπρίω	(2)	I am infuriated, cut to the quick (pass. in NT)

πρό

πρωτεύω	(1)	I am the first, have first place
φιλοπρωτεύω	(1)	I wish to be first, like to be leader
πρωΐα, ας, ἡ	(2)	(early) morning
πρῷρα, ης, ἡ	(2)	bow (of a ship)
πρωτοκαθεδία, ας, ἡ	(4)	place of honor, best seat
πρωτοκλισία, ας, ἡ	(5)	place of honor
πρωτοστάτης, ου, ὁ	(1)	leader, ringleader
πρωτοτόκια, ων, τά	(1)	birthright
πρωϊνός, ή, όν	(2)	early, belonging to the morning, morning
πρῶτος, η, ον	(155)	first, earlier, foremost; first, before (neut. as adv.)
πρόϊμος, ον	(1)	early; early or autumn rain (subst. in NT)
πρότερος, α, ον	(11)	earlier, former; before, once, formerly (neut. as adv.)
πρωτότοκος, ον	(8)	first-born
πόρρω	(4)	far away, far
πόρρωθεν	(2)	from or at a distance
πρίν	(13)	before
πρωΐ	(12)	early, early in the morning, morning
πρώτως	(1)	for the first time
πρό	(47)	before, in front of, at, above

πρός

ἔμπροσθεν	(48)	in front, ahead; in front of, before (impr. prep.)
πρός	(700)	for (gen.); at (dat.); to, for, against, with, at, by (acc.)

προσκυνέω

προσκυνέω	(60)	I worship, prostrate myself before, do reverence to
προσκυνητής, οῦ, ὁ	(1)	worshiper

πταίω

πταίω	(5)	I stumble, trip, go wrong, sin, am ruined or lost
ἄπταιστος, ον	(1)	without stumbling

πτοέω

πτοέω	(2)	I terrify; am terrified or startled (pass. in NT)
πτόησις, εως, ἡ	(1)	intimidation, fear, terror

πτύσσω

πτύσσω	(1)	I fold up, roll up
ἀναπτύσσω	(1)	I unroll

πτύω

πτύω	(3)	I spit
ἐκπτύω	(1)	I spit (out), disdain
ἐμπτύω	(6)	I spit on or at
πτύον, ου, τό	(2)	winnowing shovel
πτύσμα, ατος, τό	(1)	saliva, spit

πτωχός

πτωχεύω	(1)	I am or become poor
πτωχεία, ας, ἡ	(3)	poverty
πτωχός, ή, όν	(34)	poor, miserable, impotent; poor person (subst.)

πυγμή

πυκτεύω	(1)	I fight with fists, box
πυγμή, ῆς, ἡ	(1)	fist
πυκνός, ή, όν	(3)	frequent, numerous; often, frequently (neut. pl. as adv.)

πύλη

πύλη, ης, ἡ	(10)	gate, door
πυλών, ῶνος, ὁ	(18)	gate, gateway, vestibule, entrance

πῦρ

πυρέσσω	(2)	I suffer with a fever
πυρόω	(6)	I burn, am inflamed, make red hot (pass. in NT)
πυρράζω	(2)	I am red (of the sky)
ἀναζωπυρέω	(1)	I rekindle, kindle, inflame
πῦρ, ός, τό	(71)	fire
πυρά, ᾶς, ἡ	(2)	fire, pile of combustible or burning material
πυρετός, οῦ, ἡ	(6)	fever
πύρωσις, εως, ἡ	(3)	burning, fiery test
πύρινος, η, ον	(1)	fiery, color of fire
πυρρός, ά, όν	(2)	red

[πω]

μηδέπω	(1)	not yet
μήπω	(2)	not yet
οὐδέπω	(4)	not yet
οὔπω	(26)	not yet
πώποτε	(6)	ever, at any time

πωλέω

πωλέω	(22)	I sell; am offered for sale or sold (pass.)
πορφυρόπωλις, ιδος, ἡ	(1)	(woman) dealer in purple cloth

πωρόω

πωρόω	(5)	I harden, make dull or blind
πώρωσις, εως, ἡ	(3)	hardening, dullness, insensibility, obstinacy

ῥαββί

ῥαββί	(15)	rabbi, master, teacher
ραββουνι	(2)	my master, my teacher

ῥάβδος

ῥαβδίζω	(2)	I beat (with a rod)
ῥαπίζω	(2)	I strike, slap
ῥάβδος, ου, ἡ	(12)	rod, staff, stick, scepter
ῥάπισμα, ατος, τό	(3)	blow with a club, slap in the face
ῥαβδοῦχος, ου, ὁ	(2)	constable, policeman

ῥαντίζω

ῥαντίζω	(4)	I sprinkle; cleanse or wash myself (mid.)
ῥαντισμός, οῦ, ὁ	(2)	sprinkling

ῥαφίς

ἐπιράπτω	(1)	I sew on
ῥαφίς, ίδος, ἡ	(2)	needle
ἄραφος, ον	(1)	seamless

ῥέω

ῥέω	(1)	I flow
αἱμορροέω	(1)	I suffer with hemorrhage, bleed
παραρρέω	(1)	I am washed away, drift away
ῥύσις, εως, ἡ	(3)	flow, flowing
χειμάρρους, ου, ὁ	(1)	winter stream or torrent, ravine, wadi, valley

ῥήγνυμι

ῥήγνυμι	(7)	I tear, burst, tear loose, break out, throw down
διαρρήγνυμι	(5)	I tear, break
περιρήγνυμι	(1)	I tear off
προσρήγνυμι	(2)	I burst upon
ῥῆγμα, ατος, τό	(1)	wreck, ruin, collapse

ῥῆμα

παρρησιάζομαι	(9)	I speak freely, have courage
ῥῆμα, ατος, τό	(68)	word, saying, expression, thing, object, matter
ῥήτωρ, ορος, ὁ	(1)	orator, advocate, attorney
παρρησία, ας, ἡ	(31)	outspokenness, openness, confidence, boldness
ἀναντίρρητος, ον	(1)	not to be contradicted, undeniable
ἄρρητος, ον	(1)	inexpressible, not to be spoken
ῥητῶς	(1)	expressly, explicitly
ἀναντιρρήτως	(1)	without objection

ῥίζα

ῥιζόω	(2)	I cause to take root; am firmly rooted (pass. in NT)
ἐκριζόω	(4)	I uproot, pull out by the roots
ῥίζα, ης, ἡ	(17)	root, source, shoot, descendant

ῥίπτω

ῥιπίζω	(1)	I toss; am tossed about (pass. in NT)
ῥίπτω	(8)	I throw, throw down or off, put or lay down
ἀπορίπτω	(1)	I throw down, jump off
ἐπιρίπτω	(2)	I throw on
ῥιπή, ῆς, ἡ	(1)	rapid movement, blinking, twinkling

ῥύπος

ῥυπαίνω	(1)	I defile, pollute; am defiled or polluted (pass. in NT)
ῥυπαρία, ας, ἡ	(1)	moral uncleanness, greediness
ῥύπος, ου, ὁ	(1)	dirt
ῥυπαρός, ά, όν	(2)	dirty, unclean, defiled

ῥώννυμι

ῥώννυμι	(1)	I am strong; farewell, good-bye (imper. in NT)
ἄρρωστος, ον	(5)	sick, ill

σάββατον

σαββατισμός, οῦ, ὁ	(1)	Sabbath rest or observance
σάββατον, ου, τό	(68)	Sabbath (seventh day of the week), week
προσάββατον, ου, τό	(1)	day before the Sabbath, Friday

σαλπίζω

σαλπίζω	(12)	I sound the trumpet
σάλπιγξ, ιγγος, ἡ	(11)	trumpet, trumpet call
σαλπιστής, οῦ, ὁ	(1)	trumpeter

σάρδιον

σάρδιον, ου, τό	(2)	carnelian, sardius
σαρδόνυξ, υχος, ὁ	(1)	sardonyx

σάρξ

σάρξ, σαρκός, ἡ	(147)	flesh, body, person, human or mortal nature, earthly life
σαρκικός, ή, όν	(7)	fleshly, earthly, material, pertaining to the flesh
σάρκινος, η, ον	(4)	(made) of flesh, fleshly

σβέννυμι

σβέννυμι	(6)	I extinguish, put out, quench, stifle, suppress
ἄσβεστος, ον	(3)	inextinguishable, unquenchable

σέβω

σεβάζομαι	(1)	I worship, show reverence to
σέβω	(10)	I worship (mid. in NT)
ἀσεβέω	(1)	I act impiously, live in an ungodly way
εὐσεβέω	(2)	I am reverent or devout, show piety, worship
σέβασμα, ατος, τό	(2)	object of worship, sanctuary

σεμνότης, ητος, ἡ	(3)	reverence, dignity, holiness, seriousness
ἀσέβεια, ας, ἡ	(6)	godlessness, impiety
εὐσέβεια, ας, ἡ	(15)	piety, godliness, religion; godly acts (pl.)
θεοσέβεια, ας, ἡ	(1)	reverence for God, piety, religion
σεβαστός, ή, όν	(3)	imperial, Augustan; emperor, Imperial Majesty (subst.)
σεμνός, ή, όν	(4)	worthy of respect or honor, noble, serious, honorable
ἀσεβής, ές	(9)	godless, impious
εὐσεβής, ές	(3)	godly, devout, pious, reverent
θεοσεβής, ές	(1)	god-fearing, devout, religious, pious
εὐσεβῶς	(2)	in a godly manner, piously, religiously

σείω

σείω	(5)	I shake; am shaken, quake, am stirred, tremble (pass.)
ἀνασείω	(2)	I stir up, incite
διασείω	(1)	I extort money by violence
κατασείω	(4)	I shake, wave, make a sign, motion
σεισμός, οῦ, ὁ	(14)	shaking, earthquake, storm

σελήνη

σεληνιάζομαι	(2)	I am moon-struck; am an epileptic (fig. in NT)
σελήνη, ης, ἡ	(9)	moon

σημεῖον

σημαίνω	(6)	I make known, report, foretell
σημειόω	(1)	I note, take notice of (mid. in NT)
σημεῖον, ου, τό	(77)	sign, distinguishing mark, miracle, wonder, portent
σύσσημον, ου, τό	(1)	signal, sign, token
ἄσημος, ον	(1)	without mark, obscure, insignificant
ἐπίσημος, ον	(2)	well-known, outstanding, splendid, notorious
εὔσημος, ον	(1)	clear, easily recognizable, distinct
παράσημος, ον	(1)	distinguished, marked

σήπω

σήπω	(1)	I decay, rot
σαπρός, ά, όν	(8)	decayed, rotten, bad, evil

σής

σής, σητός, ὁ	(3)	moth
σητόβρωτος, ον	(1)	moth-eaten

σθενόω

σθενόω	(1)	I strengthen, make strong
ἀσθενέω	(33)	I am weak, powerless, sick, in need
ἀσθένεια, ας, ἡ	(24)	weakness, sickness, disease, timidity
ἀσθένημα, ατος, τό	(1)	weakness
ἀσθενής, ές	(26)	weak, powerless, sick, ill, feeble

σιγή

σιγάω	(10)	I am silent, become or keep silent, keep secret
σιγή, ῆς, ἡ	(2)	silence, quiet

σίδηρος

σίδηρος, ου, ὁ	(1)	iron
σιδηροῦς, ᾶ, οῦν	(5)	made of iron

σῖτος

σιτίον, ου, τό	(1)	grain; food (pl. in NT)
σῖτος, ου, ὁ	(14)	wheat, grain
ἀσιτία, ας, ἡ	(1)	lack of appetite, abstinence from food
ἐπισιτισμός, οῦ, ὁ	(1)	provisions, food
σιτομέτριον, ου, τό	(1)	grain or food allowance, ration
σιτευτός, ή, όν	(3)	fattened
σιτιστός, ή, όν	(1)	fattened; fattened cattle (pl. subst. in NT)
ἄσιτος, ον	(1)	without eating, fasting

σκάνδαλον

σκανδαλίζω	(29)	I cause to fall or sin, anger, shock; take offense (pass.)
σκάνδαλον, ου, τό	(15)	trap, temptation, that which offends, stumbling block

σκάπτω

σκάπτω	(3)	I dig
κατασκάπτω	(2)	I tear down, destroy
σκάφη, ης, ἡ	(3)	small boat, skiff

σκεῦος

ἀνασκευάζω	(1)	I tear down, upset, unsettle
ἐπισκευάζομαι	(1)	I make preparations, get ready
κατασκευάζω	(11)	I make ready, prepare, build, furnish
παρασκευάζω	(4)	I prepare; prepare myself, am ready (mid.)
σκευή, ῆς, ἡ	(1)	equipment, tackle, rigging (of a ship)
σκεῦος, ους, τό	(23)	object, vessel, jar, instrument, body, wife; property (pl.)
παρασκευή, ῆς, ἡ	(6)	preparation, day of preparation
ἀπαρασκεύαστος, ον	(1)	not ready, unprepared

σκηνή

σκηνόω	(5)	I live, dwell
ἐπισκηνόω	(1)	I take up residence, live in
κατασκηνόω	(4)	I live, dwell, nest
σκηνή, ῆς, ἡ	(20)	tent, booth, dwelling, tabernacle
σκῆνος, ους, τό	(2)	tent, lodging
σκήνωμα, ατος, τό	(3)	tent, dwelling, dwelling place, body
κατασκήνωσις, εως, ἡ	(2)	a place to live, nest
σκηνοπηγία, ας, ἡ	(1)	Feast of Tabernacles or Booths
σκηνοποιός, οῦ, ὁ	(1)	tentmaker

σκιά

ἐπισκιάζω	(5)	I overshadow, cast a shadow, cover
κατασκιάζω	(1)	I overshadow
σκιά, ᾶς, ἡ	(7)	shadow, shade, foreshadowing
ἀποσκίαμα, ατος, τό	(1)	shadow

σκληρός

σκληρύνω	(6)	I harden; am stubborn, harden myself (pass.)

σκληρότης, ητος, ἡ	(1)	hardness (of heart), stubbornness
σκληροκαρδία, ας, ἡ	(3)	hardness of heart, stubbornness
σκληρός, ά, όν	(5)	hard, rough, harsh, strong
σκληροτράχηλος, ον	(1)	stiff-necked, stubborn

σκοπός

σκοπέω	(6)	I look our for, keep my eyes on, consider
ἐπισκέπτομαι	(11)	I examine, look for, visit, care for, am concerned about
ἐπισκοπέω	(2)	I look at, take care, oversee, care for
κατασκοπέω	(1)	I spy out, lie in wait for
σκοπός, οῦ, ὁ	(1)	goal, mark
ἀλλοτριεπίσκοπος, ου, ὁ	(1)	one who meddles in the affairs of others, busybody
ἐπισκοπή, ῆς, ἡ	(4)	visitation, office, office of a bishop
ἐπίσκοπος, ου, ὁ	(5)	overseer, guardian, bishop
κατάσκοπος, ου, ὁ	(1)	spy

σκορπίζω

σκορπίζω	(5)	I scatter, disperse, distribute
διασκορπίζω	(9)	I scatter, disperse, waste, squander

σκότος

σκοτίζω	(5)	I am or become dark, am darkened (pass. in NT)
σκοτόω	(3)	I darken; am or become darkened (pass. in NT)
σκοτία, ας, ἡ	(16)	darkness, gloom
σκότος, ους, τό	(31)	darkness, gloom, instrument of darkness
σκοτεινός, ή, όν	(3)	dark

σκύλλω

σκύλλω	(4)	I harass, trouble, annoy; trouble myself (pass.)
σκῦλον, ου, τό	(1)	booty, spoils (pl. in NT)

σκώληξ

σκώληξ, ηκος, ὁ	(1)	worm
σκωληκόβρωτος, ον	(1)	eaten by worms

σμάραγδος

σμάραγδος, ου, ὁ	(1)	emerald
σμαράγδινος, η, ον	(1)	made of emerald

σμύρνα

σμυρνίζω	(1)	I treat with myrrh
σμύρνα, ης, ἡ	(2)	myrrh

σοφός

σοφίζω	(2)	I make wise; am cleverly devised (pass.)
κατασοφίζομαι	(1)	I take advantage of by trickery
σοφία, ας, ἡ	(51)	wisdom, insight, intelligence
φιλοσοφία, ας, ἡ	(1)	philosophy
φιλόσοφος, ου, ὁ	(1)	philosopher
σοφός, ή, όν	(20)	clever, skillful, wise, learned
ἄσοφος, ον	(1)	unwise, foolish

σπάω

σπαράσσω	(3)	I tear, pull to and fro, throw into convulsions
σπάω	(2)	I draw, pull (mid. in NT)
ἀνασπάω	(2)	I draw, pull up
ἀποσπάω	(4)	I draw away, pull away; withdraw (pass.)
διασπάω	(2)	I tear apart, tear up
ἐπισπάομαι	(1)	I pull over the foreskin, conceal circumcision
περισπάω	(1)	I am distracted, overburdened (pass. in NT)
συσπαράσσω	(2)	I tear (to pieces), pull about, throw into convulsions
ἀπερισπάστως	(1)	without distraction

σπείρω

σπείρω	(52)	I sow
διασπείρω	(3)	I scatter
ἐπισπείρω	(1)	I sow upon or after
σπέρμα, ατος, τό	(43)	seed, survivors, descendants, children, nature
σπορά, ᾶς, ἡ	(1)	sowing, seed, origin
σπόρος, ου, ὁ	(6)	seed, supply of seed
διασπορά, ᾶς, ἡ	(3)	dispersion
σπόριμος, ον	(3)	sown; standing grain, grain fields (pl. subst. in NT)
σπερμολόγος, ον	(1)	picking up seeds; babbler (subst. in NT)

σπένδω

σπένδω	(2)	I am poured out as a drink-offering (pass. in NT)
ἄσπονδος, ον	(1)	irreconcilable

σπεύδω

σπεύδω	(6)	I hurry, make haste, hasten, strive for
σπουδάζω	(11)	I hasten, am zealous or eager, make every effort
σπουδή, ῆς, ἡ	(12)	haste, speed, eagerness, earnestness
σπουδαῖος, α, ον	(3)	eager, earnest, diligent
σπουδαίως	(4)	with urgency, earnestly, zealously, eagerly

σπίλος

σπιλόω	(2)	I stain, defile
σπιλάς, άδος, ἡ	(1)	spot, stain, blemish, danger
σπίλος, ου, ὁ	(2)	spot, stain, blemish
ἄσπιλος, ον	(4)	spotless, without blemish

σπλάγχνον

σπλαγχνίζομαι	(12)	I have pity, feel sympathy
σπλάγχνον, ου, τό	(11)	inward parts, entrails, heart, love, affection (pl. in NT)
εὔσπλαγχος, ον	(2)	tenderhearted, compassionate, courageous
πολύσπλαγχνος, ον	(1)	very sympathetic or compassionate

σταυρόω

σταυρόω	(46)	I crucify
ἀνασταυρόω	(1)	I crucify, crucify again
συσταυρόω	(5)	I crucify with; am crucified together with (pass. in NT)
σταυρός, οῦ, ὁ	(27)	cross

στέγω

στέγω	(4)	I cover, pass over in silence, endure, bear
ἀποστεγάζω	(1)	I unroof, remove the roof
στέγη, ης, ἡ	(3)	roof
τρίστεγον, ου, τό	(1)	third story or floor

στέλλω

στέλλω	(2)	I keep away, avoid, try to avoid (mid. in NT)
ἀποστέλλω	(132)	I send, send out, send away
διαστέλλω	(8)	I order, give orders (mid. in NT)
ἐξαποστέλλω	(13)	I send out, send away
ἐπιστέλλω	(3)	I inform or instruct by letter, write
καταυτέλλω	(2)	I restrain, quiet, calm
συναποστέλλω	(1)	I send with
συστέλλω	(2)	I limit, shorten, cover, pack up, remove
ὑποστέλλω	(4)	I draw back; shrink from, avoid, keep silent (mid.)
στολή, ῆς, ἡ	(9)	long robe
ἀποστολή, ῆς, ἡ	(4)	apostleship, office of an apostle
ἀπόστολος, ου, ὁ	(80)	apostle, envoy, messenger
διαστολή, ῆς, ἡ	(3)	difference, distinction
ἐπιστολή, ῆς, ἡ	(24)	letter, epistle
καταστολή, ῆς, ἡ	(1)	deportment, clothing
ὑποστολή, ῆς, ἡ	(1)	shrinking, timidity
ψευδαπόστολος, ου, ὁ	(1)	false apostle

στενός

στενάζω	(6)	I sigh, groan, complain
ἀναστενάζω	(1)	I sigh deeply
στενοχωρέω	(3)	I restrict; am confined, restricted, crushed (pass. in NT)
συστενάζω	(1)	I lament or groan together
στεναγμός, οῦ, ὁ	(2)	sigh, groan, groaning
στενοχωρία, ας, ἡ	(4)	distress, difficulty, anguish, trouble
στενός, ή, όν	(3)	narrow

[στέργω]

ἄστοργος, ον	(2)	unloving
φιλόστοργος, ον	(1)	loving dearly, devoted

στερεός

στερεόω	(3)	I make strong; am strengthened (pass.)
στεῖρα, ας, ἡ	(5)	barren woman; barren (adj.)
στερέωμα, ατος, τό	(1)	firmness, steadfastness
στερεός, ά, όν	(4)	firm, solid, strong

στέφανος

στεφανόω	(3)	I crown, honor, reward
στέμμα. ατος, τό	(1)	wreath or garland (of flowers)
στέφανος, ου, ὁ	(18)	wreath, crown, prize, reward, reason for pride

στηρίζω

στηρίζω	(13)	I fix, establish, support, strengthen
ἐπιστηρίζω	(4)	I strengthen

| στηριγμός, οῦ, ὁ | (1) | firmness, firm footing |
| ἀστήρικτος, ον | (2) | unstable, weak |

στίγμα

| στίγμα, ατος, τό | (1) | mark, brand, scar |
| στιγμή, ῆς, ἡ | (1) | moment |

στοιχέω

στοιχέω	(5)	I agree with, hold to, follow
συστοιχέω	(1)	I correspond to
στοιχεῖον, ου, τό	(7)	elements, fundamental principles, elemental spirits

στόμα

ἀποστοματίζω	(1)	I question closely, interrogate, ask hostile questions
ἐπιστομίζω	(1)	I stop the mouth, silence
στόμα, ατος, τό	(78)	mouth, speech, eloquence, edge (of a sword)
στόμαχος, ου, ὁ	(1)	stomach
δίστομος, ον	(3)	double-edged

στρατιά

στρατεύομαι	(7)	I serve as a soldier, fight, wage war
ἀντιστρατεύομαι	(1)	I am at war against
στρατολογέω	(1)	I gather an army, enlist soldiers, enlist
στρατεία, ας, ἡ	(2)	expedition, campaign, warfare, fight
στράτευμα, ατος, τό	(8)	army, troops
στρατιά, ᾶς, ἡ	(2)	army, host
στρατιώτης, ου, ὁ	(26)	soldier
στρατηγός, οῦ, ὁ	(10)	chief magistrate, captain
στρατόπεδον, ου, τό	(1)	body of troops, army, legion
συστρατιώτης, ου, ὁ	(2)	fellow soldier, comrade in arms

στρέφω

στρεβλόω	(1)	I twist, distort
στρέφω	(21)	I turn, change, return; turn around, am converted (pass.)
ἀναστρέφω	(9)	I overturn, return; behave, conduct myself (pass.)
ἀποστρέφω	(9)	I turn away, return; turn away (mid. and 2 aor. pass.)
διαστρέφω	(7)	I make crooked, pervert, mislead
ἐκστρέφω	(1)	I turn aside, pervert; am corrupt (pass. in NT)
ἐπιστρέφω	(36)	I turn, turn around or back, return
καταστρέφω	(2)	I upset, overturn
μεταστρέφω	(2)	I change, alter, pervert
συστρέφω	(2)	I gather up, gather, come together
ὑποστρέφω	(35)	I turn back, return
ἀναστροφή, ῆς, ἡ	(13)	way of life, conduct, behavior
ἐπιστροφή, ῆς, ἡ	(1)	turning, conversion
καταστροφή, ῆς, ἡ	(2)	ruin, destruction
συστροφή, ῆς, ἡ	(2)	mob, disorderly gathering, commotion, plot

στρῆνος

στρηνιάω	(2)	I live in luxury or sensuality
καταστρηνιάω	(1)	I have sensual desires against
στρῆνος, ους, τό	(1)	sensuality, luxury

στρωννύω

στρωννύω	(6)	I spread out, make (a bed), furnish (a room)
καταστρώννυμι	(1)	I strike down, kill
ὑποστρωννύω	(1)	I spread out underneath
λιθόστρωτος, ον	(1)	paved with stones; stone pavement (neut. subst. in NT)

στυγητός

στυγνάζω	(2)	I am shocked, dark, gloomy
ἀποστυγέω	(1)	I hate, abhor
στυγητός, ή, όν	(1)	hated, hateful
θεοστυγής, ές	(1)	hating god

σύ

σός, σή, σόν	(27)	your, yours (sing.)
ὑμέτερος, α, ον	(11)	your (pl.)
σύ, σού; ὑμεῖς, ὑμῶν	(2905)	you (sing.); you (pl.)
σεαυτοῦ, ῆς	(43)	(of) yourself

σῦκον

συκοφαντέω	(2)	I accuse falsely, slander, extort
συκῆ, ῆς, ἡ	(16)	fig tree
σῦκον, ου, τό	(4)	fig, ripe fig
συκομορέα, ας, ἡ	(1)	fig-mulberry tree, sycamore tree

συλάω

συλάω	(1)	I rob
ἱεροσυλέω	(1)	I rob temples, commit sacrilege
συλαγωγέω	(1)	I carry off as a captive
ἱερόσυλος, ον	(1)	temple robber, sacrilegious person (subst. in NT)

σύν

συναντάω	(6)	I meet, happen
μεταξύ	(9)	meanwhile, after; between, in the middle (impr. prep.)
σύν	(128)	with, together with, accompany, besides

σύρω

σύρω	(5)	I drag, pull, draw, drag or sweep away
κατασύρω	(1)	I drag (away by force)

σφάζω

σφάζω	(10)	I slaughter, murder
κατασφάζω	(1)	I slaughter, strike down
σφαγή, ῆς, ἡ	(3)	slaughter
σφάγιον, ου, τό	(1)	(sacrificial) victim, offering

[σφάλλω]

ἀσφαλίζω	(4)	I guard, secure
ἀσφάλεια, ας, ἡ	(3)	firmness, certainty, security
ἀσφαλής, ές	(5)	firm, certain, secure
ἐπισφαλής, ές	(1)	unsafe, dangerous
ἀσφαλῶς	(3)	securely, beyond a doubt

σφόδρα

| σφόδρα | (11) | extremely, greatly, very (much) |
| σφοδρῶς | (1) | greatly, violently |

σφραγίς

σφραγίζω	(15)	I put a seal on, seal, mark, certify
κατασφραγίζω	(1)	I seal (up)
σφραγίς, ῖδος, ἡ	(16)	seal, signet, mark, inscription, that which confirms

σχίζω

| σχίζω | (11) | I split, tear; am divided or split (pass.) |
| σχίσμα, ατος, τό | (8) | tear, crack, division, dissension, schism |

σχολή

| σχολάζω | (2) | I spend time in, stand empty |
| σχολή, ῆς, ἡ | (1) | school, lecture hall |

σώζω

σώζω	(106)	I save, rescue, deliver, preserve, heal
διασώζω	(8)	I bring safely through, save, rescue, cure
σωτήρ, ῆρος, ὁ	(24)	Savior, deliverer, preserver, rescuer
σωτηρία, ας, ἡ	(46)	salvation, deliverance, preservation
ἀσωτία, ας, ἡ	(3)	debauchery, dissipation, reckless living
σωτήριος, ον	(5)	bringing salvation, delivering; salvation (neut. subst.)
ἀσώτως	(1)	dissolutely, loosely

σῶμα

σῶμα, ατος, τό	(142)	body, corpse, reality; slaves (pl.)
σωματικός, ή, όν	(2)	bodily, pertaining to the body
σύσσωμος, ον	(1)	belonging to the same body
σωματικῶς	(1)	bodily, in reality

σωρεύω

| σωρεύω | (2) | I heap up, fill with |
| ἐπισωρεύω | (1) | I heap up, accumulate |

ταλαίπωρος

ταλαιπωρέω	(1)	I lament, complain
ταλαιπωρία, ας, ἡ	(2)	distress, trouble, misery
ταλαίπωρος, ον	(2)	miserable, wretched, distressed

τάλαντον

| τάλαντον, ου, τό | (14) | talent (Greek monetary unit) |
| ταλαντιαῖος, α, ον | (1) | weighing a talent |

ταπεινός

ταπεινόω	(14)	I lower, humble, humiliate; have little (mid.)
ταπείνωσις, εως, ἡ	(4)	humiliation, humility
ταπεινοφροσύνη, ης, ἡ	(7)	humility, modesty
ταπεινός, ή, όν	(8)	poor, subservient, humble; lowly, downcast one (subst.)
ταπεινόφρων, ον	(1)	humble

ταράσσω

ταράσσω	(17)	I stir up, disturb, unsettle, trouble, frighten
διαταράσσω	(1)	I am confused, perplexed greatly (pass. in NT)
ἐκταράσσω	(1)	I agitate, throw into confusion
τάραχος, ου, ὁ	(2)	consternation, disturbance, commotion

τάσσω

τάσσω	(8)	I appoint, order, determine; set, direct (mid.)
ἀνατάσσομαι	(1)	I repeat in proper order, compile
ἀντιτάσσω	(5)	I oppose, resist (mid. in NT)
ἀποτάσσω	(6)	I say farewell, take leave, renounce (mid. in NT)
ἀτακτέω	(1)	I am idle, lazy
διατάσσω	(16)	I order, direct, command, arrange
ἐπιδιατάσσομαι	(1)	I add to (a will)
ἐπιτάσσω	(10)	I order, command
προστάσσω	(7)	I command, order, prescribe
συντάσσω	(3)	I order, direct, prescribe
ὑποτάσσω	(38)	I subject, subordinate; am or become subject (pass.)
τάγμα, ατος, τό	(1)	order, class, group
τάξις, εως, ἡ	(9)	order, good order, nature, quality, manner
διαταγή, ῆς, ἡ	(2)	ordinance, direction
διάταγμα, ατος, τό	(1)	edict, command
ἐπιταγή, ῆς, ἡ	(7)	command, order, injunction
ὑποταγή, ῆς, ἡ	(4)	subjection, subordination, obedience
τακτός, ή, όν	(1)	fixed, appointed
ἀνυπότακτος, ον	(4)	not subject, independent, undisciplined, disobedient
ἄτακτος, ον	(1)	disorderly, insubordinate, lazy
ἀτάκτως	(2)	in a disorderly manner, lazily

ταχύς

τάχος, ους, τό	(8)	speed, quickness, swiftness, haste
ταχινός, ή, όν	(2)	imminent, coming soon, swift
ταχύς, εῖα, ύ	(13)	quick, swift; quickly, soon (neut. sing. as adv.)
τάχα	(2)	perhaps, possibly, probably
ταχέως	(15)	quickly, soon, hastily, too quickly

τέ

ἑκάστοτε	(1)	at any time, always
οὔτε	(87)	and not, neither, nor, no
πάντοτε	(41)	always, at all times
τότε	(160)	then, thereafter
τέ	(215)	and, and so, so
εἴτε	(65)	if, whether
μήτε	(34)	and not, nor
ὅτε	(103)	when, while, as long as
ὥστε	(83)	for this reason, therefore, so, so that, in order that

[τείνω]

ἀποτινάσσω	(2)	I shake off
ἀτενίζω	(14)	I look intently
ἐκτείνω	(16)	I stretch out
ἐκτινάσσω	(4)	I shake off, shake out
ἐπεκτείνομαι	(1)	I stretch out, strain

παρατείνω	(1)	I extend, prolong
προτείνω	(1)	I stretch or spread out
προχειροτονέω	(1)	I choose or appoint beforehand (pass. in NT)
ὑπερεκτείνω	(1)	I stretch out beyond, overextend
χειροτονέω	(2)	I choose or elect by raising hands, choose
ἐκτένεια, ας, ἡ	(1)	perseverance, earnestness
ἐκτενής, ές	(1)	eager, earnest, constant, unfailing
ἐκτενῶς	(3)	eagerly, fervently, constantly
εὐτόνως	(2)	powerfully, vehemently, vigorously

τεῖχος

τεῖχος, ους, τό	(9)	wall
τοίχος, ου, ὁ	(1)	wall
μεσότοιχον, ου, τό	(1)	dividing wall

τέλος

τελειόω	(23)	I complete, accomplish, make perfect, fulfill, initiate
τελευτάω	(11)	I come to an end, die
τελέω	(28)	I finish, complete, accomplish, fulfill, keep, pay
ἀποτελέω	(2)	I finish, complete, perform
διατελέω	(1)	I continue, remain
ἐκτελέω	(2)	I finish, complete
ἐπιτελέω	(10)	I finish, complete, bring about, perform, erect, lay upon
λυσιτελέω	(1)	I am advantageous or better; it is better (impers. in NT)
συντελέω	(6)	I complete, finish, come to an end, fulfill, accomplish
τελεσφορέω	(1)	I bear fruit to maturity, produce ripe fruit
τελειότης, ητος, ἡ	(2)	perfection, completeness, maturity
τελείωσις, εως, ἡ	(2)	perfection, fulfillment
τελειωτής, οῦ, ὁ	(1)	perfecter
τελευτή, ῆς, ἡ	(1)	end, death
τέλος, ους, τό	(40)	end, goal, conclusion, outcome, tax
ἀρχιτελώνης, ου, ὁ	(1)	chief tax collector
συντέλεια, ας, ἡ	(6)	completion, close, end
τελώνης, ου, ὁ	(21)	tax collector, revenue officer
τελώνιον, ου, τό	(3)	revenue or tax office
τέλειος, α, ον	(19)	perfect, complete, mature, adult, initiated
ἀλυσιτελής, ές	(1)	unprofitable
ὁλοτελής, ές	(1)	quite complete, wholly
παντελής, ές	(2)	complete; completely, fully, at all (w. εἰς τό in NT)
πολυτελής, ές	(3)	very expensive, costly
τελείως	(1)	fully, perfectly, completely, altogether

τέσσαρες

τετρααρχέω	(3)	I am tetrarch or ruler
τετράδιον, ου, τό	(1)	detachment of four soldiers
τετραάρχης, ου, ὁ	(4)	tetrarch
τράπεζα, ης, ἡ	(15)	table, meal, food, bank
τραπεζίτης, ου, ὁ	(1)	money changer, banker
τέσσαρες, α	(41)	four
τεσσεράκοντα	(22)	forty
τεταρταῖος, α, ον	(1)	happening on the fourth day
τέταρτος, η, ον	(10)	fourth
τετρακόσιοι, αι, α	(4)	four hundred
τετραπλοῦς, ῆ, οῦν	(1)	four times (as much), fourfold

δεκατέσσαρες	(5)	fourteen
τεσσαρεσκαιδέκατος, η, ον	(2)	fourteenth
τεσσερακονταετής, ές	(2)	forty years
τετράγωνος, ον	(1)	square
τετρακισχίλιοι, αι, α	(5)	four thousand
τετράμηνος, ον	(1)	lasting four months; period of four months (subst. in NT)
τετράπους, ουν	(3)	four-footed; four-footed animal (subst. in NT)

τηρέω

τηρέω	(70)	I keep, hold, guard, keep watch, observe, obey
διατηρέω	(2)	I keep
παρατηρέω	(6)	I watch closely, observe carefully, guard (act. and mid.)
συντηρέω	(3)	I protect, defend, preserve, treasure up
τήρησις, εως, ἡ	(3)	custody, keeping, observance
παρατήρησις, εως, ἡ	(1)	observation

τίθημι

θεμελιόω	(5)	I found, lay the foundation of, establish, strengthen
θησαυρίζω	(8)	I store up, gather, save, reserve
τίθημι	(100)	I put, place, lay, serve, remove, appoint, make
ἀθετέω	(16)	I declare invalid, nullify, set aside, reject
ἀναθεματίζω	(4)	I bind under a curse, curse
ἀνατίθημι	(2)	I declare, lay before (mid. in NT)
ἀντιδιατίθημι	(1)	I oppose myself, am opposed (mid. in NT)
ἀποθησαυρίζω	(1)	I store up, lay up
ἀποτίθημι	(9)	I put off, take off, lay aside (mid. in NT)
διατίθημι	(7)	I decree, ordain, assign, make a will (mid. in NT)
ἐκτίθημι	(4)	I expose, abandon; explain (mid.)
ἐπιτίθημι	(39)	I lay or put upon, inflict upon, add; give, attack (mid.)
καταθεματίζω	(1)	I curse
κατατίθημι	(2)	I place; grant, do (mid. in NT)
μετατίθημι	(6)	I change, take up; desert, turn away (mid.)
νομοθετέω	(2)	I receive the law, enact by law
νουθετέω	(8)	I admonish, warn, instruct
παρατίθημι	(19)	I place or put before; entrust, demonstrate (mid.)
περιτίθημι	(8)	I put or place around, put on, show honor
προσανατίθημι	(2)	I add, contribute, consult with (mid. in NT)
προστίθημι	(18)	I add, add to, increase, do again, provide, give, grant
προτίθημι	(3)	I display publicly, plan, intend (mid. in NT)
συγκατατίθημι	(1)	I agree with, consent to (mid. in NT)
συνεπιτίθημι	(1)	I join in an attack (mid. in NT)
συντίθημι	(3)	I put with; agree, decide (mid. in NT)
ὑποτίθημι	(2)	I lay down, risk; put before, make known, teach (mid.)
θεμέλιον, ου, τό	(1)	foundation, basis
θεμέλιος, ου, ὁ	(15)	foundation, foundation stone
θήκη, ης, ἡ	(1)	receptacle, sheath
θησαυρός, οῦ, ὁ	(17)	treasure box, storehouse, treasure
ἀθέτησις, εως, ἡ	(2)	annulment, removal
ἀνάθεμα, ατος, τό	(6)	something cursed, curse
ἀνάθημα, ατος, τό	(1)	votive offering
ἀντίθεσις, εως, ἡ	(1)	opposition, objection, contradiction
ἀπόθεσις, εως, ἡ	(2)	removal
ἀποθήκη, ης, ἡ	(6)	storehouse, barn
διαθήκη, ης, ἡ	(33)	last will and testament, covenant, decree

ἐπίθεσις, εως, ἡ	(4)	laying on
κατάθεμα, ατος, τό	(1)	something cursed
μετάθεσις, εως, ἡ	(3)	removal, change, taking up
νομοθεσία, ας, ἡ	(1)	giving of the law
νομοθέτης, ου, ὁ	(1)	lawgiver
νουθεσία, ας, ἡ	(3)	admonition, instruction, warning
ὁροθεσία, ας, ἡ	(1)	boundary
παραθήκη, ης, ἡ	(3)	deposit, what is entrusted another
περίθεσις, εως, ἡ	(1)	putting on, wearing
πρόθεσις, εως, ἡ	(12)	plan, purpose, will, (bread of) presentation
προθεσμία, ας, ἡ	(1)	appointed day, set time
συγκατάθεσις, εως, ἡ	(1)	agreement, union
υἱοθεσία, ας, ἡ	(5)	adoption
ἄθεσμος, ον	(2)	lawless, unprincipled; lawless person (subst.)
ἀθῷος, ον	(2)	innocent
ἀμετάθετος, ον	(2)	unchangeable; unchangeableness (subst.)
ἀνεύθετος, ον	(1)	poor, unfavorably situated, unsuitable
ἀσύνθετος, ον	(1)	faithless, undutiful, disloyal
ἔκθετος, ον	(1)	exposed, abandoned
εὔθετος, ον	(3)	suitable, usable, convenient

τίκτω

τίκτω	(18)	I bear, give birth, bring forth
τεκνογονέω	(1)	I bear children
τεκνοτροφέω	(1)	I bring up children
τεκνίον, ου, τό	(8)	little child
τέκνον, ου, τό	(99)	child, son; descendants, posterity (pl.)
τέκτων, ονος, ὁ	(2)	carpenter, wood worker, builder
τέχνη, ης, ἡ	(3)	skill, trade, craft
τεχνίτης, ου, ὁ	(4)	craftsman, artisan, designer
τόκος, ου, ὁ	(2)	interest (on money loaned)
ἀρχιτέκτων, ονος, ὁ	(1)	master builder
πρωτοτόκια, ων, τά	(1)	birthright
τεκνογονία, ας, ἡ	(1)	bearing of children
ἄτεκνος, ον	(2)	childless
ὁμότεχνος, ον	(1)	practicing the same trade
πρωτότοκος, ον	(8)	first-born
φιλότεκνος, ον	(1)	loving one's children

τιμή

τιμάω	(21)	I set a price on, honor, revere
ἀτιμάζω	(7)	I dishonor, treat shamefully, insult
ἐπιτιμάω	(29)	I rebuke, reprove, warn, censure, punish
τιμωρέω	(2)	I punish
φιλοτιμέομαι	(3)	I aspire
τιμή, ῆς, ἡ	(41)	price, value, honor, respect, place of honor, honorarium
τιμιότης, ητος, ἡ	(1)	costliness, abundance, wealth
ἀτιμία, ας, ἡ	(7)	dishonor, disgrace, shame
ἐπιτιμία, ας, ἡ	(1)	punishment
τιμωρία, ας, ἡ	(1)	punishment
τίμιος, α, ον	(13)	valuable, precious, costly, honorable, respected
ἄτιμος, ον	(4)	unhonored, dishonored, less honorable
ἔντιμος, ον	(5)	honored, respected, valuable, precious
ἰσότιμος, ον	(1)	equal in value, of the same kind

πολύτιμος, ον	(3)	very precious, valuable

τίνω

τίνω	(1)	I pay, undergo
ἀποτίνω	(1)	I make compensation, pay the damages

τίς

τίς, τί	(555)	who? which? what?; what sort of? (adj.); why? (adv.)
ἱνατί	(6)	why? for what reason?
ὅστις, ἥτις, ὅ τι	(153)	whoever, everyone who, who
ὅτι	(1296)	that, so that, because, for, (introduces direct discourse)

τὶς

τὶς, τὶ	(525)	someone, anyone, something, anything; some, any (adj.)
μήτι	(17)	(used in questions expecting a neg. answer)
μήτιγε	(1)	not to speak of, let alone

[τοί]

ἤτοι	(1)	or, either
καίτοι	(2)	and yet, although
καίτοιγε	(1)	and yet, although
μέντοι	(8)	really, actually, though, to be sure, indeed, but
τοιγαροῦν	(2)	then, therefore, for that very reason
τοίνυν	(3)	hence, so, indeed, therefore, then

τολμάω

τολμάω	(16)	I dare, bring myself to, presume, am courageous
ἀποτολμάω	(1)	I am bold
τολμητής, οῦ, ὁ	(1)	bold, audacious person
τολμηρότερον	(1)	rather boldly

τομός

διχοτομέω	(2)	I cut in two, punish severely
ὀρθοτομέω	(1)	I cut straight; use or interpret correctly (fig. in NT)
περιτέμνω	(17)	I circumcise
συντέμνω	(1)	I cut short, shorten, limit
ταμεῖον, ου, τό	(4)	storeroom, inner room
ἀποτομία, ας, ἡ	(2)	severity
κατατομή, ῆς, ἡ	(1)	mutilation, cutting in pieces
περιτομή, ῆς, ἡ	(36)	circumcision, those who are circumcised, Jews
τομός, ή, όν	(1)	cutting, sharp
ἀπερίτμητος, ον	(1)	uncircumcised; stubborn, obstinate (fig. in NT)
ἄτομος, ον	(1)	uncut, indivisible; moment (subst. in NT)
ἀποτόμως	(2)	severely, rigorously
συντόμως	(2)	promptly, readily, briefly

τόπος

τόπος, ου, ὁ	(94)	place, position, location, possibility; regions (pl.)
ἄτοπος, ον	(4)	out of place, unusual, evil, wrong
ἐντόπιος, α, ον	(1)	local; local resident (subst. in NT)

τραῦμα

τραυματίζω	(2)	I wound, injure
τραῦμα, ατος, τό	(1)	wound
ἔκτρωμα, ατος, τό	(1)	untimely birth, miscarriage

τράχηλος

τραχηλίζω	(1)	I am laid bare, am exposed (pass. in NT)
τράχηλος, ου, ὁ	(7)	neck, throat
σκληροτράχηλος, ον	(1)	stiff-necked, stubborn

τρεῖς

ἀρχιτρίκλινος, ου, ὁ	(3)	head waiter, butler, master of a feast
τρίβολος, ου, ὁ	(2)	thorn plant, thistle
τριετία, ας, ἡ	(1)	period of three years
τρίστεγον, ου, τό	(1)	third story or floor
τρεῖς, τρία	(68)	three
τριάκοντα	(11)	thirty
τριακόσιοι, αι, α	(2)	three hundred
τρίτος, η, ον	(56)	third; third part, a third (neut. subst.); third time (adv.)
τρίμηνος, ον	(1)	of three months; three months (subst. in NT)
τρισχίλιοι, αι, α	(1)	three thousand
τρίς	(12)	three times

τρέμω

τρέμω	(3)	I tremble, am afraid, stand in awe of, respect
τρόμος, ου, ὁ	(5)	trembling, quivering
ἔντρομος, ον	(3)	trembling, fearful

τρέφω

τρέφω	(9)	I feed, nourish, nurse, bring up, train
ἀνατρέφω	(3)	I bring up, care for, rear, train
ἐκτρέφω	(2)	I nourish, bring up, rear
ἐντρέφω	(1)	I bring up, train
τεκνοτροφέω	(1)	I bring up children
θρέμμα, ατος, τό	(1)	(domesticated) animal; cattle, flocks (pl. in NT)
θρόμβος, ου, ὁ	(1)	drop or clot (of blood)
τροφή, ῆς, ἡ	(16)	nourishment, food
τροφός, οῦ, ἡ	(1)	nurse
διατροφή, ῆς, ἡ	(1)	support; food (pl. in NT)
σύντροφος, ον	(1)	raised with; foster brother, close friend (subst. in NT)

τρέχω

τρέχω	(20)	I run, rush, strive to advance, make progress
εἰστρέχω	(1)	I run in
ἐπισυντρέχω	(1)	I run together
εὐθυδρομέω	(2)	I sail a straight course
κατατρέχω	(1)	I run down
περιτρέχω	(1)	I run around, run about
προστρέχω	(3)	I run up to
προτρέχω	(2)	I run (on) ahead
συντρέχω	(3)	I run together, plunge with
ὑποτρέχω	(1)	I run or sail under the shelter of
δρόμος, ου, ὁ	(3)	course

τροχιά, ᾶς, ἡ	(1)	course, way, path
τροχός, οῦ, ὁ	(1)	wheel, course
συνδρομή, ῆς, ἡ	(1)	running together, forming of a mob
πρόδρομος, ον	(1)	running before; forerunner (subst. in NT)

τρίβος

διατρίβω	(9)	I spend, stay, remain
συντρίβω	(7)	I shatter, crush, break, bruise
χρονοτριβέω	(1)	I spend, lose, or waste time
τρίβος, ου, ἡ	(3)	path
διαπαρατριβή, ῆς, ἡ	(1)	mutual or constant irritation
σύντριμμα, ατος, τό	(1)	destruction, ruin

τρυπή

ἀνατρέπω	(3)	I cause to fall, overturn, destroy
ἀποτρέπω	(1)	I turn away from, avoid (mid. in NT)
ἐκτρέπω	(5)	I turn, avoid, am dislocated (mid. and pass. in NT)
ἐντρέπω	(9)	I make ashamed; am ashamed, respect (pass.)
ἐπιτρέπω	(18)	I allow, permit
μετατρέπω	(1)	I turn, change
περιτρέπω	(1)	I turn, drive
προτρέπω	(1)	I urge, encourage, impel, persuade (mid. in NT)
τροποφορέω	(1)	I put up with (another's conduct)
τροπή, ῆς, ἡ	(1)	turning, variation, change
τρόπος, ου, ὁ	(13)	manner, way, kind, way of life, conduct
ἐντροπή, ῆς, ἡ	(2)	shame, humiliation
ἐπιτροπή, ῆς, ἡ	(1)	permission, commission, full power
ἐπίτροπος, ου, ὁ	(3)	manager, foreman, steward, guardian
εὐτραπελία, ας, ἡ	(1)	coarse jesting, buffoonery
πολυτρόπως	(1)	in various ways

τρυμαλιά

| τρυμαλιά, ᾶς, ἡ | (1) | hole, eye (of a needle) |
| τρύπημα, ατος, τό | (1) | hole, eye (of a needle) |

τρυφή

τρυφάω	(1)	I lead a life of luxury or self-indulgence, revel, carouse
ἐντρυφάω	(1)	I revel, carouse
συνθρύπτω	(1)	I break
τρυφή, ῆς, ἡ	(2)	indulgence, reveling, luxury

τρώγω

| τρώγω | (6) | I gnaw, nibble, eat |
| τράγος, ου, ὁ | (4) | he-goat |

τυγχάνω

τυγχάνω	(12)	I attain, obtain, experience
ἐντυγχάνω	(5)	I meet, approach, appeal, petition, plead
ἐπιτυγχάνω	(5)	I obtain, attain, reach
παρατυγχάνω	(1)	I happen to be near or present
συντυγχάνω	(1)	I come together with, meet, join
ὑπερεντυγχάνω	(1)	I plead, intercede
ἔντευξις, εως, ἡ	(2)	petition, prayer

τύπος

τυμπανίζω	(1)	I torment, torture; am tortured (pass. in NT)
τύπτω	(13)	I strike, hit, beat, wound
ἐντυπόω	(1)	I carve, engrave
τύπος, ου, ὁ	(15)	mark, image, form, pattern, type, model, example
ὑποτύπωσις, εως, ἡ	(2)	model, example, standard
ἀντίτυπος, ον	(2)	corresponding to; copy, antitype, representation (subst.)
τυπικῶς	(1)	typologically, as an example

τυφλός

τυφλόω	(3)	I blind, deprive of sight
τυφλός, ή, όν	(50)	blind; blind person, the blind (subst.)

τύφω

τεφρόω	(1)	I reduce to ashes
τυφόω	(3)	I delude; am puffed up, conceited (pass. in NT)
τύφω	(1)	I give off smoke; smoke, smolder (pass. in NT)

ὑάκινθος

ὑάκινθος, ου, ὁ	(1)	jacinth, hyacinth
ὑακίνθινος, η, ον	(1)	hyacinth-colored

ὕαλος

ὕαλος, ου, ἡ	(2)	glass, crystal
ὑάλινος, η, ον	(3)	of glass, transparent as glass

ὕβρις

ὑβρίζω	(5)	I mistreat, scoff at, insult
ἐνυβρίζω	(1)	I insult, outrage
ὕβρις, εως, ἡ	(3)	shame, insult, mistreatment, disaster, damage
ὑβριστής, οῦ, ὁ	(2)	violent or insolent person

ὑγιής

ὑγιαίνω	(12)	I am in good health, healthy, sound, or correct
ὑγιής, ές	(11)	healthy, sound

ὕδωρ

ὑδροποτέω	(1)	I drink water
ὑδρία, ας, ἡ	(3)	water jar
ὕδωρ, ατος, τό	(76)	water
ὑετός, οῦ, ὁ	(5)	rain
ὑγρός, ά, όν	(1)	moist, green (of wood)
ὑδρωπικός, ή, όν	(1)	suffering from dropsy
ἄνυδρος, ον	(4)	waterless, dry

υἱός

υἱός, οῦ, ὁ	(377)	son, male offspring, descendant, follower, Son
υἱοθεσία, ας, ἡ	(5)	adoption

ὕλη

διϋλίζω	(1)	I filter, strain out

ὕλη, ης, ἡ   (1)   forest, firewood

ὕμνος

ὑμνέω   (4)   I sing hymns of praise to; sing a hymn (intrans.)
ὕμνος, ου, ὁ   (2)   hymn, song of praise

ὑπέρ

ὑπερπερισσεύω   (2)   I am present in abundance; overflow (pass.)
ὑπερῷον, ου, τό   (4)   upper story, room upstairs
ὑπεράνω   (3)   (high) above (impr. prep. in NT)
ὑπερεκπερισσοῦ   (3)   beyond all measure; infinitely more than (impr. prep.)
ὑπερπερισσῶς   (1)   beyond all measure
ὑπέρ   (150)   for, in behalf of, about (gen.); above, beyond, than (acc.)

ὑπηρέτης

ὑπηρετέω   (3)   I serve, render service, am helpful
ὑπηρέτης, ου, ὁ   (20)   servant, helper, assistant

ὕπνος

ἀγρυπνέω   (4)   I am awake, keep watch, guard
ἀφυπνόω   (1)   I fall asleep
ἐνυπνιάζομαι   (2)   I dream
ἐξυπνίζω   (1)   I wake up, arouse
ὕπνος, ου, ὁ   (6)   sleep
ἀγρυπνία, ας, ἡ   (2)   wakefulness
ἐνύπνιον, ου, τό   (1)   dream
ἔξυπνος, ον   (1)   awake, aroused

ὑπό

ὑπαντάω   (10)   I meet, oppose
ὑπάντησις, εως, ἡ   (3)   meeting
ὑπεναντίος, α, ον   (2)   opposed, contrary, hostile; opponent (subst.)
ὑποκάτω   (11)   under, below (impr. prep. in NT)
ὑπό   (220)   by, at the hands of (gen.); under, below (acc.)

ὕστερος

ὑστερέω   (16)   I miss, lack, am inferior, fail; am lacking (pass.)
ὑστέρημα, ατος, τό   (9)   need, deficiency, absence, lack, shortcoming
ὑστέρησις, εως, ἡ   (2)   need, lack, poverty
ὕστερος, α, ον   (12)   latter, last; later, then, finally (neut. sing. as adv.)

ὕψος

ὑψόω   (20)   I lift up, raise high, exalt
ὑπερυψόω   (1)   I raise to the loftiest height or the highest position
ὑψηλοφρονέω   (1)   I am proud or haughty
ὕψος, ους, τό   (6)   height, heaven, high position
ὕψωμα, ατος, τό   (2)   height, exaltation, proud obstacle
ὑψηλός, ή, όν   (11)   high, exalted, proud, haughty
ὕψιστος, η, ον   (13)   highest; highest (heaven), the Most High (subst.)

φάγος

φάγος, ου, ὁ   (2)   glutton

προσφάγιον, ου, τό	(1)	fish

φαίνω

φαίνω	(31)	I shine; shine, appear, become visible, seem (mid.-pass.)
φανερόω	(49)	I reveal, make known, show; am revealed, appear (pass.)
φαντάζω	(1)	I make visible; appear, become visible (pass. in NT)
φάσκω	(3)	I say, assert, claim
φωτίζω	(11)	I shine; illuminate, bring to light, reveal (trans.)
ἀναφαίνω	(2)	I light up, cause to appear, come into view
ἀφανίζω	(5)	I render invisible, destroy; perish, disappear (pass.)
ἐμφανίζω	(10)	I make visible, reveal, make clear, explain, bring charges
ἐπιφαίνω	(4)	I appear; show myself (pass.)
ἐπιφαύσκω	(1)	I shine on, illuminate
ἐπιφώσκω	(2)	I shine forth, dawn, draw near
συκοφαντέω	(2)	I accuse falsely, slander, extort
φανέρωσις, εως, ἡ	(2)	disclosure, announcement
φανός, οῦ, ὁ	(1)	lamp, torch, lantern
φαντασία, ας, ἡ	(1)	pomp, pageantry
φάντασμα, ατος, τό	(2)	apparition, ghost
φάσις, εως, ἡ	(1)	information, report, announcement, news
φῶς, φωτός, τό	(73)	light, fire
φωστήρ, ῆρος, ὁ	(2)	star, splendor, radiance, brilliance
φωτισμός, οῦ, ὁ	(2)	illumination, enlightenment, light, revelation
ἀφανισμός, οῦ, ὁ	(1)	disappearance, destruction
ἐπιφάνεια, ας, ἡ	(6)	appearing, appearance, coming
κατήφεια, ας, ἡ	(1)	gloominess, dejection, depression
πρόφασις, εως, ἡ	(6)	valid reason or excuse, false motive, pretext
ὑπερηφανία, ας, ἡ	(1)	arrogance, haughtiness, pride
φανερός, ά, όν	(18)	visible, clear, plain, known; the open (subst.)
φωτεινός, ή, όν	(5)	shining, bright, radiant, illuminated
ἀφανής, ές	(1)	invisible, hidden
ἄφαντος, ον	(1)	invisible
ἐμφανής, ες	(2)	visible, revealed
ἐπιφανής, ές	(1)	splendid, glorious, remarkable
ὑπερήφανος, ον	(5)	arrogant, haughty, proud
φωσφόρος, ον	(1)	bearing light; morning star (subst. in NT)
φανερῶς	(3)	openly, publicly, clearly

φάρμακον

φαρμακεία, ας, ἡ	(2)	sorcery, magic; magical arts (pl.)
φάρμακον, ου, τό	(1)	magic potion, charm
φάρμακος, ου, ὁ	(2)	magician, sorcerer

φείδομαι

φείδομαι	(10)	I spare, refrain
ἀφειδία, ας, ἡ	(1)	severe treatment, severe discipline
φειδομένως	(2)	sparingly

φέρω

φέρω	(66)	I bear, carry, endure, produce, drive, bring, utter, lead
φορέω	(6)	I wear, bear
φορτίζω	(2)	I load, burden
ἀναφέρω	(10)	I bring up, take up, offer
ἀποφέρω	(6)	I carry away, lead away, take, bring

ἀποφορτίζομαι	(1)	I unload
διαφέρω	(13)	I carry through, spread, differ, am superior to
εἰσφέρω	(8)	I bring in, carry in, lead into
ἐκφέρω	(8)	I carry or bring out, lead or send out, produce
ἐπιφέρω	(2)	I bring upon, pronounce, inflict
εὐφορέω	(1)	I bear good crops, yield well, am fruitful
καρποφορέω	(8)	I bear fruit, am productive
καταφέρω	(4)	I cast against, bring (charges); am overcome (pass.)
παραφέρω	(4)	I take away, carry away, remove
παρεισφέρω	(1)	I apply, bring to bear
περιφέρω	(3)	I carry about, carry here and there
πληροφορέω	(6)	I fill, fulfill, accomplish, convince, fully
προσφέρω	(47)	I bring to, offer, present; deal with (pass.)
προφέρω	(2)	I bring out, produce
συμφέρω	(15)	I bring together; it is good, better, or useful (impers.)
τελεσφορέω	(1)	I bear fruit to maturity, produce ripe fruit
τροποφορέω	(1)	I put up with (another's conduct)
ὑποφέρω	(3)	I bear up under, submit to, endure
φόρος, ου, ὁ	(5)	tribute, tax
φορτίον, ου, τό	(6)	burden, load, cargo
πληροφορία, ας, ἡ	(4)	full assurance, certainty, conviction, fullness
προσφορά, ᾶς, ἡ	(9)	offering, sacrificing, sacrifice, gift
διάφορος, ον	(4)	different, outstanding, excellent
διηνεκής, ές	(4)	continuous, uninterrupted
θανατηφόρος, ον	(1)	death-bringing, deadly
καρποφόρος, ον	(1)	fruitful
ποταμοφόρητος, ον	(1)	swept away by a river or stream
σύμφορος, ον	(2)	beneficial; benefit, advantage (subst. in NT)
φωσφόρος, ον	(1)	bearing light; morning star (subst. in NT)

φεύγω

φεύγω	(29)	I flee, escape, avoid, disappear
ἀποφεύγω	(3)	I escape (from)
διαφεύγω	(1)	I escape
ἐκφεύγω	(8)	I run away, escape
καταφεύγω	(2)	I flee, take refuge
φυγή, ῆς, ἡ	(1)	flight

φημί

φημί	(66)	I say, affirm, mean
βλασφημέω	(34)	I blaspheme, revile, defame
διαφημίζω	(3)	I spread widely, disseminate
δυσφημέω	(1)	I slander, defame
προφητεύω	(28)	I prophesy, proclaim a divine message
σύμφημι	(1)	I agree with
φήμη, ης, ἡ	(2)	report, news
βλασφημία, ας, ἡ	(18)	blasphemy, slander, defamation
δυσφημία, ας, ἡ	(1)	slander, ill repute
εὐφημία, ας, ἡ	(1)	good report or repute
προφητεία, ας, ἡ	(19)	prophecy, prophetic activity, gift of prophecy
προφήτης, ου, ὁ	(144)	prophet; prophets (pl. as a division of scripture)
προφῆτις, ιδος, ἡ	(2)	prophetess
ψευδοπροφήτης, ου, ὁ	(11)	false prophet
βλάσφημος, ον	(4)	blasphemous, slanderous; blasphemer (subst.)

| εὔφημος, ον | (1) | well-sounding, auspicious |
| προφητικός, ή, όν | (2) | prophetic |

φθάνω

| φθάνω | (7) | I precede, arrive, come upon or to |
| προφθάνω | (1) | I come before, anticipate |

φθέγγομαι

φθέγγομαι	(3)	I call out loudly, speak, utter, proclaim
ἀποφθέγγομαι	(3)	I speak out, declare
φθόγγος, ου, ὁ	(2)	sound, tone, voice

φθείρω

φθείρω	(9)	I destroy, ruin, corrupt, spoil, seduce
διαφθείρω	(6)	I spoil, destroy, ruin
καταφθείρω	(1)	I ruin, corrupt
φθορά, ᾶς, ἡ	(9)	ruin, destruction, that which is perishable, depravity
ἀφθαρσία, ας, ἡ	(7)	incorruptibility, immorality
ἀφθορία, ας, ἡ	(1)	soundness, integrity
διαφθορά, ᾶς, ἡ	(6)	destruction, corruption
φθαρτός, ή, όν	(6)	subject to decay, perishable, mortal
ἄφθαρτος, ον	(8)	imperishable, incorruptible, immoral
φθινοπωρινός, ή, όν	(1)	belonging to late autumn

φθόνος

| φθονέω | (1) | I envy, am jealous |
| φθόνος, ου, ὁ | (9) | envy, jealousy |

φίλος

φιλέω	(25)	I love, like, kiss
καταφιλέω	(6)	I kiss
φιλοπρωτεύω	(1)	I wish to be first, like to be leader
φιλοτιμέομαι	(3)	I aspire
φίλημα, ατος, τό	(7)	kiss
φιλία, ας, ἡ	(1)	friendship, love
φιλαδελφία, ας, ἡ	(6)	brotherly love, love of brother or sister
φιλανθρωπία, ας, ἡ	(2)	love for people, kindness, hospitality
φιλαργυρία, ας, ἡ	(1)	love of money, miserliness, avarice
φιλονεικία, ας, ἡ	(1)	dispute, strife
φιλοξενία, ας, ἡ	(2)	hospitality
φιλοσοφία, ας, ἡ	(1)	philosophy
φιλόσοφος, ου, ὁ	(1)	philosopher
φίλος, η, ον	(29)	beloved, loving, friendly; friend (subst.)
ἀφιλάγαθος, ον	(1)	not loving the good
ἀφιλάργυρος, ον	(2)	not loving money, not greedy
προσφιλής, ές	(1)	pleasing, agreeable, lovely
φιλάγαθος, ον	(1)	loving what is good
φιλάδελφος, ον	(1)	loving one's brother or sister
φίλανδρος, ον	(1)	loving one's husband
φιλάργυρος, ον	(2)	fond of money, avaricious
φίλαυτος, ον	(1)	loving oneself, selfish
φιλήδονος, ον	(1)	loving pleasure, given over to pleasure
φιλόθεος, ον	(1)	loving God, devout

φιλόνεικος, ον	(1)	quarrelsome, contentious
φιλόξενος, ον	(3)	hospitable
φιλόστοργος, ον	(1)	loving dearly, devoted
φιλότεκνος, ον	(1)	loving one's children
φιλανθρώπως	(1)	benevolently, kindly
φιλοφρόνως	(1)	friendly, hospitably

φλόξ

φλογίζω	(2)	I set on fire
φλόξ, φλογός, ἡ	(7)	flame

φλύαρος

φλυαρέω	(1)	I talk nonsense about, charge unjustly against
οἰνοφλυγία, ας, ἡ	(1)	drunkenness
φλύαρος, ον	(1)	gossipy, foolish

φόβος

φοβέω	(95)	I am afraid, fear, reverence, respect (pass. in NT)
ἐκφοβέω	(1)	I frighten, terrify
φόβητρον, ου, τό	(1)	terrible sight or event, horror
φόβος, ου, ὁ	(47)	cause of fear, fear, reverence, respect
φοβερός, ά, όν	(3)	fearful, terrible, frightful
ἔκφοβος, ον	(2)	terrified
ἔμφοβος, ον	(5)	afraid, startled, terrified
ἀφόβως	(4)	fearlessly, boldly, shamelessly

φονεύω

φονεύω	(12)	I murder, kill
φονεύς, έως, ὁ	(7)	murderer
φόνος, ου, ὁ	(9)	murder, killing
ἀνδροφόνος, ου, ὁ	(1)	murderer
πρόσφατος, ον	(1)	new, recent
προσφάτως	(1)	recently

φραγέλλιον

φραγελλόω	(2)	I flog, scourge, beat with a whip
φραγέλλιον, ου, τό	(1)	whip, lash

φράσσω

φράσσω	(3)	I shut, stop, close, silence, block
φραγμός, οῦ, ὁ	(4)	fence, wall, hedge, lane

φρήν

φρονέω	(26)	I think, ponder, set my mind on, have thoughts
φροντίζω	(1)	I think of, am intent on, am concerned about
εὐφραίνω	(14)	I cheer, gladden; rejoice, make merry (pass.)
καταφρονέω	(9)	I look down on, despise, think lightly of, disregard
παραφρονέω	(1)	I am beside myself, irrational
περιφρονέω	(1)	I disregard, look down on, despise
σωφρονέω	(6)	I am of sound mind, sensible, serious
σωφρονίζω	(1)	I encourage, advise, urge
ὑπερφρονέω	(1)	I think too highly of myself, am haughty

ὑψηλοφρονέω	(1)	I am proud or haughty
φρεναπατάω	(1)	I deceive
φρήν, φρενός, ἡ	(2)	thinking, understanding (pl. in NT)
φρόνημα, ατος, τό	(4)	way of thinking, aim, aspiration
φρόνησις, εως, ἡ	(2)	way of thinking, understanding, insight
ἀφροσύνη, ης, ἡ	(4)	foolishness, lack of sense
εὐφροσύνη, ης, ἡ	(2)	joy, gladness, cheerfulness
καταφρονητής, οῦ, ὁ	(1)	despiser, scoffer
παραφρονία, ας, ἡ	(1)	madness, insanity
σωφρονισμός, οῦ, ὁ	(1)	good judgment, moderation, advice
σωφροσύνη, ης, ἡ	(3)	reasonableness, self-control, decency, modesty
ταπεινοφροσύνη, ης, ἡ	(7)	humility, modesty
φρεναπάτης, ου, ὁ	(1)	deceiver, one who misleads
φρόνιμος, ον	(14)	sensible, thoughtful, wise
ἄφρων, ον	(11)	foolish, ignorant
ὁμόφρων, ον	(1)	like-minded, united
σώφρων, ον	(4)	thoughtful, moderate, self-controlled, decent, modest
ταπεινόφρων, ον	(1)	humble
φρονίμως	(1)	wisely, shrewdly
σωφρόνως	(1)	soberly, moderately, showing self-control
φιλοφρόνως	(1)	friendly, hospitably

φυλάσσω

φυλακίζω	(1)	I imprison
φυλάσσω	(31)	I watch, guard, protect, keep, observe; avoid, keep (mid.)
διαφυλάσσω	(1)	I guard, protect
φυλακή, ῆς, ἡ	(47)	watch, guard, prison, haunt, watch (period of the night)
φυλακτήριον, ου, τό	(1)	amulet, phylactery
φύλαξ, ακος, ὁ	(3)	guard, sentinel
γαζοφυλάκιον, ου, τό	(5)	treasure room, treasury, contribution box
δεσμοφύλαξ, ακος, ὁ	(3)	jailer, keeper of the prison

φύω

φυσιόω	(7)	I puff up, make arrogant; become conceited (pass.)
φυτεύω	(11)	I plant
φύω	(3)	I grow up, come up
ἐκφύω	(2)	I put forth
ἐμφυσάω	(1)	I breathe on
συμφύω	(1)	I grow up with (pass. in NT)
φυλή, ῆς, ἡ	(31)	tribe, nation, people
φύσις, εως, ἡ	(14)	nature, natural endowment or characteristics, creature
φυσίωσις, εως, ἡ	(1)	pride, conceit
φυτεία, ας, ἡ	(1)	plant
δωδεκάφυλον, ου, τό	(1)	the twelve tribes
συμφυλέτης, ου, ὁ	(1)	fellow countryman, compatriot
φυσικός, ή, όν	(3)	belonging to nature, natural
ἀλλόφυλος, ον	(1)	foreign; a heathen, Gentile (subst. in NT)
ἔμφυτος, ον	(1)	implanted
νεόφυτος, ον	(1)	newly converted
σύμφυτος, ον	(1)	grown together, united with
φυσικῶς	(1)	naturally, by instinct

φωνή

φωνέω	(43)	I call, call or cry out, crow, address, summon, invite

ἀναφωνέω	(1)	I cry out
ἐπιφωνέω	(4)	I cry out, shout
προσφωνέω	(7)	I call out, address, call to myself
συμφωνέω	(6)	I agree with, agree, settle with, match
φωνή, ῆς, ἡ	(139)	sound, noise, voice, call, cry, language
ἀλεκτοροφωνία, ας, ἡ	(1)	crowing of a cock, cockcrow, before dawn
κενοφωνία, ας, ἡ	(2)	empty talk, chatter
συμφώνησις, εως, ἡ	(1)	agreement
συμφωνία, ας, ἡ	(1)	music
ἀσύμφωνος, ον	(1)	not harmonious
ἄφωνος, ον	(4)	silent, dumb, incapable of speech, without meaning
σύμφωνος, ον	(1)	agreeing; agreement (subst. in NT)

χαίρω

χαίρω	(74)	I rejoice, am glad; hail, greetings (greeting form.)
χαρίζομαι	(23)	I give freely, grant, cancel, remit, forgive, pardon
χαριτόω	(2)	I bestow favor upon, favor highly, bless
εὐχαριστέω	(38)	I am thankful, give thanks, offer a prayer of thanks
συγχαίρω	(7)	I rejoice with, congratulate
χαρά, ᾶς, ἡ	(59)	joy, cause for joy, joyfulness, gladness
χάρις, ιτος, ἡ	(155)	grace, favor, goodwill, gift, thanks, kindness
χάρισμα, ατος, τό	(17)	gift, favor
εὐχαριστία, ας, ἡ	(15)	thankfulness, thanksgiving, prayer of thanksgiving
ἀχάριστος, ον	(2)	ungrateful
εὐχάριστος, ον	(1)	thankful
χάριν	(9)	for the sake of, because of, by reason of (impr. prep.)

χαλάω

χαλάω	(7)	I let down, lower
χαλιναγωγέω	(2)	I guide with bit and bridle, hold in check, control
χαλινός, οῦ, ὁ	(2)	bit, bridle

χαλκός

χαλκεύς, έως, ὁ	(1)	coppersmith, metal worker
χαλκηδών, όνος, ὁ	(1)	chalcedony, agate
χαλκίον, ου, τό	(1)	(copper) vessel, kettle
χαλκός, οῦ, ὁ	(5)	copper, brass, bronze, gong, copper coin, money
χαλκολίβανον, ου, τό	(2)	fine brass or bronze
χαλκοῦς, ῆ, οῦν	(1)	made of copper, brass, or bronze

χάραγμα

χάραγμα, ατος, τό	(8)	mark, stamp, thing formed, image
χαρακτήρ, ῆρος, ὁ	(1)	reproduction, representation
χάραξ, ακος, ὁ	(1)	palisade, barricade
χάρτης, ου, ὁ	(1)	sheet of papyrus, papyrus roll

χειμών

χειμάζω	(1)	I toss in a storm; undergo bad weather (pass. in NT)
χειμών, ῶνος, ὁ	(6)	rainy and stormy weather, bad weather, storm, winter
χειμάρρους, ου, ὁ	(1)	winter stream or torrent, ravine, wadi, valley

χείρ

διαχειρίζω	(2)	I lay violent hands on, kill, murder (mid. in NT)

ἐπιχειρέω	(3)	I set my hand to, attempt, try
προχειρίζομαι	(3)	I choose for myself, select, appoint
προχειροτονέω	(1)	I choose or appoint beforehand (pass. in NT)
χειραγωγέω	(2)	I take or lead by the hand
χειροτονέω	(2)	I choose or elect by raising hands, choose
χείρ, χειρός, ἡ	(177)	hand, arm, finger, power, activity
χειραγωγός, οῦ, ὁ	(1)	one who leads another by the hand, leader
χειρόγραφον, ου, τό	(1)	handwritten document, document of indebtedness, bond
αὐτόχειρ, ρος	(1)	with one's own hand
ἀχειροποίητος, ον	(3)	not made by hand, spiritual
χειροποίητος, ον	(6)	made by human hands

[χέω]

ἐκχέω	(27)	I pour out, shed, spill, scatter; abandon myself (pass.)
ἐπιχέω	(1)	I pour on or over
καταχέω	(2)	I pour out, pour down over
συγχέω	(5)	I confuse, trouble, stir up
ὑπερεκχύννω	(1)	I overflow (pass. in NT)
χοῦς, χοός, ὁ	(2)	soil, dust
αἱματεκχυσία, ας, ἡ	(1)	shedding of blood
ἀνάχυσις, εως, ἡ	(1)	wide stream, flood
πρόσχυσις, εως, ἡ	(1)	sprinkling, pouring, spreading
σύγχυσις, εως, ἡ	(1)	confusion, tumult
χοϊκός, ή, όν	(4)	made of earth or dust, earthly

χίλιοι

χιλιάς, αδος, ἡ	(23)	(group of) a thousand
χιλίαρχος, ου, ὁ	(21)	military tribune, high ranking officer
χίλιοι, αι, α	(11)	thousand
δισχίλιοι, αι, α	(1)	two thousand
ἑπτακισχίλιοι, αι, α	(1)	seven thousand
πεντακισχίλιοι, αι, α	(6)	five thousand
τετρακισχίλιοι, αι, α	(5)	four thousand
τρισχίλιοι, αι, α	(1)	three thousand

χιών

παραχειμάζω	(4)	I winter, spend the winter
χιών, όνος, ἡ	(2)	snow
παραχειμασία, ας, ἡ	(1)	wintering

χλευάζω

| χλευάζω | (1) | I mock, sneer, scoff |
| διαχλευάζω | (1) | I deride, mock |

χολή

| χολάω | (1) | I am angry |
| χολή, ῆς, ἡ | (2) | gall, bile |

χορός

ἐπιχορηγέω	(5)	I provide, give, grant, support
χορηγέω	(2)	I provide, supply
χορός, οῦ, ὁ	(1)	dance, dancing

| ἐπιχορηγία, ας, ἡ | (2) | support, supply, help |

χόρτος

χορτάζω	(16)	I feed, fill, satisfy; eat my fill, am satisfied (pass.)
χόρτασμα, ατος, τό	(1)	food
χόρτος, ου, ὁ	(15)	grass, hay

χράομαι

κίχρημι	(1)	I lend
χράομαι	(11)	I use, employ, proceed, act, treat
χρή	(1)	it is necessary, it ought (impers.)
χρῄζω	(5)	I need, have need of
χρηματίζω	(9)	I impart a revelation, injunction, or warning, am named
χρηστεύομαι	(1)	I am kind, loving, merciful
ἀχρειόω	(1)	I make useless; become depraved (pass. in NT)
καταχράομαι	(2)	I use, make full use of
συγχράομαι	(1)	I have dealings with, associate on friendly terms
χρεία, ας, ἡ	(49)	need, necessity, lack, want, office, duty, service
χρῆμα, ατος, τό	(6)	money; property, wealth, means, money (pl.)
χρηματισμός, οῦ, ὁ	(1)	divine statement or answer
χρῆσις, εως, ἡ	(2)	(sexual) relations or function
χρηστότης, ητος, ἡ	(10)	goodness, uprightness, kindness, generosity
ἀπόχρησις, εως, ἡ	(1)	consuming, using up
χρεοφειλέτης, ου, ὁ	(2)	debtor
χρηστολογία, ας, ἡ	(1)	smooth talk, plausible speech
χρήσιμος, η, ον	(1)	useful, beneficial, advantageous
χρηστός, ή, όν	(7)	useful, good, easy, kind, loving; kindness (subst.)
ἀχρεῖος, ον	(2)	useless, worthless, unworthy
ἄχρηστος, ον	(1)	useless, worthless
εὔχρηστος, ον	(3)	useful, serviceable
παραχρῆμα	(18)	at once, immediately

χρίω

χρίω	(5)	I anoint
ἐγχρίω	(1)	I rub on, anoint
ἐπιχρίω	(2)	I spread or smear on, anoint
χρῖσμα, ατος, τό	(3)	anointing
ἀντίχριστος, ου, ὁ	(5)	Antichrist
ψευδόχριστος, ου, ὁ	(2)	false Christ, false Messiah

χρόνος

χρονίζω	(5)	I take time, linger, delay, take a long time
χρονοτριβέω	(1)	I spend, lose, or waste time
χρόνος, ου, ὁ	(54)	time, period of time, occasion, delay
μακροχρόνιος, ον	(1)	long-lived

χρυσός

χρυσόω	(2)	I make golden, adorn with gold, gild
χρυσίον, ου, τό	(12)	gold, gold ornaments, jewelry
χρυσός, οῦ, ὁ	(10)	gold
χρυσόλιθος, ου, ὁ	(1)	chrysolite
χρυσόπρασος, ου, ὁ	(1)	chrysoprase
χρυσοῦς, ῆ, οῦν	(18)	golden, made of gold

| χρυσοδακτύλιος, ον | (1) | wearing a gold ring |

χωρέω

χωρέω	(10)	I make room, go, make progress, hold, contain, accept
ἀναχωρέω	(14)	I go away, return, withdraw, retire
ἀποχωρέω	(3)	I go away, leave, depart
ἐκχωρέω	(1)	I go out, go away, depart
στενοχωρέω	(3)	I restrict; am confined, restricted, crushed (pass. in NT)
ὑποχωρέω	(2)	I retreat, withdraw, retire
χώρα, ας, ἡ	(28)	country, land, region, inhabitants, countryside, field
χωρίον, ου τό	(10)	place, piece of land, field
στενοχωρία, ας, ἡ	(4)	distress, difficulty, anguish, trouble
εὐρύχωρος, ον	(1)	spacious, broad, roomy
περίχωρος, ον	(9)	neighboring; neighborhood, surrounding region (subst.)

χωρίς

χωρίζω	(13)	I divide, separate; separate myself, go away (pass.)
ἀποχωρίζω	(2)	I separate; am separated, am split (pass. in NT)
διαχωρίζω	(1)	I separate from; part, go away (pass. in NT)
χωρίς	(41)	separately; without, apart from, besides (impr. prep.)

ψάλλω

| ψάλλω | (5) | I sing, sing praise, make melody |
| ψαλμός, οῦ, ὁ | (7) | song of praise, psalm |

ψεύδομαι

ψεύδομαι	(12)	I lie, deceive by lying
ψευδομαρτυρέω	(5)	I bear false witness, give false testimony
ψεῦδος, ους, τό	(10)	lie, falsehood
ψεῦσμα, ατος, τό	(1)	lie, falsehood, lying, untruthfulness
ψεύστης, ου, ὁ	(10)	liar
ψευδάδελφος, ου, ὁ	(2)	false brother
ψευδαπόστολος, ου, ὁ	(1)	false apostle
ψευδοδιδάσκαλος, ου, ὁ	(1)	false teacher, one who teaches falsehoods
ψευδομαρτυρία, ας, ἡ	(2)	false testimony
ψευδόμαρτυς, υρος, ὁ	(2)	one who gives false testimony, false witness
ψευδοπροφήτης, ου, ὁ	(11)	false prophet
ψευδόχριστος, ου, ὁ	(2)	false Christ, false Messiah
ψευδής, ές	(3)	false, lying; liar (subst.)
ἀψευδής, ές	(1)	free from deceit, truthful, trustworthy
ψευδολόγος, ον	(1)	speaking falsely; liar (subst. in NT)
ψευδώνυμος, ον	(1)	falsely called or named

ψιθυρισμός

| ψιθυρισμός, οῦ, ὁ | (1) | whispering, gossip |
| ψιθυριστής, οῦ, ὁ | (1) | whisperer, gossiper |

ψύχω

ψύχω	(1)	I make cool; become cold, am extinguished (pass. in NT)
ἀναψύχω	(1)	I revive, refresh
ἀποψύχω	(1)	I faint, die
ἐκψύχω	(3)	I breathe my last, die
εὐψυχέω	(1)	I am glad, have courage

καταψύχω	(1)	I cool off, refresh
ψυχή, ῆς, ἡ	(103)	soul, self, life, person, living being, life principle
ψῦχος, ους, τό	(3)	cold
ἀνάψυξις, εως, ἡ	(1)	breathing space, relaxation, relief
ψυχικός, ή, όν	(6)	physical, unspiritual; worldly person (subst.)
ψυχρός, ά, όν	(4)	cold, cool; cold water (subst.)
ἄψυχος, ον	(1)	inanimate, lifeless
δίψυχος, ον	(2)	double-minded, doubting, hesitating
ἰσόψυχος, ον	(1)	of like soul or mind
ὀλιγόψυχος, ον	(1)	fainthearted, discouraged
σύμψυχος, ον	(1)	harmonious, united in spirit

ψώχω

ψηλαφάω	(4)	I feel (about for), touch, handle, grope after
ψηφίζω	(2)	I count, calculate, reckon, figure out
ψωμίζω	(2)	I feed, give away
ψώχω	(1)	I rub (grain)
προσψαύω	(1)	I touch
συγκαταψηφίζομαι	(1)	I am chosen together with, am added (pass. in NT)
συμψηφίζω	(1)	I count up, compute
ψῆφος, ου, ἡ	(3)	pebble, vote, stone
ψωμίον, ου, τό	(4)	piece of bread
περίψημα, ατος, τό	(1)	dirt, off-scouring

ᾠδή

ᾄδω	(5)	I sing
ᾠδή, ῆς, ἡ	(7)	song
κιθαρῳδός, οῦ, ὁ	(2)	lyre player, harpist

ὠδίν

ὠδίνω	(3)	I suffer birth pains
συνωδίνω	(1)	I suffer agony together
ὠδίν, ῖνος, ἡ	(4)	birth pains, suffering

[ὠθέω]

ἀπωθέω	(6)	I push aside, reject, repudiate (mid. in NT)
ἐξωθέω	(2)	I push out, expel, run aground

ὠνέομαι

ὠνέομαι	(1)	I buy
ὀψώνιον, ου, τό	(4)	pay, wages, support, compensation
τελώνης, ου, ὁ	(21)	tax collector, revenue officer
τελώνιον, ου, τό	(3)	revenue or tax office

ὥρα

ὥρα, ας, ἡ	(106)	hour, occasion, short time period, moment, time
ἡμίωρον, ου, τό	(1)	half hour
ὡραῖος, α, ον	(4)	beautiful, pleasant, timely

ὡς

καθώς	(182)	as, just as, even as, so far as, since, when
καθώσπερ	(1)	as, just as

ὡσαύτως	(17)	similarly, likewise
ὡς	(504)	as, like, because, when, while, in order that, that, about
ὡσεί	(21)	as, like, about
ὥσπερ	(36)	as, just as, even as
ὡσπερεί	(1)	like, as though, as it were
ὥστε	(83)	for this reason, therefore, so, so that, in order that

ὠφελέω

ὠφελέω	(15)	I help, aid, benefit, achieve, gain
ὄφελος, ους, τό	(3)	benefit, good
ὠφέλεια, ας, ἡ	(2)	use, gain, advantage
ὠφέλιμος, ον	(4)	useful, beneficial, advantageous
ἀνωφελής, ές	(2)	useless, harmful

Section Two

Frequency List of Words

The complete vocabulary of the NT is listed in this section in descending order according to frequency of use. Words that have the same frequency number are arranged alphabetically.

The main sources for the frequency information are the *Concordance to the Novum Testamentum Graece* and GRAMCORD, with the former taking precedence in cases of discrepancy. However, only the words that appear in the text of UBS[3], whether or not they are found within square brackets, are included in the frequency count. This means that the words in the longer and shorter endings of Mark and in John 7:53-8:11 are included. Conversely, the words in the following texts, found only in the apparatus of UBS[3], are not included: Matthew 17:21; 18:11; 23:14; Mark 7:16; 9:44, 46; 11:26; 15:28; Luke 17:36; 23:17; John 5:4; Acts 8:37; 15:34; 24:7; 28:29; Romans 16:24.

Crasis forms have their own frequency numbers. However, the individual parts of these contracted words are also counted in computing the frequency of the separate words. For example, κἀκεῖ, which is a crasis of καί and ἐκεῖ, occurs ten times. These uses are also included in the frequency count of καί and ἐκεῖ.

The list has been arranged in blocks of ten to provide for ease of use and to assist with memorization.

The spelling and accentuation of words follow what appears in UBS[3]. This includes the representation of certain Aramaic and Hebrew words used in direct quotations without accents or breathing marks, e.g., αββα and ηλι.

Several vocabulary items involve two words. Except for the Aramaic expression μαρανα θα, these all involve double place names, e.g., Ἀππίου Φόρον, Τρεῖς Ταβέρναι, and Καλοὶ Λιμένες.

The following contains information about alternate forms and other matters that pertain to certain words other than verbs and proper words. For similar information about verbs and proper words, see Section Three and Section Four.

ἄγαμος	Some lexica classify this word as a second declension noun, that may be masc. or fem.. However, it is actually an adj., ἄγαμος, ον.
ἀλάβαστρον	The form ἀλάβαστρος, ου, ἡ also occurs.
ἄχρι	The form ἄχρις sometimes occurs before vowels.
δεσμός	The pl. is the neut. τὰ δέσμα.
ἑκατοντάρχης	The form ἑκατοντάρχος, ου, ὁ also occurs.
ἕνεκα	Other spellings include ἕνεκεν and εἵνεκεν.
ζῆλος	The form ζῆλος, ους, τό also occurs.

κρείττων	The form κρείσσων, ον also occurs.
μέχρι	The form μέχρις usually occurs before vowels.
μηδείς	The neut. form μηθέν also occurs.
ὀστέον	The contracted form ὀστοῦν, οῦ, τό also occurs.
οὐδείς	The form οὐθείς, with related inflections, also occurs.
οὕτως	The form οὕτω also occurs.
στάδιον	The masc. pl. σταδίους also occurs.
ὕσσωπος	The form ὕσσωπος, ου, τό is also possible.
φοῖνιξ	The form φοῖνιξ, ικος, ὁ is also possible.
χαλκολίβανον	The form χαλκολίβανος, ου, ὁ, ἡ is also possible.
χειμάρρους	The form χειμάρρος, ου, ὁ is also possible.

ὁ, ἡ, τό	(19870)	the
καί	(9153)	and, even, also, but, and then, and yet, namely, both
αὐτός, ή, ό	(5595)	self, even, same (adj.); he, she, it (prn.)
σύ, σού; ὑμεῖς, ὑμῶν	(2905)	you (sing.); you (pl.)
δέ	(2792)	but, and, rather, now, then, so
ἐν	(2752)	in, on, at, near, to, by, before, among, with, within, when
ἐγώ, ἐμοῦ; ἡμεῖς, ἡμῶν	(2666)	I; we
εἰμί	(2460)	I am, exist, occur, mean, live, stay, am present
λέγω	(2354)	I say, speak, tell, mean, ask, answer, declare, call, name
εἰς	(1768)	into, in, toward, to, among, near, on, for, against, as, at
οὐ	(1606)	not (gener. used w. ind. verbs and pos. answer questions)
οὗτος, αὕτη, τοῦτο	(1388)	this; this person or thing, he, she, it (subst.)
ὅς, ἥ, ὅ	(1365)	who, which, what, that, the one who, this one, he
θεός, οῦ, ὁ, ἡ	(1317)	God, god; goddess (fem.)
ὅτι	(1296)	that, so that, because, for, (introduces direct discourse)
πᾶς, πᾶσα, πᾶν	(1244)	every, each, any, full, all; everyone, everything (subst.)
μή	(1042)	not (used w. non-ind. verbs and neg. answer questions)
γάρ	(1041)	for, so, then
Ἰησοῦς, οῦ, ὁ	(917)	Jesus, Joshua
ἐκ	(914)	from, out of, away from, by, of, because of
ἐπί	(890)	on, over, when (gen.); on, at, in (dat.); on, to, for (acc.)
κύριος, ου, ὁ	(717)	lord, Lord, master, owner, sir
ἔχω	(708)	I have, hold, wear, keep, cause, consider; am (intrans.)
πρός	(700)	for (gen.); at (dat.); to, for, against, with, at, by (acc.)
γίνομαι	(669)	I become, am born or made, happen, come, go, am, exist
διά	(667)	through, during, with, at, by (gen.); because of (acc.)
ἵνα	(663)	in order that, that, so that
ἀπό	(646)	from, away from, because of, with, for, of, by
ἀλλά	(638)	but, yet, rather, nevertheless, at least
ἔρχομαι	(634)	I come, appear, go

ποιέω	(568)	I do, make
τίς, τί	(555)	who? which? what?; what sort of? (adj.); why? (adv.)
ἄνθρωπος, ου, ὁ	(550)	human being, man, adult male, husband
Χριστός, οῦ, ὁ	(529)	Christ, Anointed One, Messiah
τὶς, τὶ	(525)	someone, anyone, something, anything; some, any (adj.)
ὡς	(504)	as, like, because, when, while, in order that, that, about
εἰ	(503)	if, that, whether
οὖν	(499)	so, therefore, consequently, accordingly, then
κατά	(473)	down from, against (gen.); along, to, according to (acc.)
μετά	(469)	with, among, against (gen.); after, behind (acc.)

ὁράω	(454)	I see, notice, experience, perceive, see to; appear (pass.)
ἀκούω	(428)	I hear, listen to, learn, obey, understand
πολύς, πολλή, πολύ	(416)	much, many, large, great; often (adv.); many (subst.)
δίδωμι	(415)	I give, grant, give out, entrust, give back, put, give up
πατήρ, πατρός, ὁ	(413)	father, ancestor, forefather, Father
ἡμέρα, ας, ἡ	(389)	day (opp. night), daylight, day (24 hours), time
πνεῦμα, ατος, τό	(379)	wind, breath, spirit, inner life, spirit (being), Spirit
υἱός, οῦ, ὁ	(377)	son, male offspring, descendant, follower, Son
ἐάν	(351)	if, when
εἷς, μία, ἕν	(344)	one, a, single, someone, anyone

ἀδελφός, οῦ, ὁ	(343)	brother, fellow believer, fellow countryman, neighbor
ἤ	(343)	or, either, nor, what, than
περί	(333)	about, concerning, for (gen.); around, near (acc.)
λόγος, ου, ὁ	(330)	word, statement, message, subject, account, Word
ἑαυτοῦ, ῆς, οῦ	(319)	(of) himself, herself, itself
οἶδα	(318)	I know, am acquainted with, know how, understand
λαλέω	(296)	I speak, say, proclaim, whisper, sound
οὐρανός, οῦ, ὁ	(273)	heaven, sky; God (fig.)
ἐκεῖνος, η, ο	(265)	that; that person or thing, he, she, it (subst.)
μαθητής, οῦ, ὁ	(261)	disciple, learner, pupil, follower

λαμβάνω	(258)	I take, remove, seize, collect, receive, obtain, put on
γῆ, γῆς, ἡ	(250)	earth, soil, ground, land, region, humankind
μέγας, μεγάλη, μέγα	(243)	large, great, loud, important, strong, high
πίστις, εως, ἡ	(243)	faith, trust, faithfulness, belief, conviction, doctrine
πιστεύω	(241)	I believe (in), have faith (in), trust, entrust
οὐδείς, οὐδεμία, οὐδέν	(234)	no; no one, nothing (subst.); in no way (neut.acc.)
ἅγιος, α, ον	(233)	dedicated to God, holy, pure; saints, sanctuary (subst.)
ἀποκρίνομαι	(231)	I answer, reply, continue, begin
ὄνομα, ατος, τό	(231)	name, title, category, person, reputation, Name
γινώσκω	(222)	I know, learn, understand, perceive, acknowledge

ὑπό	(220)	by, at the hands of (gen.); under, below (acc.)
ἐξέρχομαι	(218)	I go out or away, come out, disembark, leave
ἀνήρ, ἀνδρός, ὁ	(216)	man (male), husband, grown man, someone
γυνή, αικός, ἡ	(215)	woman, wife, bride
τέ	(215)	and, and so, so
δύναμαι	(210)	I can, am able
θέλω	(208)	I wish, desire, want, will, like, enjoy, maintain
οὕτως	(208)	in this manner, thus, so, as follows, just; such (adj.)
ἰδού	(200)	look, see, behold, consider, here is (imper. of εἶδον)
Ἰουδαῖος, α, ον	(195)	Jewish; a Jew, Jewess (subst.)

εἰσέρχομαι	(194)	I come in or into, go in or into, enter, share in, fall into
νόμος, ου, ὁ	(194)	law, rule, principle, norm, (Jewish) religion
παρά	(194)	from (gen); beside, with (dat.); at, on, more than (acc.)
γράφω	(191)	I write, record, compose
κόσμος, ου, ὁ	(186)	world, universe, earth, humankind, totality, adornment
καθώς	(182)	as, just as, even as, so far as, since, when
μέν	(179)	on the one hand, to be sure, indeed
χείρ, χειρός, ἡ	(177)	hand, arm, finger, power, activity
εὑρίσκω	(176)	I find, discover; obtain (mid.)
ἄγγελος, ου, ὁ	(175)	messenger, angel
ὄχλος, ου, ὁ	(175)	crowd, throng, (common) people, multitude
ἁμαρτία, ας, ἡ	(173)	sin, sinfulness
ἔργον, ου, τό	(169)	work, deed, action, manifestation, occupation, thing
ἄν	(167)	conditional part., part. of contingency (untrans.)
δόξα, ης, ἡ	(166)	brightness, splendor, glory, majesty, reflection, fame
βασιλεία, ας, ἡ	(162)	kingdom, kingship, royal rule, royal power, reign
ἔθνος, ους, τό	(162)	nation, people; Gentiles, heathen (pl.)
πόλις, εως, ἡ	(162)	city, town, inhabitants (of a city)
τότε	(160)	then, thereafter
ἐσθίω	(158)	I eat, consume
Παῦλος, ου, ὁ	(158)	Paul
καρδία, ας, ἡ	(156)	heart, inner self, mind, interior
Πέτρος, ου, ὁ	(156)	Peter
ἄλλος, η, ο	(155)	other, another, different, more
πρῶτος, η, ον	(155)	first, earlier, foremost; first, before (neut. as adv.)
χάρις, ιτος, ἡ	(155)	grace, favor, goodwill, gift, thanks, kindness
ἵστημι	(154)	I set, make stand; stand, stop, stand firm (intrans.)
ὅστις, ἥτις, ὅ τι	(153)	whoever, everyone who, who
πορεύομαι	(153)	I go, proceed, travel, journey, live, die (mid.-pass. in NT)
ὑπέρ	(150)	for, in behalf of, about (gen.); above, beyond, than (acc.)
καλέω	(148)	I call, address as, name, invite, summon, call in
νῦν	(147)	now, as things now stand; the present, now (subst.)
σάρξ, σαρκός, ἡ	(147)	flesh, body, person, human or mortal nature, earthly life
ἕως	(146)	until, while (conj.); until, as far as (impr. prep.)
ἐγείρω	(144)	I raise up, restore, wake; rise, awaken, appear (pass.)
προφήτης, ου, ὁ	(144)	prophet; prophets (pl. as a division of scripture)
ἀγαπάω	(143)	I love, cherish, show love, long for
ἀφίημι	(143)	I let go, give up, divorce, cancel, forgive, leave, tolerate
οὐδέ	(143)	and not, neither, nor, not even
λαός, οῦ, ὁ	(142)	people, crowd, populace
σῶμα, ατος, τό	(142)	body, corpse, reality; slaves (pl.)
πάλιν	(141)	back, again, once more, furthermore, on the other hand
ζάω	(140)	I live, become alive again, recover, remain alive
φωνή, ῆς, ἡ	(139)	sound, noise, voice, call, cry, language
δύο	(135)	two
ζωή, ῆς, ἡ	(135)	life
Ἰωάννης, ου, ὁ	(135)	John
βλέπω	(133)	I see, look at, am able to see, take care, watch, perceive
ἀποστέλλω	(132)	I send, send out, send away
ἀμήν	(129)	amen, so let it be, truly

νεκρός, ά, όν	(128)	dead, useless; dead person (subst.)
σύν	(128)	with, together with, accompany, besides
δοῦλος, ου, ὁ	(124)	slave, minister
ὅταν	(123)	at the time that, whenever, when
αἰών, ῶνος, ὁ	(122)	very long time, eternity, age, world
ἀρχιερεύς, έως, ὁ	(122)	high priest; chief priests, ruling priests (pl.)
βάλλω	(122)	I throw, cast, pour, let fall, put, bring, sweep down
θάνατος, ου, ὁ	(120)	death
δύναμις, εως, ἡ	(119)	power, ability, miracle, army, power (supernatural)
παραδίδωμι	(119)	I entrust, give up, hand over (into custody), hand down
μένω	(118)	I remain, stay, abide, live, dwell, last; wait for (trans.)
ἀπέρχομαι	(117)	I go away, depart, pass away, go, go after
ζητέω	(117)	I seek, look for, investigate, try to obtain, wish, request
ἀγάπη, ης, ἡ	(116)	love, love feast
βασιλεύς, έως, ὁ	(115)	king
ἐκκλησία, ας, ἡ	(114)	assembly, church, congregation
ἴδιος, α, ον	(114)	one's own; home, property (subst.); individually (adv.)
κρίνω	(114)	I judge, prefer, consider, decide, condemn
μόνος, η, ον	(114)	only, alone, deserted, isolated; only, alone (neut as adv.)
οἶκος, ου, ὁ	(114)	house, home, household, family, nation, property, temple
ἀποθνῄσκω	(111)	I die, decay, face death, am mortal
ὅσος, η, ον	(110)	as or how great, as or how much, as or how far
ἀλήθεια, ας, ἡ	(109)	truth, truthfulness, reality
μέλλω	(109)	I am about, intend, must, am going; future (partic.)
ὅλος, η, ον	(109)	whole, entire, complete, altogether
παρακαλέω	(109)	I call, invite, urge, implore, request, comfort, cheer up
ἀνίστημι	(108)	I raise, erect, bring to life, rise, stand up, arise, appear
σῴζω	(106)	I save, rescue, deliver, preserve, heal
ὥρα, ας, ἡ	(106)	hour, occasion, short time period, moment, time
ἐκεῖ	(105)	there, in that place, to that place
ὅτε	(103)	when, while, as long as
πῶς	(103)	how? in what way? in what sense? how is it possible?
ψυχή, ῆς, ἡ	(103)	soul, self, life, person, living being, life principle
ἀγαθός, ή, όν	(102)	good, useful, fit; good, possessions, good things (subst.)
ἐξουσία, ας, ἡ	(102)	authority, right, ability, power, official, jurisdiction
αἴρω	(101)	I take, take up, take away, remove, raise; arise (pass.)
δεῖ	(101)	it is necessary, one must, one should (impers.)
ὁδός, οῦ, ἡ	(101)	way, road, journey, way of life, conduct, Way, teaching
ἀλλήλων	(100)	each other, one another, mutually
καλός, ή, όν	(100)	beautiful, good, useful, fine, noble, blameless, better
ὀφθαλμός, οῦ, ὁ	(100)	eye, sight
τίθημι	(100)	I put, place, lay, serve, remove, appoint, make
τέκνον, ου, τό	(99)	child, son; descendants, posterity (pl.)
ἕτερος, α, ον	(98)	other, another, different; next day, neighbor (subst.)
Φαρισαῖος, ου, ὁ	(98)	Pharisee
αἷμα, ατος, τό	(97)	blood, death, murder
ἄρτος, ου, ὁ	(97)	bread, loaf, food
γεννάω	(97)	I beget, become the father of, bear, give birth, produce
διδάσκω	(97)	I teach
περιπατέω	(95)	I go (about), walk (around), live, conduct myself

φοβέω	(95)	I am afraid, fear, reverence, respect (pass. in NT)
ἐνώπιον	(94)	before, in the presence of, in the opinion of (impr. prep.)
τόπος, ου, ὁ	(94)	place, position, location, possibility; regions (pl.)
ἔτι	(93)	still, yet, more
οἰκία, ας, ἡ	(93)	house, home, dwelling, household, family
πούς, ποδός, ὁ	(93)	foot
δικαιοσύνη, ης, ἡ	(92)	righteousness, uprightness, justice
εἰρήνη, ης, ἡ	(92)	peace, harmony, order, health
θάλασσα, ης, ἡ	(91)	sea, lake
κάθημαι	(91)	I sit, sit down, stay, live, reside
ἀκολουθέω	(90)	I follow, accompany, am a disciple
ἀπόλλυμι	(90)	I ruin, destroy, lose; am destroyed, die, am lost (mid.)
μηδείς, μηδεμία, μηδέν	(90)	no; no one, nobody, nothing (subst.); in no way (adv.)
πίπτω	(90)	I fall, fall down, fall to pieces, collapse, perish
ἑπτά	(88)	seven
οὔτε	(87)	and not, neither, nor, no
ἄρχω	(86)	I rule; begin (mid.)
πληρόω	(86)	I fill, complete, finish, fulfill; pass, elapse (pass.)
προσέρχομαι	(86)	I come or go to, approach, agree with
καιρός, οῦ, ὁ	(85)	time, point or period of time, season, age, right time
προσεύχομαι	(85)	I pray
κἀγώ	(84)	and I, but I, I also, I myself, I in turn (= καὶ ἐγώ)
μήτηρ, τρός, ἡ	(83)	mother
ὥστε	(83)	for this reason, therefore, so, so that, in order that
ἀναβαίνω	(82)	I go up, ascend, embark, come up, grow up
ἕκαστος, η, ον	(82)	each, every; each one, every one (subst.)
ὅπου	(82)	where, in so far as, since
ἐκβάλλω	(81)	I drive out, send out, lead out, take out
καταβαίνω	(81)	I come down, go down, climb down, fall down
μᾶλλον	(81)	more, more than ever, rather, more surely
ἀπόστολος, ου, ὁ	(80)	apostle, envoy, messenger
Μωϋσῆς, έως, ὁ	(80)	Moses
δίκαιος, α, ον	(79)	upright, just, righteous, honest, good, innocent, right
πέμπω	(79)	I send, instruct, commission, appoint
ὑπάγω	(79)	I go away, go home, go
πονηρός, ά, όν	(78)	evil, bad, wicked, sick; evil person, evil one, evil (subst.)
στόμα, ατος, τό	(78)	mouth, speech, eloquence, edge (of a sword)
ἀνοίγω	(77)	I open
βαπτίζω	(77)	I dip, immerse, baptize
Ἰερουσαλήμ, ἡ	(77)	Jerusalem
σημεῖον, ου, τό	(77)	sign, distinguishing mark, miracle, wonder, portent
ἐμός, ή, όν	(76)	my, mine; my property (subst.)
εὐαγγέλιον, ου, τό	(76)	good news, gospel
μαρτυρέω	(76)	I bear witness, testify, am a witness, confirm, approve
πρόσωπον, ου, τό	(76)	face, countenance, presence, appearance, surface, person
ὕδωρ, ατος, τό	(76)	water
δώδεκα	(75)	twelve
κεφαλή, ῆς, ἡ	(75)	head, extremity, point
Σίμων, ωνος, ὁ	(75)	Simon
ἀποκτείνω	(74)	I kill, put to death

χαίρω	(74)	I rejoice, am glad; hail, greetings (greeting form.)
'Αβραάμ, ὁ	(73)	Abraham
πίνω	(73)	I drink
φῶς, φωτός, τό	(73)	light, fire
αἰώνιος, α, ον	(71)	eternal
ἱερόν, οῦ, τό	(71)	temple, sanctuary
πῦρ, ός, τό	(71)	fire
αἰτέω	(70)	I ask, ask for, demand
τηρέω	(70)	I keep, hold, guard, keep watch, observe, obey
'Ισραήλ, ὁ	(68)	Israel
πλοῖον, ου, τό	(68)	ship, boat
ῥῆμα, ατος, τό	(68)	word, saying, expression, thing, object, matter
σάββατον, ου, τό	(68)	Sabbath (seventh day of the week), week
τρεῖς, τρία	(68)	three
ἄγω	(67)	I lead, bring, arrest, guide, spend time, celebrate, go
ἐντολή, ῆς, ἡ	(67)	commandment, command, order, law
πιστός, ή, όν	(67)	faithful, reliable, believing, trusting; believer (subst.)
ἀπολύω	(66)	I set free, release, divorce, dismiss; go away (mid.)
καρπός, οῦ, ὁ	(66)	fruit, crop, result, advantage
πρεσβύτερος, α, ον	(66)	older; older person, ancestor, elder, presbyter (subst.)
φέρω	(66)	I bear, carry, endure, produce, drive, bring, utter, lead
φημί	(66)	I say, affirm, mean
εἴτε	(65)	if, whether
γραμματεύς, έως, ὁ	(63)	secretary, clerk, expert in the law, scribe, scholar
δαιμόνιον, ου, τό	(63)	demon, evil spirit, deity
ἔξω	(63)	outside, outer, out; outside, out of (impr. prep.)
ἐρωτάω	(63)	I ask, ask a question, request
ὄρος, ους, τό	(63)	mountain, hill, mount
δοκέω	(62)	I think, suppose, seem, have a reputation
θέλημα, ατος, τό	(62)	will, wish, desire
θρόνος, ου, ὁ	(62)	throne
'Ιεροσόλυμα, τά, ἡ	(62)	Jerusalem
ἀγαπητός, ή, όν	(61)	beloved, dear
Γαλιλαία, ας, ἡ	(61)	Galilee
δοξάζω	(61)	I praise, honor, glorify
ἤδη	(61)	now, already
κηρύσσω	(61)	I proclaim, announce, preach
νύξ, νυκτός, ἡ	(61)	night
ὧδε	(61)	here, hither, to this place, in this case
ἱμάτιον, ου, τό	(60)	garment, cloak, coat, robe; clothing (pl.)
προσκυνέω	(60)	I worship, prostrate myself before, do reverence to
ὑπάρχω	(60)	I am, exist, am present, am at one's disposal
ἀσπάζομαι	(59)	I greet, welcome, take leave, cherish, hail, pay respects
Δαυίδ, ὁ	(59)	David
διδάσκαλος, ου, ὁ	(59)	teacher
λίθος, ου, ὁ	(59)	stone
συνάγω	(59)	I gather, bring together, invite as a guest
χαρά, ᾶς, ἡ	(59)	joy, cause for joy, joyfulness, gladness
θεωρέω	(58)	I look at, perceive, see, notice, observe, experience
μέσος, η, ον	(58)	middle; the middle (subst.); in the middle of (impr. prep.)

τοιοῦτος, αύτη, οῦτον	(57)	of such a kind, such; such a person or thing (subst.)
δέχομαι	(56)	I take, receive, welcome, grasp, tolerate, accept
ἐπερωτάω	(56)	I ask, ask for
κράζω	(56)	I cry out, call out
μηδέ	(56)	and not, but not, nor, not even
συναγωγή, ῆς, ἡ	(56)	synagogue, assembly, meeting (for worship)
τρίτος, η, ον	(56)	third; third part, a third (neut. subst.); third time (adv.)
ἀρχή, ῆς, ἡ	(55)	beginning, origin, first cause, ruler, authority, domain
λοιπός, ή, όν	(55)	remaining, other, rest; finally, henceforth (neut. as adv.)
Πιλᾶτος, ου, ὁ	(55)	Pilate
δεξιός, ά, όν	(54)	right; right hand, right side (subst.)
εὐαγγελίζω	(54)	I bring or announce good news, proclaim, preach
οὐχί	(54)	not, no (used with pos. answer questions)
χρόνος, ου, ὁ	(54)	time, period of time, occasion, delay
διό	(53)	therefore, for this reason
ἐλπίς, ίδος, ἡ	(53)	hope, expectation, something hoped for
ὅπως	(53)	how, in what way, that, in order that
ἐπαγγελία, ας, ἡ	(52)	promise, pledge, offer, what is promised
ἔσχατος, η, ον	(52)	last, least; end (subst.); finally (neut. acc.)
παιδίον, ου, τό	(52)	child, infant
πείθω	(52)	I convince, persuade, satisfy; trust (perf.); obey (pass.)
σπείρω	(52)	I sow
εὐθύς, εῖα, ύ	(51)	straight, right, upright
σοφία, ας, ἡ	(51)	wisdom, insight, intelligence
γλῶσσα, ης, ἡ	(50)	tongue, language
γραφή, ῆς, ἡ	(50)	writing, scripture; scriptures (pl.)
κακός, ή, όν	(50)	bad, evil, dangerous; evil, misfortune, harm (subst.)
μακάριος, α, ον	(50)	blessed, happy, fortunate
παραβολή, ῆς, ἡ	(50)	parable, comparison, type, symbol, figure
τυφλός, ή, όν	(50)	blind; blind person, the blind (subst.)
ἄρα	(49)	so, then, consequently, perhaps
ἄχρι	(49)	until, to, as far as (impr. prep.); until (conj.)
ἔτος, ους, τό	(49)	year
παραλαμβάνω	(49)	I take, take along, receive, accept
φανερόω	(49)	I reveal, make known, show; am revealed, appear (pass.)
χρεία, ας, ἡ	(49)	need, necessity, lack, want, office, duty, service
ἀποδίδωμι	(48)	I give away, give up, pay, return, reward; sell (mid.)
ἔμπροσθεν	(48)	in front, ahead; in front of, before (impr. prep.)
ἔρημος, ον	(48)	abandoned, desolate; desert, wilderness (fem. subst.)
ποῦ	(48)	where(?) at or to what place (?)
ἁμαρτωλός, όν	(47)	sinful; sinner (subst.)
κρατέω	(47)	I grasp, attain, hold, hold fast or back, arrest, retain
κρίσις, εως, ἡ	(47)	judging, judgment, condemnation, punishment, court
οὐκέτι	(47)	no longer, no more, then not
πρό	(47)	before, in front of, at, above
προσφέρω	(47)	I bring to, offer, present; deal with (pass.)
φόβος, ου, ὁ	(47)	cause of fear, fear, reverence, respect
φυλακή, ῆς, ἡ	(47)	watch, guard, prison, haunt, watch (period of the night)
θηρίον, ου, τό	(46)	animal, beast, snake; monster (fig.)
καθίζω	(46)	I cause to sit down, appoint; stay, live (intrans.)

μικρός, ά, όν	(46)	small, humble, short; little, child, little while (subst.)
οὐαί	(46)	woe, alas; woe (subst.); woe, disaster (fem. noun)
σταυρόω	(46)	I crucify
σωτηρία, ας, ἡ	(46)	salvation, deliverance, preservation
ἀπαγγέλλω	(45)	I report, announce, tell, proclaim
διώκω	(45)	I hasten, persecute, drive away, pursue, seek after
θλῖψις, εως, ἡ	(45)	oppression, affliction, tribulation, trouble
ναός, οῦ, ὁ	(45)	temple, sanctuary, shrine
ὅμοιος, α, ον	(45)	of the same nature, like, similar
ἐπιγινώσκω	(44)	I know, understand, recognize, learn, notice, know well
Ἰούδας, α, ὁ	(44)	Judah, Judas
κατοικέω	(44)	I live, dwell, reside; inhabit (trans.)
ἁμαρτάνω	(43)	I do wrong, sin
γενεά, ᾶς, ἡ	(43)	family, descent, clan, race, generation, age
δεύτερος, α, ον	(43)	second, secondly; second time (subst.)
δέω	(43)	I bind, tie
διέρχομαι	(43)	I go through, cross over, come, go about, spread
Ἡρῴδης, ου, ὁ	(43)	Herod
θαυμάζω	(43)	I wonder, marvel, am amazed; admire (trans.)
θεραπεύω	(43)	I serve, am a servant, heal, restore
Ἰουδαία, ας, ἡ	(43)	Judea
σεαυτοῦ, ῆς	(43)	(of) yourself
σπέρμα, ατος, τό	(43)	seed, survivors, descendants, children, nature
φωνέω	(43)	I call, call or cry out, crow, address, summon, invite
ἀνάστασις, εως, ἡ	(42)	rise, resurrection
ἐγγίζω	(42)	I approach, come near
εὐλογέω	(42)	I speak well of, praise, bless, consecrate
Ἰάκωβος, ου, ὁ	(42)	James
καινός, ή, όν	(42)	new, unused, unknown
λύω	(42)	I loose, untie, set free, destroy, abolish, allow
μέρος, ους, τό	(42)	part, piece, party, matter, share; district, side (pl.)
πάσχω	(42)	I suffer, die, endure, experience
ἄξιος, α, ον	(41)	comparable, worthy, proper, fit, deserving
ἐργάζομαι	(41)	I work, do, perform, bring about
πάντοτε	(41)	always, at all times
παρίστημι	(41)	I place beside, present, render, approach, stand by
σήμερον	(41)	today; today (subst.)
τέσσαρες, α	(41)	four
τιμή, ῆς, ἡ	(41)	price, value, honor, respect, place of honor, honorarium
χωρίς	(41)	separately; without, apart from, besides (impr. prep.)
ἑτοιμάζω	(40)	I prepare, put or keep in readiness
κλαίω	(40)	I weep, cry; week for (trans.)
λογίζομαι	(40)	I calculate, count, credit, evaluate, consider, think
μισέω	(40)	I hate, detest, abhor
μνημεῖον, ου, τό	(40)	monument, grave, tomb
οἰκοδομέω	(40)	I build, erect, restore, rebuild, build up, edify, benefit
ὀλίγος, η, ον	(40)	small, little, short; small amount (subst.); few (pl.)
τέλος, ους, τό	(40)	end, goal, conclusion, outcome, tax
ἅπτω	(39)	I kindle; touch, take hold, injure (mid.)
δικαιόω	(39)	I justify, vindicate, treat as just, acquit, make free

ἐπιτίθημι	(39)	I lay or put upon, inflict upon, add; give, attack (mid.)
θύρα, ας, ἡ	(39)	door, gate, entrance
ἱκανός, ή, όν	(39)	sufficient, large, many, able, fit; bond (subst.)
περισσεύω	(39)	I am left over, exceed, overflow, abound, cause to abound
πλανάω	(39)	I lead astray, mislead, deceive; go astray, wander (pass.)
πράσσω	(39)	I do, accomplish, practice, collect; act, do, am (intrans.)
πρόβατον, ου, τό	(39)	sheep
ἐπιθυμία, ας, ἡ	(38)	desire, longing, craving, lust
εὐχαριστέω	(38)	I am thankful, give thanks, offer a prayer of thanks
πειράζω	(38)	I try, attempt, test, tempt
πέντε	(38)	five
ὑποτάσσω	(38)	I subject, subordinate; am or become subject (pass.)
ἄρχων, οντος, ὁ	(37)	ruler, lord, prince, authority, official, judge
βούλομαι	(37)	I wish, want, desire
διάβολος, ον	(37)	slanderous; the devil (subst.)
διακονέω	(37)	I wait at table, serve, care for, help, serve as deacon
ἐκεῖθεν	(37)	from there
ἐμαυτοῦ, ῆς	(37)	(of) myself
καλῶς	(37)	well, beautifully, fitly, commendably, rightly
καυχάομαι	(37)	I boast, glory, pride myself; boast about (trans.)
μαρτυρία, ας, ἡ	(37)	testimony, witness, reputation
παραγίνομαι	(37)	I come, arrive, appear, stand by, come to the aid of
ἀγρός, οῦ, ὁ	(36)	field, country; farms (pl.)
ἄρτι	(36)	now, just, at once, immediately
ἐπιστρέφω	(36)	I turn, turn around or back, return
εὐθέως	(36)	immediately, at once
ὀργή, ῆς, ἡ	(36)	anger, indignation, wrath, punishment, judgment
οὖς, ὠτός, τό	(36)	ear, hearing
περιτομή, ῆς, ἡ	(36)	circumcision, those who are circumcised, Jews
προσευχή, ῆς, ἡ	(36)	prayer, place of prayer
Σατανᾶς, ᾶ, ὁ	(36)	Satan, the Adversary
Φίλιππος, ου, ὁ	(36)	Philip
ὥσπερ	(36)	as, just as, even as
Ἰωσήφ, ὁ	(35)	Joseph
μάρτυς, υρος, ὁ	(35)	witness, martyr
ὀπίσω	(35)	behind, back; behind, after (impr. prep.)
ὀφείλω	(35)	I owe, am indebted, ought, am obligated, commit a sin
ὑποστρέφω	(35)	I turn back, return
ἅπας, ασα, αν	(34)	all, whole; everybody, everything (pl.)
βιβλίον, ου, τό	(34)	book, scroll, document, record
βλασφημέω	(34)	I blaspheme, revile, defame
διακονία, ας, ἡ	(34)	service, office, ministry, aid, office of deacon
μέλος, ους, τό	(34)	member, part, limb
μετανοέω	(34)	I repent, change my mind, feel remorse, am converted
μήτε	(34)	and not, nor
οἶνος, ου, ὁ	(34)	wine, vineyard
πτωχός, ή, όν	(34)	poor, miserable, impotent; poor person (subst.)
ἀρνέομαι	(33)	I refuse, deny, repudiate, disown, reject
ἀσθενέω	(33)	I am weak, powerless, sick, in need
δείκνυμι	(33)	I point out, show, explain, prove

διαθήκη, ης, ἡ	(33)	last will and testament, covenant, decree
ἐκπορεύομαι	(33)	I go out, come out
ναί	(33)	yes, indeed, of course, certainly
ποῖος, α, ον	(33)	of what kind? which? what?
ἀκάθαρτος, ον	(32)	impure, unclean; vicious
ἀναγινώσκω	(32)	I read, read aloud
δυνατός, ή, όν	(32)	powerful, strong, mighty, able
ἐχθρός, ά, όν	(32)	hostile, hated, hating; enemy (subst.)
ἥλιος, ου, ὁ	(32)	sun
παραγγέλλω	(32)	I give orders, command, instruct, direct
ὑπομονή, ῆς, ἡ	(32)	patience, endurance, perseverance
ἄνεμος, ου, ὁ	(31)	wind
ἐγγύς	(31)	near, close to; near, close to (impr. prep.)
ἐλπίζω	(31)	I hope, expect
ἔξεστι	(31)	it is permitted, it is possible, it is proper (impers.)
ἱερεύς, έως, ὁ	(31)	priest
καθαρίζω	(31)	I make or declare clean, cleanse, purity
παρρησία, ας, ἡ	(31)	outspokenness, openness, confidence, boldness
πλῆθος, ους, τό	(31)	number, large amount, crowd, people, community
πλήν	(31)	but, yet, only, however (conj.); except (impr. prep.)
ποτήριον, ου, τό	(31)	cup, drinking vessel
σκότος, ους, τό	(31)	darkness, gloom, instrument of darkness
φαίνω	(31)	I shine; shine, appear, become visible, seem (mid.-pass.)
φυλάσσω	(31)	I watch, guard, protect, keep, observe; avoid, keep (mid.)
φυλή, ῆς, ἡ	(31)	tribe, nation, people
ἀγοράζω	(30)	I buy, purchase
ἀρνίον, ου, τό	(30)	lamb, sheep
διδαχή, ῆς, ἡ	(30)	teaching (both act and content), instruction
ἐπικαλέω	(30)	I call, name; call upon, appeal (mid.)
ὁμοίως	(30)	likewise, so, similarly, in the same way
συνείδησις, εως, ἡ	(30)	conscience, consciousness
συνέρχομαι	(30)	I come together, come or go with, have sexual relations
γνῶσις, εως, ἡ	(29)	knowledge, Gnosis
διάκονος, ου, ὁ, ἡ	(29)	servant, helper, deacon (masc.); helper, deaconess (fem.)
ἐλεέω	(29)	I have mercy, am merciful; find mercy (pass.)
ἐπιτιμάω	(29)	I rebuke, reprove, warn, censure, punish
Ἠλίας, ου, ὁ	(29)	Elijah
ἴδε	(29)	look, see, behold, here is, here (imper. of εἶδον)'
ἰσχυρός, ά, όν	(29)	strong, mighty, powerful, loud, severe, weighty
Καῖσαρ, αρος, ὁ	(29)	Caesar, emperor
μάχαιρα, ης, ἡ	(29)	sword, saber
μισθός, οῦ, ὁ	(29)	pay, wages, reward, punishment
παράκλησις, εως, ἡ	(29)	encouragement, appeal, comfort, consolation
παρέρχομαι	(29)	I go or pass by, pass, pass away, neglect, disobey, come
πάσχα, τό	(29)	Passover, Passover meal, Passover lamb
πόθεν	(29)	from where? from which? whence?
ποτέ	(29)	at some time, once, formerly, ever
προσκαλέω	(29)	I summon, call to myself, invite, call (mid. in NT)
σκανδαλίζω	(29)	I cause to fall or sin, anger, shock; take offense (pass.)
φεύγω	(29)	I flee, escape, avoid, disappear

φίλος, η, ον	(29)	beloved, loving, friendly; friend (subst.)
ἁγιάζω	(28)	I make holy, consecrate, sanctify, dedicate, reverence
ἀδικέω	(28)	I do wrong, am in the wrong, treat unjustly, injure
ἀληθινός, ή, όs	(28)	true, dependable, real, genuine
Βαρναβᾶς, ᾶ, ὁ	(28)	Barnabas
γαμέω	(28)	I marry
ἡγέομαι	(28)	I lead, guide, rule, think, consider
θυγάτηρ, τρός, ἡ	(28)	daughter, girl, female descendant, female inhabitant
θυσία, ας, ἡ	(28)	act of offering, sacrifice, offering
ἰσχύω	(28)	I am strong, powerful, healthy, able, valid
μυστήριον, ου, τό	(28)	secret, mystery
νικάω	(28)	I conquer, prevail, win (a verdict), overcome
πλούσιος, α, ον	(28)	rich, wealthy
προφητεύω	(28)	I prophesy, proclaim a divine message
τελέω	(28)	I finish, complete, accomplish, fulfill, keep, pay
χώρα, ας, ἡ	(28)	country, land, region, inhabitants, countryside, field
βαστάζω	(27)	I take up, carry, bear, endure, remove, steal
ἐκχέω	(27)	I pour out, shed, spill, scatter; abandon myself (pass.)
ἔλεος, ους, τό	(27)	mercy, compassion, pity
ἐνδύω	(27)	I dress, clothe; put on, wear (mid.)
Ἰακώβ, ὁ	(27)	Jacob
καθαρός, ά, όν	(27)	clean, pure, ritually pure, guiltless
καταργέω	(27)	I make ineffective, nullify, abolish; cease (pass.)
κρίμα, ατος, τό	(27)	judgment, decision, lawsuit, verdict, condemnation
κώμη, ης, ἡ	(27)	village, small town, inhabitants of a village
Μαρία, ας, ἡ	(27)	Mary
Μαριάμ, ἡ	(27)	Mary
πόσος, η, ον	(27)	how great(?) how much (?) how many (?)
σός, σή, σόν	(27)	your, yours (sing.)
σταυρός, οῦ, ὁ	(27)	cross
ἀδελφή, ῆς, ἡ	(26)	sister, fellow believer
ἀληθής, ές	(26)	true, righteous, honest, truthful, real, genuine
ἀποκαλύπτω	(26)	I uncover, reveal, disclose
ἀσθενής, ές	(26)	weak, powerless, sick, ill, feeble
ἕνεκα	(26)	because of, on account of, for the sake of (impr. prep.)
ἐπεί	(26)	because, since, for, for otherwise
ἥκω	(26)	I have come, am present, come
ἰάομαι	(26)	I heal, cure, restore
λυπέω	(26)	I grieve, pain, offend; become sad, grieve (pass.)
ὀμνύω	(26)	I swear, take an oath
ὁμολογέω	(26)	I confess, promise, admit, declare, acknowledge, praise
οὔπω	(26)	not yet
πνευματικός, ή, όν	(26)	pertaining to the spirit, spiritual
στρατιώτης, ου, ὁ	(26)	soldier
συνίημι	(26)	I understand, comprehend
φρονέω	(26)	I think, ponder, set my mind on, have thoughts
χήρα, ας, ἡ	(26)	widow
ἀδικία, ας, ἡ	(25)	wrongdoing, unrighteousness, wickedness, injustice
Αἴγυπτος, ου, ἡ	(25)	Egypt
ἀναβλέπω	(25)	I look up, see again, receive sight

γέ	(25)	indeed, even, at least
γνωρίζω	(25)	I make known, reveal, know
δέκα	(25)	ten
δένδρον, ου, τό	(25)	tree
δουλεύω	(25)	I am a slave, serve, obey
Ἕλλην, ηνος, ὁ	(25)	a Greek, Gentile, pagan, heathen
ἑορτή, ῆς, ἡ	(25)	festival
κελεύω	(25)	I command, order, urge
λευκός, ή, όν	(25)	white, bright, shining
μανθάνω	(25)	I learn, find out

μήποτε	(25)	never, lest, that . . . not, whether perhaps, perhaps
νεφέλη, ης, ἡ	(25)	cloud
πορνεία, ας, ἡ	(25)	unlawful sexual intercourse, (sexual) immorality
φιλέω	(25)	I love, like, kiss
ἀκοή, ῆς, ἡ	(24)	hearing, listening, ear, fame, report, account
ἀναιρέω	(24)	I take away, do away with, destroy, kill; take up (mid.)
ἀσθένεια, ας, ἡ	(24)	weakness, sickness, disease, timidity
ἀστήρ, έρος, ὁ	(24)	star
ἐπιστολή, ῆς, ἡ	(24)	letter, epistle
καταλείπω	(24)	I leave, leave behind, abandon, neglect; remain (pass.)

κεῖμαι	(24)	I lie, recline, stand, am laid, am appointed, exist, am
νοῦς, νοός ὁ	(24)	mind, understanding, intellect, attitude, thought, opinion
οὗ	(24)	where, to which
παῖς, παιδός, ὁ, ἡ	(24)	boy, son, child, servant, slave; girl, child (fem.)
πάρειμι	(24)	I am present or here, have come
παρουσία, ας, ἡ	(24)	presence, coming, advent, arrival
πίμπλημι	(24)	I fill, fulfill; am fulfilled, come to an end (pass.)
προσέχω	(24)	I pay attention to, care for, devote myself to, officiate
σωτήρ, ῆρος, ὁ	(24)	Savior, deliverer, preserver, rescuer
Τιμόθεος, ου, ὁ	(24)	Timothy

ἀμπελών, ῶνος, ὁ	(23)	vineyard
ἀνάγω	(23)	I lead up, bring up, restore; put out to sea (mid. or pass.)
ἄπιστος, ον	(23)	unbelievable, faithless, unbelieving
αὐξάνω	(23)	I grow, increase
διότι	(23)	because, therefore, for, that
εἰκών, όνος, ἡ	(23)	image, likeness, form, appearance
ἐλεύθερος, α, ον	(23)	free, independent; free person (subst.)
ζῷον, ου, τό	(23)	living thing or being, animal
θυσιαστήριον, ου, τό	(23)	altar
κατηγορέω	(23)	I accuse, bring charges against

κοπιάω	(23)	I become tired or weary, work hard, labor, struggle
κωλύω	(23)	I hinder, prevent, forbid, restrain, withhold
μιμνήσκομαι	(23)	I remember, keep in mind, think of
νέος, α, ον	(23)	new, fresh, young
πεινάω	(23)	I hunger, am hungry
πέραν	(23)	on the other side; other side (subst.); across (impr. prep.)
περιβάλλω	(23)	I put on, clothe, dress
σκεῦος, ους, τό	(23)	object, vessel, jar, instrument, body, wife; property (pl.)
τελειόω	(23)	I complete, accomplish, make perfect, fulfill, initiate
χαρίζομαι	(23)	I give freely, grant, cancel, remit, forgive, pardon

χιλιάς, αδος, ἡ	(23)	(group of) a thousand
ἀγνοέω	(22)	I do not know, am ignorant, do not understand
ἀντί	(22)	instead of, for, in behalf of
γρηγορέω	(22)	I am awake, keep awake, am alert, am watchful
δέομαι	(22)	I ask, beg, pray
δοκιμάζω	(22)	I put to the test, examine, prove by testing, approve
ἐκλέγομαι	(22)	I choose, select
ἐκλεκτός, ἡ, όν	(22)	chosen, select, choice, excellent
Ἡσαΐας, ου, ὁ	(22)	Isaiah
θεάομαι	(22)	I see, look at, behold, visit
καθεύδω	(22)	I sleep
κἀκεῖνος, η, ο	(22)	and that one or he, that one or he also (= καὶ ἐκεῖνος)
κατεργάζομαι	(22)	I do, achieve, accomplish, produce, prepare, conquer
κοιλία, ας, ἡ	(22)	body cavity, belly, stomach, womb, uterus, heart
Μακεδονία, ας, ἡ	(22)	Macedonia
μετάνοια, ας, ἡ	(22)	repentance, change of mind, remorse, conversion
μηκέτι	(22)	no longer, not from now on
πληγή, ῆς, ἡ	(22)	blow, stroke, plague, wound, bruise
πλοῦτος, ου, ὁ, τό	(22)	wealth, riches, abundance
πωλέω	(22)	I sell; am offered for sale or sold (pass.)
συνέδριον, ου, τό	(22)	Sanhedrin, council
τεσσεράκοντα	(22)	forty
βασιλεύω	(21)	I am king, rule, become king
διδασκαλία, ας, ἡ	(21)	teaching (both act and content), instruction
ἐνεργέω	(21)	I work, am at work, produce
εὐδοκέω	(21)	I am well pleased, consent, resolve, like, approve
ἐφίστημι	(21)	I stand by, appear, attack; am present, imminent (perf.)
θερίζω	(21)	I reap, harvest
καθίστημι	(21)	I bring, appoint, ordain, make
λατρεύω	(21)	I serve, worship
μνημονεύω	(21)	I remember, keep in mind, think of, mention
πειρασμός, οῦ, ὁ	(21)	test, trial, temptation, enticement, testing
στρέφω	(21)	I turn, change, return; turn around, am converted (pass.)
τελώνης, ου, ὁ	(21)	tax collector, revenue officer
τιμάω	(21)	I set a price on, honor, revere
ὑπακούω	(21)	I obey, follow, am subject to, answer (the door)
χιλίαρχος, ου, ὁ	(21)	military tribune, high ranking officer
ὡσεί	(21)	as, like, about
αἰτία, ας, ἡ	(20)	cause, reason, relationship, charge, accusation
ἀκροβυστία, ας, ἡ	(20)	foreskin, uncircumcision, Gentile(s)
ἀργύριον, ου, τό	(20)	silver, money
γένος, ους, τό	(20)	race, descendant(s), family, nation, class
γονεύς, έως, ὁ	(20)	parent; parents (pl. in NT)
ἑκατοντάρχης, ου, ὁ	(20)	centurion, captain, officer
ἐπίγνωσις, εως, ἡ	(20)	knowledge, recognition
ἡγεμών, όνος, ὁ	(20)	prince, governor, ruler
Ἰσαάκ, ὁ	(20)	Isaac
ἰχθύς, ύος, ὁ	(20)	fish
νηστεύω	(20)	I fast, go without food
νυνί	(20)	now

ξύλον, ου, τό	(20)	wood, stocks, pole, club, cross, tree
προάγω	(20)	I lead forward or out; go or come before (intrans.)
σκηνή, ῆς, ἡ	(20)	tent, booth, dwelling, tabernacle
σοφός, ή, όν	(20)	clever, skillful, wise, learned
τοσοῦτος, αύτη, οῦτον	(20)	so great, so large, so many, so far, so much
τρέχω	(20)	I run, rush, strive to advance, make progress
ὑπηρέτης, ου, ὁ	(20)	servant, helper, assistant
ὑψόω	(20)	I lift up, raise high, exalt
ἀπέχω	(19)	I receive in full, am enough, am distant; abstain (mid.)
βάπτισμα, ατος, τό	(19)	baptism
γεωργός, οῦ, ὁ	(19)	farmer, vine dresser, tenant farmer
διακρίνω	(19)	I differentiate, judge; dispute, waver (mid.)
δῶρον, ου, τό	(19)	gift, present, offering, offering
ἐπαίρω	(19)	I lift up; am in opposition, am presumptuous (pass.)
ἐπάνω	(19)	above, over, more than; over, above, on (impr. prep.)
ἐπιλαμβάνομαι	(19)	I take hold of, catch, arrest, am concerned with, help
ἐπουράνιος, ον	(19)	heavenly; heaven, heavenly places or things (pl. subst.)
κοινωνία, ας, ἡ	(19)	fellowship, close relationship, participation, gift
κρείττων, ον	(19)	better, higher in rank, more useful; better (adv.)
κριτής, οῦ, ὁ	(19)	judge
κτίσις, εως, ἡ	(19)	creation, creature, world, act of creation
μαρτύριον, ου, τό	(19)	testimony, proof
μεριμνάω	(19)	I have anxiety, am anxious, care for
παλαιός, ά, όν	(19)	old, former
παράπτωμα, ατος, τό	(19)	false step, trespass, transgression, sin
παρατίθημι	(19)	I place or put before; entrust, demonstrate (mid.)
πότε	(19)	when?
προφητεία, ας, ἡ	(19)	prophecy, prophetic activity, gift of prophecy
τέλειος, α, ον	(19)	perfect, complete, mature, adult, initiated
ἀληθῶς	(18)	truly, in truth, really, actually
Ἀντιόχεια, ας, ἡ	(18)	Antioch
ἀποκάλυψις, εως, ἡ	(18)	revelation, disclosure
ἀπώλεια, ας, ἡ	(18)	destruction, waste, ruin
ἀριθμός, οῦ, ὁ	(18)	number, total
Ἀσία, ας, ἡ	(18)	Asia
βλασφημία, ας, ἡ	(18)	blasphemy, slander, defamation
δέησις, εως, ἡ	(18)	prayer, entreaty, petition
δεσμός, οῦ, ὁ	(18)	bond, fetter; bonds, imprisonment, prison (pl.)
εἰσπορεύομαι	(18)	I go in, come in, enter
ἐπιβάλλω	(18)	I throw over, lay on, put on, sew on, beat upon, belong to
ἐπιτρέπω	(18)	I allow, permit
θυμός, οῦ, ὁ	(18)	passion, anger, rage, wrath
καταγγέλλω	(18)	I proclaim, make known
κατακρίνω	(18)	I condemn, pass judgment on
κενός, ή, όν	(18)	empty, empty-handed, without content or result, vain
κληρονομέω	(18)	I inherit, acquire, obtain, receive
κοιμάω	(18)	I sleep, fall asleep, die (pass. in NT)
κόπος, ου, ὁ	(18)	trouble, work, labor
κρύπτω	(18)	I hide, conceal, cover, keep secret
μήν	(18)	indeed, surely

οἰκοδομή, ῆς, ἡ	(18)	building up, edification, building, edifice
παραχρῆμα	(18)	at once, immediately
ποιμήν, ένος, ὁ	(18)	shepherd
πόλεμος, ου, ὁ	(18)	war, battle, fight, conflict, strife
πολλάκις	(18)	many times, often, frequently
προστίθημι	(18)	I add, add to, increase, do again, provide, give, grant
πυλών, ῶνος, ὁ	(18)	gate, gateway, vestibule, entrance
στέφανος, ου, ὁ	(18)	wreath, crown, prize, reward, reason for pride
τίκτω	(18)	I bear, give birth, bring forth
φανερός, ά, όν	(18)	visible, clear, plain, known; the open (subst.)
χρυσοῦς, ῆ, οῦν	(18)	golden, made of gold
ἀνάγκη, ης, ἡ	(17)	necessity, compulsion, distress, calamity
ἀρέσκω	(17)	I strive to please, please
ἄφεσις, εως, ἡ	(17)	release, pardon, forgiveness
βρῶμα, ατος, τό	(17)	food
ἑκατόν	(17)	one hundred
ἐλέγχω	(17)	I bring to light, expose, convince, reprove, punish
ἐξίστημι	(17)	I confuse, amaze, lose my mind, am astonished
ἐπαύριον	(17)	tomorrow, the next day
ἔτοιμος, η, ον	(17)	ready, prepared
θησαυρός, οῦ, ὁ	(17)	treasure box, storehouse, treasure
ἵππος, ου, ὁ	(17)	horse, steed
Καισάρεια, ας, ἡ	(17)	Caesarea
κἄν	(17)	and if, even if, if only (= καὶ ἐάν)
καταλύω	(17)	I throw down, tear down, destroy, abolish, find lodging
κατέχω	(17)	I hold back, suppress, restrain, hold fast, possess
κερδαίνω	(17)	I gain, profit, spare myself
κρυπτός, ή, όν	(17)	hidden, secret; hidden thing or place (subst.)
μέχρι	(17)	until (conj); until, as far as, to the point of (impr. prep.)
μήτι	(17)	(used in questions expecting a neg. answer)
νίπτω	(17)	I wash
οὔ	(17)	no
περιτέμνω	(17)	I circumcise
πλήρωμα, ατος, τό	(17)	fullness, fulfilling, fulfillment, contents, patch, total
πλησίον	(17)	neighbor, fellow (subst.); near, close to (impr. prep.)
ποταμός, οῦ, ὁ	(17)	river, stream
ῥίζα, ης, ἡ	(17)	root, source, shoot, descendant
ῥύομαι	(17)	I save, rescue, deliver, preserve; Deliverer (partic.)
ταράσσω	(17)	I stir up, disturb, unsettle, trouble, frighten
ὑποκριτής, οῦ, ὁ	(17)	hypocrite, pretender
ὑπομένω	(17)	I remain, hold out, endure
χάρισμα, ατος, τό	(17)	gift, favor
ὦ	(17)	O!
ὡσαύτως	(17)	similarly, likewise
ἀθετέω	(16)	I declare invalid, nullify, set aside, reject
ἀνακρίνω	(16)	I question, examine, judge, call to account
γάμος, ου, ὁ	(16)	wedding, wedding banquet, marriage, wedding hall
δεῖπνον, ου, τό	(16)	dinner, supper, main meal, banquet
δέσμιος, ου, ὁ	(16)	prisoner
δηνάριον, ου, τό	(16)	denarius (Roman silver coin)

διαλογίζομαι	(16)	I consider, ponder, reason, argue
διατάσσω	(16)	I order, direct, command, arrange
διψάω	(16)	I am thirsty, thirst, long for
ἐκτείνω	(16)	I stretch out
ἐμβαίνω	(16)	I go in, step in, embark
ἔπειτα	(16)	then, thereupon, next
ἐπιθυμέω	(16)	I desire, long for, lust for
ἐπιμένω	(16)	I stay, remain, continue, persist, persevere
ἐργάτης, ου, ὁ	(16)	workman, laborer, doer
εὐλογία, ας, ἡ	(16)	praise, flattery, blessing, consecration, bounty
Ἔφεσος, ου, ἡ	(16)	Ephesus
ζῆλος, ου, ὁ	(16)	zeal, ardor, jealousy
κακῶς	(16)	badly, wrongly, wickedly
κατέρχομαι	(16)	I come down, arrive, put in
Καφαρναούμ, ἡ	(16)	Capernaum
κλείω	(16)	I shut, lock, bar, close
κλέπτης, ου, ὁ	(16)	thief
λύπη, ης, ἡ	(16)	grief, sorrow, pain, affliction
νυμφίος, ου, ὁ	(16)	bridegroom
οὐδέποτε	(16)	never
πάθημα, ατος, τό	(16)	suffering, misfortune, passion
παρέχω	(16)	I offer, grant, cause; show myself, grant, get (mid.)
περισσότερος, α, ον	(16)	greater, more, even more; more, even more (adv.)
πλήρης, ες	(16)	filled, full, complete, fully ripened, covered with
προσδοκάω	(16)	I wait for, look for, expect
σκοτία, ας, ἡ	(16)	darkness, gloom
συκῆ, ῆς, ἡ	(16)	fig tree
συλλαμβάνω	(16)	I arrest, catch, become pregnant; seize, help (mid.)
συνίστημι	(16)	I recommend, commend, show, stand by, hold together
σφραγίς, ῖδος, ἡ	(16)	seal, signet, mark, inscription, that which confirms
τέρας, ατος, τό	(16)	portent, omen, wonder
τολμάω	(16)	I dare, bring myself to, presume, am courageous
τροφή, ῆς, ἡ	(16)	nourishment, food
ὑστερέω	(16)	I miss, lack, am inferior, fail; am lacking (pass.)
χορτάζω	(16)	I feed, fill, satisfy; eat my fill, am satisfied (pass.)
ἀνέχω	(15)	I endure, bear with, put up with, accept (mid. in NT)
ἀνομία, ας, ἡ	(15)	lawlessness, lawless deed
ἀπάγω	(15)	I lead away, bring before, lead; am misled (pass.)
γεύομαι	(15)	I taste, partake of, eat; come to know, experience (fig.)
γνωστός, ή, όν	(15)	known, notable, intelligible; acquaintance, (subst.)
γυμνός, ή, όν	(15)	naked, without an outer garment, poorly dressed
Δαμασκός, οῦ, ἡ	(15)	Damascus
δέρω	(15)	I skin; beat (fig. in NT)
διαμαρτύρομαι	(15)	I charge, warn, testify, bear witness
εἶτα	(15)	then, next, furthermore
ἐντέλλομαι	(15)	I command
ἐπαγγέλλομαι	(15)	I announce, proclaim, promise, offer, profess
εὐσέβεια, ας, ἡ	(15)	piety, godliness, religion; godly acts (pl.)
εὐχαριστία, ας, ἡ	(15)	thankfulness, thanksgiving, prayer of thanksgiving
θεμέλιος, ου, ὁ	(15)	foundation, foundation stone

θρίξ, τριχός, ἡ	(15)	hair
Ἰορδάνης, ου, ὁ	(15)	Jordan
καταλαμβάνω	(15)	I seize, win, attain, overtake, catch; grasp (mid.)
κληρονόμος, ου, ὁ	(15)	heir
κτίζω	(15)	I create, make; Creator (partic.)
Λάζαρος, ου, ὁ	(15)	Lazarus
λῃστής, οῦ, ὁ	(15)	bandit, robber, revolutionary, insurrectionist
μοιχεύω	(15)	I commit adultery
νήπιος, α, ον	(15)	infant, minor, immature, innocent; child (subst.)
νομίζω	(15)	I think, believe, suppose; am the custom (pass.)
ξηραίνω	(15)	I dry; dry up, wither, stop, become stiff
ὅθεν	(15)	from where, where, whence, from which, therefore
οἰκουμένη, ης, ἡ	(15)	world, inhabited earth, humankind, Roman Empire
ὁμοιόω	(15)	I make like, compare; be like, resemble (pass.)
ὄψιος, α, ον	(15)	late; evening (fem. subst.)
παρθένος, ου, ἡ, ὁ	(15)	virgin (female or male)
παύω	(15)	I stop, keep; stop, cease (mid.)
πέτρα, ας, ἡ	(15)	rock, stone, rocky grotto or ground
ποτίζω	(15)	I give to drink, water
προλέγω	(15)	I tell beforehand or in advance, say before or already
πώς	(15)	somehow, in some way, perhaps
ῥαββί	(15)	rabbi, master, teacher
σαλεύω	(15)	I shake, cause to move to and fro, incite
Σαῦλος, ου, ὁ	(15)	Saul
σκάνδαλον, ου, τό	(15)	trap, temptation, that which offends, stumbling block
συμφέρω	(15)	I bring together; it is good, better, or useful (impers.)
σφραγίζω	(15)·	I put a seal on, seal, mark, certify
ταχέως	(15)	quickly, soon, hastily, too quickly
τράπεζα, ης, ἡ	(15)	table, meal, food, bank
τύπος, ου, ὁ	(15)	mark, image, form, pattern, type, model, example
ὑπακοή, ῆς, ἡ	(15)	obedience
χόρτος, ου, ὁ	(15)	grass, hay
ὠφελέω	(15)	I help, aid, benefit, achieve, gain
ἄκανθα, ης, ἡ	(14)	thorn plant, thorn
ἀλλότριος, α, ον	(14)	belonging to another, strange, hostile; stranger (subst.)
ἀμφότεροι, αι, α	(14)	both, all
ἀναγγέλλω	(14)	I report, disclose, announce, proclaim
ἀνάκειμαι	(14)	I lie, recline, am at table
ἀναχωρέω	(14)	I go away, return, withdraw, retire
ἀνθίστημι	(14)	I set myself against, oppose, resist, withstand
ἅπαξ	(14)	once, once for all
ἀπειθέω	(14)	I disobey, am disobedient, disbelieve
ἁρπάζω	(14)	I snatch, seize, steal
ἀτενίζω	(14)	I look intently
αὔριον	(14)	tomorrow, next day, soon
ἀφίστημι	(14)	I mislead, go away, fall away, keep away
γράμμα, ατος, τό	(14)	letter (of alphabet); document, epistle, book (mostly pl.)
διαλογισμός, οῦ, ὁ	(14)	thought, opinion, reasoning, doubt, dispute
ἕκτος, η, ον	(14)	sixth
ἐλάχιστος, η, ον	(14)	smallest, least, very small, insignificant, very few

ἐνιαυτός, οῦ, ὁ	(14)	year, era
ἐπίσταμαι	(14)	I understand, know
εὐφραίνω	(14)	I cheer, gladden; rejoice, make merry (pass.)
θύω	(14)	I sacrifice, slaughter, kill, celebrate
κατανοέω	(14)	I notice, look, consider, contemplate
κατεσθίω	(14)	I eat up, consume, devour, destroy
κλάω	(14)	I break (bread)
κληρονομία, ας, ἡ	(14)	inheritance, possession, property, salvation
κοινός, ή, όν	(14)	common, ordinary, profane, unclean
κοινόω	(14)	I make common, defile, desecrate, consider unclean
κωφός, ή, όν	(14)	dull, dumb, mute, deaf
λύχνος, ου, ὁ	(14)	lamp
μακρόθεν	(14)	from far away, from a distance, far off
μακροθυμία, ας, ἡ	(14)	patience, steadfastness, endurance, forbearance
μερίζω	(14)	I divide, separate, distribute, apportion; share (mid.)
μέτρον, ου, τό	(14)	measure, quantity, number
μύρον, ου, τό	(14)	ointment, perfume
νοέω	(14)	I perceive, understand, comprehend, consider, think
ξένος, η, ον	(14)	strange, foreign, unusual; stranger, alien, host (subst.)
οἶος, α, ον	(14)	of what sort, as, such as
ὄφις, εως, ὁ	(14)	snake, serpent
πετεινόν, οῦ, τό	(14)	bird
προσδέχομαι	(14)	I receive, welcome, expect, wait for
Σαδδουκαῖος, ου, ὁ	(14)	Sadducee
σεισμός, οῦ, ὁ	(14)	shaking, earthquake, storm
σῖτος, ου, ὁ	(14)	wheat, grain
τάλαντον, ου, τό	(14)	talent (Greek monetary unit)
ταπεινόω	(14)	I lower, humble, humiliate; have little (mid.)
φρόνιμος, ον	(14)	sensible, thoughtful, wise
φύσις, εως, ἡ	(14)	nature, natural endowment or characteristics, creature
χωλός, ή, όν	(14)	lame, crippled; what is lame, lame leg (subst.)
ἀνά	(13)	upwards, up, each; among, between (w. μέσον)
ἀναλαμβάνω	(13)	I take up, take along
ἀναστροφή, ῆς, ἡ	(13)	way of life, conduct, behavior
Ἀνδρέας, ου, ὁ	(13)	Andrew
ἄνωθεν	(13)	from above, from heaven, for a long time, again, anew
δαιμονίζομαι	(13)	I am possessed by a demon
διαλέγομαι	(13)	I discuss, speak, preach
διαφέρω	(13)	I carry through, spread, differ, am superior to
δράκων, οντος, ὁ	(13)	dragon, serpent
ἐκπλήσσω	(13)	I am amazed, overwhelmed (pass. in NT)
ἐλαία, ας, ἡ	(13)	olive tree, olive
ἐλεημοσύνη, ης, ἡ	(13)	kind deed, alms, charitable giving
ἐμπαίζω	(13)	I ridicule, make fun of, mock, deceive, trick
ἔξ	(13)	six
ἐξαποστέλλω	(13)	I send out, send away
ἔξωθεν	(13)	from the outside, outside; (from) outside (impr. prep)
ἐπιζητέω	(13)	I search, wish for, demand
ζύμη, ης, ἡ	(13)	yeast, leaven
θερισμός, οῦ, ὁ	(13)	reaping, harvest, crop

καθάπερ	(13)	just as
καπνός, οῦ, ὁ	(13)	smoke
καταισχύνω	(13)	I dishonor, put to shame; am disappointed (pass.)
καταντάω	(13)	I come, arrive, attain
καταρτίζω	(13)	I restore, make complete, prepare, make
κλέπτω	(13)	I steal
Μάρθα, ας, ἡ	(13)	Martha
Ναζωραῖος, ου, ὁ	(13)	inhabitant of Nazareth, a Nazarene
παιδεύω	(13)	I bring up, train, educate, discipline, correct, whip
παιδίσκη, ης, ἡ	(13)	maid, servant girl, female slave
παράδοσις, εως, ἡ	(13)	tradition
πρίν	(13)	before
στηρίζω	(13)	I fix, establish, support, strengthen
συνεργός, όν	(13)	working together; helper, fellow worker (subst. in NT)
ταχύς, εῖα, ύ	(13)	quick, swift; quickly, soon (neut. sing. as adv.)
τίμιος, α, ον	(13)	valuable, precious, costly, honorable, respected
Τίτος, ου, ὁ	(13)	Titus
τρόπος, ου, ὁ	(13) .	manner, way, kind, way of life, conduct
τύπτω	(13)	I strike, hit, beat, wound
ὕψιστος, η, ον	(13)	highest; highest (heaven), the Most High (subst.)
Φῆστος, ου, ὁ	(13)	Festus
χωρίζω	(13)	I divide, separate; separate myself, go away (pass.)
ἄδικος, ον	(12)	unjust, dishonest, untrustworthy
ἀλέκτωρ, ορος, ὁ	(12)	cock, rooster
ἀναπαύω	(12)	I cause to rest, give rest, refresh; rest (mid.)
ἀναπίπτω	(12)	I lie down, recline, lean, lean back
ἀσκός, οῦ, ὁ	(12)	leather bag, wineskin
αὐλή, ῆς, ἡ	(12)	courtyard, palace, farm, house
Βαβυλών, ῶνος, ἡ	(12)	Babylon
βαπτιστής, οῦ, ὁ	(12)	Baptist, Baptizer
βασανίζω	(12)	I torture, torment, harass
Βηθανία, ας, ἡ	(12)	Bethany
βῆμα, ατος, τό	(12)	step, judicial bench, speaker's platform,
βοάω	(12)	I call, shout, cry out
βουλή, ῆς, ἡ	(12)	purpose, counsel, resolution, decision
βροντή, ῆς, ἡ	(12)	thunder
γέεννα, ης, ἡ	(12)	Gehenna, valley of the sons of Hinnom, hell
γόνυ, ατος, τό	(12)	knee
δεῦτε	(12)	come (serves as pl. of δεῦρο)
διάνοια, ας, ἡ	(12)	understanding, mind, insight, thought
δίκτυον, ου, τό	(12)	fish net
ἔθος, ους, τό	(12)	habit, usage, custom, law
ἐμβλέπω	(12)	I look at, consider
ἐξάγω	(12)	I lead out, bring out
ἔσωθεν	(12)	from inside, within; inside, inner nature (subst.)
Ζεβεδαῖος, ου, ὁ	(12)	Zebedee
καίω	(12)	I light, burn, keep burning
κάλαμος, ου, ὁ	(12)	reed, measuring rod, reed pen
κατακαίω	(12)	I burn down, burn up, consume
κατάκειμαι	(12)	I lie down, recline, dine

κολλάω	(12)	I unite; cling to, join, join myself to (pass. in NT)
κράτος, ους, τό	(12)	power, might, mighty deed, sovereignty, rule
λίαν	(12)	very much, exceedingly, very, quite
λιμός, οῦ, ὁ, ἡ	(12)	hunger, famine
λυχνία, ας, ἡ	(12)	lampstand
Μαγδαληνή, ῆς, ἡ	(12)	Magdalene
μάλιστα	(12)	most of all, above all, especially, particularly
μεταβαίνω	(12)	I go or pass over, move
μωρός, ά, όν	(12)	foolish, stupid, fool; foolishness (subst.)
ὀδούς, ὀδόντος, ὁ	(12)	tooth
οἰκοδεσπότης, ου, ὁ	(12)	master of the house
ὅραμα, ατος, τό	(12)	vision
ὅριον, ου, τό	(12)	boundary; region, district (pl. in NT)
παραιτέομαι	(12)	I ask for, excuse, decline, reject, refuse, dismiss, avoid
περισσοτέρως	(12)	even more, far greater, so much more, especially
πιάζω	(12)	I take hold of, seize, grasp, arrest, catch
πληθύνω	(12)	I increase, multiply; grow (pass.)
πλουτέω	(12)	I am rich, become rich, am generous
πόρνη, ης, ἡ	(12)	prostitute, harlot
πρόθεσις, εως, ἡ	(12)	plan, purpose, will, (bread of) presentation
προσλαμβάνω	(12)	I take aside, accept, receive, take along (mid. in NT)
πρωΐ	(12)	early, early in the morning, morning
πυνθάνομαι	(12)	I inquire, ask, learn
πῶλος, ου, ὁ	(12)	colt, young donkey, horse
ῥάβδος, ου, ἡ	(12)	rod, staff, stick, scepter
Ῥωμαῖος, α, ον	(12)	Roman; Roman person or citizen (subst. in NT)
σαλπίζω	(12)	I sound the trumpet
Σιλᾶς, ᾶ, ὁ	(12)	Silas
Σολομών, ῶνος, ὁ	(12)	Solomon
σπλαγχνίζομαι	(12)	I have pity, feel sympathy
σπουδή, ῆς, ἡ	(12)	haste, speed, eagerness, earnestness
συνέχω	(12)	I torment, stop, press hard, hold prisoner, embrace, rule
τρίς	(12)	three times
τυγχάνω	(12)	I attain, obtain, experience
ὑγιαίνω	(12)	I am in good health, healthy, sound, or correct
ὕστερος, α, ον	(12)	latter, last; later, then, finally (neut. sing. as adv.)
φιάλη, ης, ἡ	(12)	bowl
φονεύω	(12)	I murder, kill
χοῖρος, ου, ὁ	(12)	swine, pig
χρυσίον, ου, τό	(12)	gold, gold ornaments, jewelry
ψεύδομαι	(12)	I lie, deceive by lying
ἀγαλλιάω	(11)	I exult, am glad, overjoyed
ἀγορά, ᾶς, ἡ	(11)	market place
Ἀγρίππας, α, ὁ	(11)	Agrippa
ἅλυσις, εως, ἡ	(11)	chain, imprisonment
Ἀνανίας, ου, ὁ	(11)	Ananias
ἀνατολή, ῆς, ἡ	(11)	rising, east; east (pl.)
ἀντιλέγω	(11)	I speak against, contradict, oppose, refuse
ἀπαρνέομαι	(11)	I deny, reject
ἀπιστία, ας, ἡ	(11)	unfaithfulness, unbelief

ἀρχαῖος, α, ον	(11)	ancient, old
ἄφρων, ον	(11)	foolish, ignorant
Βαραββᾶς, ᾶ, ὁ	(11)	Barabbas
βρῶσις, εως, ἡ	(11)	eating, food, corrosion, rust
Γαλιλαῖος, α, ον	(11)	Galilean; a Galilean (subst.)
γέμω	(11)	I am full
διαμερίζω	(11)	I divide, separate, distribute, share
δόλος, ου, ὁ	(11)	deceit, treachery, cunning
δωρεά, ᾶς, ἡ	(11)	gift, bounty
ἐάω	(11)	I let, permit, let go, leave alone
εἴδωλον, ου, τό	(11)	image, idol
εἴκοσι	(11)	twenty
εἰσάγω	(11)	I bring in, lead in
ἔλαιον, ου, τό	(11)	olive oil, oil
ἐλευθερία, ας, ἡ	(11)	freedom, liberty
ἐνδείκνυμι	(11)	I show, demonstrate, do (mid. in NT)
ἐξουθενέω	(11)	I despise, reject, treat with contempt
ἔπαινος, ου, ὁ	(11)	praise, approval, thing worthy of praise
ἐπαισχύνομαι	(11)	I am ashamed
ἐπιπίπτω	(11)	I fall upon, approach eagerly, press close, come upon
ἐπισκέπτομαι	(11)	I examine, look for, visit, care for, am concerned abou
Ζαχαρίας, ου, ὁ	(11)	Zechariah
ζηλόω	(11)	I strive, desire, show zeal, am filled with jealousy
ζωοποιέω	(11)	I make alive, give life to
θανατόω	(11)	I put to death, kill
θάπτω	(11)	I bury
Θωμᾶς, ᾶ, ὁ	(11)	Thomas
κακία, ας, ἡ	(11)	badness, wickedness, malice, trouble
καταβολή, ῆς, ἡ	(11)	foundation, beginning
κατασκευάζω	(11)	I make ready, prepare, build, furnish
καύχημα, ατος, τό	(11)	boast, object of boasting, pride, boasting
καύχησις, εως, ἡ	(11)	boasting, pride, object of boasting
κέρας, ατος, τό	(11)	horn, corner, end
κλάδος, ου, ὁ	(11)	branch
κλῆρος, ου, ὁ	(11)	lot, portion, share, place
κλῆσις, εως, ἡ	(11)	call, calling, invitation, position, vocation
κράβαττος, ου, ὁ	(11)	mattress, pallet, bed, cot
λίμνη, ης, ἡ	(11)	lake
μετρέω	(11)	I measure, give out, apportion
νεανίσκος, ου, ὁ	⸄(11)	youth, young man, servant
νόσος, ου, ἡ	(11)	disease, illness
ὁμοθυμαδόν	(11)	with one mind, by common consent, together
πηγή, ῆς, ἡ	(11)	spring, fountain, well, flow
ποιμαίνω	(11)	I tend (sheep); guide, protect, nurture (fig.)
πρᾶγμα, ατος, τό	(11)	deed, thing, event, undertaking, matter, affair, lawsui
πραΰτης, ητος, ἡ	(11)	gentleness, humility, courtesy
πρότερος, α, ον	(11)	earlier, former; before, once, formerly (neut. as adv.)
σάλπιγξ, ιγγος, ἡ	(11)	trumpet, trumpet call
Σαμάρεια, ας, ἡ	(11)	Samaria
σπλάγχνον, ου, τό	(11)	inward parts, entrails, heart, love, affection (pl. in NT)

σπουδάζω	(11)	I hasten, am zealous or eager, make every effort
συγγενής, ές	(11)	related; relative, fellow countryman (subst. in NT)
σφόδρα	(11)	extremely, greatly, very (much)
σχίζω	(11)	I split, tear; am divided or split (pass.)
τελευτάω	(11)	I come to an end, die
τριάκοντα	(11)	thirty
Τύρος, ου, ή	(11)	Tyre
ὑγιής, ές	(11)	healthy, sound
ὑμέτερος, α, ον	(11)	your (pl.)
ὑποκάτω	(11)	under, below (impr. prep. in NT)
ὑψηλός, ή, όν	(11)	high, exalted, proud, haughty
φυτεύω	(11)	I plant
φωτίζω	(11)	I shine; illuminate, bring to light, reveal (trans.)
χείρων, ον	(11)	worse, more severe
χίλιοι, αι, α	(11)	thousand
χιτών, ῶνος, ὁ	(11)	tunic, shirt; clothes (pl.)
χράομαι	(11)	I use, employ, proceed, act, treat
ψευδοπροφήτης, ου, ὁ	(11)	false prophet
ἁγιασμός, οῦ, ὁ	(10)	holiness, consecration, sanctification
ᾅδης, ου, ὁ	(10)	Hades, underworld, death
ἀδύνατος, ον	(10)	powerless, impotent, impossible
ἀκαθαρσία, ας, ή	(10)	impurity, dirt, refuse, immorality, viciousness
ἅμα	(10)	at the same time, together; together with (impr. prep.)
ἀναφέρω	(10)	I bring up, take up, offer
ἀπολαμβάνω	(10)	I receive, recover, take aside
Ἀπολλῶς, ῶ, ὁ	(10)	Apollos
ἀπολογέομαι	(10)	I speak in my own defense, defend myself
ἀπολύτρωσις, εως, ή	(10)	release, redemption
ἀσέλγεια, ας, ή	(10)	licentiousness, debauchery, sensuality
ἀσπασμός, οῦ, ὁ	(10)	greeting
ἀφαιρέω	(10)	I take away, cut off
ἀφορίζω	(10)	I separate, excommunicate, appoint
Ἀχαΐα, ας, ή	(10)	Achaia
βίβλος, ου, ή	(10)	book, sacred book, record
βίος, ου, ὁ	(10)	life, conduct, property
δάκρυον, ου, τό	(10)	tear; weeping (pl.)
δεσπότης, ου, ὁ	(10)	lord, master, owner
δικαίωμα, ατος, τό	(10)	regulation, requirement, righteous deed
διωγμός, οῦ, ὁ	(10)	persecution
ἐγκαταλείπω	(10)	I leave behind, abandon, leave
ἐκκόπτω	(10)	I cut off or down, remove
ἐκπίπτω	(10)	I fall off, fall from, lose, fail, run aground
ἐμφανίζω	(10)	I make visible, reveal, make clear, explain, bring charges
ἔνατος, η, ον	(10)	ninth
ἔνοχος, ον	(10)	caught in, subject to, liable, guilty, deserving
ἐντεῦθεν	(10)	from here, from this
ἐξομολογέω	(10)	I promise, consent; confess, admit, praise
ἐπειδή	(10)	when, after, since, since then, because
ἐπιτάσσω	(10)	I order, command
ἐπιτελέω	(10)	I finish, complete, bring about, perform, erect, lay upon

θλίβω	(10)	I press upon, oppress; am narrow, afflicted (pass.)
Ἰόππη, ης, ἡ	(10)	Joppa
ἰσχύς, ύος, ἡ	(10)	strength, might, power
κἀκεῖ	(10)	and there, there also (= καὶ ἐκεῖ)
κἀκεῖθεν	(10)	and from there, and then (= καὶ ἐκεῖθεν)
κλητός, ή, όν	(10)	called, invited
κοινωνός, οῦ, ὁ, ἡ	(10)	companion, partner, sharer
κομίζω	(10)	I bring; receive, obtain, recover (mid.)
κοσμέω	(10)	I put in order, trim, adorn, decorate, do credit to
μακράν	(10)	far, far away
μακροθυμέω	(10)	I have patience, wait patiently, am patient
μέλει	(10)	it is a concern (impers.)
ξενίζω	(10)	I entertain, surprise, astonish; stay (pass.)
ὅδε, ἥδε, τόδε	(10)	this, such and such
οἰκονόμος, ου, ὁ	(10)	steward, manager, administrator, treasurer
ὀνομάζω	(10)	I name, call, pronounce; am known (pass.)
ὄντως	(10)	really, certainly, in truth; real (adj.)
ὅρκος, ου, ὁ	(10)	oath
παντοκράτωρ, ορος, ὁ	(10)	Almighty, Omnipotent One
παράγω	(10)	I pass by or away, go away; pass away, disappear (pass.)
παραλυτικός, ή, όν	(10)	lame; lame person, paralytic (subst. in NT)
παρεμβολή, ῆς, ἡ	(10)	camp, barracks, headquarters, army, battle line
πατάσσω	(10)	I strike, hit, strike down, slay
πενθέω	(10)	I am sad, grieve, mourn; mourn over (trans.)
περιστερά, ᾶς, ἡ	(10)	pigeon, dove
πλάνη, ης, ἡ	(10)	wandering, error, delusion, deception
πλεονεξία, ας, ἡ	(10)	greediness, avarice, covetousness, something forced
ποικίλος, η, ον	(10)	of various kinds, diverse
πόρνος, ου, ὁ	(10)	one who practices sexual immorality
προσκαρτερέω	(10)	I attach or devote myself to, continue in, am ready
πύλη, ης, ἡ	(10)	gate, door
σέβω	(10)	I worship (mid. in NT)
σιγάω	(10)	I am silent, become or keep silent, keep secret
σιωπάω	(10)	I keep silent, am quiet
στήκω	(10)	I stand, stand firm, am steadfast
στρατηγός, οῦ, ὁ	(10)	chief magistrate, captain
συζητέω	(10)	I discuss, dispute, debate, argue
σύνδουλος, ου, ὁ	(10)	fellow slave
σφάζω	(10)	I slaughter, murder
τέταρτος, η, ον	(10)	fourth
ὑπαντάω	(10)	I meet, oppose
ὑπόδημα, ατος, τό	(10)	sandal, footwear
φείδομαι	(10)	I spare, refrain
χρηστότης, ητος, ἡ	(10)	goodness, uprightness, kindness, generosity
χρυσός, οῦ, ὁ	(10)	gold
χωρέω	(10)	I make room, go, make progress, hold, contain, accept
χωρίον, ου τό	(10)	place, piece of land, field
ψεῦδος, ους, τό	(10)	lie, falsehood
ψεύστης, ου, ὁ	(10)	liar
ἄβυσσος, ου, ἡ	(9)	abyss, depth, underworld

ἀγαθοποιέω	(9)	I do good, what is right
Ἀδάμ, ὁ	(9)	Adam
ἄζυμος, ον	(9)	unleavened; festival of unleavened bread (subst.)
αἵρεσις, εως, ἡ	(9)	sect, party, school, dissension, faction, opinion
ἀκριβῶς	(9)	accurately, carefully, well
ἀλείφω	(9)	I anoint
ἄμπελος, ου, ἡ	(9)	vine, grapevine
ἀναγκάζω	(9)	I compel, force, invite, strongly urge
ἀναστρέφω	(9)	I overturn, return; behave, conduct myself (pass.)
ἀνατέλλω	(9)	I cause to spring up, rise, spring up, am descended
ἄνομος, ον	(9)	lawless, wicked, Gentile; criminal, lawless one (subst.)
ἄνω	(9)	above, up, upwards
ἀπαρχή, ῆς, ἡ	(9)	first fruits, first portion, first, birth certificate
ἀποδοκιμάζω	(9)	I reject, declare useless
ἀποστρέφω	(9)	I turn away, return; turn away (mid. and 2 aor. pass.)
ἀποτίθημι	(9)	I put off, take off, lay aside (mid. in NT)
ἄρσην, εν	(9)	male
ἀρχισυνάγωγος, ου, ὁ	(9)	leader or president of a synagogue
ἀσεβής, ές	(9)	godless, impious
ἀστραπή, ῆς, ἡ	(9)	lightning, light
βόσκω	(9)	I feed, tend; graze (pass.)
γαστήρ, τρός, ἡ	(9)	belly, glutton, womb
γνώμη, ης, ἡ	(9)	purpose, opinion, consent, decision
γωνία, ας, ἡ	(9)	corner
δεῦρο	(9)	come, until now
διασκορπίζω	(9)	I scatter, disperse, waste, squander
διατρίβω	(9)	I spend, stay, remain
δωρεάν	(9)	as a gift, without payment, undeservedly, in vain
ἕβδομος, η, ον	(9)	seventh; the seventh (subst.)
εἰδωλόθυτος, ον	(9)	meat offered to an idol (subst. in NT)
ἐκδίκησις, εως, ἡ	(9)	vengeance, punishment
Ἐλισάβετ, ἡ	(9)	Elizabeth
ἐντρέπω	(9)	I make ashamed; am ashamed, respect (pass.)
ἑξήκοντα	(9)	sixty
ἐπέρχομαι	(9)	I come, come along, appear, approach, come upon, attack
ἐπιδίδωμι	(9)	I give, hand over, deliver, give up or over, surrender
ἐπιποθέω	(9)	I long for, desire, yearn over
ἔρις, ιδος, ἡ	(9)	strife, discord, contention
ἔσω	(9)	in, inside; inside, into (impr. prep.); insider (subst.)
εὐάρεστος, ον	(9)	pleasing, acceptable
εὐδοκία, ας, ἡ	(9)	good will, favor, good pleasure, wish, desire
εὐώνυμος, ον	(9)	left (as opposed to right)
θνήσκω	(9)	I die; have died, am dead (perf. in NT)
Ἰσραηλίτης, ου, ὁ	(9)	an Israelite
Ἰωνᾶς, ᾶ, ὁ	(9)	Jonah
καθαιρέω	(9)	I take or bring down, conquer, destroy
Καϊάφας, α, ὁ	(9)	Caiaphas
κατάγω	(9)	I lead or bring down; put in (pass.)
κατάπαυσις, εως, ἡ	(9)	rest, place of rest
καταφρονέω	(9)	I look down on, despise, think lightly of, disregard

κάτω	(9)	below, downwards, down
κήρυγμα, ατος, τό	(9)	proclamation, preaching, message
Κηφᾶς, ᾶ, ὁ	(9)	Cephas
κίνδυνος, ου, ὁ	(9)	danger, risk
κλάσμα, ατος, τό	(9)	fragment, piece, crumb
κλαυθμός, οῦ, ὁ	(9)	weeping, crying
κλίνη, ης, ἡ	(9)	bed, couch, pallet, stretcher, sickbed
κραυγάζω	(9)	I cry out, scream
κρούω	(9)	I strike, knock
λαμπάς, άδος, ἡ	(9)	torch, lamp
λαμπρός, ά, όν	(9)	bright, shining, radiant, clear; splendor (subst.)
λεπρός, ά, όν	(9)	leprous; leper, person with a skin disease (subst.)
λέων, οντος, ὁ	(9)	lion
λιθάζω	(9)	I stone
μαργαρίτης, ου, ὁ	(9)	pearl
μεστός, ή, όν	(9)	full
μεταξύ	(9)	meanwhile, after; between, in the middle (impr. prep.)
μεταπέμπω	(9)	I send for, summon
μνᾶ, μνᾶς, ἡ	(9)	mina (Greek monetary unit)
μονογενής, ές	(9)	only, unique
νῆσος, ου, ἡ	(9)	island
νομικός, ή, όν	(9)	pertaining to the law; legal expert, lawyer (subst.)
οἰκέω	(9)	I live, dwell; inhabit (trans.)
οἰκονομία, ας, ἡ	(9)	management, commission, plan, training, office
ὀνειδίζω	(9)	I reproach, revile, insult
οὐράνιος, ον	(9)	heavenly
παρρησιάζομαι	(9)	I speak freely, have courage
περίχωρος, ον	(9)	neighboring; neighborhood, surrounding region (subst.)
πιπράσκω	(9)	I sell
πλατεῖα, ας, ἡ	(9)	wide road, street
πλεονάζω	(9)	I grow, increase, have too much; cause to grow (trans.)
προέρχομαι	(9)	I go forward, go before, come out
προπέμπω	(9)	I accompany, escort, send or help on one's way
προσφορά, ᾶς, ἡ	(9)	offering, sacrificing, sacrifice, gift
Σαμαρίτης, ου, ὁ	(9)	a Samaritan
Σαούλ, ὁ	(9)	Saul
σελήνη, ης, ἡ	(9)	moon
Σιδών, ῶνος, ἡ	(9)	Sidon
Σόδομα, ων, τά	(9)	Sodom
στάσις, εως, ἡ	(9)	existence, standing, dissension, revolt, rebellion
στολή, ῆς, ἡ	(9)	long robe
τάξις, εως, ἡ	(9)	order, good order, nature, quality, manner
τεῖχος, ους, τό	(9)	wall
τρέφω	(9)	I feed, nourish, nurse, bring up, train
ὑστέρημα, ατος, τό	(9)	need, deficiency, absence, lack, shortcoming
Φῆλιξ, ικος, ὁ	(9)	Felix
φθείρω	(9)	I destroy, ruin, corrupt, spoil, seduce
φθόνος, ου, ὁ	(9)	envy, jealousy
φθορά, ᾶς, ἡ	(9)	ruin, destruction, that which is perishable, depravity
φόνος, ου, ὁ	(9)	murder, killing

χάριν	(9)	for the sake of, because of, by reason of (impr. prep.)
χρηματίζω	(9)	I impart a revelation, injunction, or warning, am named
ἁγνός, ή, όν	(8)	pure, holy, innocent, chaste
ἀγωνίζομαι	(8)	I engage in a contest, fight, struggle
ἀδόκιμος, ον	(8)	not standing the test, unqualified, worthless
αἰνέω	(8)	I praise
ἅλας, ατος, τό	(8)	salt
ἄμωμος, ον	(8)	unblemished, blameless
ἀναγκαῖος, α, ον	(8)	necessary
ἀντίκειμαι	(8)	I am opposed
ἀπεκδέχομαι	(8)	I await eagerly, wait
ἀπιστέω	(8)	I disbelieve, refuse to believe, am unfaithful
ἁπλότης, ητος, ἡ	(8)	simplicity, sincerity, generosity
ἀποκαθίστημι	(8)	I restore, reestablish, cure, give back, restore
ἀπολογία, ας, ἡ	(8)	defense, reply
ἀργός, ή, όν	(8)	unemployed, idle, lazy, careless, useless
ἀρκέω	(8)	I am enough, am sufficient; am satisfied (pass.)
ἄφθαρτος, ον	(8)	imperishable, incorruptible, immoral
βάθος, ους, τό	(8)	depth
βέβαιος, α, ον	(8)	firm, permanent, secure, reliable, certain, valid
βεβαιόω	(8)	I make firm, establish, confirm, strengthen
Βηθλέεμ, ἡ	(8)	Bethlehem
βοηθέω	(8)	I help
βοῦς, βοός, ὁ, ἡ	(8)	head of cattle, ox, cow
βρέφος, ους, τό	(8)	unborn child, embryo, baby, infant, childhood
γεμίζω	(8)	I fill
γογγύζω	(8)	I grumble, murmur, speak secretly, whisper
δάκτυλος, ου, ὁ	(8)	finger
διακόσιοι, αι, α	(8)	two hundred
διανοίγω	(8)	I open, explain, interpret
διαστέλλω	(8)	I order, give orders (mid. in NT)
διασῴζω	(8)	I bring safely through, save, rescue, cure
διηγέομαι	(8)	I tell, relate, describe
δουλόω	(8)	I enslave, subject, bring into bondage
δρέπανον, ου, τό	(8)	sickle, pruning hook
εἰσφέρω	(8)	I bring in, carry in, lead into
ἐκτός	(8)	outside; outside, except (impr. prep.)
ἐκφέρω	(8)	I carry or bring out, lead or send out, produce
ἐκφεύγω	(8)	I run away, escape
ἕλκω	(8)	I drag, draw
ἐναντίον	(8)	before, in the judgment of (impr. prep. in NT)
ἐναντίος, α, ον	(8)	opposite, against, contrary, hostile
ἔνδυμα, ατος, τό	(8)	garment, clothing
ἐνέργεια, ας, ἡ	(8)	working, operation, action
ἐνθάδε	(8)	here, in or to this place
ἐξαιρέω	(8)	I take out; set free, rescue, select, choose (mid.)
ἐπιλανθάνομαι	(8)	I forget, overlook
ἐπισυνάγω	(8)	I gather together
ἐσθής, ῆτος, ἡ	(8)	clothing
εὐθύς	(8)	immediately, at once, then, so then

εὐλογητός, ή, όν	(8)	blessed, praised
εὐνοῦχος, ου, ὁ	(8)	eunuch, castrated man
ζηλωτής, οῦ, ὁ	(8)	zealot, enthusiast, fanatic
ζιζάνιον, ου, τό	(8)	darnel, weed
ζώνη, ης, ἡ	(8)	belt, girdle
ἡλικία, ας, ἡ	(8)	age, time of life, years, maturity, stature
θησαυρίζω	(8)	I store up, gather, save, reserve
Ἰσκαριώτης, ου, ὁ	(8)	Iscariot
ἴσος, η, ον	(8)	equal, same, consistent; equally (neut. pl. as adv.)
καλύπτω	(8)	I cover, hide, conceal
καρποφορέω	(8)	I bear fruit, am productive
κατέναντι	(8)	opposite; opposite, in the sight of, before (impr. prep.)
κατηχέω	(8)	I make myself understood, inform, teach, instruct
Κιλικία, ας, ἡ	(8)	Cilicia
κινέω	(8)	I move, remove, shake, arouse, cause
κοινωνέω	(8)	I share, participate, give a share
κόπτω	(8)	I cut off; mourn (mid.)
κοράσιον, ου, τό	(8)	girl
Κορνήλιος, ου, ὁ	(8)	Cornelius
κύκλῳ	(8)	around, all around; nearby (adj.); around (impr. prep.)
Μᾶρκος, ου, ὁ	(8)	Mark
μεγαλύνω	(8)	I make large or long, magnify, praise, extol
μεθερμηνεύω	(8)	I translate
Μελχισέδεκ, ὁ	(8)	Melchizedek
μέντοι	(8)	really, actually, though, to be sure, indeed, but
μετέχω	(8)	I share, participate, belong, eat, drink, enjoy
μέτωπον, ου, τό	(8)	forehead
μνῆμα, ατος, τό	(8)	grave, tomb
μυριάς, άδος, ἡ	(8)	myriad, ten thousand
νουθετέω	(8)	I admonish, warn, instruct
νύμφη, ης, ἡ	(8)	bride, daughter-in-law
Νῶε, ὁ	(8)	Noah
ξηρός, ά, όν	(8)	dry, dried up; dry land, withered (subst.)
ὀκτώ	(8)	eight
ὀξύς, εῖα, ύ	(8)	sharp, swift
ὀργίζω	(8)	I am angry (pass. in NT)
ὁρίζω	(8)	I appoint, determine, set, designate
ὅσιος, α, ον	(8)	devout, pious, holy
ὀσφῦς, ύος, ἡ	(8)	waist, loins, genitals
πάντως	(8)	by all means, certainly, of course, perhaps, at least
πατρίς, ίδος, ἡ	(8)	fatherland, home town
περιτίθημι	(8)	I put or place around, put on, show honor
πορνεύω	(8)	I practice sexual immorality
πραιτώριον, ου, τό	(8)	praetorium, imperial guard
προΐστημι	(8)	I rule, manage, am concerned about, care for
προσκόπτω	(8)	I strike or beat against, stumble, take offense at, reject
προσπίπτω	(8)	I fall down before, fall or beat upon, strike against
πρωτότοκος, ον	(8)	first-born
ῥίπτω	(8)	I throw, throw down or off, put or lay down
Ῥώμη, ης, ἡ	(8)	Rome

σαπρός, ά, όν	(8)	decayed, rotten, bad, evil
στράτευμα, ατος, τό	(8)	army, troops
συγκαλέω	(8)	I call together; call to myself, summon (mid.)
συλλέγω	(8)	I collect, gather
συμβαίνω	(8)	I happen, come about
συμβούλιον, ου, τό	(8)	plan, purpose, council
Συρία, ας, ἡ	(8)	Syria
σχίσμα, ατος, τό	(8)	tear, crack, division, dissension, schism
ταπεινός, ή, όν	(8)	poor, subservient, humble; lowly, downcast one (subst.)
τάσσω	(8)	I appoint, order, determine; set, direct (mid.)
τάχος, ους, τό	(8)	speed, quickness, swiftness, haste
τεκνίον, ου, τό	(8)	little child
ὑπερβολή, ῆς, ἡ	(8)	excess, extraordinary quality or character
χάραγμα, ατος, τό	(8)	mark, stamp, thing formed, image
ἀγανακτέω	(7)	I am aroused, indignant, angry
ἀγέλη, ης, ἡ	(7)	herd
ἁγνίζω	(7)	I purify, cleanse
ἀεί	(7)	always, continually, from the beginning
ἀήρ, ἀέρος, ὁ	(7)	air, sky, space
ἄκαρπος, ον	(7)	unfruitful, fruitless, useless, unproductive
ἀνθρώπινος, η, ον	(7)	human
ἀνταποδίδωμι	(7)	I give back, repay, return
ἀξιόω	(7)	I consider worthy, make worthy, consider suitable
ἀπάτη, ης, ἡ	(7)	deception, deceitfulness, pleasure
ἀπείθεια, ας, ἡ	(7)	disobedience, disbelief
ἄπειμι	(7)	I am absent, am away
ἀποδέχομαι	(7)	I welcome, accept, recognize, praise
ἀπολείπω	(7)	I leave behind, desert; remain (pass.)
ἀτιμάζω	(7)	I dishonor, treat shamefully, insult
ἀτιμία, ας, ἡ	(7)	dishonor, disgrace, shame
ἀφθαρσία, ας, ἡ	(7)	incorruptibility, immorality
ἀφορμή, ῆς, ἡ	(7)	occasion, pretext, opportunity, excuse
Βεελζεβούλ, ὁ	(7)	Beelzebub
Βηθσαϊδά, ἡ	(7)	Bethsaida
βραχύς, εῖα, ύ	(7)	short, little, small
βρέχω	(7)	I wet, send rain; it rains (impers.)
βρυγμός, οῦ, ὁ	(7)	gnashing, chattering
γαμίζω	(7)	I give in marriage, marry
δέκατος, η, ον	(7)	tenth; tithe, tenth part, tithe (subst.)
δηλόω	(7)	I reveal, make clear, show
διαστρέφω	(7)	I make crooked, pervert, mislead
διατίθημι	(7)	I decree, ordain, assign, make a will (mid. in NT)
δοκιμή, ῆς, ἡ	(7)	character, test, ordeal, proof
δόκιμος, ον	(7)	approved, genuine, tried and true, respected
δῶμα, ατος, τό	(7)	roof, housetop
Ἑβραϊστί	(7)	in Hebrew or Aramaic
ἐγκαλέω	(7)	I accuse, bring charges against
εἰδωλολάτρης, ου, ὁ	(7)	idolater
ἐκζητέω	(7)	I seek out, search for, charge with
ἐκλογή, ῆς, ἡ	(7)	selection, election, choosing, that which is selected

ἔκστασις, εως, ἡ	(7)	astonishment, terror, trance, ecstasy
ἐλευθερόω	(7)	I free, set free
ἐμπίπτω	(7)	I fall into, among
ἐνδυναμόω	(7)	I strengthen; become or grow strong (pass.)
ἐνίστημι	(7)	I am present, impending, imminent
ἐπίγειος, ον	(7)	earthly, human
ἐπιδείκνυμι	(7)	I show, demonstrate, give proof
ἐπίκειμαι	(7)	I lie upon, press upon, am imposed
ἐπιστάτης, ου, ὁ	(7)	master
ἐπιταγή, ῆς, ἡ	(7)	command, order, injunction
ἐποικοδομέω	(7)	I build upon
ἐριθεία, ας, ἡ	(7)	selfishness, selfish ambition, selfish rivalry
εὔκοπος, ον	(7)	easy; easier (comp. in NT)
εὔχομαι	(7)	I pray, wish
ζήτησις, εως, ἡ	(7)	investigation, controversy, debate
ἡμέτερος, α, ον	(7)	our
θαρσέω	(7)	I am courageous; have courage! (imper. in NT)
θεῖον, ου, τό	(7)	sulfur
θόρυβος, ου, ὁ	(7)	noise, turmoil, excitement, uproar, disturbance, riot
ἰατρός, οῦ, ὁ	(7)	physician
Ἰεριχώ, ἡ	(7)	Jericho
καθαρισμός, οῦ, ὁ	(7)	purification
καθέζομαι	(7)	I sit, sit down, am situated
καταπίνω	(7)	I swallow, swallow up, devour; am drowned (pass.)
κλίνω	(7)	I incline, bow, lay down, draw to a close; rout (pass.)
κόκκος, ου, ὁ	(7)	seed, grain
κρεμάννυμι	(7)	I hang, crucify; hang, depend (mid.)
κτάομαι	(7)	I get, acquire, take
κυριεύω	(7)	I am lord or master, rule, control, lord it over
λάμπω	(7)	I shine, flash, shine forth
λιθοβολέω	(7)	I throw stones, stone (to death)
μαστιγόω	(7)	I whip, flog, scourge, punish
μεταλαμβάνω	(7)	I receive my share, share in, receive
μνεία, ας, ἡ	(7)	memory, remembrance, mention
μοιχαλίς, ίδος, ἡ	(7)	adulteress; adulterous (adj.)
νότος, ου, ὁ	(7)	south wind, southwest wind, south
ὄπισθεν	(7)	from behind, on the back; behind, after (impr. prep.)
ὀφειλέτης, ου, ὁ	(7)	debtor, one who is obligated or guilty, sinner
πάλαι	(7)	long ago, formerly, for a long time, already
πανταχοῦ	(7)	everywhere, in all directions
παράβασις, εως, ἡ	(7)	overstepping, transgression, violation
πεντήκοντα	(7)	fifty
περιβλέπω	(7)	I look around (mid. in NT)
πνέω	(7)	I blow
πολεμέω	(7)	I make war, fight
πονηρία, ας, ἡ	(7)	wickedness, evil
ποταπός, ή, όν	(7)	of what sort or kind, how great or glorious
πρέπω	(7)	I am fitting; it is fitting or proper (impers. in NT)
προσμένω	(7)	I remain or stay with, continue in, remain longer
προστάσσω	(7)	I command, order, prescribe

προσφωνέω	(7)	I call out, address, call to myself
πτῶμα, ατος, τό	(7)	corpse, (dead) body
ῥήγνυμι	(7)	I tear, burst, tear loose, break out, throw down
ῥομφαία, ας, ἡ	(7)	sword
σαρκικός, ή, όν	(7)	fleshly, earthly, material, pertaining to the flesh
Σιών, ἡ	(7)	Zion
σκιά, ᾶς, ἡ	(7)	shadow, shade, foreshadowing
σπεῖρα, ης, ἡ	(7)	cohort (tenth part of a legion)
στάδιον, ου, τό	(7)	stade (measure of distance), arena, stadium
Στέφανος, ου, ὁ	(7)	Stephen
στοιχεῖον, ου, τό	(7)	elements, fundamental principles, elemental spirits
στρατεύομαι	(7)	I serve as a soldier, fight, wage war
συγχαίρω	(7)	I rejoice with, congratulate
συμβιβάζω	(7)	I unite, conclude, demonstrate, teach
Συμεών, ὁ	(7)	Symeon, Simeon
συνανάκειμαι	(7)	I eat with, recline at table with
σύνεσις, εως, ἡ	(7)	intelligence, insight, understanding
συντρίβω	(7)	I shatter, crush, break, bruise
ταπεινοφροσύνη, ης, ἡ	(7)	humility, modesty
τάφος, ου, ὁ	(7)	grave, tomb
τράχηλος, ου, ὁ	(7)	neck, throat
ὑπομιμνῄσκω	(7)	I remind, call to mind; remember (pass.)
ὑποπόδιον, ου, τό	(7)	footstool
φθάνω	(7)	I precede, arrive, come upon or to
φίλημα, ατος, τό	(7)	kiss
φιμόω	(7)	I muzzle, silence; am silenced or silent (pass.)
φλόξ, φλογός, ἡ	(7)	flame
φονεύς, έως, ὁ	(7)	murderer
φρέαρ, ατος, τό	(7)	well, pit, shaft
φυσιόω	(7)	I puff up, make arrogant; become conceited (pass.)
χαλάω	(7)	I let down, lower
χεῖλος, ους, τό	(7)	lip, shore, bank
χρηστός, ή, όν	(7)	useful, good, easy, kind, loving; kindness (subst.)
ψαλμός, οῦ, ὁ	(7)	song of praise, psalm
ᾠδή, ῆς, ἡ	(7)	song
ἀγών, ῶνος, ὁ	(6)	contest, struggle, fight
αἰγιαλός, οῦ, ὁ	(6)	shore, beach
αἰσχύνη, ης, ἡ	(6)	modesty, shame, disgrace, shameful deed
ἄκρον, ου, τό	(6)	high point, top, tip, end
Ἀκύλας, ὁ	(6)	Aquila
Ἀλέξανδρος, ου, ὁ	(6)	Alexander
ἀλλάσσω	(6)	I change, alter, exchange
ἀνάθεμα, ατος, τό	(6)	something cursed, curse
ἀνακλίνω	(6)	I lay (down), put to bed; recline to eat, lie down (pass.)
ἀναμιμνῄσκω	(6)	I remind; remember (pass.)
ἀναπληρόω	(6)	I make complete, fulfill, replace
ἀνόητος, ον	(6)	unintelligent, foolish
ἀνυπόκριτος, ον	(6)	genuine, sincere
ἀξίως	(6)	worthily, suitably, properly
ἀπειθής, ές	(6)	disobedient

ἀποδημέω	(6)	I go on a journey, am away, am absent
ἀποθήκη, ης, ἡ	(6)	storehouse, barn
ἀποκόπτω	(6)	I cut off, make a eunuch of, castrate
ἀπορέω	(6)	I am at a loss, am uncertain
ἀποστερέω	(6)	I steal, rob, defraud, deprive
ἀποτάσσω	(6)	I say farewell, take leave, renounce (mid. in NT)
ἀποφέρω	(6)	I carry away, lead away, take, bring
ἀπωθέω	(6)	I push aside, reject, repudiate (mid. in NT)
ἀσέβεια, ας, ἡ	(6)	godlessness, impiety
βάρβαρος, ον	(6)	foreign, strange; non-Greek, barbarian, foreigner (subst.)
βαρέω	(6)	I weigh down, burden
βάρος, ους, τό	(6)	weight, burden, fullness
βαρύς, εῖα, ύ	(6)	heavy, burdensome, severe, weighty, important, fierce
βασανισμός, οῦ, ὁ	(6)	tormenting, torment
βδέλυγμα, ατος, τό	(6)	abomination, detestable thing
βουλεύω	(6)	I deliberate, resolve, decide (mid. in NT)
διάλεκτος, ου, ἡ	(6)	language
διαπεράω	(6)	I cross over
διαφθείρω	(6)	I spoil, destroy, ruin
διαφθορά, ᾶς, ἡ	(6)	destruction, corruption
διεγείρω	(6)	I wake up, arouse, stir up; awaken (pass.)
διερμηνεύω	(6)	I translate, explain, interpret
δίς	(6)	twice
δοκός, οῦ, ἡ	(6)	beam of wood
ἐγκακέω	(6)	I become tired, despondent, afraid
ἐγκεντρίζω	(6)	I graft
εἰκῇ	(6)	without cause, in vain, to no purpose
εἴπερ	(6)	if indeed, if after all, since
ἐκδέχομαι	(6)	I expect, wait
ἐκδικέω	(6)	I avenge, procure justice, punish
ἐκδύω	(6)	I strip, take off; undress myself (mid.)
ἐμπτύω	(6)	I spit on or at
ἕνδεκα	(6)	eleven
ἔνι	(6)	there is (= ἔνεστιν; impers. and with neg. in NT)
ἐξαπατάω	(6)	I deceive
ἐξαυτῆς	(6)	at once, immediately
ἐξηγέομαι	(6)	I explain, interpret, tell, report, describe, make known
ἐπαινέω	(6)	I praise, commend
ἐπιβαίνω	(6)	I go up or upon, mount, board, embark, arrive
ἐπιφάνεια, ας, ἡ	(6)	appearing, appearance, coming
ἐραυνάω	(6)	I search, examine, investigate
ἐργασία, ας, ἡ	(6)	practice, pursuit, trade, profit, gain, effort
ἔχθρα, ας, ἡ	(6)	enmity, hatred, hostility
ζημιόω	(6)	I suffer damage or loss, lose, am punished (pass. in NT)
ζυγός, οῦ, ὁ	(6)	yoke, balance scales
Ἡρῳδιάς, άδος, ἡ	(6)	Herodias
θαρρέω	(6)	I am confident, courageous
θαυμαστός, ή, όν	(6)	wonderful, marvelous, remarkable
θερμαίνω	(6)	I warm myself (mid. in NT)
θνητός, ή, όν	(6)	mortal

θυμίαμα, ατος, τό	(6)	incense, incense offering
Ἰκόνιον, ου, τό	(6)	Iconium
ἱνατί	(6)	why? for what reason?
καθότι	(6)	as, to the degree, because
κακόω	(6)	I harm, mistreat, make angry, embitter
κάμηλος, ου, ὁ, ἡ	(6)	camel
κάρφος, ους, τό	(6)	speck, chip
καταλλάσσω	(6)	I reconcile
καταπέτασμα, ατος, τό	(6)	curtain, veil
κατάρα, ας, ἡ	(6)	curse, something accursed
καταφιλέω	(6)	I kiss
κιβωτός, οῦ, ἡ	(6)	ark (ship), ark (covenant box)
κλείς, κλειδός, ἡ	(6)	key
κόκκινος, η, ον	(6)	red, scarlet; scarlet cloth (neut. subst.)
κόλπος, ου, ὁ	(6)	bosom, breast, chest, fold of a garment, bay, gulf
Κόρινθος, ου, ἡ	(6)	Corinth
κόφινος, ου, ὁ	(6)	basket
κραυγή, ῆς, ἡ	(6)	shouting, clamor, loud cry, crying
Κυρηναῖος, ου, ὁ	(6)	a Cyrenian
λανθάνω	(6)	I escape notice, am hidden, am unaware
Λαοδίκεια, ας, ἡ	(6)	Laodicea
λείπω	(6)	I leave, fall short, lack
λειτουργία, ας, ἡ	(6)	service, ceremonial duty, ministry
Λευίς, Λευί, ὁ	(6)	Levi
λύκος, ου, ὁ	(6)	wolf
Λύστρα, ἡ, τά	(6)	Lystra
μάγος, ου, ὁ	(6)	wise man, Magus, magician
μάστιξ, ιγος, ἡ	(6)	whip, lash, suffering; lashing (pl.)
μάταιος, α, ον	(6)	empty, idle, fruitless, useless, powerless, worthless
μέλας, αινα, αν	(6)	black; ink (neut. subst.)
μέριμνα, ης, ἡ	(6)	anxiety, worry, care
μεσίτης, ου, ὁ	(6)	mediator, arbitrator, intermediary
μεταμέλομαι	(6)	I regret, repent, change my mind
μετατίθημι	(6)	I change, take up; desert, turn away (mid.)
μέτοχος, ον	(6)	sharing or participating in; partner, companion (subst.)
μιμητής, οῦ, ὁ	(6)	imitator
μόλις	(6)	scarcely, with difficulty, only rarely
μόσχος, ου, ὁ	(6)	calf, young bull or ox
Ναζαρέθ, ἡ	(6)	Nazareth
Ναζαρηνός, ή, όν	(6)	Nazarene; inhabitant of Nazareth, a Nazarene (subst.)
Ναθαναήλ, ὁ	(6)	Nathanael
νήφω	(6)	I am well-balanced, self-controlled, sober
νόημα, ατος, τό	(6)	thought, mind, purpose, design, plot
ὁμοίωμα, ατος, τό	(6)	likeness, image, appearance
ὁμολογία, ας, ἡ	(6)	confession, confessing, acknowledgment, profession
ὄναρ, τό	(6)	dream
ὄξος, ους, τό	(6)	sour wine, wine vinegar
ὅπλον, ου, τό	(6)	tool, weapon
ὀσμή, ῆς, ἡ	(6)	fragrance, odor
παιδεία, ας, ἡ	(6)	upbringing, training, instruction, discipline

παραδέχομαι	(6)	I accept, receive, acknowledge, welcome
παρασκευή, ῆς, ἡ	(6)	preparation, day of preparation
παρατηρέω	(6)	I watch closely, observe carefully, guard (act. and mid.)
πενθερά, ᾶς, ἡ	(6)	mother-in-law
πεντακισχίλιοι, αι, α	(6)	five thousand
πεποίθησις, εως, ἡ	(6)	trust, confidence
περιάγω	(6)	I lead around, take about, go around or about
περιζώννυμι	(6)	I gird about, wrap around; dress myself (mid.)
περισσός, ή, όν	(6)	extraordinary, abundant, unnecessary; advantage (subst.)
πηλός, οῦ, ὁ	(6)	clay, mud
πήρα, ας, ἡ	(6)	knapsack, traveler's or beggar's bag
πλέω	(6)	I travel by sea, sail
πληροφορέω	(6)	I fill, fulfill, accomplish, convince, fully
ποιητής, οῦ, ὁ	(6)	doer, maker
πρᾶξις, εως, ἡ	(6)	activity, function, deed, evil deed
προκόπτω	(6)	I go forward, progress, advance, am far gone
προορίζω	(6)	I decide beforehand, predestine
πρόσκομμα, ατος, τό	(6)	stumbling, offense, obstacle
πρόφασις, εως, ἡ	(6)	valid reason or excuse, false motive, pretext
πυρετός, οῦ, ἡ	(6)	fever
πυρόω	(6)	I burn, am inflamed, make red hot (pass. in NT)
πώποτε	(6)	ever, at any time
σβέννυμι	(6)	I extinguish, put out, quench, stifle, suppress
σημαίνω	(6)	I make known, report, foretell
σινδών, όνος, ἡ	(6)	linen cloth, tunic, shirt
σκληρύνω	(6)	I harden; am stubborn, harden myself (pass.)
σκοπέω	(6)	I look our for, keep my eyes on, consider
σπεύδω	(6)	I hurry, make haste, hasten, strive for
σπήλαιον, ου, τό	(6)	cave, den
σπόρος, ου, ὁ	(6)	seed, supply of seed
στενάζω	(6)	I sigh, groan, complain
στρωννύω	(6)	I spread out, make (a bed), furnish (a room)
συλλαλέω	(6)	I talk or discuss with
συμβάλλω	(6)	I converse, consider, meet, engage; help (mid.)
συμφωνέω	(6)	I agree with, agree, settle with, match
συναντάω	(6)	I meet, happen
συνευδοκέω	(6)	I agree with, approve of, sympathize with
συντέλεια, ας, ἡ	(6)	completion, close, end
συντελέω	(6)	I complete, finish, come to an end, fulfill, accomplish
σωφρονέω	(6)	I am of sound mind, sensible, serious
Τρῳάς, άδος, ἡ	(6)	Troas
τρώγω	(6)	I gnaw, nibble, eat
ὕπνος, ου, ὁ	(6)	sleep
ὑπόδειγμα, ατος, τό	(6)	example, model, pattern, copy, imitation
ὑποδείκνυμι	(6)	I show, give direction, prove, warn
ὑπόκρισις, εως, ἡ	(6)	hypocrisy, pretense, outward show
ὕψος, ους, τό	(6)	height, heaven, high position
φαῦλος, η, ον	(6)	worthless, bad, evil
φθαρτός, ή, όν	(6)	subject to decay, perishable, mortal
φιλαδελφία, ας, ἡ	(6)	brotherly love, love of brother or sister

φορέω	(6)	I wear, bear
φορτίον, ου, τό	(6)	burden, load, cargo
φύλλον, ου, τό	(6)	leaf
χειμών, ῶνος, ὁ	(6)	rainy and stormy weather, bad weather, storm, winter
χειροποίητος, ον	(6)	made by human hands
χρῆμα, ατος, τό	(6)	money; property, wealth, means, money (pl.)
ψυχικός, ή, όν	(6)	physical, unspiritual; worldly person (subst.)
ὡσαννά	(6)	hosanna
Ἀαρών, ὁ	(5)	Aaron
ἀγαλλίασις, εως, ἡ	(5)	exultation, extreme joy
ᾄδω	(5)	I sing
ἀετός, οῦ, ὁ	(5)	eagle, vulture
Αἰγύπτιος, α, ον	(5)	Egyptian; an Egyptian (subst.)
αἰσχύνω	(5)	I am ashamed, disgraced (pass. in NT)
αἴτιος, α, ον	(5)	responsible, guilty; cause, guilt (subst. in NT)
ἀκαταστασία, ας, ἡ	(5)	disturbance, disorder, unruliness, insurrection
ἁλιεύς, έως, ὁ	(5)	fisherman
Ἀλφαῖος, ου, ὁ	(5)	Alphaeus
ἄμεμπτος, ον	(5)	blameless, faultless
ἄμμος, ου, ἡ	(5)	sand, seashore
ἀνακράζω	(5)	I cry out, shout
ἀνάπαυσις, εως, ἡ	(5)	stopping, ceasing, rest, resting place
ἀναπέμπω	(5)	I send up, send back
ἀνέγκλητος, ον	(5)	blameless, irreproachable
ἀνεκτός, όν	(5)	bearable, endurable
ἄνεσις, εως, ἡ	(5)	relaxing, rest, relaxation, relief
ἀνθύπατος, ου, ὁ	(5)	proconsul
ἀντίδικος, ου, ὁ	(5)	opponent, enemy
ἀντιτάσσω	(5)	I oppose, resist (mid. in NT)
ἀντίχριστος, ου, ὁ	(5)	Antichrist
ἀόρατος, ον	(5)	unseen, invisible
ἀπέναντι	(5)	opposite, against, contrary to (impr. prep. in NT)
ἄργυρος, ου, ὁ	(5)	silver, money
ἀρετή, ῆς, ἡ	(5)	virtue, miracle
Ἀρίσταρχυς, ου, ὁ	(5)	Aristarchus
ἅρπαξ, αγος	(5)	ravenous; swindler, robber (subst.)
ἄρρωστος, ον	(5)	sick, ill
Ἄρτεμις, ιδος, ἡ	(5)	Artemis
ἀσύνετος, ον	(5)	senseless, foolish, without understanding
ἀσφαλής, ές	(5)	firm, certain, secure
ἀφανίζω	(5)	I render invisible, destroy; perish, disappear (pass.)
βασιλικός, ή, όν	(5)	royal
βάτος, ου, ὁ, ἡ	(5)	thorn bush
βέβηλος, ον	(5)	profane, godless, irreligious
βύσσινος, η, ον	(5)	made of fine linen; fine linen (subst.)
γαζοφυλάκιον, ου, τό	(5)	treasure room, treasury, contribution box
Γάϊος, ου, ὁ	(5)	Gaius
γάλα, γάλακτος, τό	(5)	milk
γένεσις, εως, ἡ	(5)	beginning, origin, descent, birth, existence
δαπανάω	(5)	I spend, spend freely, waste

δεκατέσσαρες	(5)	fourteen
δεκτός, ή, όν	(5)	acceptable, welcome, favorable
δή	(5)	indeed, now, then, therefore
διαμένω	(5)	I remain, continue
διαπορεύομαι	(5)	I go through, pass through, walk through
διαρρήγνυμι	(5)	I tear, break
δικαίως	(5)	justly, uprightly
δόγμα, ατος, τό	(5)	decree, ordinance, decision, command
δουλεία, ας, ή	(5)	slavery
δυσμή, ῆς, ή	(5)	going down, setting (of the sun), west (pl. in NT)
ἑβδομήκοντα	(5)	seventy
ἐγκόπτω	(5)	I hinder, thwart, prevent
εἶδος, ους, τό	(5)	form, outward appearance, kind, sight
εἰσακούω	(5)	I listen to, obey, hear
εἴσοδος, ου, ή	(5)	entrance, access, coming
ἐκλύω	(5)	I become weary, give out (pass. in NT)
ἐκμάσσω	(5)	I wipe, dry
ἐκτρέπω	(5)	I turn, avoid, am dislocated (mid. and pass. in NT)
ἐλαύνω	(5)	I drive, advance, row
ἐμβριμάομαι	(5)	I scold, censure, warn sternly
ἐμπίμπλημι	(5)	I fill, satisfy, enjoy
ἔμπορος, ου, ὁ	(5)	merchant, wholesale dealer
ἔμφοβος, ον	(5)	afraid, startled, terrified
ἐννέα	(5)	nine
ἐνοικέω	(5)	I live, dwell in
ἔντιμος, ον	(5)	honored, respected, valuable, precious
ἐντυγχάνω	(5)	I meet, approach, appeal, petition, plead
ἐξαίφνης	(5)	suddenly, unexpectedly
ἐξαλείφω	(5)	I wipe away, wipe out, remove, destroy
ἑξῆς	(5)	next (day), soon after
ἔπειμι	(5)	I come after; next, next day (partic. in NT)
ἐπέχω	(5)	I hold fast, notice, fix my attention on, stop, stay
ἐπιγραφή, ῆς, ή	(5)	inscription, superscription
ἐπιγράφω	(5)	I write on or in
ἐπιεικής, ές	(5)	yielding, gentle, kind
ἐπισκιάζω	(5)	I overshadow, cast a shadow, cover
ἐπίσκοπος, ου, ὁ	(5)	overseer, guardian, bishop
ἐπιτυγχάνω	(5)	I obtain, attain, reach
ἐπιχορηγέω	(5)	I provide, give, grant, support
ἐρημόω	(5)	I am laid waste, depopulated (pass. in NT)
εὖ	(5)	well
εὐπρόσδεκτος, ον	(5)	acceptable, pleasant, welcome
εὐσχήμων, ον	(5)	proper, presentable, prominent, noble
ἐφάπαξ	(5)	at once, once for all
Ἐφέσιος, α, ον	(5)	Ephesian; an Ephesian (subst.)
ἔχιδνα, ης, ή	(5)	viper, snake
ζήτημα, ατος, τό	(5)	controversial question or issue
ζόφος, ου, ὁ	(5)	darkness, gloom
ἡδέως	(5)	gladly; very gladly (superl. ἥδιστα)
ἡδονή, ῆς, ή	(5)	pleasure, enjoyment, lust, passion

ἥμισυς, εια, υ	(5)	half; one half (neut. subst.)
ἡσυχάζω	(5)	I am quiet, rest
θεμελιόω	(5)	I found, lay the foundation of, establish, strengthen
Θεσσαλονίκη, ης, ἡ	(5)	Thessalonica
θηλάζω	(5)	I give suck, suck, nurse
θῆλυς, εια, υ	(5)	female; woman (subst.)
θώραξ, ακος, ὁ	(5)	breastplate, chest
Ἰάσων, ονος, ὁ	(5)	Jason
ἰδιώτης, ου, ὁ	(5)	layman, amateur, untrained, ungifted
Ἰεσσαί, ὁ	(5)	Jesse
ἱματισμός, οῦ, ὁ	(5)	clothing, apparel
καθεξῆς	(5)	in order, one after the other; successor (subst.)
καίπερ	(5)	though, although
καταδικάζω	(5)	I condemn, find or pronounce guilty
κατακλίνω	(5)	I cause to lie or sit down; recline at table, dine (pass.)
καταλαλέω	(5)	I speak against, defame, slander
καταπατέω	(5)	I trample, tread upon, treat with disdain
καταράομαι	(5)	I curse
κενόω	(5)	I make empty, destroy, render void
κῆπος, ου, ὁ	(5)	garden
κολαφίζω	(5)	I strike with the fist, beat, treat roughly
κονιορτός, οῦ, ὁ	(5)	dust
κράσπεδον, ου, τό	(5)	edge, border, hem, tassel
Κρήτη, ης, ἡ	(5)	Crete
κῦμα, ατος, τό	(5)	wave
Κύπρος, ου, ἡ	(5)	Cyprus
κύων, κυνός, ὁ	(5)	dog
λατρεία, ας, ἡ	(5)	service, worship, rite
λειτουργός, οῦ, ὁ	(5)	servant, minister
ληνός, οῦ, ἡ	(5)	wine press
λούω	(5)	I wash, bathe
Μαθθαῖος, ου, ὁ	(5)	Matthew
μαίνομαι	(5)	I am mad, out of my mind, insane
Μακεδών, όνος, ὁ	(5)	a Macedonian
μαρτύρομαι	(5)	I testify, bear witness, insist, implore
μεθίστημι	(5)	I remove, transfer, turn away, mislead
μεθύσκω	(5)	I get drunk, become intoxicated (pass. in NT)
μεθύω	(5)	I am drunk
μερίς, ίδος, ἡ	(5)	part, share, portion, district
μεταδίδωμι	(5)	I give, impart, share
μετασχηματίζω	(5)	I change, transform, apply
μιαίνω	(5)	I stain, defile, contaminate
μῦθος, ου, ὁ	(5)	tale, story, legend, myth, fable
μωρία, ας, ἡ	(5)	foolishness
νηστεία, ας, ἡ	(5)	fasting, abstention from food, hunger
Νικόδημος, ου, ὁ	(5)	Nicodemus
ὄγδοος, η, ον	(5)	eighth
ὁδηγέω	(5)	I lead, guide
ὁδηγός, οῦ, ὁ	(5)	leader, guide
ὀθόνιον, ου, τό	(5)	linen cloth, bandage

οἰκτιρμός, οῦ, ὁ	(5)	pity, mercy, compassion
ὀλιγόπιστος, ον	(5)	of little faith or trust
ὀνειδισμός, οῦ, ὁ	(5)	reproach, reviling, disgrace, insult
ὄνος, ου, ὁ, ἡ	(5)	donkey
ὁποῖος, α, ον	(5)	of what sort
ὁρμάω	(5)	I rush
οὐρά, ᾶς, ἡ	(5)	tail
ὀψάριον, ου, τό	(5)	fish
παγις, ίδος, ἡ	(5)	trap, snare
παίω	(5)	I strike, hit, sting
Παμφυλία, ας, ἡ	(5)	Pamphylia
πανουργία, ας, ἡ	(5)	cunning, craftiness, trickery
παραβάτης, ου, ὁ	(5)	transgressor, sinner
παραγγελία, ας, ἡ	(5)	order, command, precept, advice, instruction
παράκλητος, ου, ὁ	(5)	helper, intercessor
παρακύπτω	(5)	I bend over, stoop, look, steal a glance
παραλύω	(5)	I weaken; am weakened, paralyzed (pass. in NT)
παραπορεύομαι	(5)	I go, pass by
παροιμία, ας, ἡ	(5)	proverb, figure of speech
πατέω	(5)	I tread, trample; walk (intrans.)
πένθος, ους, τό	(5)	grief, sadness, mourning, sorrow
περιαιρέω	(5)	I take away, remove; am abandoned (pass.)
περίκειμαι	(5)	I am placed around, surrounded, bound, subject to
περίλυπος, ον	(5)	very sad, deeply grieved
περιποίησις, εως, ἡ	(5)	preserving, saving, gaining, possession
περίσσευμα, ατος, τό	(5)	abundance, fullness, what remains, scraps
πέτομαι	(5)	I fly
πίναξ, ακος, ἡ	(5)	platter, dish
πλάνος, ον	(5)	leading astray, deceitful; deceiver, impostor (subst.)
πλεονεκτέω	(5)	I take advantage of, outwit, defraud
πλευρά, ᾶς, ἡ	(5)	side
πλοιάριον, ου, τό	(5)	small boat, boat
ποίμνη, ης, ἡ	(5)	flock (esp. of sheep)
ποίμνιον, ου, τό	(5)	flock (esp. of sheep)
προβαίνω	(5)	I go on, advance
προγινώσκω	(5)	I know before or in advance, choose beforehand
προθυμία, ας, ἡ	(5)	willingness, readiness, goodwill, zeal
πρόκειμαι	(5)	I am set before, am present, publicly exhibited
πρωτοκλισία, ας, ἡ	(5)	place of honor
πταίω	(5)	I stumble, trip, go wrong, sin, am ruined or los
πτέρυξ, υγος, ἡ	(5)	wing
πωρόω	(5)	I harden, make dull or blind
σείω	(5)	I shake; am shaken, quake, am stirred, tremble (pass.)
σιδηροῦς, ᾶ, οῦν	(5)	made of iron
σίναπι, εως, τό	(5)	mustard
σκηνόω	(5)	I live, dwell
σκληρός, ά, όν	(5)	hard, rough, harsh, strong
σκορπίζω	(5)	I scatter, disperse, distribute
σκορπίος, ου, ὁ	(5)	scorpion
σκοτίζω	(5)	I am or become dark, am darkened (pass. in NT)

σπυρίς, ίδος, ἡ	(5)	basket, hamper
στάχυς, υος, ὁ	(5)	head of grain or wheat
στεῖρα, ας, ἡ	(5)	barren woman; barren (adj.)
στῆθος, ους, τό	(5)	chest, breast
στοιχέω	(5)	I agree with, hold to, follow
συγχέω	(5)	I confuse, trouble, stir up
συμπνίγω	(5)	I choke, crowd around, crush
συνεργέω	(5)	I work together with, cooperate with, help
συνεσθίω	(5)	I eat with
σύρω	(5)	I drag, pull, draw, drag or sweep away
συσταυρόω	(5)	I crucify with; am crucified together with (pass. in NT)
σωτήριος, ον	(5)	bringing salvation, delivering; salvation (neut. subst.)
τετρακισχίλιοι, αι, α	(5)	four thousand
τρόμος, ου, ὁ	(5)	trembling, quivering
Τυχικός, οῦ, ὁ	(5)	Tychicus
ὑβρίζω	(5)	I mistreat, scoff at, insult
ὑετός, οῦ, ὁ	(5)	rain
υἱοθεσία, ας, ἡ	(5)	adoption
ὑπερβάλλω	(5)	I go beyond, surpass, outdo
ὑπερέχω	(5)	I have power over, surpass, excel
ὑπερήφανος, ον	(5)	arrogant, haughty, proud
ὑπολαμβάνω	(5)	I take up, support, reply, suppose
ὑπόστασις, εως, ἡ	(5)	essence, substance, reality, situation, realization
Φαραώ, ὁ	(5)	Pharaoh
φόρος, ου, ὁ	(5)	tribute, tax
φύραμα, ατος, τό	(5)	that which is mixed, lump (of dough or clay)
φωτεινός, ή, όν	(5)	shining, bright, radiant, illuminated
χαλκός, οῦ, ὁ	(5)	copper, brass, bronze, gong, copper coin, money
χρήζω	(5)	I need, have need of
χρίω	(5)	I anoint
χρονίζω	(5)	I take time, linger, delay, take a long time
ψάλλω	(5)	I sing, sing praise, make melody
ψευδομαρτυρέω	(5)	I bear false witness, give false testimony
Ἄβελ, ὁ	(4)	Abel
ἀγαθωσύνη, ης, ἡ	(4)	goodness, uprightness, generosity
ἄγαμος, ον	(4)	unmarried; unmarried man or woman (subst. in NT)
ἄγκυρα, ας, ἡ	(4)	anchor
ἄγνοια, ας, ἡ	(4)	ignorance
ἀγρυπνέω	(4)	I am awake, keep watch, guard
ἀδιαλείπτως	(4)	constantly, unceasingly
Ἀθῆναι, ῶν, αἱ	(4)	Athens
αἰσχρός, ά, όν	(4)	ugly, shameful, disgraceful
αἰχμαλωτίζω	(4)	I capture, make captive, mislead, deceive
ἀκρίς, ίδος, ἡ	(4)	grasshopper, locust
ἀκροατής, οῦ, ὁ	(4)	hearer
ἀλάβαστρον, ου, τό	(4)	alabaster flask
ἁλληλουϊά	(4)	hallelujah, praise Yahweh
ἁμάρτημα, ατος, τό	(4)	sin, transgression
ἀμελέω	(4)	I neglect, am unconcerned, disregard
ἀμίαντος, ον	(4)	undefiled, pure

ἀμνός, οῦ, ὁ	(4)	lamb
ἀναθεματίζω	(4)	I bind under a curse, curse
ἀνακάμπτω	(4)	I return
ἀνακύπτω	(4)	I raise myself up, stand erect
ἀνάμνησις, εως, ἡ	(4)	reminder, remembrance
ἄνθος, ους, τό	(4)	blossom, flower
ἀνίημι	(4)	I loosen, unfasten, abandon, give up
Ἅννας, α, ὁ	(4)	Annas
ἀντέχω	(4)	I cling to, hold fast to, help (mid. in NT)
ἀντιλογία, ας, ἡ	(4)	contradiction, dispute, hostility, rebellion
ἀντλέω	(4)	I draw (water)
ἄνυδρος, ον	(4)	waterless, dry
ἀνυπότακτος, ον	(4)	not subject, independent, undisciplined, disobedient
ἀποβαίνω	(4)	I go away, get out, turn out, lead
ἀπογράφω	(4)	I register, record
ἀποδείκνυμι	(4)	I make, proclaim, appoint, display, prove
ἀποδεκατόω	(4)	I tithe, give one tenth, collect a tithe
ἀπόκειμαι	(4)	I am put away, am stored up; it is destined (impers.)
ἀποκεφαλίζω	(4)	I behead
ἀπόκρισις, εως, ἡ	(4)	answer
ἀποκρύπτω	(4)	I hide, conceal, keep secret
ἀποκυλίω	(4)	I roll away
ἀποπλέω	(4)	I sail away
ἀποσπάω	(4)	I draw away, pull away; withdraw (pass.)
ἀποστολή, ῆς, ἡ	(4)	apostleship, office of an apostle
ἀρεστός, ή, όν	(4)	pleasing
Ἀριμαθαία, ας, ἡ	(4)	Arimathea
ἀριστερός, ά, όν	(4)	left; left hand (subst.)
ἄρμα, ατος, τό	(4)	carriage, chariot
ἀρχηγός, οῦ, ὁ	(4)	leader, ruler, prince, originator, founder
ἄρωμα, ατος, τό	(4)	spice; spices, aromatic oils or ointments (pl.)
ἄσπιλος, ον	(4)	spotless, without blemish
ἄστρον, ου, τό	(4)	star, constellation
ἀσφαλίζω	(4)	I guard, secure
ἄτιμος, ον	(4)	unhonored, dishonored, less honorable
ἄτοπος, ον	(4)	out of place, unusual, evil, wrong
αὐτοῦ	(4)	here, there
ἀφόβως	(4)	fearlessly, boldly, shamelessly
ἀφροσύνη, ης, ἡ	(4)	foolishness, lack of sense
ἄφωνος, ον	(4)	silent, dumb, incapable of speech, without meaning
βαθύς, εῖα, ύ	(4)	deep
βαλλάντιον, ου, τό	(4)	money bag, purse
βαπτισμός, οῦ, ὁ	(4)	dipping, washing, baptism
βάπτω	(4)	I dip
Βαρθολομαῖος, ου, ὁ	(4)	Bartholomew
βασίλισσα, ης, ἡ	(4)	queen
Βενιαμίν, ὁ	(4)	Benjamin
βλαστάνω	(4)	I spout, put forth, produce
βλάσφημος, ον	(4)	blasphemous, slanderous; blasphemer (subst.)
Γαλατία, ας, ἡ	(4)	Galatia

γείτων, ονος, ὁ, ἡ	(4)	neighbor
γένημα, ατος, τό	(4)	produce, fruit, yield
γέννημα, ατος, τό	(4)	child, offspring
γλυκύς, εῖα, ύ	(4)	sweet
γνήσιος, α ον	(4)	born in wedlock, legitimate, genuine
γογγυσμός, οῦ, ὁ	(4)	complaint, displeasure, secret talk, whispering
Γόμορρα, ων, τα	(4)	Gomorrah
γονυπετέω	(4)	I kneel down
γυμνάζω	(4)	I exercise naked, train
δαμάζω	(4)	I subdue, tame, control
δανίζω	(4)	I lend (money); borrow (mid.)
δειπνέω	(4)	I eat, dine
δεσμωτήριον, ου, τό	(4)	prison, jail
δῆμος, ου, ὁ	(4)	people, populace, crowd, popular assembly
δημόσιος, α, ον	(4)	public; publicly (used as adv.)
διαδίδωμι	(4)	I distribute
διαπορέω	(4)	I am greatly perplexed, at a loss
διάφορος, ον	(4)	different, outstanding, excellent
διηνεκής, ές	(4)	continuous, uninterrupted
διορύσσω	(4)	I break through, break in
διπλοῦς, ῆ, οῦν	(4)	double, two-fold
δόμα, ατος, τό	(4)	gift
Ἑβραῖος, ου, ὁ	(4)	a Hebrew
ἐγκράτεια, ας, ἡ	(4)	self-control
ἐθνικός, ή, όν	(4)	Gentile, heathen; the Gentile (subst. in NT)
εἰδωλολατρία, ας, ἡ	(4)	idolatry
εἰρηνεύω	(4)	I keep the peace, live at peace
εἴσειμι	(4)	I go in, go into
εἴωθα	(4)	I am accustomed
ἐκδίδωμι	(4)	I let out for hire, lease, rent (mid. in NT)
ἐκθαμβέω	(4)	I am amazed, alarmed (pass. in NT)
ἐκλείπω	(4)	I fail, die out, cease, grow dark
ἐκπειράζω	(4)	I put to the test, try, tempt
ἐκριζόω	(4)	I uproot, pull out by the roots
ἐκτίθημι	(4)	I expose, abandon; explain (mid.)
ἐκτινάσσω	(4)	I shake off, shake out
ἐλάσσων, ον	(4)	smaller, younger, inferior, lesser
ἐμμένω	(4)	I stay, remain, stand by, remain true
ἔνδειξις, εως, ἡ	(4)	sign, proof
ἔνδοξος, ον	(4)	honored, distinguished, glorious, splendid
ἐνενήκοντα	(4)	ninety
ἐνθύμησις, εως, ἡ	(4)	thought, reflection, idea
ἐξαγοράζω	(4)	I buy, redeem; make the most of (mid.)
ἔξειμι	(4)	I go out or away, go on a journey
ἐξουσιάζω	(4)	I have the right or power over
ἐπακολουθέω	(4)	I follow, come after, devote myself to
ἐπίβλημα, ατος, τό	(4)	patch
ἐπιβουλή, ῆς, ἡ	(4)	plot
ἐπίθεσις, εως, ἡ	(4)	laying on
ἐπισκοπή, ῆς, ἡ	(4)	visitation, office, office of a bishop

ἐπιστηρίζω	(4)	I strengthen
ἐπιφαίνω	(4)	I appear; show myself (pass.)
ἐπιφωνέω	(4)	I cry out, shout
ἑπτάκις	(4)	seven times
ἐρημία, ας, ἡ	(4)	uninhabited region, desert
ἑρπετόν, οῦ, τό	(4)	reptile
εὐλαβής, ές	(4)	devout, God-fearing
εὐοδόω	(4)	I prosper, succeed (pass. in NT)
ζημία, ας, ἡ	(4)	damage, loss
ζυμόω	(4)	I ferment, leaven, cause to rise
ἡσυχία, ας, ἡ	(4)	quietness, rest, silence
Θεσσαλονικεύς, έως, ὁ	(4)	a Thessalonian
θορυβέω	(4)	I throw into disorder; am troubled, distressed (pass.)
θρηνέω	(4)	I mourn, lament, sing a dirge; mourn for (trans.)
θρησκεία, ας, ἡ	(4)	religion, worship
Θυάτειρα, ων, τά	(4)	Thyatira
θυρωρός, οῦ, ὁ, ἡ	(4)	doorkeeper
ἴασπις, ιδος, ἡ	(4)	jasper
ἱμάς, άντος, ὁ	(4)	strap, thong, whip
Ἰταλία, ας, ἡ	(4)	Italy
καθίημι	(4)	I let down
καθό	(4)	as, in so far as
κακολογέω	(4)	I speak evil of, revile, insult
κακοποιέω	(4)	I do wrong, harm, injure
κακοῦργος, ον	(4)	evil doing; criminal, evildoer (subst. in NT)
κάλυμμα, ατος, τό	(4)	covering, veil
κάμινος, ου, ἡ	(4)	oven, furnace
κάμπτω	(4)	I bend, bow
Κανά, ἡ	(4)	Cana
κανών, όνος, ὁ	(4)	rule, standard, sphere, limits
κατάγνυμι	(4)	I break
κατακαυχάομαι	(4)	I boast against, brag, exult over, triumph over
κατακλυσμός, οῦ, ὁ	(4)	flood, deluge
κατακυριεύω	(4)	I subdue, gain power over, rule over
καταλλαγή, ῆς, ἡ	(4)	reconciliation
καταπαύω	(4)	I bring to rest, stop, rest
κατασείω	(4)	I shake, wave, make a sign, motion
κατασκηνόω	(4)	I live, dwell, nest
καταφέρω	(4)	I cast against, bring (charges); am overcome (pass.)
κατήγορος, ου, ὁ	(4)	accuser
καυματίζω	(4)	I burn, scorch
κείρω	(4)	I shear; have my hair cut (mid.)
κέντρον, ου, τό	(4)	sting, goad
κῆνσος, ου, ὁ	(4)	tax
κιθάρα, ας, ἡ	(4)	lyre, harp
κινδυνεύω	(4)	I am in danger, run a risk
κλῆμα, ατος, τό	(4)	branch
κοίτη, ης, ἡ	(4)	bed, marriage bed, sexual intercourse, semen
κολοβόω	(4)	I curtail, shorten
κρανίον, ου, τό	(4)	skull

κραταιόω	(4)	I strengthen; become strong, grow strong (pass. in NT)
κράτιστος, η, ον	(4)	most noble, most excellent
κτῆμα, ατος, τό	(4)	property, possession, piece of land
κτῆνος, ους, τό	(4)	domesticated animal, animal used for riding; cattle (pl.)
κτίσμα, ατος, τό	(4)	creature, what is created
κυκλόω	(4)	I surround, encircle, go around
κυλλός, ή, όν	(4)	crippled, deformed
κυνάριον, ου, τό	(4)	little dog, dog
κυριότης, ητος, ἡ	(4)	lordship, dominion, ruling power
λαγχάνω	(4)	I receive, am appointed by lot, cast lots
λάθρᾳ	(4)	secretly
λάχανον, ου, τό	(4)	vegetable, garden herb
λεγιών, ῶνος, ἡ	(4)	legion
λέπρα, ας, ἡ	(4)	leprosy, skin disease
λόγιον, ου, τό	(4)	saying; oracles, sayings (pl. in NT)
λοιδορέω	(4)	I revile, insult
Λώτ, ὁ	(4)	Lot
μαθητεύω	(4)	I make a disciple of; become a disciple (pass.)
μακρός, ά, όν	(4)	long, far away, distant
μαλακός, ή, όν	(4)	soft, homosexual
μαμωνᾶς, ᾶ, ὁ	(4)	wealth, property
μάννα, τό	(4)	manna
μάχη, ης, ἡ	(4)	battle; fighting, quarrels, strife (pl. in NT)
μάχομαι	(4)	I fight, quarrel, dispute
μέλι, ιτος, τό	(4)	honey
μεσονύκτιον, ου, τό	(4)	midnight
μετακαλέω	(4)	I call to myself, summon, invite (mid. in NT)
μεταμορφόω	(4)	I am transformed, changed
μετοικεσία, ας, ἡ	(4)	deportation
μηνύω	(4)	I make known, reveal, inform, report
μίγνυμι	(4)	I mingle, mix
μιμέομαι	(4)	I imitate, follow
μοιχάω	(4)	I commit adultery (pass. in NT)
μύλος, ου, ὁ	(4)	mill, millstone
μωραίνω	(4)	I make foolish; become foolish or tasteless (pass.)
Ναζαρέτ, ἡ	(4)	Nazareth
νεότης, ητος, ἡ	(4)	youth
νῖκος, ους, τό	(4)	victory
ὀδυνάω	(4)	I suffer pain, am deeply distressed (pass. in NT)
οἰκέτης, ου, ὁ	(4)	house slave, domestic, servant
ὄλεθρος, ου, ὁ	(4)	destruction, ruin, death
ὅλως	(4)	generally speaking, actually, everywhere
ὁμιλέω	(4)	I speak, talk, converse
ὁμοῦ	(4)	together
ὀπτασία, ας, ἡ	(4)	vision
ὅρασις, εως, ἡ	(4)	appearance, vision
ὀρθῶς	(4)	rightly, correctly, properly
ὀρκωμοσία, ας, ἡ	(4)	oath, taking an oath
ὀρχέομαι	(4)	I dance
ὀστέον, ου, τό	(4)	bone

οὐδέπω	(4)	not yet
ὄφελον	(4)	O that, would that
ὀψώνιον, ου, τό	(4)	pay, wages, support, compensation
παλαιόω	(4)	I make old, treat as obsolete; become old (pass.)
παραζηλόω	(4)	I make jealous
παρακολουθέω	(4)	I follow, accompany, follow closely, investigate
παραμένω	(4)	I remain, stay, serve, continue in office
παραμυθέομαι	(4)	I encourage, cheer up, console, comfort
παρασκευάζω	(4)	I prepare; prepare myself, am ready (mid.)
παραφέρω	(4)	I take away, carry away, remove
παραχειμάζω	(4)	I winter, spend the winter
πάροικος, ον	(4)	strange; stranger, alien (subst.)
πατριάρχης, ου, ὁ	(4)	patriarch, father of a nation
πειθαρχέω	(4)	I obey, follow
πέμπτος, η, ον	(4)	fifth
πέρας, ατος, τό	(4)	end, limit, boundary; finally (adv.)
περιΐστημι	(4)	I stand around; avoid, shun (mid.)
περισσεία, ας, ἡ	(4)	surplus, abundance
περισσῶς	(4)	exceedingly, beyond measure, very, even more
πετρώδης, ες	(4)	rocky; rocky ground (subst. in NT)
πῆχυς, εως, ὁ	(4)	cubit (measure of length)
πικραίνω	(4)	I make bitter, embitter
πικρία, ας, ἡ	(4)	bitterness, harshness
πλάτος, ους, τό	(4)	breadth, width
πλεονέκτης, ου, ὁ	(4)	greedy or covetous person
πληροφορία, ας, ἡ	(4)	full assurance, certainty, conviction, fullness
πλουσίως	(4)	richly, abundantly
πολίτης, ου, ὁ	(4)	citizen, fellow citizen
πόνος, ου, ὁ	(4)	toil, pain, distress, affliction
πόρρω	(4)	far away, far
πορφύρα, ας, ἡ	(4)	purple cloth or garment
πορφυροῦς, ᾶ, οῦν	(4)	purple; purple garment (subst.)
πού	(4)	somewhere, about, approximately
πραΰς, πραεῖα, πραΰ	(4)	gentle, humble, considerate
προγράφω	(4)	I write before, mark out, portray publicly
προοράω	(4)	I see previously, foresee; see before me (mid.)
προσάγω	(4)	I bring forward or to
προσήλυτος, ου, ὁ	(4)	proselyte, convert
πρόσκαιρος, ον	(4)	lasting only for a time, temporary
προσωπολημψία, ας, ἡ	(4)	partiality
πρωτοκαθεδία, ας, ἡ	(4)	place of honor, best seat
πύργος, ου, ὁ	(4)	tower, watchtower, farm building
ῥαντίζω	(4)	I sprinkle; cleanse or wash myself (mid.)
ῥύμη, ης, ἡ	(4)	narrow street, lane, alley
σάκκος, ου, ὁ	(4)	sack, sackcloth
σάρκινος, η, ον	(4)	(made) of flesh, fleshly
Σάρρα, ας, ἡ	(4)	Sarah
σεμνός, ή, όν	(4)	worthy of respect or honor, noble, serious, honorable
Σιλουανός, οῦ, ὁ	(4)	Silvanus
Σινά	(4)	Sinai

σκολιός, ά, όν	(4)	crooked, unscrupulous, dishonest, harsh
σκύλλω	(4)	I harass, trouble, annoy; trouble myself (pass.)
σουδάριον, ου, τό	(4)	face cloth, handkerchief
σπουδαίως	(4)	with urgency, earnestly, zealously, eagerly
στέγω	(4)	I cover, pass over in silence, endure, bear
στένοχωρία, ας, ή	(4)	distress, difficulty, anguish, trouble
στερεός, ά, όν	(4)	firm, solid, strong
στοά, ᾶς, ή	(4)	colonnade, portico, porch
στρουθίον, ου, τό	(4)	sparrow
στῦλος, ου, ὁ	(4)	pillar, column
συγκλείω	(4)	I enclose, confine, imprison, catch
συγκληρονόμος, ον	(4)	inheriting together with; fellow heir (subst. in NT)
συγκοινωνός, οῦ, ὁ	(4)	participant, partner, sharer
σῦκον, ου, τό	(4)	fig, ripe fig
συμβουλεύω	(4)	I advise; consult, plot (mid.)
συμπαραλαμβάνω	(4)	I take along with
συμπορεύομαι	(4)	I go along with, come together, flock
συναρπάζω	(4)	I seize, drag away
σύνδεσμος, ου, ὁ	(4)	that which binds together, bond, fetter
συνετός, ή, όν	(4)	intelligent, wise
σώφρων, ον	(4)	thoughtful, moderate, self-controlled, decent, modest
ταμεῖον, ου, τό	(4)	storeroom, inner room
ταπείνωσις, εως, ή	(4)	humiliation, humility
ταῦρος, ου, ὁ	(4)	bull, ox
τετραάρχης, ου, ὁ	(4)	tetrarch
τετρακόσιοι, αι, α	(4)	four hundred
τεχνίτης, ου, ὁ	(4)	craftsman, artisan, designer
τηλικοῦτος, αύτη, οῦτο	(4)	so great, so large, so important
τράγος, ου, ὁ	(4)	he-goat
ὑμνέω	(4)	I sing hymns of praise to; sing a hymn (intrans.)
ὑπερῷον, ου, τό	(4)	upper story, room upstairs
ὑποδέχομαι	(4)	I receive, welcome
ὑποστέλλω	(4)	I draw back; shrink from, avoid, keep silent (mid.)
ὑποταγή, ῆς, ή	(4)	subjection, subordination, obedience
φάτνη, ης, ή	(4)	manger, stall, stable, feeding place
Φίλιπποι, ων, οἱ	(4)	Philippi
φραγμός, οῦ, ὁ	(4)	fence, wall, hedge, lane
φρόνημα, ατος, τό	(4)	way of thinking, aim, aspiration
φρουρέω	(4)	I guard, hold in custody, protect, keep
χάλαζα, ης, ή	(4)	hail
χλωρός, ά, όν	(4)	(light) green, pale; plant (subst.)
χοϊκός, ή, όν	(4)	made of earth or dust, earthly
ψηλαφάω	(4)	I feel (about for), touch, handle, grope after
ψυχρός, ά, όν	(4)	cold, cool; cold water (subst.)
ψωμίον, ου, τό	(4)	piece of bread
ὠδίν, ῖνος, ή	(4)	birth pains, suffering
ὡραῖος, α, ον	(4)	beautiful, pleasant, timely
ὠφέλιμος, ον	(4)	useful, beneficial, advantageous
αββα	(3)	father, abba
Ἀβιά, ὁ	(3)	Abijah

ἀγγαρεύω	(3)	I press into service, force, compel
ἁγιωσύνη, ης, ἡ	(3)	holiness
ἄγριος, α, ον	(3)	found in the open field, wild, stormy
ἀδημονέω	(3)	I am distressed, troubled, anxious
ἀδίκημα, ατος, τό	(3)	wrong, crime, misdeed
ἀθανασία, ας, ἡ	(3)	immortality
αἱρέω	(3)	I choose, prefer
αἴτημα, ατος, τό	(3)	request
αἰχμαλωσία, ας, ἡ	(3)	captivity, prisoners of war
ἀκέραιος, ον	(3)	pure, innocent
ἀκυρόω	(3)	I make void
ἄλαλος, ον	(3)	mute, dumb; mute person (subst.)
ἅλλομαι	(3)	I leap, spring up, well up, bubble up
ἀλοάω	(3)	I thresh
ἄλογος, ον	(3)	without reason, contrary to reason
Ἄλφα, τό	(3)	alpha
ἀλώπηξ, εκος, ἡ	(3)	fox
Ἀμιναδάβ, ὁ	(3)	Amminadab
ἀμφιέννυμι	(3)	I clothe, dress, adorn
Ἀμώς, ὁ	(3)	Amos
ἀνάγνωσις, εως, ἡ	(3)	reading, public reading
ἀναζητέω	(3)	I look, search
ἀναστατόω	(3)	I disturb, trouble, upset
ἀνατρέπω	(3)	I cause to fall, overturn, destroy
ἀνατρέφω	(3)	I bring up, care for, rear, train
ἀνεπίλημπτος, ον	(3)	irreproachable
ἀνέρχομαι	(3)	I go up, come up
ἄνευ	(3)	without (impr. prep.)
ἀνήκω	(3)	it is proper, fitting (impers. in NT)
ἀνθρωποκτόνος, ου, ὁ	(3)	murderer
ἀνορθόω	(3)	I rebuild, restore
ἀντιλαμβάνω	(3)	I help, take part in, practice, benefit by (mid. in NT)
ἀπαίρω	(3)	I take away (pass. in NT)
ἀπαλλάσσω	(3)	I free, release; am cured, leave, depart (pass.)
ἀπαλλοτριόω	(3)	I estrange; am estranged (pass. in NT)
ἀπάντησις, εως, ἡ	(3)	meeting; to meet (w. εἰς in NT)
ἀπατάω	(3)	I deceive, cheat, mislead
ἀπειλή, ῆς, ἡ	(3)	threat
ἀποκαταλλάσσω	(3)	I reconcile
ἀπόκρυφος, ον	(3)	hidden, secret
ἀποστάσιον, ου, τό	(3)	notice of divorce
ἀποσυνάγωγος, ον	(3)	expelled from the synagogue, excommunicated
ἀποφεύγω	(3)	I escape (from)
ἀποφθέγγομαι	(3)	I speak out, declare
ἀποχωρέω	(3)	I go away, leave, depart
ἀπρόσκοπος, ον	(3)	undamaged, blameless, giving no offense
ἆρα	(3)	interrog. part. of anxiety (untrans.)
ἀργυροῦς, ᾶ, οῦν	(3)	made of silver
ἀριθμέω	(3)	I count
ἀριστάω	(3)	I eat breakfast, eat a meal, dine

ἄριστον, ου, τό	(3)	breakfast, noon meal, meal
ἀρκετός, ή, όν	(3)	enough, sufficient, adequate
ἀροτριάω	(3)	I plow
ἁρπαγή, ῆς, ή	(3)	robbery, what has been stolen, plunder
ἀρραβών, ῶνος, ὁ	(3)	first installment, deposit, down payment
ἀρτύω	(3)	I prepare, season, salt
ἀρχιτρίκλινος, ου, ὁ	(3)	head waiter, butler, master of a feast
ἄσβεστος, ον	(3)	inextinguishable, unquenchable
ἀστοχέω	(3)	I miss the mark, miss, fail, deviate
ἀσφάλεια, ας, ή	(3)	firmness, certainty, security
ἀσφαλῶς	(3)	securely, beyond a doubt
ἀσωτία, ας, ή	(3)	debauchery, dissipation, reckless living
αὐλέω	(3)	I play the flute
ἄφνω	(3)	suddenly, immediately
ἀχειροποίητος, ον	(3)	not made by hand, spiritual
Βαλαάμ, ὁ	(3)	Balaam
βάσανος, ου, ή	(3)	torture, torment, severe pain
Βερνίκη, ης, ή	(3)	Bernice
Βηθφαγή, ή	(3)	Bethphage
βία, ας, ή	(3)	force, use of force, violence
βιβλαρίδιον, ου, τό	(3)	little book, little scroll
βιωτικός, ή, όν	(3)	belonging to life
βόθυνος, ου, ὁ	(3)	pit, ditch
βούλημα, ατος, τό	(3)	intention, purpose
βραδύς, εῖα, ύ	(3)	slow
βραχίων, ονος, ὁ	(3)	arm
βυρσεύς, έως, ὁ	(3)	tanner
γαλήνη, ης, ή	(3)	calm
Γαλλίων, ωνος, ὁ	(3)	Gallio
Γεννησαρέτ, ή	(3)	Gennesaret
Γερασηνός, ή, όν	(3)	Gerasene; a Gerasene (subst.)
Γολγοθᾶ, ή	(3)	Golgotha
γόμος, ου, ὁ	(3)	load, cargo
γυμνότης, ητος, ή	(3)	nakedness, destitution, lack of sufficient clothing
δειλός, ή, όν	(3)	cowardly, timid
δεκαπέντε	(3)	fifteen
Δεκάπολις, εως, ή	(3)	Decapolis
δελεάζω	(3)	I lure, entice
Δέρβη, ης, ή	(3)	Derbe
δεσμεύω	(3)	I bind, tie up
δεσμοφύλαξ, ακος, ὁ	(3)	jailer, keeper of the prison
δῆλος, η, ον	(3)	clear, plain, evident
Δημᾶς, ᾶ, ὁ	(3)	Demas
Δημήτριος, ου ὁ	(3)	Demetrius
διαβαίνω	(3)	I go through, cross, come over
διαβλέπω	(3)	I look intently, see clearly
διαγγέλλω	(3)	I proclaim far and wide, give notice of
διαγίνομαι	(3)	I pass, elapse
διάδημα, ατος, τό	(3)	diadem, crown
διαζώννυμι	(3)	I tie around

διαίρεσις, εως, ἡ	(3)	apportionment, division, difference
διάκρισις, εως, ἡ	(3)	distinguishing, ability to discriminate, quarrel
διαρπάζω	(3)	I plunder thoroughly, rob
διασπείρω	(3)	I scatter
διασπορά, ᾶς, ἡ	(3)	dispersion
διαστολή, ῆς, ἡ	(3)	difference, distinction
διαφημίζω	(3)	I spread widely, disseminate
διδακτός, ή, όν	(3)	instructed, imparted, taught
Δίδυμος, ου, ὁ	(3)	Didymus
διΐστημι	(3)	I go away, part, pass
δίκη, ης, ἡ	(3)	penalty, punishment; Justice (pers.)
δίστομος, ον	(3)	double-edged
δούλη, ης, ἡ	(3)	female slave, bondmaid
δραχμή, ῆς, ἡ	(3)	drachma (Greek silver coin)
δρόμος, ου, ὁ	(3)	course
δυνάστης, ου, ὁ	(3)	ruler, sovereign, court official
δυνατέω	(3)	I am strong, able
δυσκόλως	(3)	hardly, with difficulty
δωρέομαι	(3)	I give, present, bestow
ἐάνπερ	(3)	if indeed, if only, supposing that
Ἑβραΐς, ίδος, ἡ	(3)	Hebrew language (Aramaic)
ἐγγράφω	(3)	I write in, record
ἑδραῖος, α, ον	(3)	seated; firm, steadfast (met. in NT)
εἰλικρίνεια, ας, ἡ	(3)	sincerity, purity of motive
ἑκατονταπλασίων, ον	(3)	a hundred fold
ἐκδημέω	(3)	I leave my country or home, am away from home
ἐκκλάω	(3)	I break off
ἐκκλίνω	(3)	I turn away, turn aside, shun
ἐκπλέω	(3)	I sail away
ἐκπνέω	(3)	I breath out, expire, die
ἐκτενῶς	(3)	eagerly, fervently, constantly
ἐκψύχω	(3)	I breathe my last, die
ἐλαιών, ῶνος, ὁ	(3)	olive grove, olive orchard
ἐλαττόω	(3)	I make lower, inferior; diminish (pass.)
ἐλεάω	(3)	I have mercy on, show kindness
Ἑλιακίμ, ὁ	(3)	Eliakim
ἕλκος, ους, τό	(3)	sore, abscess, ulcer
Ἑλληνιστής, οῦ, ὁ	(3)	a Hellenist, Greek-speaking Jew
ἑνδέκατος, η, ον	(3)	eleventh
ἐνδημέω	(3)	I am at home
ἐνεργής, ές	(3)	effective, active, powerful
ἐνέχω	(3)	I have a grudge against; am subject to (pass.)
ἔνταλμα, ατος, τό	(3)	commandment
ἔντρομος, ον	(3)	trembling, fearful
ἐντυλίσσω	(3)	I wrap up, fold up
Ἑνώχ, ὁ	(3)	Enoch
ἐξακολουθέω	(3)	I follow, obey
ἐξανίστημι	(3)	I raise up, beget, stand up
ἐξετάζω	(3)	I examine, inquire
ἔξοδος, ου, ἡ	(3)	the Exodus, departure, death

ἐξώτερος, α, ον	(3)	farthest, extreme
ἐπάγω	(3)	I bring upon
ἐπάν	(3)	when, as soon as
ἐπανάγω	(3)	I put out (so sea), go out, return
ἐπαρκέω	(3)	I help, aid
Ἐπαφρᾶς, ᾶ, ὁ	(3)	Epaphras
ἐπιβαρέω	(3)	I weigh down, burden
ἐπιβιβάζω	(3)	I cause to mount
ἐπιβλέπω	(3)	I look at, consider, care about
ἐπιμελέομαι	(3)	I care for, take care of
ἐπιστέλλω	(3)	I inform or instruct by letter, write
ἐπίτροπος, ου, ὁ	(3)	manager, foreman, steward, guardian
ἐπιχειρέω	(3)	I set my hand to, attempt, try
Ἔραστος, ου, ὁ	(3)	Erastus
ἐρήμωσις, εως, ἡ	(3)	devastation, destruction, depopulation
ἑρμηνεύω	(3)	I explain, interpret, translate
ἑσπέρα, ας, ἡ	(3)	evening
Ἑσρώμ, ὁ	(3)	Hezron
ἑταῖρος, ου, ὁ	(3)	companion, friend
ἑτοίμως	(3)	readily
εὐαγγελιστής, οῦ, ὁ	(3)	one who proclaims good news, evangelist
εὐαρεστέω	(3)	I please, am pleasing
εὐγενής, ές	(3)	well-born, noble-minded, open-minded
εὔθετος, ον	(3)	suitable, usable, convenient
εὐθυμέω	(3)	I am cheerful, keep up my courage
εὐκαιρέω	(3)	I have time or opportunity, spend time
εὐσεβής, ές	(3)	godly, devout, pious, reverent
εὐσχημόνως	(3)	decently, becomingly
εὐχή, ῆς, ἡ	(3)	prayer, oath, vow
εὔχρηστος, ον	(3)	useful, serviceable
εὐωδία, ας, ἡ	(3)	fragrance, aroma
ἐχθές	(3)	yesterday
Ζαβουλών, ὁ	(3)	Zebulun
Ζακχαῖος, ου, ὁ	(3)	Zacchaeus
ζεστός, ή, όν	(3)	hot
Ζοροβαβέλ, ὁ	(3)	Zerubbabel
ζώννυμι	(3)	I gird, dress
ζωογονέω	(3)	I give life to, make alive, keep alive
ἡλίκος, η, ον	(3)	how great, how large, how small
Ἡρῳδιανοί, ῶν, οἱ	(3)	Herodians
Ἡσαῦ, ὁ	(3)	Esau
ἦχος, ου, ὁ	(3)	sound, tone, noise, report, news
θαμβέω	(3)	I am astounded, amazed (pass. in NT)
θάμβος, ους, τό	(3)	astonishment, fear
θέατρον, ου, τό	(3)	theater, play, spectacle
θεῖος, α, ον	(3)	divine; divine being, divinity (neut. subst.)
θεραπεία, ας, ἡ	(3)	serving, service, care, healing, servants
θέρος, ους, τό	(3)	summer
θιγγάνω	(3)	I touch
θροέω	(3)	I am disturbed, frightened (pass. in NT)

ἴαμα, ατος, τό	(3)	healing
ἴασις, εως, ἡ	(3)	healing
Ἰερεμίας, ου, ὁ	(3)	Jeremiah
ἱερός, ά, όν	(3)	holy; the holy things (neut. subst.)
ἱερωσύνη, ης, ἡ	(3)	priestly office, priesthood
ἰός, οῦ, ὁ	(3)	poison, rust
Ἰοῦστος, ου, ὁ	(3)	Justus
Ἰσκαριώθ, ὁ	(3)	Iscariot
ἰσότης, ητος, ἡ	(3)	equality, fairness
ἴχνος, ους, τό	(3)	footprint
Ἰωβήδ, ὁ	(3)	Obed
Ἰωσῆς, ῆτος, ὁ	(3)	Joses
καθαίρεσις, εως, ἡ	(3)	tearing down, destruction
καθέδρα, ας, ἡ	(3)	chair, seat
Κάϊν, ὁ	(3)	Cain
κακοπαθέω	(3)	I suffer misfortune, bear hardship patiently
κακοποιός, όν	(3)	doing evil; evildoer, criminal, sorcerer (subst. in NT)
καταγελάω	(3)	I laugh at, ridicule
καταγινώσκω	(3)	I condemn, convict
κατακαλύπτω	(3)	I cover, veil; cover myself (mid. in NT)
κατάκριμα, ατος, τό	(3)	punishment, doom
κατάλυμα, ατος, τό	(3)	inn, lodging, guest room, dining room
καταμαρτυρέω	(3)	I bear witness against, testify against
καταναρκάω	(3)	I burden, am a burden to
καταξιόω	(3)	I consider worthy
καταπίπτω	(3)	I fall (down)
κατενώπιον	(3)	before, in the presence of (impr. prep. in NT)
κατευθύνω	(3)	I make straight, lead, direct
κατηγορία, ας, ἡ	(3)	accusation, charge
κατισχύω	(3)	I am strong, prevail, am able, am victorious over
καύσων, ωνος, ὁ	(3)	heat, burning
κεντυρίων, ωνος, ὁ	(3)	centurion
κεραμεύς, έως, ὁ	(3)	potter
κεράννυμι	(3)	I mix, pour
κέρδος, ους, τό	(3)	gain
κῆρυξ, υκος, ὁ	(3)	herald, preacher
Κλαύδιος, ου, ὁ	(3)	Claudius
κλίμα, ατος, τό	(3)	district, region
κολλυβιστής, οῦ, ὁ	(3)	money-changer
κολυμβήθρα, ας, ἡ	(3)	pool, swimming pool
κοπάζω	(3)	I stop, abate, rest
κουστωδία, ας, ἡ	(3)	guard
κρημνός, οῦ, ὁ	(3)	steep slope or bank, cliff
κριτήριον, ου, τό	(3)	court, tribunal, lawsuit
κυκλόθεν	(3)	all around, from all sides; around (impr. prep.)
Κύπριος, ου, ὁ	(3)	a Cyprian
κῶμος, ου, ὁ	(3)	excessive feasting, carousing, revelry
λαῖλαψ, απος, ἡ	(3)	whirlwind, hurricane, storm, squall
λαλιά, ᾶς, ἡ	(3)	speech, speaking, accent, way of speaking
λειτουργέω	(3)	I perform a service, serve

λεπτός, ή, όν	(3)	small; lepton, small copper coin (subst. in NT)
Λευίτης, ου, ὁ	(3)	Levite
λίθινος, η, ον	(3)	(made of) stone
λοιδορία, ας, ἡ	(3)	abuse (verbal), reproach, reviling
Λουκᾶς, ᾶ, ὁ	(3)	Luke
Λύδδα, ας, ἡ	(3)	Lydda
λυτρόω	(3)	I set free, redeem, rescue (mid.); am ransomed (pass.)
λύτρωσις, εως, ἡ	(3)	redemption, ransoming, releasing
μακαρισμός, οῦ, ὁ	(3)	blessing, happiness
μαλακία, ας, ἡ	(3)	weakness, sickness
Μανασσῆς, ῆ, ὁ	(3)	Manasseh
μαστός, οῦ, ὁ	(3)	breast, chest
ματαιότης, ητος, ἡ	(3)	emptiness, futility, purposelessness, worthlessness
μεγαλειότης, ητος, ἡ	(3)	grandeur, greatness, majesty
μεγαλωσύνη, ης, ἡ	(3)	majesty, greatness, Majesty
μεγιστάν, ᾶνος, ὁ	(3)	great person, courtier
μέθη, ης, ἡ	(3)	drunkenness
μενοῦνγε	(3)	rather, on the contrary, indeed
μεσουράνημα, ατος, τό	(3)	midheaven, zenith
μετάθεσις, εως, ἡ	(3)	removal, change, taking up
μῆκος, ους, τό	(3)	length
Μίλητος, ου, ἡ	(3)	Miletus
μισθαποδοσία, ας, ἡ	(3)	reward, punishment, retribution
μισθωτός, οῦ, ὁ	(3)	hired worker
μνημόσυνον, ου, τό	(3)	memory, memorial offering
μνηστεύω	(3)	I betroth; am betrothed, become engaged
μόδιος, ίου, ὁ	(3)	basket, container (for measuring grain)
μοιχεία, ας, ἡ	(3)	adultery
μοιχός, οῦ, ὁ	(3)	adulterer
μολύνω	(3)	I stain, defile, make unclean
μορφή, ῆς, ἡ	(3)	form, outward appearance, shape
μόχθος, ου, ὁ	(3)	labor, exertion, hardship
Ναασσών, ὁ	(3)	Nahshon
ναύτης, ου, ὁ	(3)	sailor
νεανίας, ου, ὁ	(3)	youth, young man, servant
νεκρόω	(3)	I put to death; am as good as dead (pass.)
Νεφθαλίμ, ὁ	(3)	Naphtali
νηφάλιος, α, ον	(3)	temperate, sober, clear-headed, self-controlled
Νινευίτης, ου, ὁ	(3)	a Ninevite
νομοδιδάσκαλος, ου, ὁ	(3)	teacher of the law
νοσφίζω	(3)	I keep back for myself, embezzle (mid. in NT)
νουθεσία, ας, ἡ	(3)	admonition, instruction, warning
νυμφών, ῶνος, ὁ	(3)	wedding hall, bridal chamber
ξυράω	(3)	I have myself shaved (mid.); am shaved (pass.)
οἰκεῖος, α, ον	(3)	member of the household (subst. in NT)
οἰκτίρμων, ον	(3)	merciful, compassionate
οἴομαι	(3)	I think, suppose, expect
ὀκνηρός, ά, όν	(3)	lazy, indolent, troublesome
ὁλοκαύτωμα, ατος, τό	(3)	whole burnt offering
ὅμως	(3)	nevertheless, yet, likewise, also

ὀρέγω	(3)	I stretch myself, aspire to, desire, long for (mid. in NT)
ὄρθρος, ου, ὁ	(3)	dawn, early morning
ὄρνεον, ου, τό	(3)	bird
ὀρύσσω	(3)	I dig
ὁσάκις	(3)	as often as, whenever
ὀφειλή, ῆς, ἡ	(3)	debt, one's due, duty
ὄφελος, ους, τό	(3)	benefit, good
ὀψέ	(3)	late in the day, in the evening; after (impr. prep.)
ὄψις, εως, ἡ	(3)	outward appearance, face
πάθος, ους, τό	(3)	passion
παιδαγωγός, οῦ, ὁ	(3)	attendant, custodian, guide
πανοπλία, ας, ἡ	(3)	full armor, panoply
πάντοθεν	(3)	from all directions, on all sides, entirely
παραβαίνω	(3)	I turn aside; transgress, break (trans.)
παράδεισος, ου, ὁ	(3)	paradise
παραθήκη, ης, ἡ	(3)	deposit, what is entrusted another
παρακοή, ῆς, ἡ	(3)	disobedience, disloyalty
παρακούω	(3)	I overhear, ignore, disobey
παρεκτός	(3)	besides, outside; apart from, except for (impr. prep.)
παρεπίδημος, ον	(3)	sojourning; stranger, exile, alien (subst. in NT)
πατριά, ᾶς, ἡ	(3)	family, clan, nation, people
πατρῷος, α, ον	(3)	paternal, belonging to one's ancestors
πέδη, ης, ἡ	(3)	fetter, shackle
πεντηκοστή, ῆς, ἡ	(3)	Pentecost
Πέργη, ης, ἡ	(3)	Perga
περιέρχομαι	(3)	I go around, wander
περικαλύπτω	(3)	I cover, conceal
περιπίπτω	(3)	I fall in with, encounter, fall into, strike
περιποιέω	(3)	I preserve, acquire, gain (mid. in NT)
περιφέρω	(3)	I carry about, carry here and there
πλάξ, πλακός, ἡ	(3)	flat stone, tablet, table
πλατύνω	(3)	I make broad, enlarge, open wide
πλέκω	(3)	I weave, plait
πλοῦς, πλοός, ὁ	(3)	voyage, navigation
πλουτίζω	(3)	I make rich
πλύνω	(3)	I wash
πνίγω	(3)	I choke, strangle; drown (pass.)
πνικτός, ή, όν	(3)	strangled, choked to death
πολυτελής, ές	(3)	very expensive, costly
πολύτιμος, ον	(3)	very precious, valuable
Πόντιος, ου, ὁ	(3)	Pontius
πορθέω	(3)	I destroy, try to destroy
ποσάκις	(3)	how many times? how often?
πόσις, εως, ἡ	(3)	drinking, drink
πρεσβυτέριον, ου, τό	(3)	council of elders
πρεσβύτης, ου, ὁ	(3)	old or elderly man
Πρίσκα, ης, ἡ	(3)	Prisca
Πρίσκιλλα, ης, ἡ	(3)	Priscilla
πρόδηλος, ον	(3)	clear, evident, known to all
προδότης, ου, ὁ	(3)	traitor, betrayer

πρόθυμος, ον	(3)	ready, willing, eager; eagerness, desire (subst.)
προκοπή, ῆς, ἡ	(3)	progress, advancement
προλαμβάνω	(3)	I do before, anticipate, take, detect
προνοέω	(3)	I think of beforehand, care for, have regard for
προσαγωγή, ῆς, ἡ	(3)	approach, access
προστρέχω	(3)	I run up to
προτίθημι	(3)	I display publicly, plan, intend (mid. in NT)
προχειρίζομαι	(3)	I choose for myself, select, appoint
πρύμνα, ης, ἡ	(3)	stern (of a ship)
πτύω	(3)	I spit
πτωχεία, ας, ἡ	(3)	poverty
πυκνός, ή, όν	(3)	frequent, numerous; often, frequently (neut. pl. as adv.)
πύρωσις, εως, ἡ	(3)	burning, fiery test
πώρωσις, εως, ἡ	(3)	hardening, dullness, insensibility, obstinacy
ῥάπισμα, ατος, τό	(3)	blow with a club, slap in the face
ῥύσις, εως, ἡ	(3)	flow, flowing
Σαλαθιήλ, ὁ	(3)	Shealtiel, Salathiel
Σαμουήλ, ὁ	(3)	Samuel
Σάρδεις, εων, αἱ	(3)	Sardis
σαρόω	(3)	I sweep (clean)
σεβαστός, ή, όν	(3)	imperial, Augustan; emperor, Imperial Majesty (subst.)
σεμνότης, ητος, ἡ	(3)	reverence, dignity, holiness, seriousness
σής, σητός, ὁ	(3)	moth
Σιλωάμ, ὁ	(3)	Siloam
σιτευτός, ή, όν	(3)	fattened
σκάπτω	(3)	I dig
σκάφη, ης, ἡ	(3)	small boat, skiff
σκέλος, ους, τό	(3)	leg
σκήνωμα, ατος, τό	(3)	tent, dwelling, dwelling place, body
σκιρτάω	(3)	I leap, spring about, jump for joy, move
σκληροκαρδία, ας, ἡ	(3)	hardness of heart, stubbornness
σκοτεινός, ή, όν	(3)	dark
σκοτόω	(3)	I darken; am or become darkened (pass. in NT)
σπαράσσω	(3)	I tear, pull to and fro, throw into convulsions
σπόγγος, ου, ὁ	(3)	sponge
σποδός, οῦ, ἡ	(3)	ashes
σπόριμος, ον	(3)	sown; standing grain, grain fields (pl. subst. in NT)
σπουδαῖος, α, ον	(3)	eager, earnest, diligent
σταφυλή, ῆς, ἡ	(3)	(bunch of) grapes
στέγη, ης, ἡ	(3)	roof
στενός, ή, όν	(3)	narrow
στενοχωρέω	(3)	I restrict; am confined, restricted, crushed (pass. in NT)
στερεόω	(3)	I make strong; am strengthened (pass.)
Στεφανᾶς, ᾶ, ὁ	(3)	Stephanas
στεφανόω	(3)	I crown, honor, reward
συγγένεια, ας, ἡ	(3)	relationship, kinship, relatives
συγκοινωνέω	(3)	I participate in
συγκρίνω	(3)	I compare, explain, interpret, combine
συζάω	(3)	I live with or together
συμμαρτυρέω	(3)	I testify with, confirm, testify in support of

συμπληρόω	(3)	I am swamped, approach, come (pass. in NT)
συναίρω	(3)	I settle
συναιχμάλωτος, ου, ὁ	(3)	fellow prisoner
συνακολουθέω	(3)	I follow, accompany
συναναμίγνυμι	(3)	I mix up together; mingle or associate with (pass. in NT)
συναπάγω	(3)	I am led or carried away (pass. in NT)
συναποθνήσκω	(3)	I die with
συνεγείρω	(3)	I raise together with
συνήθεια, ας, ἡ	(3)	being accustomed, custom, habit
συντάσσω	(3)	I order, direct, prescribe
συντηρέω	(3)	I protect, defend, preserve, treasure up
συντίθημι	(3)	I put with; agree, decide (mid. in NT)
συντρέχω	(3)	I run together, plunge with
σφαγή, ῆς, ἡ	(3)	slaughter
σχεδόν	(3)	nearly, almost
σωφροσύνη, ης, ἡ	(3)	reasonableness, self-control, decency, modesty
Ταρσός, οῦ, ἡ	(3)	Tarsus
τελώνιον, ου, τό	(3)	revenue or tax office
τετρααρχέω	(3)	I am tetrarch or ruler
τετράπους, ουν	(3)	four-footed; four-footed animal (subst. in NT)
τέχνη, ης, ἡ	(3)	skill, trade, craft
τήρησις, εως, ἡ	(3)	custody, keeping, observance
Τιβεριάς, άδος, ἡ	(3)	Tiberias
τίλλω	(3)	I pluck, pick
τοίνυν	(3)	hence, so, indeed, therefore, then
τοὐναντίον	(3)	on the other hand, rather (= τὸ ἐναντίον)
τρέμω	(3)	I tremble, am afraid, stand in awe of, respect
τρίβος, ου, ἡ	(3)	path
Τρόφιμος, ου, ὁ	(3)	Trophimus
τρυγάω	(3)	I pick, gather
τυφλόω	(3)	I blind, deprive of sight
τυφόω	(3)	I delude; am puffed up, conceited (pass. in NT)
ὑάλινος, η, ον	(3)	of glass, transparent as glass
ὕβρις, εως, ἡ	(3)	shame, insult, mistreatment, disaster, damage
ὑδρία, ας, ἡ	(3)	water jar
ὑπάντησις, εως, ἡ	(3)	meeting
ὑπεραίρω	(3)	I exalt myself, am puffed up with pride (mid. in NT)
ὑπεράνω	(3)	(high) above (impr. prep. in NT)
ὑπερεκπερισσοῦ	(3)	beyond all measure; infinitely more than (impr. prep.)
ὑπήκοος, ον	(3)	obedient
ὑπηρετέω	(3)	I serve, render service, am helpful
ὑποδέω	(3)	I tie or bind beneath, put on shoes (mid. in NT)
ὑπόμνησις, εως, ἡ	(3)	remembering, reminding, remembrance
ὑπονοέω	(3)	I suspect, suppose
ὑποφέρω	(3)	I bear up under, submit to, endure
φανερῶς	(3)	openly, publicly, clearly
Φάρες, ὁ	(3)	Perez
φάσκω	(3)	I say, assert, claim
φθέγγομαι	(3)	I call out loudly, speak, utter, proclaim
φιλόξενος, ον	(3)	hospitable

φιλοτιμέομαι	(3)	I aspire
φοβερός, ά, όν	(3)	fearful, terrible, frightful
Φοινίκη, ης, ή	(3)	Phoenicia
φράσσω	(3)	I shut, stop, close, silence, block
Φρυγία, ας, ή	(3)	Phrygia
φύλαξ, ακος, ὁ	(3)	guard, sentinel
φυσικός, ή, όν	(3)	belonging to nature, natural
φύω	(3)	I grow up, come up
χρῖσμα, ατος, τό	(3)	anointing
Χριστιανός, οῦ, ὁ	(3)	a Christian
ψευδής, ές	(3)	false, lying; liar (subst.)
ψῆφος, ου, ἡ	(3)	pebble, vote, stone
ψῦχος, ους, τό	(3)	cold
Ω	(3)	omega
ὠδίνω	(3)	I suffer birth pains
ὠτίον, ου, τό	(3)	ear
Ἀβιούδ, ὁ	(2)	Abiud
Ἄγαβος, ου, ὁ	(2)	Agabus
Ἀγάρ, ἡ	(2)	Hagar
ἀγγελία, ας, ἡ	(2)	message, command
ἄγε	(2)	come! (pres. imper. of ἄγω)
ἄγναφος, ον	(2)	unbleached, unshrunken, new
ἁγνεία, ας, ἡ	(2)	purity, chastity
ἁγνότης, ητος, ἡ	(2)	purity, sincerity
ἀγνωσία, ας, ἡ	(2)	ignorance, lack of spiritual discernment
ἀγοραῖος, ον	(2)	pertaining to a market; loafer, court session (subst.)
ἄγρα, ας, ἡ	(2)	catching, catch
ἀγριέλαιος, ου, ἡ	(2)	wild olive tree
ἀγρυπνία, ας, ἡ	(2)	wakefulness
ἀδελφότης, ητος, ἡ	(2)	brotherhood
ἄδηλος, ον	(2)	not clear, unseen, indistinct
ἀδιάλειπτος, ον	(2)	unceasing, constant
ἀδυνατέω	(2)	I am powerless; it is impossible (impers. in NT)
Ἀζώρ, ὁ	(2)	Azor
ἀθέμιτος, ον	(2)	unlawful, lawless, wanton
ἄθεσμος, ον	(2)	lawless, unprincipled; lawless person (subst.)
ἀθέτησις, εως, ἡ	(2)	annulment, removal
Ἀθηναῖος, α, ον	(2)	Athenian; an Athenian (subst.)
ἀθλέω	(2)	I compete in a contest
ἀθῷος, ον	(2)	innocent
ἀίδιος, ον	(2)	eternal
Αἰθίοψ, οπος, ὁ	(2)	an Ethiopian
Αἰνέας, ου, ὁ	(2)	Aeneas
αἶνος, ου, ὁ	(2)	praise
αἰσχροκερδής, ές	(2)	fond of dishonest gain, greedy for money
αἰφνίδιος, ον	(2)	sudden
ἄκακος, ον	(2)	innocent, guileless, unsuspecting
ἀκάνθινος, η, ον	(2)	thorny
ἀκατακάλυπτος, ον	(2)	uncovered
ἀκατάκριτος, ον	(2)	uncondemned, without a proper trial

ἀκατάστατος, ον	(2)	unstable, restless
ἀκρασία, ας, ἡ	(2)	lack of self-control, self-indulgence
ἀκριβόω	(2)	I ascertain, inquire with exactness
ἀκρογωνιαῖος, α, ον	(2)	lying at the extreme corner; cornerstone (subst.)
ἀλαζονεία, ας, ἡ	(2)	pretension, arrogance, pride
ἀλαζών, όνος, ὁ	(2)	boaster, braggart
ἀλαλάζω	(2)	I cry out loudly, clang
Ἀλεξανδρεύς, έως, ὁ	(2)	an Alexandrian
Ἀλεξανδρῖνος, η, ον	(2)	Alexandrian
ἄλευρον, ου, τό	(2)	wheat flour
ἀληθεύω	(2)	I am truthful, tell the truth
ἀλήθω	(2)	I grind
ἁλίζω	(2)	I salt
ἅλων, ωνος, ἡ	(2)	threshing floor, threshed grain
ἄμαχος, ον	(2)	peaceable
ἀμέμπτως	(2)	blamelessly, blameless
ἀμέριμνος, ον	(2)	free from care, without worry
ἀμετάθετος, ον	(2)	unchangeable; unchangeableness (subst.)
ἀμεταμέλητος, ον	(2)	not to be regretted, without regret, irrevocable
ἄμετρος, ον	(2)	immeasurable
ἀναβαθμός, οῦ, ὁ	(2)	step; flight of stairs (pl.)
ἀνάγαιον, ου, τό	(2)	room upstairs
ἀναγεννάω	(2)	I beget again, cause to be born again
ἀναδείκνυμι	(2)	I show forth, show clearly, appoint, commission
ἀναδέχομαι	(2)	I accept, receive, welcome
ἀναζάω	(2)	I come to life again, spring into life
ἀναθεωρέω	(2)	I examine, observe carefully
ἀναίτιος, ον	(2)	innocent
ἀνακαθίζω	(2)	I sit up
ἀνακαινόω	(2)	I renew
ἀνακαίνωσις, εως, ἡ	(2)	renewal
ἀνακαλύπτω	(2)	I uncover, unveil
ἀνακεφαλαιόω	(2)	I sum up, recapitulate
ἀναλίσκω	(2)	I consume
ἀναλύω	(2)	I depart, return, die
ἀνάπειρος, ον	(2)	crippled
ἀναπολόγητος, ον	(2)	without excuse, inexcusable
ἀνάπτω	(2)	I kindle, set fire
ἀνασείω	(2)	I stir up, incite
ἀνασπάω	(2)	I draw, pull up
ἀνατίθημι	(2)	I declare, lay before (mid. in NT)
ἀναφαίνω	(2)	I light up, cause to appear, come into view
ἀνεξιχνίαστος, ον	(2)	inscrutable, incomprehensible
ἀνετάζω	(2)	I give a hearing
ἀνευρίσκω	(2)	I find by searching
ἀνθρακιά, ᾶς, ἡ	(2)	charcoal fire
ἀνθρωπάρεσκος, ον	(2)	trying to please people
ἄνιπτος, ον	(2)	unwashed
ἄνοια, ας, ἡ	(2)	folly, foolishness, fury
ἀνοικοδομέω	(2)	I build up again, rebuild

ἀνόμως	(2)	without the law
ἀνόσιος, ον	(2)	unholy, wicked
ἀνοχή, ῆς, ἡ	(2)	forbearance, clemency, tolerance
ἀντάλλαγμα, ατος, τό	(2)	something given in exchange
ἀνταπόδομα, ατος, τό	(2)	repayment, retribution
ἀνταποκρίνομαι	(2)	I answer in turn, answer back
ἀντιμισθία, ας, ἡ	(2)	reward, penalty, exchange
ἀντιπαρέρχομαι	(2)	I pass by on the opposite side
ἀντίτυπος, ον	(2)	corresponding to; copy, antitype, representation (subst.)
ἀνώτερος, α, ον	(2)	higher, above, earlier (neut. as adv. in NT)
ἀνωφελής, ές	(2)	useless, harmful
ἀξίνη, ης, ἡ	(2)	ax
ἀπαιτέω	(2)	I ask for, demand
ἀπαλός, ή, όν	(2)	tender
ἀπαντάω	(2)	I meet
ἀπειλέω	(2)	I threaten, warn
ἀπεκδύομαι	(2)	I take off, strip off, disarm
ἀπλοῦς, ῆ, οῦν	(2)	single, simple, sincere, healthy, generous
ἀποβάλλω	(2)	I throw away, take off, lose
ἀποβολή, ῆς, ἡ	(2)	rejection, loss
ἀπογραφή, ῆς, ἡ	(2)	list, census, registration
ἀπόδεκτος, ον	(2)	pleasing, acceptable
ἀποδοχή, ῆς, ἡ	(2)	acceptance, approval
ἀπόθεσις, εως, ἡ	(2)	removal
ἀποκαραδοκία, ας, ἡ	(2)	eager expectation
ἀποκυέω	(2)	I give birth to, bear, bring into being
ἀπόλαυσις, εως, ἡ	(2)	enjoyment
ἀπολούω	(2)	I wash away; wash myself (mid. in NT)
ἀποπλανάω	(2)	I mislead; wander away (pass.)
ἀποπνίγω	(2)	I choke, drown
ἀποστασία, ας, ἡ	(2)	rebellion, apostasy
ἀποτελέω	(2)	I finish, complete, perform
ἀποτινάσσω	(2)	I shake off
ἀποτομία, ας, ἡ	(2)	severity
ἀποτόμως	(2)	severely, rigorously
ἀποχωρίζω	(2)	I separate; am separated, am split (pass. in NT)
Ἀραβία, ας, ἡ	(2)	Arabia
Ἀράμ, ὁ	(2)	Aram
Ἄρειος Πάγος, ὁ	(2)	Areopagus, Hill of Ares
ἀρσενοκοίτης, ου, ὁ	(2)	male homosexual
ἀρχάγγελος, ου, ὁ	(2)	archangel
Ἄρχιππος, ου, ὁ	(2)	Archippus
ἀσάλευτος, ον	(2)	immovable, unshaken
Ἀσάφ	(2)	Asaph
Ἀσήρ, ὁ	(2)	Asher
ἀσσάριον, ου, τό	(2)	assarion (Roman copper coin)
Ἄσσος, ου, ἡ	(2)	Assos
ἀστεῖος, α, ον	(2)	beautiful, well-formed, acceptable
ἀστήρικτος, ον	(2)	unstable, weak
ἄστοργος, ον	(2)	unloving

ἀστράπτω	(2)	I flash, gleam
ἀσχημονέω	(2)	I behave disgracefully, behave indecently
ἀσχημοσύνη, ης, ἡ	(2)	shameless deed, shame (= γενιταλσ)
ἀτάκτως	(2)	in a disorderly manner, lazily
ἄτεκνος, ον	(2)	childless
ἄτερ	(2)	without, apart from (impr. prep.)
ἀτμίς, ίδος, ἡ	(2)	mist, vapor, steam
αὐθάδης, ες	(2)	self-willed, stubborn, arrogant
αὐθαίρετος, ον	(2)	of one's own accord
αὐλητής, οῦ, ὁ	(2)	flute player
αὐλίζομαι	(2)	I spend the night, find lodging
αὔξησις, εως, ἡ	(2)	growth, increase
αὐστηρός, ά, όν	(2)	severe, austere, exacting, strict
αὐτάρκεια, ας, ἡ	(2)	sufficiency, contentment
αὐτόματος, η, ον	(2)	by itself
ἀφεδρών, ῶνος, ὁ	(2)	latrine, toilet
ἀφή, ῆς, ἡ	(2)	ligament
ἀφιλάργυρος, ον	(2)	not loving money, not greedy
ἀφοράω	(2)	I look away, see
ἀφρίζω	(2)	I foam at the mouth
Ἀχάζ, ὁ	(2)	Ahaz
ἀχάριστος, ον	(2)	ungrateful
Ἀχίμ, ὁ	(2)	Achim
ἀχρεῖος, ον	(2)	useless, worthless, unworthy
ἄχυρον, ου, τό	(2)	chaff
ἄψινθος, ου, ὁ, ἡ	(2)	wormwood
βαρέως	(2)	with difficulty
Βαρσαββᾶς, ᾶ, ὁ	(2)	Barsabbas
βασίλειος, ον	(2)	royal
βδελύσσομαι	(2)	I abhor, detest
βεβαίωσις, εως, ἡ	(2)	confirmation, establishment, verification
βεβηλόω	(2)	I desecrate, profane
Βέροια, ας, ἡ	(2)	Beroea
βιάζομαι	(2)	I use force, violence (mid. dep.); suffer violence (pass.)
Βιθυνία, ας, ἡ	(2)	Bithynia
βλάπτω	(2)	I harm, injure
Βόες, ὁ	(2)	Boaz
βοήθεια, ας, ἡ	(2)	help, support
βολίζω	(2)	I take a sounding, heave the lead
βορρᾶς, ᾶ, ὁ	(2)	north
βουλευτής, οῦ, ὁ	(2)	council member
βουνός, οῦ, ὁ	(2)	hill
βραβεῖον, ου, τό	(2)	prize
βραδύνω	(2)	I hesitate, delay, hold back
βροχή, ῆς, ἡ	(2)	rain
βυθίζω	(2)	I sink, plunge
Γαβριήλ, ὁ	(2)	Gabriel
Γαλατικός, ή, όν	(2)	Galatian
Γαμαλιήλ, ὁ	(2)	Gamaliel
Γεθσημανί	(2)	Gethsemane

γελάω	(2)	I laugh
γενεαλογία, ας, ἡ	(2)	genealogy
γενέσια, ων, τά	(2)	birthday celebration (pl. from subst. adj.)
γεννητός, ή, όν	(2)	born, begotten
γηράσκω	(2)	I grow old
γλωσσόκομον, ου, τό	(2)	money box
δειγματίζω	(2)	I expose, make an example of, disgrace
δεινῶς	(2)	fearfully, terribly
δεκαοκτώ	(2)	eighteen
δεκατόω	(2)	I collect or receive tithes; pay tithes (pass.)
δερμάτινος, η, ον	(2)	(made of) leather
δεσμώτης, ου, ὁ	(2)	prisoner
διαβεβαιόομαι	(2)	I speak confidently, insist
διαγινώσκω	(2)	I decide, determine
διαγογγύζω	(2)	I complain, grumble
διάγω	(2)	I spend my life, live
διαιρέω	(2)	I distribute, divide
διαλαλέω	(2)	I discuss
διαπονέομαι	(2)	I am greatly disturbed, annoyed
διαπρίω	(2)	I am infuriated, cut to the quick (pass. in NT)
διασαφέω	(2)	I explain, tell plainly, report
διασπάω	(2)	I tear apart, tear up
διαταγή, ῆς, ἡ	(2)	ordinance, direction
διατηρέω	(2)	I keep
διαχειρίζω	(2)	I lay violent hands on, kill, murder (mid. in NT)
διδακτικός, ή, όν	(2)	able to teach
δίδραχμον, ου, τό	(2)	two-drachma piece (Greek silver coin)
διετία, ας, ἡ	(2)	period of two years
διϊσχυρίζομαι	(2)	I insist, maintain firmly
δικαίωσις, εως, ἡ	(2)	justification, vindication, acquittal
δικαστής, οῦ, ὁ	(2)	judge
διοδεύω	(2)	I go, travel through, go about
διόπερ	(2)	therefore, for this very reason
διστάζω	(2)	I doubt
διχοστασία, ας, ἡ	(2)	dissension
διχοτομέω	(2)	I cut in two, punish severely
δίψυχος, ον	(2)	double-minded, doubting, hesitating
δοκίμιον, ου, τό	(2)	testing, means of testing; genuineness (subst. neut. adj.)
Δορκάς, άδος, ἡ	(2)	Dorcas
δόσις, εως, ἡ	(2)	gift, giving
δοῦλος, η, ον	(?)	slavish, servile, subject
δοχή, ῆς, ἡ	(2)	reception, banquet
δυναμόω	(2)	I strengthen
δύνω	(2)	I go down, set (of the sun)
δυσβάστακτος, ον	(2)	difficult to carry, hard to bear
δώρημα, ατος, τό	(2)	gift, present
ἐγκαινίζω	(2)	I renew, inaugurate, dedicate
ἔγκλημα, ατος, τό	(2)	charge, accusation
ἐγκρατεύομαι	(2)	I control myself
ἐγκρύπτω	(2)	I hide, conceal in, put into

Ἐζεκίας, ου, ὁ	(2)	Hezekiah
εἰλικρινής, ές	(2)	pure, sincere
εἰρηνικός, ή, όν	(2)	peaceable, peaceful
ἔκβασις, εως, ἡ	(2)	way out, end, outcome
ἐκδιηγέομαι	(2)	I tell (in detail)
ἔκδικος, ον	(2)	avenging; avenger, one who punishes (subst. in NT)
ἐκεῖσε	(2)	there, at that place
ἐκκαθαίρω	(2)	I clean out, cleanse
ἐκκεντέω	(2)	I pierce
ἐκκλείω	(2)	I shut out, exclude
ἐκμυκτηρίζω	(2)	I ridicule, sneer
ἐκουσίως	(2)	willingly, intentionally
ἔκπαλαι	(2)	for a long time, long ago
ἐκπέμπω	(2)	I send out
ἐκτελέω	(2)	I finish, complete
ἐκτρέφω	(2)	I nourish, bring up, rear
ἔκφοβος, ον	(2)	terrified
ἐκφύω	(2)	I put forth
ἑκών, οῦσα, όν	(2)	willing, of one's own free will
ἐλαφρός, ά, όν	(2)	light, insignificant
Ἐλεάζαρ, ὁ	(2)	Eleazar
ἐλεεινός, ή, όν	(2)	miserable, pitiable
ἐλεήμων, ον	(2)	merciful, sympathetic
Ἐλιούδ, ὁ	(2)	Eliud
ἑλίσσω	(2)	I roll up
Ἑλληνίς, ίδος, ἡ	(2)	Greek or Gentile woman
Ἑλληνιστί	(2)	in the Greek language
ἐλλογέω	(2)	I charge to someone's account
ελωι	(2)	my God!
ἐμβάπτω	(2)	I dip in
ἐμπαίκτης, ου, ὁ	(2)	mocker
ἐμπλέκω	(2)	I am entangled (pass. in NT)
ἐμπορεύομαι	(2)	I carry on business, buy and sell, exploit
ἐμφανής, ές	(2)	visible, revealed
ἐναγκαλίζομαι	(2)	I take in my arms, embrace
ἔναντι	(2)	opposite, before, in the judgment of (impr. prep. in NT)
ἐνάρχομαι	(2)	I begin, make a beginning
ἐνδιδύσκω	(2)	I dress, put on
ἔνδικος, ον	(2)	just, deserved
ἐνδοξάζομαι	(2)	I am glorified, honored
ἐνέδρα, ας, ἡ	(2)	plot, ambush
ἐνεδρεύω	(2)	I lie in wait, plot
ἐνέργημα, ατος, τό	(2)	working, activity
ἐνευλογέω	(2)	I bless
ἔνθεν	(2)	from here
ἐνθυμέομαι	(2)	I consider, think
ἐνισχύω	(2)	I grow strong, strengthen
ἔννοια, ας, ἡ	(2)	thought, knowledge, insight, intention
ἔννομος, ον	(2)	legal, lawful, subject to law, regular
ἑνότης, ητος, ἡ	(2)	unity

ἐνοχλέω	(2)	I trouble
ἐνταφιάζω	(2)	I prepare for burial, bury
ἐνταφιασμός, οῦ, ὁ	(2)	preparation for burial, burial
ἔντευξις, εως, ἡ	(2)	petition, prayer
ἐντός	(2)	inside, within, among (impr. prep. in NT)
ἐντροπή, ῆς, ἡ	(2)	shame, humiliation
ἐνυπνιάζομαι	(2)	I dream
ἐξαγγέλλω	(2)	I proclaim, report, tell
ἐξακόσιοι, αι, α	(2)	six hundred
ἐξανατέλλω	(2)	I spring up, sprout
ἐξαπορέομαι	(2)	I am in great difficulty, despair
ἐξαρτίζω	(2)	I complete, equip
ἐξεγείρω	(2)	I awaken, raise, cause to appear, bring into being
ἐξορύσσω	(2)	I dig out, tear out
ἐξωθέω	(2)	I push out, expel, run aground
ἔοικα	(2)	I am like, resemble
ἐπάγγελμα, ατος, τό	(2)	promise
ἐπαιτέω	(2)	I beg
ἐπαναπαύομαι	(2)	I rest, find rest of comfort
ἐπανέρχομαι	(2)	I return
ἐπανίστημι	(2)	I set up, rise up, rise in rebellion
ἐπαρχεία, ας, ἡ	(2)	province
Ἐπαφρόδιτος, ου, ὁ	(2)	Epaphraditus
ἐπεγείρω	(2)	I awaken, arouse, excite
ἐπενδύομαι	(2)	I put on (in addition)
ἐπηρεάζω	(2)	I threaten, mistreat, abuse
ἐπιδέχομαι	(2)	I receive as a guest, welcome, accept, recognize
ἐπιδημέω	(2)	I stay in a place as a stranger, visit, live in a place
ἐπιείκεια, ας, ἡ	(2)	clemency, gentleness, graciousness
ἐπικατάρατος, ον	(2)	cursed
ἐπιλέγω	(2)	I call, name; choose, select (mid.)
ἐπιλύω	(2)	I set free, explain, interpret, settle, resolve
ἐπιούσιος, ον	(2)	for today, for tomorrow, necessary for existence
ἐπιπόθησις, εως, ἡ	(2)	longing
ἐπιρίπτω	(2)	I throw on
ἐπίσημος, ον	(2)	well-known, outstanding, splendid, notorious
ἐπισκοπέω	(2)	I look at, take care, oversee, care for
ἐπίστασις, εως, ἡ	(2)	attack, pressure, attention, care, superintendence, delay
ἐπισυναγωγή, ῆς, ἡ	(2)	assembling, meeting
ἐπιφέρω	(2)	I bring upon, pronounce, inflict
ἐπιφώσκω	(2)	I shine forth, dawn, draw near
ἐπιχορηγία, ας, ἡ	(2)	support, supply, help
ἐπιχρίω	(2)	I spread or smear on, anoint
ἐποπτεύω	(2)	I observe, see
ἐρεθίζω	(2)	I arouse, provoke, irritate, embitter
ἔριον, ου, τό	(2)	wool
ἔριφος, ου, ὁ	(2)	kid, goat
ἑρμηνεία, ας, ἡ	(2)	translation, interpretation
Ἑρμῆς, οῦ, ὁ	(2)	Hermes
ἐρυθρός, ά, όν	(2)	red

ἔσοπτρον, ου, τό	(2)	mirror
ἐσώτερος, α, ον	(2)	inner; inside (adv. as impr. prep.)
ἑτεροδιδασκαλέω	(2)	I teach a different doctrine
Εὕα, ας, ἡ	(2)	Eve
εὐεργεσία, ας, ἡ	(2)	doing good, service, good deed, kindness
εὐθυδρομέω	(2)	I sail a straight course
εὐθύνω	(2)	I straighten, guide straight
εὐκαιρία, ας, ἡ	(2)	favorable opportunity, right moment
εὔκαιρος, ον	(2)	well-timed, suitable
εὐκαίρως	(2)	conveniently
εὐλάβεια, ας, ἡ	(2)	fear (of God), reverence, awe, anxiety
εὐνουχίζω	(2)	I castrate, emasculate, make a eunuch of myself
εὐσεβέω	(2)	I am reverent or devout, show piety, worship
εὐσεβῶς	(2)	in a godly manner, piously, religiously
εὔσπλαγχος, ον	(2)	tenderhearted, compassionate, courageous
εὐτόνως	(2)	powerfully, vehemently, vigorously
Εὐφράτης, ου, ὁ	(2)	Euphrates
εὐφροσύνη, ης, ἡ	(2)	joy, gladness, cheerfulness
ἐφημερία, ας, ἡ	(2)	class or division (of priests)
ἐφικνέομαι	(2)	I come to, reach
ἐφοράω	(2)	I gaze upon, look at, concern myself with
ζεῦγος, ους, τό	(2)	yoke, pair
Ζεύς, Διός, ὁ	(2)	Zeus
ζέω	(2)	I boil (fig. in NT)
ζωγρέω	(2)	I capture alive, catch
ἡγεμονεύω	(2)	I am governor, command, rule
ἡδύοσμον, ου, τό	(2)	mint (plant)
ηλι	(2)	my God
ἧλος, ου, ὁ	(2)	nail
ἡνίκα	(2)	when, at the time when
ἥσσων, ον	(2)	worse (subst.); less (neut. as adv.)
ἡσύχιος, ον	(2)	quiet, peaceful
ἡττάομαι	(2)	I am defeated, succumb
ἥττημα, ατος, τό	(2)	defeat, failure
Θαδδαῖος, ου, ὁ	(2)	Thaddaeus
θάλπω	(2)	I cherish, comfort, take care of
θαῦμα, ατος, τό	(2)	wonder, marvel, amazement
Θεόφιλος, ου, ὁ	(2)	Theophilus
θεριστής, οῦ, ὁ	(2)	reaper, harvester
θριαμβεύω	(2)	I lead in triumph, triumph over, cause to triumph
θυγάτριον, ου, τό	(2)	little daughter
θυρίς, ίδος, ἡ	(2)	window
Ἰάϊρος, ου, ὁ	(2)	Jairus
ἱερατεία, ας, ἡ	(2)	priestly office or service
ἱεράτευμα, ατος, τό	(2)	priesthood
Ἱεροσολυμίτης, ου, ὁ	(2)	inhabitant of Jerusalem
Ἰεχονίας, ου, ὁ	(2)	Jechoniah
ἱκανόω	(2)	I make sufficient, qualify, empower, authorize
ἱλάσκομαι	(2)	I expiate, make atonement for; am merciful (pass.)
ἱλασμός, οῦ, ὁ	(2)	expiation, propitiation, means of forgiveness

ἱλαστήριον, ου, τό	(2)	means of expiation or forgiveness, mercy seat
ἵλεως, ων	(2)	gracious, merciful
ἱματίζω	(2)	I dress, clothe
Ἰουδαϊσμός, οῦ, ὁ	(2)	Judaism
Ἰούλιος, ου, ὁ	(2)	Julius
ἱππεύς, έως, ὁ	(2)	horseman, cavalryman
ἶρις, ιδος, ἡ	(2)	rainbow, halo, radiance
ἰχθύδιον, ου, τό	(2)	little fish
Ἰωαθάμ, ὁ	(2)	Jotham
Ἰωάννα, ας, ἡ	(2)	Joanna
Ἰωράμ, ὁ	(2)	Joram
Ἰωσαφάτ, ὁ	(2)	Jehoshaphat
Ἰωσίας, ου, ὁ	(2)	Josiah
καθηγητής, οῦ, ὁ	(2)	teacher
καθήκω	(2)	it is proper (impers. in NT)
Καϊνάμ, ὁ	(2)	Cainan
καινότης, ητος, ἡ	(2)	newness
καίτοι	(2)	and yet, although
κακουχέω	(2)	I mistreat, torment
καμμύω	(2)	I close
κάμνω	(2)	I am weary, ill
Καναναῖος, ου, ὁ	(2)	a Cananaean, enthusiast, zealot
Καππαδοκία, ας, ἡ	(2)	Cappadocia
καρδιογνώστης, ου, ὁ	(2)	knower of hearts
καταβάλλω	(2)	I throw down, strike down; lay (mid.)
καταδουλόω	(2)	I enslave, reduce to slavery, take advantage of
καταδυναστεύω	(2)	I oppress, exploit, dominate
κατακλάω	(2)	I break in pieces
κατακλείω	(2)	I shut up, lock up
κατακολουθέω	(2)	I follow
κατάκρισις, εως, ἡ	(2)	condemnation
καταλαλιά, ᾶς, ἡ	(2)	evil speech, slander, insult
καταπονέω	(2)	I subdue, oppress, torment, mistreat
καταποντίζω	(2)	I drown, sink
κατασκάπτω	(2)	I tear down, destroy
κατασκήνωσις, εως, ἡ	(2)	a place to live, nest
καταστέλλω	(2)	I restrain, quiet, calm
καταστρέφω	(2)	I upset, overturn
καταστροφή, ῆς, ἡ	(2)	ruin, destruction
κατάσχεσις, εως, ἡ	(2)	possession, taking possession
κατατίθημι	(2)	I place; grant, do (mid. in NT)
καταφεύγω	(2)	I flee, take refuge
καταχέω	(2)	I pour out, pour down over
καταχράομαι	(2)	I use, make full use of
κατεξουσιάζω	(2)	I exercise authority, tyrannize
κατοικητήριον, ου, τό	(2)	dwelling place, house, home
καῦμα, ατος, τό	(2)	burning, heat
καυσόω	(2)	I am consumed by heat, burn up (pass. in NT)
Κεγχρεαί, ῶν, αἱ	(2)	Cenchreae
κενοφωνία, ας, ἡ	(2)	empty talk, chatter

κεραία, ας, ἡ	(2)	projection, serif, stroke (part of a letter)
κεράμιον, ου, τό	(2)	earthenware vessel, jar
κεφάλαιον, ου, τό	(2)	main point, sum of money
κιθαρίζω	(2)	I play the lyre or harp
κιθαρῳδός, οῦ, ὁ	(2)	lyre player, harpist
κλάσις, εως, ἡ	(2)	breaking
κλίβανος, ου, ὁ	(2)	oven, furnace
κλινίδιον, ου, τό	(2)	bed, pallet, stretcher
κλοπή, ῆς, ἡ	(2)	theft, stealing
κλύδων, ωνος, ὁ	(2)	rough water, waves
κοδράντης, ου, ὁ	(2)	quadrans, penny (Roman copper coin)
κολάζω	(2)	I punish
κόλασις, εως, ἡ	(2)	punishment
κομάω	(2)	I wear long hair
κονιάω	(2)	I whitewash
κορέννυμι	(2)	I satiate; am satiated or full, have enough (pass. in NT)
Κορίνθιος, ου, ὁ	(2)	a Corinthian
κοσμικός, ή, όν	(2)	earthly, worldly
κόσμιος, ον	(2)	respectable, honorable, modest
κρέας, κρέως, τό	(2)	meat
Κρής, ητός, ὁ	(2)	a Cretan
κρίθινος, η, ον	(2)	made of barley flour
κρίνον, ου, τό	(2)	lily
Κρίσπος, ου, ὁ	(2)	Crispus
κρύσταλλος, ου, ὁ	(2)	crystal, ice
κρυφαῖος, α, ον	(2)	hidden, secret
κυβερνήτης, ου, ὁ	(2)	captain, steersman, pilot
κύπτω	(2)	I bend down
κυρία, ας, ἡ	(2)	lady, mistress
κυριακός, ή, όν	(2)	belonging to the Lord, Lord's
κυρόω	(2)	I confirm, ratify, decide in favor of
λατομέω	(2)	I hew, cut, shape
λεμα	(2)	why?
λέντιον, ου, τό	(2)	towel
Λευί, ὁ	(2)	Levi
λευκαίνω	(2)	I make white
λίβανος, ου, ὁ	(2)	frankincense
λιβανωτός, οῦ, ὁ	(2)	censer
λικμάω	(2)	I crush
λιμήν, ένος, ὁ	(2)	harbor
λίνον, ου, τό	(2)	linen garment, wick
λίτρα, ας, ἡ	(2)	Roman pound
λογεία, ας, ἡ	(2)	collection
λογικός, ή, όν	(2)	rational, spiritual
λογισμός, οῦ, ὁ	(2)	thought, reasoning
λοίδορος, ου, ὁ	(2)	reviler, slanderer
λοιμός, οῦ, ὁ	(2)	pestilence, plague, disease, trouble maker
Λούκιος, ου, ὁ	(2)	Lucius
λουτρόν, οῦ, τό	(2)	bath, washing
Λυδία, ας, ἡ	(2)	Lydia

Λυσίας, ου, ὁ	(2)	Lysias
λύτρον, ου, τό	(2)	price of release, ransom
Μαθθάτ, ὁ	(2)	Matthat
Μαθθίας, ου, ὁ	(2)	Matthias
μακαρίζω	(2)	I call or consider blessed, happy, fortunate
μάτην	(2)	in vain, to no end
Ματθάν, ὁ	(2)	Matthan
Ματταθίας, ου, ὁ	(2)	Mattathias
μεθοδεία, ας, ἡ	(2)	scheming, craftiness
μέθυσος, ου, ὁ	(2)	drunkard
μελετάω	(2)	I practice, think about
Μελχί, ὁ	(2)	Melchi
μέμφομαι	(2)	I find fault, blame
μερισμός, οῦ, ὁ	(2)	separation, distribution, apportionment
μεσημβρία, ας, ἡ	(2)	midday, noon, south
Μεσοποταμία, ας, ἡ	(2)	Mesopotamia
Μεσσίας, ου, ὁ	(2)	Messiah
μετάγω	(2)	I guide, steer, control
μεταίρω	(2)	I go away, leave
μεταλλάσσω	(2)	I exchange
μεταστρέφω	(2)	I change, alter, pervert
μετοικίζω	(2)	I cause to migrate, resettle, remove, deport
μηδαμῶς	(2)	by no means, certainly not, no
μήπω	(2)	not yet
μήτρα, ας, ἡ	(2)	womb
μίσθιος, ου, ὁ	(2)	day laborer, hired worker
μισθόω	(2)	I hire (mid. in NT)
Μιχαήλ, ὁ	(2)	Michael
μονή, ῆς, ἡ	(2)	staying, room, abode
μονόφθαλμος, ον	(2)	one-eyed
μόρφωσις, εως, ἡ	(2)	embodiment, formulation, outward form, appearance
μύριοι, αι, α	(2)	ten thousand
Μυσία, ας, ἡ	(2)	Mysia
μωμάομαι	(2)	I find fault with, censure, blame
Ναζαρά, ἡ	(2)	Nazareth
νάρδος, ου, ἡ	(2)	nard, oil of nard
ναυαγέω	(2)	I suffer shipwreck
νέκρωσις, εως, ἡ	(2)	death, putting to death, deadness, deadening
νεύω	(2)	I nod, motion
νήθω	(2)	I spin
νῆστις, ιδος, ὁ, ἡ	(2)	not eating, hungry
Νικολαΐτης, ου, ὁ	(2)	Nicolaitan
νομή, ῆς, ἡ	(2)	pasture, spreading
νομίμως	(2)	in accordance with the rules, lawfully
νομοθετέω	(2)	I receive the law, enact by law
νυστάζω	(2)	I nod, become drowsy, doze, am sleepy or idle
νωθρός, ά, όν	(2)	lazy, sluggish, hard (of hearing)
ξενία, ας, ἡ	(2)	hospitality, guest room, place of lodging
ξύλινος, η, ον	(2)	wooden
ὀγδοήκοντα	(2)	eighty

ὁδοιπορία, ας, ἡ	(2)	walking, journey
ὀδύνη, ης, ἡ	(2)	pain, woe, sorrow
ὀδυρμός, οῦ, ὁ	(2)	lamentation, mourning
Ὀζίας, ου, ὁ	(2)	Uzziah
ὀθόνη, ης, ἡ	(2)	linen cloth, sheet
οἰκητήριον, ου, τό	(2)	dwelling, habitation
οἰκιακός, οῦ, ὁ	(2)	member of a household
οἰκτίρω	(2)	I have compassion
οἰνοπότης, ου, ὁ	(2)	wine drinker, drunkard
ὁλόκληρος, ον	(2)	whole, complete, sound, blameless
ὄμμα, ατος, τό	(2)	eye
ὁμοιοπαθής, ές	(2)	with the same nature, like in every way
ὁμοιότης, ητος, ἡ	(2)	likeness, similarity
Ὀνήσιμος, ου, ὁ	(2)	Onesimus
Ὀνησίφορος, ου, ὁ	(2)	Onesiphorus
ὀνικός, ή, όν	(2)	pertaining to a donkey
ὀπή, ῆς, ἡ	(2)	opening, hole
ὀργυιά, ᾶς, ἡ	(2)	fathom (nautical measure)
ὀρεινός, ή, όν	(2)	mountainous; hill country (subst. in NT)
ὀρθός, ή, όν	(2)	straight, upright
ὁρκίζω	(2)	I put under oath, implore, beg
ὁρμή, ῆς, ἡ	(2)	impulse, inclination, desire, attempt
ὄρνις, ιθος, ὁ, ἡ	(2)	bird, cock or hen
ὀρφανός, ή, όν	(2)	orphaned; orphan (subst.)
ὁσιότης, ητος, ἡ	(2)	devoutness, piety, holiness
ὀστράκινος, η, ον	(2)	made of earth or clay
οὐρανόθεν	(2)	from heaven
οὐσία, ας, ἡ	(2)	property, wealth
ὀφείλημα, ατος, τό	(2)	debt, one's due, sin
ὀφθαλμοδουλία, ας, ἡ	(2)	eyeservice, service to attract attention
παιδευτής, οῦ, ὁ	(2)	instructor, teacher, one who disciplines
παλιγγενεσία, ας, ἡ	(2)	rebirth, regeneration, new age
παντελής, ές	(2)	complete; completely, fully, at all (w. εἰς τό in NT)
παραβιάζομαι	(2)	I use force, urge strongly
παραινέω	(2)	I advise, recommend, urge
παράκειμαι	(2)	I am ready, at hand
παραλέγομαι	(2)	I sail past, coast along
παραλογίζομαι	(2)	I deceive, delude
παραπικρασμός, οῦ, ὁ	(2)	revolt, rebellion
παρεισέρχομαι	(2)	I slip in, come in
παρίημι	(2)	I neglect; am weakened, listless, drooping (pass.)
παροικέω	(2)	I inhabit or live as a stranger, migrate
παροικία, ας, ἡ	(2)	stay, sojourn, exile
πάροινος, ον	(2)	drunken, addicted to wine; drunkard (subst. in NT)
παροξύνω	(2)	I irritate; become irritated or angry (pass. in NT)
παροξυσμός, οῦ, ὁ	(2)	provoking, encouragement, sharp disagreement
παροργίζω	(2)	I make angry
Πάφος, ου, ἡ	(2)	Paphos
παχύνω	(2)	I make dull; become dull (pass. in NT)
πεζῇ	(2)	by land

πεῖρα, ας, ἡ	(2)	attempt, trial, experience
πέλαγος, ους, τό	(2)	sea, open sea
πεντακόσιοι, αι, α	(2)	five hundred
Πέργαμος, ου, ἡ	(2)	Pergamum
περιαστράπτω	(2)	I shine around
περιβόλαιον, ου, τό	(2)	covering, cloak, robe
περίεργος, ον	(2)	meddlesome; busybody, magic (subst. in NT)
περιέχω	(2)	I seize; stand, say (intrans.)
περικεφαλαία, ας, ἡ	(2)	helmet
περιλάμπω	(2)	I shine around
περιλείπομαι	(2)	I remain, am left behind
πέρυκτι	(2)	last year, a year ago
πηδάλιον, ου, τό	(2)	rudder
πηλίκος, η, ον	(2)	how large, how great
πικρός, ά, όν	(2)	bitter
πικρῶς	(2)	bitterly
πιστικός, ή, όν	(2)	genuine, unadulterated
πλάσσω	(2)	I form, mold
πλήκτης, ου, ὁ	(2)	combative person, bully
πνευματικῶς	(2)	spiritually
πνοή, ῆς, ἡ	(2)	wind
ποίημα, ατος, τό	(2)	what is made, work, creation
πολιτάρχης, ου, ὁ	(2)	civic magistrate, politarch
πολιτεία, ας, ἡ	(2)	citizenship, commonwealth, state
πολιτεύομαι	(2)	I live, conduct myself
πόμα, ατος, τό	(2)	drink
Πόντος, ου, ὁ	(2)	Pontus
Πόπλιος, ου, ὁ	(2)	Publius
πορεία, ας, ἡ	(2)	journey, trip, way, conduct
πορισμός, οῦ, ὁ	(2)	means of gain
πόρρωθεν	(2)	from or at a distance
πράκτωρ, ορος, ὁ	(2)	officer (of a court)
πρασιά, ᾶς, ἡ	(2)	garden plot (lit.); group (fig. in NT)
πρεσβεία, ας, ἡ	(2)	embassy, delegation, ambassadors
πρεσβεύω	(2)	I am an ambassador or representative
προαμαρτάνω	(2)	I sin before
προβάλλω	(2)	I put forward, put out (leaves)
πρόγνωσις, εως, ἡ	(2)	foreknowledge
πρόγονος, ον	(2)	born before; forefathers, ancestors (pl. subst. in NT)
προενάρχομαι	(2)	I begin (beforehand)
προεπαγγέλλω	(2)	I promise beforehand or previously (mid. pass. in NT)
προετοιμάζω	(2)	I prepare beforehand
προκαταγγέλλω	(2)	I announce beforehand, foretell
πρόνοια, ας, ἡ	(2)	foresight, care, provision
προπετής, ές	(2)	rash, reckless, thoughtless
προπορεύομαι	(2)	I go before
προσαίτης, ου, ὁ	(2)	beggar
προσαναπληρόω	(2)	I fill up, replenish, supply
προσανατίθημι	(2)	I add, contribute, consult with (mid. in NT)
προσδοκία, ας, ἡ	(2)	expectation

προσκολλάω	(2)	I am faithfully devoted to, join (pass. in NT)
προσκυλίω	(2)	I roll against or to
προσλαλέω	(2)	I speak to or with, address
προσοχθίζω	(2)	I am angry, offended, provoked
προσρήγνυμι	(2)	I burst upon
προτρέχω	(2)	I run (on) ahead
προϋπάρχω	(2)	I exist before
προφέρω	(2)	I bring out, produce
προφητικός, ή, όν	(2)	prophetic
προφῆτις, ιδος, ἡ	(2)	prophetess
πρωΐα, ας, ἡ	(2)	(early) morning
πρωϊνός, ή, όν	(2)	early, belonging to the morning, morning
πρῷρα, ης, ἡ	(2)	bow (of a ship)
πτερύγιον, ου, τό	(2)	end, edge, pinnacle, summit
πτοέω	(2)	I terrify; am terrified or startled (pass. in NT)
πτύον, ου, τό	(2)	winnowing shovel
πτῶσις, εως, ἡ	(2)	falling, fall
πυρά, ᾶς, ἡ	(2)	fire, pile of combustible or burning material
πυρέσσω	(2)	I suffer with a fever
πυρράζω	(2)	I am red (of the sky)
πυρρός, ά, όν	(2)	red
Ῥαάβ, ἡ	(2)	Rahab
ῥαββουνι	(2)	my master, my teacher
ῥαβδίζω	(2)	I beat (with a rod)
ῥαβδοῦχος, ου, ὁ	(2)	constable, policeman
ῥάκος, ους, τό	(2)	piece of cloth, patch
ῥαντισμός, οῦ, ὁ	(2)	sprinkling
ῥαπίζω	(2)	I strike, slap
ῥαφίς, ίδος, ἡ	(2)	needle
ῥιζόω	(2)	I cause to take root; am firmly rooted (pass. in NT)
Ῥοβοάμ, ὁ	(2)	Rehoboam
Ῥοῦφος, ου, ὁ	(2)	Rufus
ῥυπαρός, ά, όν	(2)	dirty, unclean, defiled
σαβαχθανι	(2)	you have forsaken me
Σαβαώθ	(2)	Sabaoth, Almighty
Σαδώκ, ὁ	(2)	Zadok
Σαλά, ὁ	(2)	Shelah
Σαλήμ, ἡ	(2)	Salem
Σαλμών, ὁ	(2)	Salmon
Σαλώμη, ης, ἡ	(2)	Salome
Σαμαρῖτις, ιδος, ἡ	(2)	a Samaritan woman
σανδάλιον, ου, τό	(2)	sandal
σάρδιον, ου, τό	(2)	carnelian, sardius
σάτον, ου, τό	(2)	seah (Hebrew dry measure), measure (for grain)
σέβασμα, ατος, τό	(2)	object of worship, sanctuary
σεληνιάζομαι	(2)	I am moon-struck; am an epileptic (fig. in NT)
σιαγών, όνος, ἡ	(2)	cheek
σιγή, ῆς, ἡ	(2)	silence, quiet
Σιδώνιος, α, ον	(2)	Sidonian; country around Sidon, a Sidonian (subst.)
σκῆνος, ους, τό	(2)	tent, lodging

σκυθρωπός, ή, όν	(2)	sad, gloomy
σμύρνα, ης, ἡ	(2)	myrrh
Σμύρνα, ης, ἡ	(2)	Smyrna
σοφίζω	(2)	I make wise; am cleverly devised (pass.)
Σπανία, ας, ἡ	(2)	Spain
σπαργανόω	(2)	I wrap in swaddling cloths
σπαταλάω	(2)	I live luxuriously
σπάω	(2)	I draw, pull (mid. in NT)
σπένδω	(2)	I am poured out as a drink-offering (pass. in NT)
σπίλος, ου, ὁ	(2)	spot, stain, blemish
σπιλόω	(2)	I stain, defile
στέλλω	(2)	I keep away, avoid, try to avoid (mid. in NT)
στεναγμός, οῦ, ὁ	(2)	sigh, groan, groaning
στρατεία, ας, ἡ	(2)	expedition, campaign, warfare, fight
στρατιά, ᾶς, ἡ	(2)	army, host
στρηνιάω	(2)	I live in luxury or sensuality
στυγνάζω	(2)	I am shocked, dark, gloomy
συγκάθημαι	(2)	I sit with
συγκαθίζω	(2)	I cause to sit down with, sit down with
συγκακοπαθέω	(2)	I suffer together with, share in hardship with
συγκεράννυμι	(2)	I blend, unite, arrange
συζεύγνυμι	(2)	I yoke together, join together
συζωοποιέω	(2)	I make alive together with
συκοφαντέω	(2)	I accuse falsely, slander, extort
συμβασιλεύω	(2)	I rule (as king) or reign with
συμμέτοχος, ον	(2)	sharing with; sharer (subst. in NT)
σύμμορφος, ον	(2)	having the same form, similar in form
συμπαθέω	(2)	I sympathize with, have sympathy for
συμπάσχω	(2)	I suffer together with
συμπέμπω	(2)	I send with
συμπόσιον, ου, τό	(2)	group (eating together), party
σύμφορος, ον	(2)	beneficial; benefit, advantage (subst. in NT)
συναθλέω	(2)	I fight or work together with
συναθροίζω	(2)	I gather, bring together; am gathered, meet (pass.)
συναναβαίνω	(2)	I come or go up with
συναντιλαμβάνομαι	(2)	I help, come to the aid of
συναρμολογέω	(2)	I join together; am joined or fit together (pass. in NT)
σύνειμι	(2)	I am with
συνεισέρχομαι	(2)	I enter or go in with
συνέκδημος, ου, ὁ	(2)	traveling companion
συνευωχέομαι	(2)	I feast together
συνθάπτω	(2)	I bury with; am buried with (pass. in NT)
συνθλάω	(2)	I dash to pieces; am broken to pieces (pass. in NT)
συνθλίβω	(2)	I press together or upon
σύνοιδα	(2)	I share knowledge with, am aware of
συνοράω	(2)	I perceive, realize
συνοχή, ῆς, ἡ	(2)	distress, dismay, anguish
συντόμως	(2)	promptly, readily, briefly
συσπαράσσω	(2)	I tear (to pieces), pull about, throw into convulsions
συστέλλω	(2)	I limit, shorten, cover, pack up, remove

συστρατιώτης, ου, ὁ	(2)	fellow soldier, comrade in arms
συστρέφω	(2)	I gather up, gather, come together
συστροφή, ῆς, ἡ	(2)	mob, disorderly gathering, commotion, plot
συσχηματίζω	(2)	I form; am formed like, conformed to (pass. in NT)
Συχέμ, ἡ	(2)	Shechem
σχῆμα, ατος, τό	(2)	outward appearance, form, shape, present form
σχοινίον, ου, τό	(2)	rope, cord
σχολάζω	(2)	I spend time in, stand empty
σωματικός, ή, όν	(2)	bodily, pertaining to the body
σωρεύω	(2)	I heap up, fill with
Σωσθένης, ους, ὁ	(2)	Sosthenes
Ταβιθά, ἡ	(2)	Tabitha
ταλαιπωρία, ας, ἡ	(2)	distress, trouble, misery
ταλαίπωρος, ον	(2)	miserable, wretched, distressed
τάραχος, ου, ὁ	(2)	consternation, disturbance, commotion
Ταρσεύς, έως, ὁ	(2)	person from Tarsus
τάχα	(2)	perhaps, possibly, probably
ταχινός, ή, όν	(2)	imminent, coming soon, swift
τέκτων, ονος, ὁ	(2)	carpenter, wood worker, builder
τελειότης, ητος, ἡ	(2)	perfection, completeness, maturity
τελείωσις, εως, ἡ	(2)	perfection, fulfillment
Τέρτυλλος, ου, ὁ	(2)	Tertullus
τεσσαρεσκαιδέκατος, η, ον	(2)	fourteenth
τεσσερακονταετής, ές	(2)	forty years
τιμωρέω	(2)	I punish
τίτλος, ου, ὁ	(2)	inscription, notice
τοιγαροῦν	(2)	then, therefore, for that very reason
τόκος, ου, ὁ	(2)	interest (on moncy loancd)
τραυματίζω	(2)	I wound, injure
τραχύς, εῖα, ύ	(2)	rough, uneven
τριακόσιοι, αι, α	(2)	three hundred
τρίβολος, ου, ὁ	(2)	thorn plant, thistle
τρύβλιον, ου, τό	(2)	bowl, dish
τρυφή, ῆς, ἡ	(2)	indulgence, reveling, luxury
ὕαλος, ου, ἡ	(2)	glass, crystal
ὑβριστής, οῦ, ὁ	(2)	violent or insolent person
Ὑμέναιος, ου, ὁ	(2)	Hymenaeus
ὕμνος, ου, ὁ	(2)	hymn, song of praise
ὕπαρξις, εως, ἡ	(2)	property, possession
ὑπεναντίος, α, ον	(2)	opposed, contrary, hostile; opponent (subst.)
ὑπερλίαν	(2)	exceedingly; special (adj. in NT)
ὑπέρογκος, ον	(2)	puffed up, haughty, bombastic, boastful
ὑπεροχή, ῆς, ἡ	(2)	abundance, superiority, place of prominence or authority
ὑπερπερισσεύω	(2)	I am present in abundance; overflow (pass.)
ὑποζύγιον, ου, τό	(2)	pack animal, donkey
ὑποπλέω	(2)	I sail under the shelter of
ὑποτίθημι	(2)	I lay down, risk; put before, make known, teach (mid.)
ὑποτύπωσις, εως, ἡ	(2)	model, example, standard
ὑποχωρέω	(2)	I retreat, withdraw, retire
ὑπωπιάζω	(2)	I wear out, treat roughly, keep under control

ὕσσωπος, ου, ὁ, ἡ	(2)	hyssop
ὑστέρησις, εως, ἡ	(2)	need, lack, poverty
ὕψωμα, ατος, τό	(2)	height, exaltation, proud obstacle
φάγος, ου, ὁ	(2)	glutton
φανέρωσις, εως, ἡ	(2)	disclosure, announcement
φάντασμα, ατος, τό	(2)	apparition, ghost
φαρμακεία, ας, ἡ	(2)	sorcery, magic; magical arts (pl.)
φάρμακος, ου, ὁ	(2)	magician, sorcerer
φέγγος, ους, τό	(2)	light, radiance
φειδομένως	(2)	sparingly
φήμη, ης, ἡ	(2)	report, news
φθόγγος, ου, ὁ	(2)	sound, tone, voice
Φιλαδέλφεια, ας, ἡ	(2)	Philadelphia
φιλανθρωπία, ας, ἡ	(2)	love for people, kindness, hospitality
φιλάργυρος, ον	(2)	fond of money, avaricious
φιλοξενία, ας, ἡ	(2)	hospitality
φλογίζω	(2)	I set on fire
φοῖνιξ, ικος, ὁ	(2)	palm tree, palm branch
φορτίζω	(2)	I load, burden
φραγελλόω	(2)	I flog, scourge, beat with a whip
φρήν, φρενός, ἡ	(2)	thinking, understanding (pl. in NT)
φρόνησις, εως, ἡ	(2)	way of thinking, understanding, insight
φωλεός, οῦ, ὁ	(2)	den, lair, hole
φωστήρ, ῆρος, ὁ	(2)	star, splendor, radiance, brilliance
φωτισμός, οῦ, ὁ	(2)	illumination, enlightenment, light, revelation
χαλεπός, ή, όν	(2)	hard, difficult, violent, dangerous
χαλιναγωγέω	(2)	I guide with bit and bridle, hold in check, control
χαλινός, οῦ, ὁ	(2)	bit, bridle
χαλκολίβανον, ου, τό	(2)	fine brass or bronze
χαμαί	(2)	on or to the ground
Χανάαν, ἡ	(2)	Canaan
χαριτόω	(2)	I bestow favor upon, favor highly, bless
Χαρράν, ἡ	(2)	Haran
χειραγωγέω	(2)	I take or lead by the hand
χειροτονέω	(2)	I choose or elect by raising hands, choose
χιών, όνος, ἡ	(2)	snow
χλαμύς, ύδος, ἡ	(2)	cloak
χοῖνιξ, ικος, ἡ	(2)	choenix (dry measure)
χολή, ῆς, ἡ	(2)	gall, bile
Χοραζίν, ἡ	(2)	Chorazin
χορηγέω	(2)	I provide, supply
χοῦς, χοός, ὁ	(2)	soil, dust
χρεοφειλέτης, ου, ὁ	(2)	debtor
χρῆσις, εως, ἡ	(2)	(sexual) relations or function
χρυσόω	(2)	I make golden, adorn with gold, gild
ψευδάδελφος, ου, ὁ	(2)	false brother
ψευδομαρτυρία, ας, ἡ	(2)	false testimony
ψευδόμαρτυς, υρος, ὁ	(2)	one who gives false testimony, false witness
ψευδόχριστος, ου, ὁ	(2)	false Christ, false Messiah
ψηφίζω	(2)	I count, calculate, reckon, figure out

ψιχίον, ου, τό	(2)	very little bit, crumb, scrap
ψωμίζω	(2)	I feed, give away
ὦμος, ου, ὁ	(2)	shoulder
ὠτάριον, ου, τό	(2)	ear
ὠφέλεια, ας, ἡ	(2)	use, gain, advantage
Ἀβαδδών, ὁ	(1)	Abaddon
ἀβαρής, ές	(1)	light weight, not burdensome
Ἀβιαθάρ, ὁ	(1)	Abiathar
Ἀβιληνή, ῆς, ἡ	(1)	Abilene
ἀγαθοεργέω	(1)	I do good
ἀγαθοποιΐα, ας, ἡ	(1)	doing good, doing right
ἀγαθοποιός, όν	(1)	doing good, upright; one who does good (subst.)
ἀγαθουργέω	(1)	I do good (contr. of ἀγαθοεργέω)
ἀγανάκτησις, εως, ἡ	(1)	indignation
ἀγγεῖον, ου, τό	(1)	vessel, flask, container
ἀγγέλλω	(1)	I announce
ἄγγος, ους, τό	(1)	vessel, container
ἀγενεαλόγητος, ον	(1)	without genealogy
ἀγενής, ές	(1)	base, low, insignificant
ἁγιότης, ητος, ἡ	(1)	holiness
ἀγκάλη, ης, ἡ	(1)	arm
ἄγκιστρον, ου, τό	(1)	fishhook
ἁγνισμός, οῦ, ὁ	(1)	purification
ἀγνόημα, ατος, τό	(1)	sin committed in ignorance
ἁγνῶς	(1)	purely, sincerely
ἄγνωστος, ον	(1)	unknown
ἀγράμματος, ον	(1)	unable to write, illiterate, uneducated
ἀγραυλέω	(1)	I live outdoors
ἀγρεύω	(1)	I catch
ἀγωγή, ῆς, ἡ	(1)	way of life, conduct
ἀγωνία, ας, ἡ	(1)	agony, anxiety
ἀδάπανος, ον	(1)	free of charge
Ἀδδί, ὁ	(1)	Addi
ἀδηλότης, ητος, ἡ	(1)	uncertainty
ἀδήλως	(1)	uncertainly
ἀδιάκριτος, ον	(1)	unwavering, impartial
ἀδίκως	(1)	unjustly
Ἀδμίν, ὁ	(1)	Admin
ἄδολος, ον	(1)	without deceit, unadulterated, pure
Ἀδραμυττηνός, ή, όν	(1)	of Adramyttium
Ἀδρίας, ου, ὁ	(1)	Adriatic Sea
ἁδρότης, ητος, ἡ	(1)	abundance
Ἄζωτος, ου, ἡ	(1)	Azotus
ἄθεος, ον	(1)	without God, godless
ἄθλησις, εως, ἡ	(1)	contest, hard struggle
ἀθροίζω	(1)	I collect, gather
ἀθυμέω	(1)	I am discouraged, lose heart
αἴγειος, α, ον	(1)	of a goat
αἰδώς, οῦς, ἡ	(1)	modesty
αἱματεκχυσία, ας, ἡ	(1)	shedding of blood

αἱμορροέω	(1)	I suffer with hemorrhage, bleed
αἴνεσις, εως, ἡ	(1)	praise
αἴνιγμα, ατος, τό	(1)	riddle, obscure image
Αἰνών, ἡ	(1)	Aenon
αἱρετίζω	(1)	I choose
αἱρετικός, ή, όν	(1)	factious, causing divisions
αἰσθάνομαι	(1)	I understand
αἴσθησις, εως, ἡ	(1)	insight, experience
αἰσθητήριον, ου, τό	(1)	sense, faculty
αἰσχροκερδῶς	(1)	greedily
αἰσχρολογία, ας, ἡ	(1)	evil speech, obscene speech
αἰσχρότης, ητος, ἡ	(1)	ugliness, wickedness
αἰτίωμα, ατος, τό	(1)	charge, complaint
αἰχμαλωτεύω	(1)	I capture, take captive
αἰχμάλωτος, ου, ὁ	(1)	captive
ἀκαιρέομαι	(1)	I have no time, no opportunity
ἀκαίρως	(1)	out of season, unseasonably
ἀκατάγνωστος, ον	(1)	beyond reproach, above criticism
ἀκατάλυτος, ον	(1)	indestructible, endless
ἀκατάπαυστος, ον	(1)	unceasing, restless
Ἀκελδαμάχ	(1)	Akeldama, Field of Blood
ἀκλινής, ές	(1)	without wavering, firmly
ἀκμάζω	(1)	I am ripe
ἀκμήν	(1)	even yet, still
ἀκρατής, ές	(1)	without self-control, dissolute
ἄκρατος, ον	(1)	unmixed, pure
ἀκρίβεια, ας, ἡ	(1)	exactness, precision
ἀκριβής, ές	(1)	exact, strict
ἀκροατήριον, ου, τό	(1)	audience room, auditorium
ἀκροθίνιον, ου τό	(1)	first fruits, booty, spoils (pl.)
ἀκωλύτως	(1)	without hindrance, freely
ἄκων, ουσα, ον	(1)	unwilling; unwillingly (adv.)
ἀλάλητος, ον	(1)	unexpressed, wordless
ἀλεκτοροφωνία, ας, ἡ	(1)	crowing of a cock, cockcrow, before dawn
ἁλιεύω	(1)	I fish
ἀλίσγημα, ατος, τό	(1)	pollution
ἀλλαχόθεν	(1)	from another place
ἀλλαχοῦ	(1)	elsewhere, in another direction
ἀλληγορέω	(1)	I speak allegorically
ἀλλογενής, ές	(1)	foreign; foreigner (subst.)
ἀλλοτριεπίσκοπος, ου, ὁ	(1)	one who meddles in the affairs of others, busybody
ἀλλόφυλος, ον	(1)	foreign; a heathen, Gentile (subst.)
ἄλλως	(1)	otherwise, in another way
ἀλόη, ης, ἡ	(1)	aloes
ἁλυκός, ή, όν	(1)	salty
ἄλυπος, ον	(1)	free from anxiety
ἀλυσιτελής, ές	(1)	unprofitable
ἅλωσις, εως, ἡ	(1)	capture, catching
ἀμαθής, ές	(1)	ignorant
ἀμαράντινος, η, ον	(1)	unfading

ἀμάραντος, ον	(1)	unfading
ἀμάρτυρος, ον	(1)	without witness
ἀμάω	(1)	I mow
ἀμέθυστος, ου, ἡ	(1)	amethyst
ἀμετακίνητος, ον	(1)	immovable, firm
ἀμετανόητος, ον	(1)	unrepentant
ἀμήτωρ, ορος	(1)	without a mother
ἀμοιβή, ῆς, ἡ	(1)	return, recompense, repayment
ἀμπελουργός, οῦ, ὁ	(1)	vine dresser, gardener
Ἀμπλιᾶτος, ου, ὁ	(1)	Ampliatus
ἀμύνομαι	(1)	I retaliate, help
ἀμφιβάλλω	(1)	I cast a fishnet
ἀμφίβληστρον, ου, τό	(1)	casting-net
ἀμφιέζω	(1)	I clothe
Ἀμφίπολις, εως, ἡ	(1)	Amphipolis
ἄμφοδον, ου, τό	(1)	street
ἀμώμητος, ον	(1)	blameless, unblemished
ἄμωμον, ου, τό	(1)	amomum (an Indian spice plant)
ἀναβάλλω	(1)	I postpone, adjourn
ἀναβιβάζω	(1)	I bring up, pull up
ἀνάβλεψις, εως, ἡ	(1)	recovery of sight
ἀναβοάω	(1)	I cry out, shout
ἀναβολή, ῆς, ἡ	(1)	delay, postponement
ἀναγκαστῶς	(1)	by compulsion
ἀναγνωρίζω	(1)	I learn to know again
ἀνάδειξις, εως, ἡ	(1)	commissioning, installation, revelation
ἀναδίδωμι	(1)	I deliver, hand over
ἀναζώννυμι	(1)	I bind up, gird up
ἀναζωπυρέω	(1)	I rekindle, kindle, inflame
ἀναθάλλω	(1)	I cause to grow again, revive
ἀνάθημα, ατος, τό	(1)	votive offering
ἀναίδεια, ας, ἡ	(1)	shamelessness, persistence, impudence
ἀναίρεσις, εως, ἡ	(1)	murder, killing
ἀνακαινίζω	(1)	I renew, restore
ἀνάκρισις, εως, ἡ	(1)	investigation, hearing
ἀνάλημψις, εως, ἡ	(1)	ascension
ἀναλογία, ας, ἡ	(1)	right relationship, proportion
ἀναλογίζομαι	(1)	I consider carefully
ἄναλος, ον	(1)	without salt, saltless
ἀνάλυσις, εως, ἡ	(1)	departure, death
ἀναμάρτητος, ον	(1)	without sin
ἀναμένω	(1)	I wait for, expect
ἀνανεόω	(1)	I renew
ἀνανήφω	(1)	I become sober again, return to my senses
ἀναντίρρητος, ον	(1)	not to be contradicted, undeniable
ἀναντιρρήτως	(1)	without objection
ἀνάξιος, ον	(1)	unworthy
ἀναξίως	(1)	in an unworthy manner, unworthily, improperly
ἀναπείθω	(1)	I persuade, incite
ἀναπηδάω	(1)	I jump up, stand up

ἀναπτύσσω	(1)	I unroll
ἀναρίθμητος, ον	(1)	innumerable, countless
ἀνασκευάζω	(1)	I tear down, upset, unsettle
ἀνασταυρόω	(1)	I crucify, crucify again
ἀναστενάζω	(1)	I sigh deeply
ἀνατάσσομαι	(1)	I repeat in proper order, compile
ἀναφωνέω	(1)	I cry out
ἀνάχυσις, εως, ἡ	(1)	wide stream, flood
ἀνάψυξις, εως, ἡ	(1)	breathing space, relaxation, relief
ἀναψύχω	(1)	I revive, refresh
ἀνδραποδιστής, οῦ, ὁ	(1)	slave dealer, kidnapper
ἀνδρίζομαι	(1)	I act like a man, act courageously
Ἀνδρόνικος, ου, ὁ	(1)	Andronicus
ἀνδροφόνος, ου, ὁ	(1)	murderer
ἀνεκδιήγητος, ον	(1)	indescribable
ἀνεκλάλητος, ον	(1)	inexpressible
ἀνέκλειπτος, ον	(1)	unfailing, inexhaustible
ἀνελεήμων, ον	(1)	unmerciful
ἀνέλεος, ον	(1)	merciless
ἀνεμίζω	(1)	I am moved by the wind (pass. in NT)
ἀνένδεκτος, ον	(1)	impossible
ἀνεξεραύνητος, ον	(1)	unfathomable, unsearchable
ἀνεξίκακος, ον	(1)	bearing evil without resentment, patient
ἀνεπαίσχυντος, ον	(1)	unashamed
ἀνεύθετος, ον	(1)	poor, unfavorably situated, unsuitable
ἀνεψιός, οῦ, ὁ	(1)	cousin
ἄνηθον, ου, τό	(1)	dill
ἀνήμερος, ον	(1)	savage, brutal
ἀνθομολογέομαι	(1)	I praise, thank
ἄνθραξ, ακος, ὁ	(1)	charcoal
Ἅννα, ας, ἡ	(1)	Anna
ἄνοιξις, εως, ἡ	(1)	opening
ἀνταγωνίζομαι	(1)	I struggle
ἀνταναπληρόω	(1)	I fill up, complete
ἀνταπόδοσις, εως, ἡ	(1)	repaying, reward
ἀντιβάλλω	(1)	I put against, place against, exchange
ἀντιδιατίθημι	(1)	I oppose myself, am opposed (mid. in NT)
ἀντίθεσις, εως, ἡ	(1)	opposition, objection, contradiction
ἀντικαθίστημι	(1)	I place against, oppose, resist
ἀντικαλέω	(1)	I invite in return
ἀντικρυς	(1)	opposite (impr. prep. in NT)
ἀντίλημψις, εως, ἡ	(1)	help
ἀντιλοιδορέω	(1)	I revile or insult in return
ἀντίλυτρον, ου, τό	(1)	ransom
ἀντιμετρέω	(1)	I measure in return, repay
Ἀντιοχεύς, έως, ὁ	(1)	an Antiochean
Ἀντιπᾶς, ᾶ, ὁ	(1)	Antipas
Ἀντιπατρίς, ίδος, ἡ	(1)	Antipatris
ἀντιπέρα	(1)	opposite (impr. prep. in NT)
ἀντιπίπτω	(1)	I resist, oppose

ἀντιστρατεύομαι	(1)	I am at war against
ἄντλημα, ατος, τό	(1)	bucket
ἀντοφθαλμέω	(1)	I look directly at, face into
ἀνωτερικός, ή, όν	(1)	upper, inland
ἀπάγχω	(1)	I hang myself (mid. in NT)
ἀπαίδευτος, ον	(1)	uninstructed, uneducated, ignorant
ἀπαλγέω	(1)	I become callous, languish
ἀπαράβατος, ον	(1)	permanent, unchangeable
ἀπαρασκεύαστος, ον	(1)	not ready, unprepared
ἀπαρτισμός, οῦ, ὁ	(1)	completion
ἀπασπάζομαι	(1)	I take leave of, say farewell to
ἀπάτωρ, ορος	(1)	fatherless, without a father
ἀπαύγασμα, ατος, τό	(1)	radiance, reflection
ἄπειμι	(1)	I go, come
ἀπείραστος, ον	(1)	without temptation, unable to be tempted
ἄπειρος, ον	(1)	unacquainted with, unaccustomed to
ἀπέκδυσις, εως, ἡ	(1)	removal, stripping off
ἀπελαύνω	(1)	I drive away
ἀπελεγμός, οῦ, ὁ	(1)	refutation, exposure, discredit
ἀπελεύθερος, ου, ὁ	(1)	freed person
Ἀπελλῆς, οῦ, ὁ	(1)	Apelles
ἀπελπίζω	(1)	I despair, expect in return
ἀπέραντος, ον	(1)	endless, limitless
ἀπερισπάστως	(1)	without distraction
ἀπερίτμητος, ον	(1)	uncircumcised; stubborn, obstinate (fig. in NT)
ἁπλῶς	(1)	generously
ἀποβλέπω	(1)	I look, pay attention
ἀπόβλητος, ον	(1)	rejected
ἀπογίνομαι	(1)	I die
ἀπόδειξις, εως, ἡ	(1)	proof
ἀπόδημος, ον	(1)	away on a journey
ἀποδιορίζω	(1)	I divide, separate
ἀποθησαυρίζω	(1)	I store up, lay up
ἀποθλίβω	(1)	I press upon, crowd
ἀποκατάστασις, εως, ἡ	(1)	restoration
ἀποκλείω	(1)	I close, shut
ἀπόκριμα, ατος, τό	(1)	official report, decision, verdict
ἀπολέγω	(1)	I disown, renounce (mid. in NT)
Ἀπολλύων, ονος, ὁ	(1)	Apollyon, Destroyer
Ἀπολλωνία, ας, ἡ	(1)	Apollonia
ἀπομάσσω	(1)	I wipe off (mid. in NT)
ἀπονέμω	(1)	I show (honor)
ἀπονίπτω	(1)	I wash off
ἀποπίπτω	(1)	I fall away
ἀπορία, ας, ἡ	(1)	perplexity, anxiety
ἀπορίπτω	(1)	I throw down, jump off
ἀπορφανίζω	(1)	I make an orphan of, separate from
ἀποσκίαμα, ατος, τό	(1)	shadow
ἀποστεγάζω	(1)	I unroof, remove the roof
ἀποστοματίζω	(1)	I question closely, interrogate, ask hostile questions

ἀποστυγέω	(1)	I hate, abhor
ἀποτίνω	(1)	I make compensation, pay the damages
ἀποτολμάω	(1)	I am bold
ἀποτρέπω	(1)	I turn away from, avoid (mid. in NT)
ἀπουσία, ας, ἡ	(1)	absence
ἀποφορτίζομαι	(1)	I unload
ἀπόχρησις, εως, ἡ	(1)	consuming, using up
ἀποψύχω	(1)	I faint, die
Ἀππίου Φόρον	(1)	Appii Forum, Forum of Appius
ἀπρόσιτος, ον	(1)	unapproachable
ἀπροσωπολήμπτως	(1)	impartially
ἄπταιστος, ον	(1)	without stumbling
Ἀπφία, ας, ἡ	(1)	Apphia
ἀρά, ᾶς, ἡ	(1)	curse
ἄραφος, ον	(1)	seamless
Ἄραψ, βος, ὁ	(1)	an Arab
ἀργέω	(1)	I am idle, grow weary
ἀργυροκόπος, ου, ὁ	(1)	silversmith
Ἀρεοπαγίτης, ου, ὁ	(1)	an Areopagite
ἀρεσκεία, ας, ἡ	(1)	desire to please
Ἀρέτας, α, ὁ	(1)	Aretas
ἀρήν, ἀρνός, ὁ	(1)	lamb
Ἀριστόβουλος, ου, ὁ	(1)	Aristobulus
ἄρκος, ου, ὁ, ἡ	(1)	bear
Ἁρμαγεδών	(1)	Armageddon
ἁρμόζω	(1)	I betroth, join in marriage (mid. in NT)
ἁρμός, οῦ, ὁ	(1)	joint
Ἀρνί, ὁ	(1)	Arni
ἄροτρον, ου, τό	(1)	plow
ἁρπαγμός, οῦ, ὁ	(1)	something to hold, prize
ἄρρητος, ον	(1)	inexpressible, not to be spoken
Ἀρτεμᾶς, ᾶ, ὁ	(1)	Artemas
ἀρτέμων, ωνος, ὁ	(1)	sail, foresail
ἀρτιγέννητος, ον	(1)	new born
ἄρτιος, α, ον	(1)	complete, capable, proficient
Ἀρφαξάδ, ὁ	(1)	Arphaxad
Ἀρχέλαος, ου, ὁ	(1)	Archelaus
ἀρχιερατικός, όν	(1)	high-priestly
ἀρχιποίμην, ενος, ὁ	(1)	chief shepherd
ἀρχιτέκτων, ονος, ὁ	(1)	master builder
ἀρχιτελώνης, ου, ὁ	(1)	chief tax collector
ἀσεβέω	(1)	I act impiously, live in an ungodly way
ἄσημος, ον	(1)	without mark, obscure, insignificant
ἀσθένημα, ατος, τό	(1)	weakness
Ἀσιανός, οῦ, ὁ	(1)	an Asian
Ἀσιάρχης, ου, ὁ	(1)	Asiarch
ἀσιτία, ας, ἡ	(1)	lack of appetite, abstinence from food
ἄσιτος, ον	(1)	without eating, fasting
ἀσκέω	(1)	I practice, engage in, do my best
ἀσμένως	(1)	gladly

ἄσοφος, ον	(1)	unwise, foolish
ἀσπίς, ίδος, ἡ	(1)	asp, Egyptian cobra, snake
ἄσπονδος, ον	(1)	irreconcilable
ἆσσον	(1)	nearer, closer, close
ἀστατέω	(1)	I am unsettled, homeless
Ἀσύγκριτος, ου, ὁ	(1)	Asyncritus
ἀσύμφωνος, ον	(1)	not harmonious
ἀσύνθετος, ον	(1)	faithless, undutiful, disloyal
ἀσχήμων, ον	(1)	shameful, unpresentable, indecent; genitals (subst.)
ἀσώτως	(1)	dissolutely, loosely
ἀτακτέω	(1)	I am idle, lazy
ἄτακτος, ον	(1)	disorderly, insubordinate, lazy
ἄτομος, ον	(1)	uncut, indivisible; moment (subst.)
Ἀττάλεια, ας, ἡ	(1)	Attalia
αὐγάζω	(1)	I see, shine forth
αὐγή, ῆς, ἡ	(1)	dawn
Αὐγοῦστος, ου, ὁ	(1)	Augustus
αὐθεντέω	(1)	I have authority, domineer, control
αὐλός, οῦ, ὁ	(1)	flute
αὐτάρκης, ες	(1)	content, self-sufficient
αὐτοκατάκριτος, ον	(1)	self-condemned
αὐτόπτης, ου, ὁ	(1)	eyewitness
αὐτόφωρος, ον	(1)	in the act
αὐτόχειρ, ρος	(1)	with one's own hand
αὐχέω	(1)	I boast
αὐχμηρός, ά, όν	(1)	dry, dirty, dark
ἀφανής, ές	(1)	invisible, hidden
ἀφανισμός, οῦ, ὁ	(1)	disappearance, destruction
ἄφαντος, ον	(1)	invisible
ἀφειδία, ας, ἡ	(1)	severe treatment, severe discipline
ἀφελότης, ητος, ἡ	(1)	simplicity, humility
ἀφθορία, ας, ἡ	(1)	soundness, integrity
ἀφικνέομαι	(1)	I reach, become known
ἀφιλάγαθος, ον	(1)	not loving the good
ἄφιξις, εως, ἡ	(1)	departure
ἀφομοιόω	(1)	I make like, become like, resemble
ἀφρός, οῦ, ὁ	(1)	foam
ἀφυπνόω	(1)	I fall asleep
Ἀχαϊκός, οῦ, ὁ	(1)	Achaicus
ἀχλύς, ύος, ἡ	(1)	mistiness
ἀχρειόω	(1)	I make useless; become depraved (pass.)
ἄχρηστος, ον	(1)	useless, worthless
ἀψευδής, ές	(1)	free from deceit, truthful, trustworthy
ἄψυχος, ον	(1)	inanimate, lifeless
Βάαλ, ὁ	(1)	Baal
βαθμός, οῦ, ὁ	(1)	step, rank
βαθύνω	(1)	I make deep, go down deep
βάϊον, ου, τό	(1)	palm branch
Βαλάκ, ὁ	(1)	Balak
Βαράκ, ὁ	(1)	Barak

Βαραχίας, ου, ὁ	(1)	Barachiah
Βαριησοῦς, οῦ, ὁ	(1)	Bar-Jesus
Βαριωνᾶ, ὁ	(1)	Bar-Jona
Βαρτιμαῖος, ου, ὁ	(1)	Bartimaeus
βαρύτιμος, ον	(1)	very expensive, very precious
βασανιστής, οῦ, ὁ	(1)	torturer, jailer
βάσις, εως, ἡ	(1)	foot
βασκαίνω	(1)	I bewitch
βάτος, ου, ὁ	(1)	bath (Hebrew liquid measure)
βάτραχος, ου, ὁ	(1)	frog
βατταλογέω	(1)	I babble, use many words
βδελυκτός, ή, όν	(1)	abominable, detestable
Βελιάρ, ὁ	(1)	Belial
βελόνη, ης, ἡ	(1)	needle
βέλος, ους, τό	(1)	arrow
βελτίων, ον	(1)	better, very well (neut. as adv. in NT)
Βεροιαῖος, α, ον	(1)	Beroean; a Beroean (subst.)
Βηθζαθά, ἡ	(1)	Bethzatha
βήρυλλος, ου, ὁ, ἡ	(1)	beryl
βίαιος, α, ον	(1)	violent, forcible, strong
βιαστής, οῦ, ὁ	(1)	violent person
βιβρώσκω	(1)	I eat
βιόω	(1)	I live
βίωσις, εως, ἡ	(1)	manner of life
βλαβερός, ά, όν	(1)	harmful
Βλάστος, ου, ὁ	(1)	Blastus
βλέμμα, ατος, τό	(1)	glance, look
βλητέος, α, ον	(1)	must be put
Βοανηργές	(1)	Boanerges
βοή, ῆς, ἡ	(1)	cry, shout
βοηθός, όν	(1)	helpful; helper (subst. in NT)
βολή, ῆς, ἡ	(1)	throw
Βόος, ὁ	(1)	Boaz
βόρβορος, ου, ὁ	(1)	mud, mire, filth, slime
Βοσόρ, ὁ	(1)	Bosor
βοτάνη, ης, ἡ	(1)	fodder, herb, plant
βότρυς, υος, ὁ	(1)	bunch of grapes
βραβεύω	(1)	I rule, control
βραδυπλοέω	(1)	I sail slowly
βραδύτης, ητος, ἡ	(1)	slowness
βρόχος, ου, ὁ	(1)	noose; restriction (fig. in NT)
βρύχω	(1)	I gnash
βρύω	(1)	I pour forth, gush
βρώσιμος, ον	(1)	eatable
βυθός, οῦ, ὁ	(1)	depth, open sea
βύσσος, ου, ἡ	(1)	fine linen
βωμός, ου, ὁ	(1)	altar
Γαββαθᾶ	(1)	Gabbatha
γάγγραινα, ης, ἡ	(1)	gangrene
Γάδ, ὁ	(1)	Gad

Γαδαρηνός, ή, όν	(1)	Gadarene; a Gadarene (subst.)
Γάζα, ης, ἡ	(1)	Gaza
γάζα, ης, ἡ	(1)	treasury, treasure
Γαλάτης, ου, ὁ	(1)	a Galatian
γαμίσκω	(1)	I give in marriage
Γεδεών, ὁ	(1)	Gideon
γέλως, ωτος, ὁ	(1)	laughter
γενεαλογέω	(1)	I trace descent; am descended from (pass.)
γενετή, ῆς, ἡ	(1)	birth
γερουσία, ας, ἡ	(1)	council of elders (Sanhedrin)
γέρων, οντος, ὁ	(1)	old man
γεωργέω	(1)	I cultivate, till
γεώργιον, ου, τό	(1)	cultivated land, field
γῆρας, ως, τό	(1)	old age
γλεῦκος, ους, τό	(1)	sweet new wine
γναφεύς, έως, ὁ	(1)	bleacher, fuller
γνησίως	(1)	sincerely, genuinely
γνόφος, ου, ὁ	(1)	darkness
γνώστης, ου, ὁ	(1)	one acquainted, expert
γογγυστής, οῦ, ὁ	(1)	grumbler
γόης, ητος, ὁ	(1)	sorcerer, swindler, cheat, impostor
γραπτός, ή, όν	(1)	written
γραώδης, ες	(1)	characteristic of old women
γυμνασία, ας, ἡ	(1)	training
γυμνιτεύω	(1)	I am poorly clothed
γυναικάριον, ου, τό	(1)	idle or silly woman
γυναικεῖος, α, ον	(1)	feminine, female
Γώγ, ὁ	(1)	Gog
δαιμονιώδης, ες	(1)	demonic
δαίμων, ονος, ὁ	(1)	demon, evil spirit
δάκνω	(1)	I bite
δακρύω	(1)	I weep
δακτύλιος, ου, ὁ	(1)	ring
Δαλμανουθά, ἡ	(1)	Dalmanutha
Δαλματία, ας, ἡ	(1)	Dalmatia
δάμαλις, εως, ἡ	(1)	heifer, young cow
Δάμαρις, ιδος, ἡ	(1)	Damaris
Δαμασκηνός, ή, όν	(1)	Damascene; a Damascene (subst.)
δάνειον, ου, τό	(1)	loan, debt
Δανιήλ, ὁ	(1)	Daniel
δανιστής, οῦ, ὁ	(1)	money lender, creditor
δαπάνη, ης, ἡ	(1)	cost, expense
δεῖγμα, ατος, τό	(1)	example
δειλία, ας, ἡ	(1)	cowardice
δειλιάω	(1)	I am cowardly, timid
δεῖνα, ὁ, ἡ, τό	(1)	so-and-so, a certain person, somebody (masc. in NT)
δεισιδαιμονία, ας, ἡ	(1)	religion
δεισιδαίμων, ον	(1)	religious
δεξιολάβος, ου, ὁ	(1)	spearman or slinger
δέος, ους, τό	(1)	fear, awe, reverence

Δερβαῖος, α, ον	(1)	Derbean; a Derbean (subst.)
δέρμα, ατος, τό	(1)	skin
δέσμη, ης, ἡ	(1)	bundle
δευτεραῖος, α, ον	(1)	on the second day
δημηγορέω	(1)	I deliver a public address, make a speech
δημιουργός, οῦ, ὁ	(1)	craftsman, maker, creator, builder
δήπου	(1)	of course, surely
διαβάλλω	(1)	I bring charges
διάγνωσις, εως, ἡ	(1)	decision
διαγρηγορέω	(1)	I keep awake

διαδέχομαι	(1)	I receive possession of
διάδοχος, ου, ὁ	(1)	successor
διακαθαίρω	(1)	I clean out
διακαθαρίζω	(1)	I clean out
διακατελέγχομαι	(1)	I refute
διακούω	(1)	I give a hearing
διακωλύω	(1)	I prevent
διαλείπω	(1)	I stop, cease
διαλλάσσομαι	(1)	I become reconciled
διαλύω	(1)	I break up, dissolve, scatter

διαμάχομαι	(1)	I contend sharply
διαμερισμός, οῦ, ὁ	(1)	dissension, disunity
διανέμω	(1)	I distribute
διανεύω	(1)	I nod, beckon
διανόημα, ατος, τό	(1)	thought
διανυκτερεύω	(1)	I spend the night
διανύω	(1)	I complete, continue, arrive, travel
διαπαρατριβή, ῆς, ἡ	(1)	mutual or constant irritation
διαπλέω	(1)	I sail through, sail across
διαπραγματεύομαι	(1)	I gain by trading, earn

διασείω	(1)	I extort money by violence
διάστημα, ατος, τό	(1)	interval
διάταγμα, ατος, τό	(1)	edict, command
διαταράσσω	(1)	I am confused, perplexed greatly (pass. in NT)
διατελέω	(1)	I continue, remain
διατροφή, ῆς, ἡ	(1)	support; food (pl. in NT)
διαυγάζω	(1)	I shine through, dawn
διαυγής, ές	(1)	transparent, pure
διαφεύγω	(1)	I escape
διαφυλάσσω	(1)	I guard, protect

διαχλευάζω	(1)	I deride, mock
διαχωρίζω	(1)	I separate from; part, go away (pass.)
διενθυμέομαι	(1)	I consider, reflect, ponder
διέξοδος, ου, ἡ	(1)	outlet (used of streets)
διερμηνευτής, οῦ, ὁ	(1)	interpreter, translator
διερωτάω	(1)	I learn by inquiry
διετής, ές	(1)	two years old
διήγησις, εως, ἡ	(1)	narrative, account
διθάλασσος, ον	(1)	with the sea on both sides, between the seas
διϊκνέομαι	(1)	I pierce, penetrate

δικαιοκρισία, ας, ἡ	(1)	righteous judgment, just verdict
δίλογος, ον	(1)	double-tongued, insincere
Διονύσιος, ου, ὁ	(1)	Dionysius
διοπετής, ές	(1)	fallen from heaven
διόρθωμα, ατος, τό	(1)	reform
διόρθωσις, εως, ἡ	(1)	improvement, reformation, new order
Διόσκουροι, ων, οἱ	(1)	the Dioscuri (twin sons of Zeus)
Διοτρέφης, ους, ὁ	(1)	Diotrephes
διπλόω	(1)	I double, pay back double
δισμυριάς, άδος, ἡ	(1)	double myriad, twenty thousand
δισχίλιοι, αι, α	(1)	two thousand
διϋλίζω	(1)	I filter, strain out
διχάζω	(1)	I separate, turn against
δίψος, ους, τό	(1)	thirst
διώκτης, ου, ὁ	(1)	persecutor
δογματίζω	(1)	I submit to rules and regulations (pass. in NT)
δοκιμασία, ας, ἡ	(1)	testing, examination
δόλιος, α, ον	(1)	deceitful, treacherous
δολιόω	(1)	I deceive
δολόω	(1)	I falsify, adulterate
δότης, ου, ὁ	(1)	giver
δουλαγωγέω	(1)	I enslave, bring into subjection
δράσσομαι	(1)	I catch, seize
Δρούσιλλα, ης, ἡ	(1)	Drusilla
δυσεντέριον, ου, τό	(1)	dysentery
δυσερμήνευτος, ον	(1)	hard to explain
δύσις, εως, ἡ	(1)	setting (of the sun), west
δύσκολος, ον	(1)	hard, difficult
δυσνόητος, ον	(1)	hard to understand
δυσφημέω	(1)	I slander, defame
δυσφημία, ας, ἡ	(1)	slander, ill repute
δωδέκατος, η, ον	(1)	twelfth
δωδεκάφυλον, ου, τό	(1)	the twelve tribes
ἔα	(1)	ah! ha! (poss. pres. imper. of ἐάω)
ἑβδομηκοντάκις	(1)	seventy times
Ἔβερ, ὁ	(1)	Eber
ἔγγυος, ου, ὁ	(1)	surety, guarantee, guarantor
ἔγερσις, εως, ἡ	(1)	resurrection
ἐγκάθετος, ον	(1)	hired to lie in wait; spy (subst.)
ἐγκαίνια, ων, τά	(1)	Festival of Rededication, Feast of Lights, Hanukkah
ἐγκατοικέω	(1)	I live, dwell
ἐγκαυχάομαι	(1)	I boast
ἐγκομβόομαι	(1)	I gird, put on myself
ἐγκοπή, ῆς, ἡ	(1)	hindrance, obstacle
ἐγκρατής, ές	(1)	self-controlled, disciplined
ἐγκρίνω	(1)	I class
ἔγκυος, ον	(1)	pregnant
ἐγχρίω	(1)	I rub on, anoint
ἐδαφίζω	(1)	I dash or raze to the ground, completely destroy
ἔδαφος, ους, τό	(1)	ground

ἑδραίωμα, ατος, τό	(1)	foundation, support
ἐθελοθρησκία, ας, ἡ	(1)	self-made or would-be religion
ἐθίζω	(1)	I accustom
ἐθνάρχης, ου, ὁ	(1)	ethnarch, governor, official
ἐθνικῶς	(1)	in Gentile fashion, like the heathen
εἰδέα, ας, ἡ	(1)	appearance
εἰδωλεῖον, ου, τό	(1)	idol's temple
εἴκω	(1)	I yield
εἰρηνοποιέω	(1)	I make peace
εἰρηνοποιός, ον	(1)	making peace; peacemaker (subst.)
εἰσδέχομαι	(1)	I take in, receive, welcome
εἰσκαλέομαι	(1)	I invite in
εἰσπηδάω	(1)	I leap in, rush in
εἰστρέχω	(1)	I run in
ἑκάστοτε	(1)	at any time, always
ἑκατονταετής, ές	(1)	a hundred years old
ἐκβαίνω	(1)	I go out, come from
ἐκβολή, ῆς, ἡ	(1)	throwing out, jettisoning
ἔκγονος, ον	(1)	born of; descendants, grandchildren (subst. pl. in NT)
ἐκδαπανάω	(1)	I spend, exhaust
ἔκδηλος, ον	(1)	quite evident, plain
ἐκδιώκω	(1)	I persecute severely
ἔκδοτος, ον	(1)	given up, delivered up, handed over
ἐκδοχή, ῆς, ἡ	(1)	expectation
ἐκζήτησις, εως, ἡ	(1)	useless speculation
ἔκθαμβος, ον	(1)	utterly astonished
ἐκθαυμάζω	(1)	I wonder greatly
ἔκθετος, ον	(1)	exposed, abandoned
ἐκκαίω	(1)	I kindle; am inflamed (pass. in NT)
ἐκκολυμβάω	(1)	I swim away
ἐκκομίζω	(1)	I carry out
ἐκκρεμάννυμι	(1)	I hang out; hang on (mid. in NT)
ἐκλαλέω	(1)	I tell
ἐκλάμπω	(1)	I shine (out)
ἐκλανθάνομαι	(1)	I forget (altogether)
ἐκνεύω	(1)	I turn, withdrew
ἐκνήφω	(1)	I became sober
ἑκούσιος, α, ον	(1)	voluntary, willing
ἐκπερισσῶς	(1)	excessively
ἐκπετάννυμι	(1)	I spread, hold out
ἐκπηδάω	(1)	I rush out
ἐκπληρόω	(1)	I fulfill
ἐκπλήρωσις, εως, ἡ	(1)	completion
ἐκπορνεύω	(1)	I engage in illicit sex, indulge in immorality
ἐκπτύω	(1)	I spit (out), disdain
ἐκστρέφω	(1)	I turn aside, pervert; am corrupt (pass. in NT)
ἐκταράσσω	(1)	I agitate, throw into confusion
ἐκτένεια, ας, ἡ	(1)	perseverance, earnestness
ἐκτενής, ές	(1)	eager, earnest, constant, unfailing
ἔκτρωμα, ατος, τό	(1)	untimely birth, miscarriage

ἐκφοβέω	(1)	I frighten, terrify
ἐκχωρέω	(1)	I go out, go away, depart
Ἐλαμίτης, ου, ὁ	(1)	an Elamite
ἐλαττονέω	(1)	I have less, too little
ἐλαφρία, ας, ἡ	(1)	vacillation, levity
ἐλεγμός, οῦ, ὁ	(1)	conviction, reproof, punishment
ἔλεγξις, εως, ἡ	(1)	conviction, rebuke, reproof
ἔλεγχος, ου, ὁ	(1)	proof, proving, inner conviction
ἔλευσις, εως, ἡ	(1)	coming, advent
ἐλεφάντινος, η, ον	(1)	made of ivory
Ἐλιέζερ, ὁ	(1)	Eliezer
Ἐλισαῖος, ου, ὁ	(1)	Elisha
ἑλκόω	(1)	I cause sores; am covered with sores (pass. in NT)
Ἑλλάς, άδος, ἡ	(1)	Greece
Ἑλληνικός, ή, όν	(1)	Greek
Ἐλμαδάμ, ὁ	(1)	Elmadam
Ἐλύμας, α, ὁ	(1)	Elymas
ἐμβάλλω	(1)	I throw in
ἐμβατεύω	(1)	I enter, possess, go into detail, take my stand on
ἐμβιβάζω	(1)	I put in, aboard
ἐμέω	(1)	I spit out
ἐμμαίνομαι	(1)	I am enraged
Ἐμμανουήλ, ὁ	(1)	Emmanuel
Ἐμμαοῦς, ἡ	(1)	Emmaus
Ἐμμώρ, ὁ	(1)	Hamor
ἐμπαιγμονή, ῆς, ἡ	(1)	mocking
ἐμπαιγμός, οῦ, ὁ	(1)	scorn, mocking, derisive torture
ἐμπεριπατέω	(1)	I walk about, move, live
ἐμπίμπρημι	(1)	I set on fire, burn
ἐμπλοκή, ῆς, ἡ	(1)	braiding, braid
ἐμπνέω	(1)	I breathe
ἐμπορία, ας, ἡ	(1)	business, trade
ἐμπόριον, ου, τό	(1)	market
ἐμφυσάω	(1)	I breathe on
ἔμφυτος, ον	(1)	implanted
ἐνάλιος, ον	(1)	belong to the sea; sea creature (subst. in NT)
ἐνδεής, ές	(1)	poor, impoverished
ἔνδειγμα, ατος, τό	(1)	evidence, plain indication, proof
ἐνδέχομαι	(1)	it is possible (impers. in NT)
ἐνδύνω	(1)	I go in, enter, creep in, worm into
ἔνδυσις, εως, ἡ	(1)	putting on, wearing
ἐνδώμησις, εως, ἡ	(1)	interior structure, material, foundation
ἐνειλέω	(1)	I wrap, confine
ἔνειμι	(1)	I am in or inside
ἐνεός, ά, όν	(1)	speechless
ἐννεύω	(1)	I nod, make signals, gesture
ἔννυχος, ον	(1)	at night (acc. neut. pl. as adv. in NT)
ἐνορκίζω	(1)	I put under oath
ἐντόπιος, α, ον	(1)	local; local resident (subst.)
ἐντρέφω	(1)	I bring up, train

ἐντρυφάω	(1)	I revel, carouse
ἐντυπόω	(1)	I carve, engrave
ἐνυβρίζω	(1)	I insult, outrage
ἐνύπνιον, ου, τό	(1)	dream
Ἐνώς, ὁ	(1)	Enos
ἐνωτίζομαι	(1)	I give ear, pay attention
ἐξαίρω	(1)	I remove, drive away
ἐξαιτέω	(1)	I ask for, demand (mid. in NT)
ἐξάλλομαι	(1)	I jump up
ἐξανάστασις, εως, ἡ	(1)	resurrection
ἐξάπινα	(1)	suddenly
ἐξαστράπτω	(1)	I flash, gleam
ἐξέλκω	(1)	I drag away, lure away
ἐξέραμα, ατος, τό	(1)	vomit
ἐξεραυνάω	(1)	I inquire carefully
ἐξηχέω	(1)	I ring out, sound forth (pass. in NT)
ἕξις, εως, ἡ	(1)	exercise, practice
ἐξισχύω	(1)	I am able, strong
ἐξολεθρεύω	(1)	I destroy, root out
ἐξορκίζω	(1)	I put under oath
ἐξορκιστής, οῦ, ὁ	(1)	exorcist
ἐξουδενέω	(1)	I treat with contempt
ἐξοχή, ῆς, ἡ	(1)	prominence
ἐξυπνίζω	(1)	I wake up, arouse
ἔξυπνος, ον	(1)	awake, aroused
ἑορτάζω	(1)	I celebrate
ἐπαγωνίζομαι	(1)	I fight, contend
ἐπαθροίζω	(1)	I collect in addition, gather more (pass. in NT)
Ἐπαίνετος, ου, ὁ	(1)	Epaenetus
ἐπακούω	(1)	I hear, listen to
ἐπακροάομαι	(1)	I listen to
ἐπάναγκες	(1)	by compulsion, necessarily
ἐπαναμιμνῄσκω	(1)	I remind
ἐπανόρθωσις, εως, ἡ	(1)	correcting, restoration, improvement
ἐπάρατος, ον	(1)	accursed
ἔπαυλις, εως, ἡ	(1)	farm, homestead, residence
ἐπαφρίζω	(1)	I cause to foam up
ἐπειδήπερ	(1)	inasmuch as, since
ἐπεισαγωγή, ῆς, ἡ	(1)	introduction
ἐπεισέρχομαι	(1)	I come upon, rush in suddenly and forcibly
ἐπέκεινα	(1)	farther on, beyond (impr. prep. in NT)
ἐπεκτείνομαι	(1)	I stretch out, strain
ἐπενδύτης, ου, ὁ	(1)	outer garment, coat
ἐπερώτημα, ατος, τό	(1)	question, request, appeal
ἐπιγαμβρεύω	(1)	I marry as next of kin
ἐπιγίνομαι	(1)	I come up or on, happen
ἐπιδιατάσσομαι	(1)	I add to (a will)
ἐπιδιορθόω	(1)	I finish setting right, correct
ἐπιδύω	(1)	I set (of the sun)
ἐπιθανάτιος, ον	(1)	condemned to death

ἐπιθυμητής, οῦ, ὁ	(1)	one who desires
ἐπικαθίζω	(1)	I sit, sit on
ἐπικάλυμμα, ατος, τό	(1)	cover, veil, pretext
ἐπικαλύπτω	(1)	I cover
ἐπικέλλω	(1)	I bring to shore, run aground
Ἐπικούρειος, ου, ὁ	(1)	Epicurean
ἐπικουρία, ας, ἡ	(1)	help
ἐπικρίνω	(1)	I decide, determine
ἐπιλείπω	(1)	I fail
ἐπιλείχω	(1)	I lick
ἐπιλησμονή, ῆς, ἡ	(1)	forgetfulness
ἐπίλοιπος, ον	(1)	left, remaining
ἐπίλυσις, εως, ἡ	(1)	explanation, interpretation
ἐπιμαρτυρέω	(1)	I bear witness, testify
ἐπιμέλεια, ας, ἡ	(1)	care, attention
ἐπιμελῶς	(1)	carefully
ἐπινεύω	(1)	I consent, agree
ἐπίνοια, ας, ἡ	(1)	thought, conception, intent
ἐπιορκέω	(1)	I swear falsely, break my oath
ἐπίορκος, ον	(1)	perjured; perjurer (subst. in NT)
ἐπιπλήσσω	(1)	I strike at, rebuke, reprove
ἐπιπόθητος, ον	(1)	longed for, desired
ἐπιποθία, ας, ἡ	(1)	longing, desire
ἐπιπορεύομαι	(1)	I come or go to
ἐπιράπτω	(1)	I sew on
ἐπισιτισμός, οῦ, ὁ	(1)	provisions, food
ἐπισκευάζομαι	(1)	I make preparations, get ready
ἐπισκηνόω	(1)	I take up residence, live in
ἐπισπάομαι	(1)	I pull over the foreskin, conceal circumcision
ἐπισπείρω	(1)	I sow upon or after
ἐπιστήμων, ον	(1)	expert, learned, understanding
ἐπιστομίζω	(1)	I stop the mouth, silence
ἐπιστροφή, ῆς, ἡ	(1)	turning, conversion
ἐπισυντρέχω	(1)	I run together
ἐπισφαλής, ές	(1)	unsafe, dangerous
ἐπισχύω	(1)	I grow strong, insist
ἐπισωρεύω	(1)	I heap up, accumulate
ἐπιτήδειος, α, ον	(1)	necessary, proper
ἐπιτιμία, ας, ἡ	(1)	punishment
ἐπιτροπή, ῆς, ἡ	(1)	permission, commission, full power
ἐπιφανής, ές	(1)	splendid, glorious, remarkable
ἐπιφαύσκω	(1)	I shine on, illuminate
ἐπιχέω	(1)	I pour on or over
ἐπονομάζω	(1)	I call, name; call myself (pass. in NT)
ἐπόπτης, ου, ὁ	(1)	eyewitness
ἔπος, ους, τό	(1)	word
ἑπτακισχίλιοι, αι, α	(1)	seven thousand
ἐρείδω	(1)	I jam fast, become fixed
ἐρεύγομαι	(1)	I utter, proclaim
ἐρίζω	(1)	I quarrel, wrangle

ἐρίφιον, ου, τό	(1)	kid, goat
Ἑρμᾶς, ᾶ, ὁ	(1)	Hermas
Ἑρμογένης, ους, ὁ	(1)	Hermogenes
Ἐσλί, ὁ	(1)	Esli
ἐσσόομαι	(1)	I am defeated, inferior, treated worse
ἐσχάτως	(1)	finally
ἑτερόγλωσσος, ον	(1)	speaking a foreign or strange language
ἑτεροζυγέω	(1)	I am unevenly yoked, mismated
ἑτέρως	(1)	differently, otherwise
ἑτοιμασία, ας, ἡ	(1)	readiness, preparation
εὐαρέστως	(1)	acceptably, pleasingly
Εὔβουλος, ου, ὁ	(1)	Eubulus
εὖγε	(1)	well done! excellent!
εὐδία, ας, ἡ	(1)	fair weather
εὐεργετέω	(1)	I do good
εὐεργέτης, ου, ὁ	(1)	benefactor
εὔθυμος, ον	(1)	cheerful, encouraged
εὐθύμως	(1)	cheerfully
εὐθύτης, ητος, ἡ	(1)	straightness; uprightness (fig. in NT)
εὐλαβέομαι	(1)	I am afraid, concerned
εὐμετάδοτος, ον	(1)	generous
Εὐνίκη, ης, ἡ	(1)	Eunice
εὐνοέω	(1)	I make friends
εὔνοια, ας, ἡ	(1)	good will, zeal, enthusiasm
Εὐοδία, ας, ἡ	(1)	Euodia
εὐπάρεδρος, ον	(1)	constant; devotion (subst. in NT)
εὐπειθής, ές	(1)	obedient, complaint
εὐπερίστατος, ον	(1)	easily ensnaring
εὐποιΐα, ας, ἡ	(1)	doing of good
εὐπορέω	(1)	I have plenty, am well off
εὐπορία, ας, ἡ	(1)	prosperity
εὐπρέπεια, ας, ἡ	(1)	fine appearance, beauty
εὐπροσωπέω	(1)	I make a good showing
Εὐρακύλων, ωνος, ὁ	(1)	Euraquilo, northeast wind
εὐρύχωρος, ον	(1)	spacious, broad, roomy
εὔσημος, ον	(1)	clear, easily recognizable, distinct
εὐσχημοσύνη, ης, ἡ	(1)	propriety, presentability, decorum
εὐτραπελία, ας, ἡ	(1)	coarse jesting, buffoonery
Εὔτυχος, ου, ὁ	(1)	Eutychus
εὐφημία, ας, ἡ	(1)	good report or repute
εὔφημος, ον	(1)	well-sounding, auspicious
εὐφορέω	(1)	I bear good crops, yield well, am fruitful
εὐχάριστος, ον	(1)	thankful
εὐψυχέω	(1)	I am glad, have courage
ἐφάλλομαι	(1)	I leap upon
ἐφευρετής, οῦ, ὁ	(1)	inventor, contriver
ἐφήμερος, ον	(1)	for the day, daily
Ἐφραίμ, ὁ	(1)	Ephraim
εφφαθα	(1)	be opened
Ζάρα, ὁ	(1)	Zerah

ζευκτηρία, ας, ἡ	(1)	bands, ropes
ζηλεύω	(1)	I am eager, earnest
Ζηνᾶς, ὁ	(1)	Zenas
ἡγεμονία, ας, ἡ	(1)	chief command, rule, government
ἦθος, ους, τό	(1)	custom, habit
Ἡλί, ὁ	(1)	Heli
ἡμιθανής, ές	(1)	half dead
ἡμίωρον, ου, τό	(1)	half hour
ἤπερ	(1)	than
ἤπιος, α, ον	(1)	gentle, kind
Ἤρ, ὁ	(1)	Er
ἤρεμος, ον	(1)	quiet, tranquil, peaceful
Ἡρῳδίων, ωνος, ὁ	(1)	Herodion
ἤτοι	(1)	or, either
ἠχέω	(1)	I sound, ring out
ἦχος, ους, τό	(1)	sound, tone, noise, roar
Θαμάρ, ἡ	(1)	Tamar
θανάσιμος, ον	(1)	deadly; deadly poison or thing (subst. in NT)
θανατηφόρος, ον	(1)	death-bringing, deadly
Θάρα, ὁ	(1)	Terah
θάρσος, ους, τό	(1)	courage
θαυμάσιος, α, ον	(1)	wonderful
θεά, ᾶς, ἡ	(1)	goddess
θεατρίζω	(1)	I put to shame, expose publicly
θειότης, ητος, ἡ	(1)	divinity, divine nature
θειώδης, ες	(1)	sulfurous yellow
θέλησις, εως, ἡ	(1)	will
θεμέλιον, ου, τό	(1)	foundation, basis
θεοδίδακτος, ον	(1)	taught by God
θεομάχος, ον	(1)	fighting against or opposing God
θεόπνευστος, ον	(1)	inspired by God
θεοσέβεια, ας, ἡ	(1)	reverence for God, piety, religion
θεοσεβής, ές	(1)	god-fearing, devout, religious, pious
θεοστυγής, ές	(1)	hating god
θεότης, ητος, ἡ	(1)	deity, divinity
θεράπων, οντος, ὁ	(1)	servant
θέρμη, ης, ἡ	(1)	heat
Θευδᾶς, ᾶ, ὁ	(1)	Theudas
θεωρία, ας, ἡ	(1)	spectacle, sight
θήκη, ης, ἡ	(1)	receptacle, sheath
θήρα, ας, ἡ	(1)	net, trap
θηρεύω	(1)	I catch, hunt
θηριομαχέω	(1)	I fight wild animals
θορυβάζω	(1)	I cause trouble; am troubled, distracted (pass. in NT)
θραύω	(1)	I break, weaken, oppress
θρέμμα, ατος, τό	(1)	(domesticated) animal; cattle, flocks (pl. in NT)
θρησκός, όν	(1)	religious
θρόμβος, ου, ὁ	(1)	drop or clot (of blood)
θύελλα, ης, ἡ	(1)	windstorm, whirlwind
θύϊνος, η, ον	(1)	from the citron tree, scented

θυμιατήριον, ου, τό	(1)	altar of incense
θυμιάω	(1)	I make an incense offering
θυμομαχέω	(1)	I am very angry
θυμόω	(1)	I make angry; become angry (pass. in NT)
θυρεός, οῦ, ὁ	(1)	shield
Ἰαμβρῆς, ὁ	(1)	Jambres
Ἰανναί, ὁ	(1)	Jannai
Ἰάννης, ὁ	(1)	Jannes
Ἰάρετ, ὁ	(1)	Jared
Ἰδουμαία, ας, ἡ	(1)	Idumea
ἱδρώς, ῶτος, ὁ	(1)	sweat, perspiration
Ἰεζάβελ, ἡ	(1)	Jezebel
Ἱεράπολις, εως, ἡ	(1)	Hierapolis
ἱερατεύω	(1)	I am a priest, perform the service of a priest
ἱερόθυτος, ον	(1)	offered in sacrifice
ἱεροπρεπής, ές	(1)	holy, worthy of reverence
ἱεροσυλέω	(1)	I rob temples, commit sacrilege
ἱερόσυλος, ον	(1)	temple robber, sacrilegious person (subst. in NT)
ἱερουργέω	(1)	I serve as a priest
Ἰεφθάε, ὁ	(1)	Jephthah
ἱκανότης, ητος, ἡ	(1)	fitness, capability, qualification
ἱκετηρία, ας, ἡ	(1)	supplication, request
ἰκμάς, άδος, ἡ	(1)	moisture
ἱλαρός, ά, όν	(1)	cheerful, glad
ἱλαρότης, ητος, ἡ	(1)	cheerfulness
Ἰλλυρικόν, οῦ, τό	(1)	Illyricum
ἰουδαΐζω	(1)	I live as a Jew or according to Jewish customs
Ἰουδαϊκός, ή, όν	(1)	Jewish
Ἰουδαϊκῶς	(1)	in a Jewish manner, like a Jew
Ἰουλία, ας, ἡ	(1)	Julia
Ἰουνιᾶς, ᾶ, ὁ	(1)	Junias
ἱππικός, ή, όν	(1)	pertaining to a horseman; cavalry (subst. in NT)
ἰσάγγελος, ον	(1)	like a angel
ἰσότιμος, ον	(1)	equal in value, of the same kind
ἰσόψυχος, ον	(1)	of like soul or mind
Ἰσσαχάρ, ὁ	(1)	Issachar
ἱστορέω	(1)	I visit
ἴσως	(1)	perhaps, probably
Ἰταλικός, ή, όν	(1)	Italian
Ἰτουραῖος, α, ον	(1)	Ituraean
Ἰωανάν, ὁ	(1)	Joanan
Ἰώβ, ὁ	(1)	Job
Ἰωδά, ὁ	(1)	Joda
Ἰωήλ, ὁ	(1)	Joel
Ἰωνάμ, ὁ	(1)	Jonam
Ἰωρίμ, ὁ	(1)	Jorim
Ἰωσήχ, ὁ	(1)	Josech
ἰῶτα, τό	(1)	iota
καθά	(1)	just as
καθαίρω	(1)	I make clean, prune

καθάπτω	(1)	I take hold of, seize, fasten on
καθαρότης, ητος, ἡ	(1)	purity, purification
καθημερινός, ή, όν	(1)	daily
καθόλου	(1)	entirely, completely
καθοπλίζω	(1)	I arm fully, equip
καθοράω	(1)	I perceive, notice
καθώσπερ	(1)	as, just as
καίτοιγε	(1)	and yet, although
κακοήθεια, ας, ἡ	(1)	malice, malignity
κακοπαθία, ας, ἡ	(1)	suffering, misfortune, misery, strenuous effort
κάκωσις, εως, ἡ	(1)	mistreatment, oppression
καλάμη, ης, ἡ	(1)	stalk, straw, stubble
καλλιέλαιος, ου, ἡ	(1)	cultivated olive tree
καλοδιδάσκαλος, ον	(1)	teaching what is good
Καλοὶ Λιμένες, οἱ	(1)	Fair Havens
καλοποιέω	(1)	I do what is right or good
Κανδάκη, ης, ἡ	(1)	Candace
καπηλεύω	(1)	I trade in, peddle
Κάρπος, ου, ὁ	(1)	Carpus
καρποφόρος, ον	(1)	fruitful
καρτερέω	(1)	I endure, persevere, am strong
καταβαρέω	(1)	I burden, am a burden
καταβαρύνω	(1)	I weigh down; am heavy (pass.)
κατάβασις, εως, ἡ	(1)	descent, road leading down, slope
καταβραβεύω	(1)	I decide against, rob of a prize, cheat, condemn
καταγγελεύς, έως, ὁ	(1)	proclaimer, preacher, herald
καταγράφω	(1)	I write
καταγωνίζομαι	(1)	I conquer, defeat, overcome
καταδέω	(1)	I bind up, bandage
κατάδηλος, ον	(1)	very clear or evident
καταδίκη, ης, ἡ	(1)	condemnation, sentence
καταδιώκω	(1)	I search for, hunt for
κατάθεμα, ατος, τό	(1)	something cursed
καταθεματίζω	(1)	I curse
κατακληρονομέω	(1)	I give as an inheritance
κατακλύζω	(1)	I flood, inundate
κατακόπτω	(1)	I beat, bruise
κατακρημνίζω	(1)	I throw down from a cliff
κατακύπτω	(1)	I bend down
κατάλαλος, ον	(1)	speaking evil of others; slanderer (subst. in NT)
καταλέγω	(1)	I select, enlist, enroll
καταλιθάζω	(1)	I stone to death
κατάλοιπος, ον	(1)	left, remaining
καταμανθάνω	(1)	I observe, notice
καταμένω	(1)	I stay, live
καταναλίσκω	(1)	I consume
κατανεύω	(1)	I signal, motion to
κατάνυξις, εως, ἡ	(1)	stupor, numbness
κατανύσσομαι	(1)	I am pierced, stabbed
καταπλέω	(1)	I sail, sail down

καταριθμέω	(1)	I count, count among; belong to (pass. in NT)
κατάρτισις, εως, ἡ	(1)	being made complete
καταρτισμός, οῦ, ὁ	(1)	equipment, equipping, training
κατασκιάζω	(1)	I overshadow
κατασκοπέω	(1)	I spy out, lie in wait for
κατάσκοπος, ου, ὁ	(1)	spy
κατασοφίζομαι	(1)	I take advantage of by trickery
κατάστημα, ατος, τό	(1)	behavior, demeanor
καταστολή, ῆς, ἡ	(1)	deportment, clothing
καταστρηνιάω	(1)	I have sensual desires against
καταστρώννυμι	(1)	I strike down, kill
κατασύρω	(1)	I drag (away by force)
κατασφάζω	(1)	I slaughter, strike down
κατασφραγίζω	(1)	I seal (up)
κατατομή, ῆς, ἡ	(1)	mutilation, cutting in pieces
κατατρέχω	(1)	I run down
καταφθείρω	(1)	I ruin, corrupt
καταφρονητής, οῦ, ὁ	(1)	despiser, scoffer
καταχθόνιος, ον	(1)	under the earth, subterranean
καταψύχω	(1)	I cool off, refresh
κατείδωλος, ον	(1)	full of idols
κατευλογέω	(1)	I bless
κατεφίσταμαι	(1)	I rise up against, attack
κατήγωρ, ορος, ὁ	(1)	accuser
κατήφεια, ας, ἡ	(1)	gloominess, dejection, depression
κατιόω	(1)	I rust over; become rusty, tarnished (pass. in NT)
κατοίκησις, εως, ἡ	(1)	living quarters, dwelling
κατοικία, ας, ἡ	(1)	dwelling place, habitation
κατοικίζω	(1)	I cause to dwell
κατοπτρίζω	(1)	I look at (as in a mirror), contemplate (mid. in NT)
κατώτερος, α, ον	(1)	lower
κατωτέρω	(1)	lower, below, under
Καῦδα	(1)	Cauda
καῦσις, εως, ἡ	(1)	burning
καυστηριάζω	(1)	I brand with a hot iron, sear
Κεδρών, ὁ	(1)	Kidron
κειρία, ας, ἡ	(1)	bandage, grave clothes
κέλευσμα, ατος, τό	(1)	signal, shout of command
κενοδοξία, ας, ἡ	(1)	vanity, conceit, excessive ambition
κενόδοξος, ον	(1)	conceited, boastful
κενῶς	(1)	in an empty manner, idly, in vain
κεραμικός, ή, όν	(1)	belonging to the potter, made of clay
κέραμος, ου, ὁ	(1)	roof tile
κεράτιον, ου, τό	(1)	carob pod
κέρμα, ατος, τό	(1)	piece of money, coin
κερματιστής, οῦ, ὁ	(1)	money-changer
κεφαλιόω	(1)	I strike on the head
κεφαλίς, ίδος, ἡ	(1)	roll
κημόω	(1)	I muzzle
κηπουρός, οῦ, ὁ	(1)	gardener

κῆτος, ους, τό	(1)	sea monster
κιννάμωμον, ου, τό	(1)	cinnamon
Κίς, ὁ	(1)	Kish
κίχρημι	(1)	I lend
Κλαυδία, ας, ἡ	(1)	Claudia
κλέμμα, ατος, τό	(1)	stealing, theft
Κλεοπᾶς, ᾶ, ὁ	(1)	Cleopas
κλέος, ους, τό	(1)	fame, glory, credit
Κλήμης, εντος, ὁ	(1)	Clement
κληρόω	(1)	I appoint by lot, choose
κλινάριον, ου, τό	(1)	bed, cot
κλισία, ας, ἡ	(1)	group (of people eating)
κλυδωνίζομαι	(1)	I am tossed by waves
Κλωπᾶς, ᾶ, ὁ	(1)	Clopas
κνήθω	(1)	I itch; feel an itching (pass. in NT)
Κνίδος, ου, ἡ	(1)	Cnidus
κοίμησις, εως, ἡ	(1)	sleep, rest
κοινωνικός, ή, όν	(1)	liberal, generous
κοιτών, ῶνος, ὁ	(1)	bedroom
κολακεία, ας, ἡ	(1)	flattery
κολλούριον, ου, τό	(1)	eye salve
Κολοσσαί, ῶν, αἱ	(1)	Colossae
κολυμβάω	(1)	I swim
κολωνία, ας, ἡ	(1)	colony
κόμη, ης, ἡ	(1)	hair
κομψότερον	(1)	better
κοπετός, οῦ, ὁ	(1)	mourning, lamentation
κοπή, ῆς, ἡ	(1)	cutting down, slaughter, defeat
κοπρία, ας, ἡ	(1)	dung heap, garbage pile
κόπριον, ου, τό	(1)	dung, manure
κόραξ, ακος, ὁ	(1)	crow, raven
κορβᾶν	(1)	corban, gift
κορβανᾶς, ᾶ, ὁ	(1)	temple treasury
Κόρε, ὁ	(1)	Korah
κόρος, ου, ὁ	(1)	cor, kor (Hebrew dry measure)
κοσμοκράτωρ, ορος, ὁ	(1)	world ruler
Κούαρτος, ου, ὁ	(1)	Quartus
κουμ	(1)	stand up
κουφίζω	(1)	I make light, lighten
κραιπάλη, ης, ἡ	(1)	drunken dissipation, intoxication, hangover, staggering
κραταιός, ά, όν	(1)	powerful, mighty
Κρήσκης, εντος, ὁ	(1)	Crescens
κριθή, ῆς, ἡ	(1)	barley
κριτικός, ή, όν	(1)	able to discern or judge
κρύπτη, ης, ἡ	(1)	dark and hidden place, cellar
κρυσταλλίζω	(1)	I shine like crystal, am as transparent as crystal
κρυφῇ	(1)	in secret, secretly
κτήτωρ, ορος, ὁ	(1)	owner
κτίστης, ου, ὁ	(1)	Creator
κυβεία, ας, ἡ	(1)	dice-playing, trickery, craftiness

κυβέρνησις, εως, ἡ	(1)	administration, ability to lead
κυκλεύω	(1)	I surround
κυλισμός, οῦ, ὁ	(1)	rolling, wallowing
κυλίω	(1)	I roll; roll myself, roll about (pass. in NT)
κύμβαλον, ου, τό	(1)	cymbal
κύμινον, ου, τό	(1)	cummin
Κυρήνη, ης, ἡ	(1)	Cyrene
Κυρήνιος, ου, ὁ	(1)	Quirinius
κῶλον, ου, τό	(1)	dead body, corpse
κωμόπολις, εως, ἡ	(1)	market town, country town, town
κώνωψ, ωπος, ὁ	(1)	gnat, mosquito
Κώς, Κῶ, ἡ	(1)	Cos
Κωσάμ, ὁ	(1)	Cosam
λακάω	(1)	I burst open
λακτίζω	(1)	I kick
Λάμεχ, ὁ	(1)	Lamech
λαμπρότης, ητος, ἡ	(1)	brilliance, splendor, brightness
λαμπρῶς	(1)	splendidly
λαξευτός, ή, όν	(1)	hewn in the rock
Λαοδικεύς, έως, ὁ	(1)	a Laodicean
λάρυγξ, γγος, ὁ	(1)	throat, gullet
Λασαία, ας, ἡ	(1)	Lasea
λεῖμμα, ατος, τό	(1)	remnant
λεῖος, α, ον	(1)	smooth, level
λειτουργικός, ή, όν	(1)	engaged in holy service, serving, ministering
λεπίς, ίδος, ἡ	(1)	fish scale; scale (fig. in NT)
Λευιτικός, ή, όν	(1)	Levitical
λήθη, ης, ἡ	(1)	forgetfulness
λῆμψις, εως, ἡ	(1)	receiving
λῆρος, ου, ὁ	(1)	idle talk, nonsense
Λιβερτῖνος, ου, ὁ	(1)	Freedman
Λιβύη, ης, ἡ	(1)	Libya
λιθόστρωτος, ον	(1)	paved with stones; stone pavement (neut. subst. in NT)
Λίνος, ου, ὁ	(1)	Linus
λιπαρός, ά, όν	(1)	rich, luxurious, costly
λίψ, λιβός, ὁ	(1)	southwest
λόγιος, α, ον	(1)	learned, cultured
λογομαχέω	(1)	I dispute about words, split hairs
λογομαχία, ας, ἡ	(1)	word battle, dispute about words
λόγχη, ης, ἡ	(1)	spear, lance
Λυκαονία, ας, ἡ	(1)	Lycaonia
Λυκαονιστί	(1)	in the Lycaonian language
Λυκία, ας, ἡ	(1)	Lycia
λυμαίνομαι	(1)	I harm, destroy
Λυσανίας, ου, ὁ	(1)	Lysanias
λύσις, εως, ἡ	(1)	release, separation, divorce
λυσιτελέω	(1)	I am advantageous or better; it is better (impers. in NT)
λυτρωτής, οῦ, ὁ	(1)	redeemer
Λωΐς, ίδος, ἡ	(1)	Lois
Μάαθ, ὁ	(1)	Maath

Μαγαδάν, ή	(1)	Magadan
μαγεία, ας, ή	(1)	magic
μαγεύω	(1)	I practice magic
Μαγώγ, ὁ	(1)	Magog
Μαδιάμ, ὁ	(1)	Midian
μαθήτρια, ας, ή	(1)	woman disciple
Μαθουσαλά, ὁ	(1)	Methuselah
μάκελλον, ου, τό	(1)	meat market, food market
μακροθύμως	(1)	patiently
μακροχρόνιος, ον	(1)	long-lived
Μαλελεήλ, ὁ	(1)	Maleleel
Μάλχος, ου, ὁ	(1)	Malchus
μάμμη, ης, ή	(1)	grandmother
Μαναήν, ὁ	(1)	Manaen
μανία, ας, ή	(1)	madness, insanity, frenzy
μαντεύομαι	(1)	I prophesy, give an oracle
μαραίνω	(1)	I destroy; die out, fade, wither (pass. in NT)
μαρανα θα	(1)	our Lord, come!
μάρμαρος, ου, ὁ	(1)	marble
μασάομαι	(1)	I bite
μαστίζω	(1)	I strike with a whip, scourge
ματαιολογία, ας, ή	(1)	empty or fruitless talk
ματαιολόγος, ον	(1)	talking idly; idle or empty talker (subst.)
ματαιόω	(1)	I think about worthless things, am foolish (pass. in NT)
Ματταθά, ὁ	(1)	Mattatha
μεγαλεῖος, α, ον	(1)	magnificent; mighty deed (neut. subst. in NT)
μεγαλοπρεπής, ές	(1)	magnificent, sublime, majestic
μεγάλως	(1)	greatly, very much
μέγεθος, ους, τό	(1)	greatness
Μελεά, ὁ	(1)	Melea
Μελίτη, ης, ή	(1)	Malta
μεμβράνα, ης, ή	(1)	parchment
μεμψίμοιρος, ον	(1)	faultfinding, complaining
Μεννά, ὁ	(1)	Menna
μενοῦν	(1)	rather, on the contrary, indeed
μεριστής, οῦ, ὁ	(1)	divider, arbitrator
μεσιτεύω	(1)	I guarantee, mediate, act as surety
μεσότοιχον, ου, τό	(1)	dividing wall
μεσόω	(1)	I am in or at the middle, am half over
μεστόω	(1)	I fill; am full (pass. in NT)
μεταβάλλω	(1)	I change my mind (mid. in NT)
μετακινέω	(1)	I shift, remove
μετάλημψις, εως, ή	(1)	sharing, taking, receiving
μετατρέπω	(1)	I turn, change
μετέπειτα	(1)	afterwards
μετεωρίζομαι	(1)	I am anxious, worry
μετοχή, ῆς, ή	(1)	sharing, participation
μετρητής, οῦ, ὁ	(1)	measure (liquid)
μετριοπαθέω	(1)	I deal gently
μετρίως	(1)	moderately

μηδέποτε	(1)	never
μηδέπω	(1)	not yet
Μῆδος, ου, ὁ	(1)	a Mede
μηκύνω	(1)	I make long; become long, grow (mid. in NT)
μηλωτή, ῆς, ἡ	(1)	sheepskin
μήν, μηνός, ὁ	(1)	month, new moon
μηρός, οῦ, ὁ	(1)	thigh
μήτιγε	(1)	not to speak of, let alone
μητρολῴας, ου, ὁ	(1)	one who murders one's mother
μίασμα, ατος, τό	(1)	defilement, corruption
μιασμός, οῦ, ὁ	(1)	defilement, corruption
μίγμα, ατος, τό	(1)	mixture, compound
μίλιον, ου, τό	(1)	mile (Roman)
μισθαποδότης, ου, ὁ	(1)	rewarder
μίσθωμα, ατος, τό	(1)	rent, rented house
Μιτυλήνη, ης, ἡ	(1)	Mitylene
Μνάσων, ωνος, ὁ	(1)	Mnason
μνήμη, ης, ἡ	(1)	remembrance, memory
μογιλάλος, ον	(1)	speaking with difficulty, having a speech impediment
μόγις	(1)	scarcely, with difficulty
Μολόχ, ὁ	(1)	Moloch
μολυσμός, οῦ, ὁ	(1)	defilement
μομφή, ῆς, ἡ	(1)	blame, cause for complaint, complaint
μονόω	(1)	I make solitary; am left alone (pass. in NT)
μορφόω	(1)	I form, shape
μοσχοποιέω	(1)	I make a calf
μουσικός, ή, όν	(1)	pertaining to music; musician (subst. in NT)
μυελός, οῦ, ὁ	(1)	marrow
μυέω	(1)	I initiate; learn the secret of (pass. in NT)
μυκάομαι	(1)	I roar
μυκτηρίζω	(1)	I treat with contempt, mock
μυλικός, ή, όν	(1)	belonging to a mill
μύλινος, η, ον	(1)	belonging to a mill; millstone (subst. in NT)
Μύρα, ων, τά	(1)	Myra
μυρίζω	(1)	I anoint
μυρίος, α, ον	(1)	innumerable, countless
μυωπάζω	(1)	I am shortsighted
μώλωψ, ωπος, ὁ	(1)	welt, bruise, wound
μῶμος, ου, ὁ	(1)	blemish, defect
μωρολογία, ας, ἡ	(1)	foolish or silly talk
Ναγγαί, ὁ	(1)	Naggai
Ναθάμ, ὁ	(1)	Nathan
Ναιμάν, ὁ	(1)	Naaman
Ναΐν, ἡ	(1)	Nain
Ναούμ, ὁ	(1)	Nahum
Νάρκισσος, ου, ὁ	(1)	Narcissus
ναύκληρος, ου, ὁ	(1)	ship owner, captain
ναῦς, ὁ	(1)	ship
Ναχώρ, ὁ	(1)	Nahor
Νέα Πόλις, ἡ	(1)	Neapolis

νεομηνία, ας, ἡ	(1)	new moon (festival)
νεόφυτος, ον	(1)	newly converted
νέφος, ους, τό	(1)	cloud, host
νεφρός, οῦ, ὁ	(1)	kidney; mind (fig. in NT)
νεωκόρος, ου, ὁ	(1)	temple keeper
νεωτερικός, ή, όν	(1)	youthful
νή	(1)	by (used w. oaths)
νηπιάζω	(1)	I am a child
Νηρεύς, εως, ὁ	(1)	Nereus
Νηρί, ὁ	(1)	Neri
νησίον, ου, τό	(1)	island, small island
Νίγερ, ὁ	(1)	Niger
Νικάνωρ, ορος, ὁ	(1)	Nicanor
νίκη, ης, ἡ	(1)	victory
Νικόλαος, ου, ὁ	(1)	Nicolaus
Νικόπολις, εως, ἡ	(1)	Nicopolis
νιπτήρ, ῆρος, ὁ	(1)	washbasin
νόθος, η, ον	(1)	illegitimate
νόμισμα, ατος, τό	(1)	coin, money
νομοθεσία, ας, ἡ	(1)	giving of the law
νομοθετης, ου, ὁ	(1)	lawgiver
νοσέω	(1)	I have an unhealthy craving
νοσσιά, ᾶς, ἡ	(1)	brood
νοσσίον, ου, τό	(1)	young bird
νοσσός, οῦ, ὁ	(1)	young bird
νουνεχῶς	(1)	wisely, thoughtfully
Νύμφα, ας, ἡ	(1)	Nympha
νύσσω	(1)	I prick, stab, pierce
νυχθήμερον, ου, τό	(1)	a day and a night
νῶτος, ου, ὁ	(1)	back
ξενοδοχέω	(1)	I show hospitality
ξέστης, ου, ὁ	(1)	pitcher, jug
ὄγκος, ου, ὁ	(1)	weight, burden, impediment
ὁδεύω	(1)	I go, travel, am on a journey
ὁδοιπορέω	(1)	I travel, am on my way
ὄζω	(1)	I smell, stink, give off an odor
οἰκετεία, ας, ἡ	(1)	slaves of a household
οἴκημα, ατος, τό	(1)	room, prison
οἰκοδεσποτέω	(1)	I manage my household, keep house
οἰκοδόμος, ου, ὁ	(1)	builder
οἰκονομέω	(1)	I am manager
οἰκουργός, όν	(1)	working at home, domestic
οἰνοφλυγία, ας, ἡ	(1)	drunkenness
ὀκνέω	(1)	I hesitate, delay
ὀκταήμερος, ον	(1)	on the eighth day
ὀλιγοπιστία, ας, ἡ	(1)	littleness of faith
ὀλιγόψυχος, ον	(1)	fainthearted, discouraged
ὀλιγωρέω	(1)	I think lightly, make light
ὀλίγως	(1)	scarcely, barely
ὀλοθρευτής, οῦ, ὁ	(1)	destroyer (angel)

ὀλοθρεύω	(1)	I destroy, ruin
ὀλοκληρία, ας, ἡ	(1)	wholeness, soundness, perfect health
ὀλολύζω	(1)	I wail, moan, cry out
ὀλοτελής, ές	(1)	quite complete, wholly
Ὀλυμπᾶς, ᾶ, ὁ	(1)	Olympas
ὄλυνθος, ου, ὁ	(1)	late or summer fig
ὄμβρος, ου, ὁ	(1)	rainstorm, thunderstorm
ὀμείρομαι	(1)	I have a kindly feeling, long for
ὁμιλία, ας, ἡ	(1)	association, company
ὁμίχλη, ης, ἡ	(1)	mist, fog
ὁμοίωσις, εως, ἡ	(1)	likeness, resemblance
ὁμολογουμένως	(1)	confessedly, undeniably
ὁμότεχνος, ον	(1)	practicing the same trade
ὁμόφρων, ον	(1)	like-minded, united
ὀνάριον, ου, τό	(1)	little donkey, donkey
ὄνειδος, ους, τό	(1)	disgrace, reproach, insult
ὀνίνημι	(1)	I profit, benefit, have joy (mid. in NT)
ὁπλίζω	(1)	I equip; arm myself (mid. in NT)
ὀπτάνομαι	(1)	I appear
ὀπτός, ή, όν	(1)	roasted, baked, broiled
ὀπώρα, ας, ἡ	(1)	fruit
ὁρατος, ή, όν	(1)	visible
ὀργίλος, η, ον	(1)	quick-tempered
ὄρεξις, εως, ἡ	(1)	longing, desire, passion
ὀρθοποδέω	(1)	I am straightforward, progress (fig. in NT)
ὀρθοτομέω	(1)	I cut straight; use or interpret correctly (fig. in NT)
ὀρθρίζω	(1)	I get up early in the morning
ὀρθρινός, ή, όν	(1)	early in the morning
ὅρμημα, ατος, τό	(1)	violent rush, violence
ὁροθεσία, ας, ἡ	(1)	boundary
ὁσίως	(1)	devoutly, in a holy manner
ὄσφρησις, εως, ἡ	(1)	sense of smell, nose
οὐά	(1)	aha!
οὐδαμῶς	(1)	by no means
οὐκοῦν	(1)	so then, so
Οὐρβανός, οῦ, ὁ	(1)	Urbanus
Οὐρίας, ου, ὁ	(1)	Uriah
ὀφρῦς, ύος, ἡ	(1)	brow, edge (of a hill)
ὀχλέω	(1)	I trouble, disturb
ὀχλοποιέω	(1)	I form a mob or crowd
ὀχύρωμα, ατος, τό	(1)	stronghold, fortress, prison
ὄψιμος, ον	(1)	late; late or spring rain (subst. in NT)
παγιδεύω	(1)	I set a snare or trap, entrap
παθητός, ή, όν	(1)	subject to suffering
παιδάριον, ου, τό	(1)	boy, youth, young slave
παιδιόθεν	(1)	from childhood
παίζω	(1)	I play, amuse myself, dance
παλαιότης, ητος, ἡ	(1)	age, oldness, obsoleteness
πάλη, ης, ἡ	(1)	struggle
παμπληθεί	(1)	all together

πανδοχεῖον, ου, τό	(1)	inn
πανδοχεύς, έως, ὁ	(1)	innkeeper
πανήγυρις, εως, ἡ	(1)	festal gathering
πανοικεί	(1)	with one's whole household
πανοῦργος, ον	(1)	clever, crafty, sly
πανταχῇ	(1)	everywhere
πάντῃ	(1)	in every way
παραβάλλω	(1)	I approach, come near, arrive
παραβολεύομαι	(1)	I risk
παραδειγματίζω	(1)	I expose, make an example of, hold up to contempt
παράδοξος, ον	(1)	strange, wonderful, remarkable, unusual
παραθαλάσσιος, α, ον	(1)	by the sea or lake
παραθεωρέω	(1)	I overlook, neglect
παρακαθέζομαι	(1)	I sit beside; have seated myself beside (pass. in NT)
παρακαλύπτω	(1)	I hide, conceal; am hidden (pass. in NT)
παράλιος, ον	(1)	by the seacoast; seacoast district (subst. in NT)
παραλλαγή, ῆς, ἡ	(1)	change, variation
παραμυθία, ας, ἡ	(1)	encouragement, comfort, consolation
παραμύθιον, ου, τό	(1)	encouragement, consolation
παρανομέω	(1)	I break or act contrary to the law
παρανομία, ας, ἡ	(1)	lawlessness, evil-doing
παραπικραίνω	(1)	I am disobedient, rebellious
παραπίπτω	(1)	I fall away commit apostasy
παραπλέω	(1)	I sail past
παραπλήσιος, α, ον	(1)	similar; nearly, almost (neut. as impr. prep. in NT)
παραπλησίως	(1)	similarly, likewise
παραρρέω	(1)	I am washed away, drift away
παράσημος, ον	(1)	distinguished, marked
παρατείνω	(1)	I extend, prolong
παρατήρησις, εως, ἡ	(1)	observation
παρατυγχάνω	(1)	I happen to be near or present
παραυτίκα	(1)	on the spot; momentary (adj. in NT)
παραφρονέω	(1)	I am beside myself, irrational
παραφρονία, ας, ἡ	(1)	madness, insanity
παραχειμασία, ας, ἡ	(1)	wintering
πάρδαλις, εως, ἡ	(1)	leopard
παρεδρεύω	(1)	I wait upon, serve
παρεισάγω	(1)	I bring in secretly or maliciously
παρείσακτος, ον	(1)	smuggled or sneaked in
παρεισδύω	(1)	I slip in stealthily, sneak in
παρεισφέρω	(1)	I apply, bring to bear
παρεμβάλλω	(1)	I set up, throw up
παρενοχλέω	(1)	I cause difficulty, trouble, annoy
πάρεσις, εως, ἡ	(1)	passing over, letting go unpunished, overlooking
παρηγορία, ας, ἡ	(1)	comfort
παρθενία, ας, ἡ	(1)	virginity
Πάρθοι, ων, οἱ	(1)	Parthians
Παρμενᾶς, ᾶ, ὁ	(1)	Parmenas
πάροδος, ου, ἡ	(1)	passage, passing by
παροίχομαι	(1)	I pass by, am gone

παρομοιάζω	(1)	I am like, resemble
παρόμοιος, ον	(1)	like, similar
παροργισμός, οῦ, ὁ	(1)	anger
παροτρύνω	(1)	I arouse, incite
παροψίς, ίδος, ή	(1)	dish
Πάταρα, ων, τά	(1)	Patara
Πάτμος, ου, ὁ	(1)	Patmos
πατρικός, ή, όν	(1)	handed down by one's father, paternal
Πατροβᾶς, ᾶ, ὁ	(1)	Patrobas
πατρολῴας, ου, ὁ	(1)	one who murders one's father
πατροπαράδοτος, ον	(1)	inherited, handed down from one's father
πεδινός, ή, όν	(1)	flat, level
πεζεύω	(1)	I travel by land
πειθός, ή, όν	(1)	persuasive
πειράομαι	(1)	I try, attempt
πεισμονή, ῆς, ή	(1)	persuasion
πελεκίζω	(1)	I behead
πένης, ητος	(1)	poor; poor person (subst. in NT)
πενθερός, οῦ, ὁ	(1)	father-in-law
πενιχρός, ά, όν	(1)	poor, needy
πεντάκις	(1)	five times
πεντεκαιδέκατος, η, ον	(1)	fifteenth
περαιτέρω	(1)	further, beyond
περιάπτω	(1)	I kindle
περιδέω	(1)	I bind, wrap
περιεργάζομαι	(1)	I am a busybody
περίθεσις, εως, ή	(1)	putting on, wearing
περικάθαρμα, ατος, τό	(1)	dirt, refuse, off-scouring
περικρατής, ές	(1)	having power, being in command or control
περικρύβω	(1)	I hide, conceal
περικυκλόω	(1)	I surround, encircle
περιμένω	(1)	I wait for
πέριξ	(1)	around, in the vicinity
περιοικέω	(1)	I live in the neighborhood of
περίοικος, ον	(1)	living around; neighbor (subst. in NT)
περιούσιος, ον	(1)	chosen, special
περιοχή, ῆς, ή	(1)	portion, section, passage
περιπείρω	(1)	I pierce through
περιρήγνυμι	(1)	I tear off
περισπάω	(1)	I am distracted, overburdened (pass. in NT)
περιτρέπω	(1)	I turn, drive
περιτρέχω	(1)	I run around, run about
περιφρονέω	(1)	I disregard, look down on, despise
περίψημα, ατος, τό	(1)	dirt, off-scouring
περπερεύομαι	(1)	I boast, brag
Περσίς, ίδος, ή	(1)	Persis
πήγανον, ου, τό	(1)	rue (a garden herb)
πήγνυμι	(1)	I set up
πιέζω	(1)	I press down
πιθανολογία, ας, ή	(1)	persuasive speech, plausible argument

πίμπρημι	(1)	I burn with fever, swell up (pass. in NT)
πινακίδιον, ου, τό	(1)	little writing tablet
πιότης, τητος, ἡ	(1)	fatness, richness
Πισιδία, ας, ἡ	(1)	Pisidia
Πισίδιος, α, ον	(1)	Pisidian
πιστόω	(1)	I feel confidence, am convinced (pass. in NT.)
πλανήτης, ου, ὁ	(1)	wanderer, roamer; wandering (adj.)
πλάσμα, ατος, τό	(1)	that which is formed or molded, image, figure
πλαστός, ή, όν	(1)	made up, fabricated, false
πλατύς, εῖα, ύ	(1)	broad, wide
πλέγμα, ατος, τό	(1)	woven, braided
πλήμμυρα, ης, ἡ	(1)	high water, flood
πλησμονή, ῆς, ἡ	(1)	satisfaction, gratification, indulgence
πλήσσω	(1)	I strike
ποδήρης, ες	(1)	reaching to the feet; robe reaching to the feet (subst.)
ποίησις, εως, ἡ	(1)	doing, working
πολίτευμα, ατος, τό	(1)	commonwealth, state
πολλαπλασίων, ον	(1)	many times as much, manifold
πολυλογία, ας, ἡ	(1)	wordiness, many words
πολυμερῶς	(1)	in many ways
πολυποίκιλος, ον	(1)	many-sided
πολύσπλαγχνος, ον	(1)	very sympathetic or compassionate
πολυτρόπως	(1)	in various ways
Ποντικός, ή, όν	(1)	Pontian; a Pontian (subst.)
Πόρκιος, ου, ὁ	(1)	Porcius
πορφυρόπωλις, ιδος, ἡ	(1)	(woman) dealer in purple cloth
ποταμοφόρητος, ον	(1)	swept away by a river or stream
πότερον	(1)	whether
Ποτίολοι, ων, οἱ	(1)	Puteoli
πότος, ου, ὁ	(1)	drinking, drinking party, carousal
Πούδης, εντος, ὁ	(1)	Pudens
πραγματεία, ας, ἡ	(1)	activity; undertakings, business, affairs (pl. in NT)
πραγματεύομαι	(1)	I conduct business, am engaged in business
πραϋπάθεια, ας, ἡ	(1)	gentleness
πρεσβῦτις, ιδος, ἡ	(1)	old or elderly woman
πρηνής, ές	(1)	forward, head first, head long
πρίζω	(1)	I saw in two
προαιρέω	(1)	I bring out; decide, make up my mind (mid. in NT)
προαιτιάομαι	(1)	I accuse beforehand
προακούω	(1)	I hear before
προαύλιον, ου, τό	(1)	porch, gateway
προβατικός, ή, όν	(1)	pertaining to sheep
προβιβάζω	(1)	I put forward, prompt, instruct
προβλέπω	(1)	I see beforehand; select, provide (mid. in NT)
προγίνομαι	(1)	I happen before
προδίδωμι	(1)	I give in advance
πρόδρομος, ον	(1)	running before; forerunner (subst. in NT)
προελπίζω	(1)	I hope before, am the first to hope
προευαγγελίζομαι	(1)	I proclaim good news in advance
προέχω	(1)	I excel; am better off, protect myself (prob. mid. in NT)

προηγέομαι	(1)	I outdo, lead the way, consider better
προθεσμία, ας, ἡ	(1)	appointed day, set time
προθύμως	(1)	willingly, eagerly, freely
πρόϊμος, ον	(1)	early; early or autumn rain (subst. in NT)
προκαλέω	(1)	I provoke, challenge (mid. in NT)
προκαταρτίζω	(1)	I prepare in advance
προκηρύσσω	(1)	I proclaim or preach beforehand
πρόκριμα, ατος, τό	(1)	prejudice, discrimination
προκυρόω	(1)	I ratify previously
προμαρτύρομαι	(1)	I bear witness to beforehand, predict
προμελετάω	(1)	I prepare
προμεριμνάω	(1)	I am anxious beforehand, worry in advance
προπάσχω	(1)	I suffer previously
προπάτωρ, ορος, ὁ	(1)	forefather
προσάββατον, ου, τό	(1)	day before the Sabbath, Friday
προσαγορεύω	(1)	I call, name, designate
προσαιτέω	(1)	I beg
προσαναβαίνω	(1)	I go or move up
προσαναλίσκω	(1)	I spend lavishly, spend
προσαπειλέω	(1)	I threaten further or in addition (mid. in NT)
προσδαπανάω	(1)	I spend in addition
προσδέομαι	(1)	I need in addition, have need
προσεάω	(1)	I permit to go farther
προσεργάζομαι	(1)	I make more, earn in addition
προσηλόω	(1)	I nail securely
προσκαρτέρησις, εως, ἡ	(1)	perseverance, patience
προσκεφάλαιον, ου, τό	(1)	pillow, cushion
προσκληρόω	(1)	I allot; am attached to, join (pass. in NT)
προσκλίνω	(1)	I incline toward, attach myself to, join (pass. in NT)
πρόσκλισις, εως, ἡ	(1)	partiality
προσκοπή, ῆς, ἡ	(1)	cause for offense
προσκυνητής, οῦ, ὁ	(1)	worshiper
πρόσλημψις, εως, ἡ	(1)	acceptance
προσορμίζω	(1)	I come into harbor, come to anchor (pass. in NT)
προσοφείλω	(1)	I owe besides, owe
πρόσπεινος, ον	(1)	hungry
προσπήγνυμι	(1)	I fasten to, nail to (the cross), crucify
προσποιέω	(1)	I act as if, pretend (mid. in NT)
προσπορεύομαι	(1)	I come up to, approach
προστάτις, ιδος, ἡ	(1)	patroness, helper
προσφάγιον, ου, τό	(1)	fish
πρόσφατος, ον	(1)	new, recent
προσφάτως	(1)	recently
προσφιλής, ές	(1)	pleasing, agreeable, lovely
πρόσχυσις, εως, ἡ	(1)	sprinkling, pouring, spreading
προσψαύω	(1)	I touch
προσωπολημπτέω	(1)	I show partiality
προσωπολήμπτης, ου, ὁ	(1)	one who shows partiality
προτείνω	(1)	I stretch or spread out
προτρέπω	(1)	I urge, encourage, impel, persuade (mid. in NT)

προφθάνω	(1)	I come before, anticipate
προχειροτονέω	(1)	I choose or appoint beforehand (pass. in NT)
Πρόχορος, ου, ὁ	(1)	Prochorus
πρωτεύω	(1)	I am the first, have first place
πρωτοστάτης, ου, ὁ	(1)	leader, ringleader
πρωτοτόκια, ων, τά	(1)	birthright
πρώτως	(1)	for the first time
πτέρνα, ης, ἡ	(1)	heel
πτηνός, ή, όν	(1)	winged; bird (subst. in NT)
πτόησις, εως, ἡ	(1)	intimidation, fear, terror
Πτολεμαΐς, ίδος, ἡ	(1)	Ptolemais
πτύρω	(1)	I am terrified, intimidated, frightened (pass. in NT)
πτύσμα, ατος, τό	(1)	saliva, spit
πτύσσω	(1)	I fold up, roll up
πτωχεύω	(1)	I am or become poor
πυγμή, ῆς, ἡ	(1)	fist
πύθων, ωνος, ὁ	(1)	spirit of divination (from the Python)
πυκτεύω	(1)	I fight with fists, box
πύρινος, η, ον	(1)	fiery, color of fire
Πύρρος, ου, ὁ	(1)	Pyrrhus
Ῥαγαύ, ὁ	(1)	Reu
ῥᾳδιούργημα, ατος, τό	(1)	crime, villainy
ῥᾳδιουργία, ας, ἡ	(1)	wickedness, villainy, unscrupulousness
Ῥαιφάν, ὁ	(1)	Rephan
ῥακά	(1)	fool, empty head
Ῥαμά, ἡ	(1)	Rama
Ῥαχάβ, ἡ	(1)	Rahab
Ῥαχήλ, ἡ	(1)	Rachel
Ῥεβέκκα, ας, ἡ	(1)	Rebecca
ῥέδη, ης, ἡ	(1)	(four-wheeled) carriage
ῥέω	(1)	I flow
Ῥήγιον, ου, τό	(1)	Rhegium
ῥῆγμα, ατος, τό	(1)	wreck, ruin, collapse
Ῥησά, ὁ	(1)	Rhesa
ῥήτωρ, ορος, ὁ	(1)	orator, advocate, attorney
ῥητῶς	(1)	expressly, explicitly
ῥιπή, ῆς, ἡ	(1)	rapid movement, blinking, twinkling
ῥιπίζω	(1)	I toss; am tossed about (pass. in NT)
Ῥόδη, ης, ἡ	(1)	Rhoda
Ῥόδος, ου, ἡ	(1)	Rhodes
ῥοιζηδόν	(1)	with a load noise, with great suddenness
Ῥουβήν, ὁ	(1)	Reuben
Ῥούθ, ἡ	(1)	Ruth
ῥυπαίνω	(1)	I defile, pollute; am defiled or polluted (pass. in NT)
ῥυπαρία, ας, ἡ	(1)	moral uncleanness, greediness
ῥύπος, ου, ὁ	(1)	dirt
ῥυτίς, ίδος, ἡ	(1)	wrinkle
Ῥωμαϊστί	(1)	in the Latin language
ῥώννυμι	(1)	I am strong; farewell, good-bye (imper. in NT)
σαββατισμός, οῦ, ὁ	(1)	Sabbath rest or observance

σαγήνη, ης, ἡ	(1)	dragnet
σαίνω	(1)	I disturb, flatter; am disturbed (pass. in NT)
Σαλαμίς, ῖνος, ἡ	(1)	Salamis
Σαλείμ, τό	(1)	Salim
Σαλμώνη, ης, ἡ	(1)	Salmone
σάλος, ου, ὁ	(1)	waves (of a rough sea)
σαλπιστής, οῦ, ὁ	(1)	trumpeter
Σαμοθρᾴκη, ης, ἡ	(1)	Samothrace
Σάμος, ου, ἡ	(1)	Samos
Σαμψών, ὁ	(1)	Samson
σανίς, ίδος, ἡ	(1)	board, plank
Σάπφιρα, ης, ἡ	(1)	Sapphira
σάπφιρος, ου, ἡ	(1)	sapphire
σαργάνη, ης, ἡ	(1)	(rope) basket
σαρδόνυξ, υχος, ὁ	(1)	sardonyx
Σάρεπτα, ων, τά	(1)	Zarephath
Σαρών, ῶνος, ὁ	(1)	Sharon
σεβάζομαι	(1)	I worship, show reverence to
σειρά, ᾶς, ἡ	(1)	rope, chain
Σεκοῦνδος, ου, ὁ	(1)	Secundus
Σελεύκεια, ας, ἡ	(1)	Seleucia
Σεμεΐν, ὁ	(1)	Semein
σεμίδαλις, εως, ἡ	(1)	fine wheat flour
Σέργιος, ου, ὁ	(1)	Sergius
Σερούχ, ὁ	(1)	Serug
Σήθ, ἡ	(1)	Seth
Σήμ, ὁ	(1)	Shem
σημειόω	(1)	I note, take notice of (mid. in NT)
σήπω	(1)	I decay, rot
σητόβρωτος, ον	(1)	moth-eaten
σθενόω	(1)	I strengthen, make strong
σίδηρος, ου, ὁ	(1)	iron
σικάριος, ου, ὁ	(1)	sicarius, assassin, terrorist
σίκερα, τό	(1)	strong drink
σιμικίνθιον, ου, τό	(1)	apron
σινιάζω	(1)	I shake in a sieve, sift
σιρικός, ή, όν	(1)	silken; silk cloth (subst. in NT)
σιτίον, ου, τό	(1)	grain; food (pl. in NT)
σιτιστός, ή, όν	(1)	fattened; fattened cattle (pl. subst. in NT)
σιτομέτριον, ου, τό	(1)	grain or food allowance, ration
σκέπασμα, ατος, τό	(1)	covering, clothing, house
Σκευᾶς, ᾶ, ὁ	(1)	Sceva
σκευή, ῆς, ἡ	(1)	equipment, tackle, rigging (of a ship)
σκηνοπηγία, ας, ἡ	(1)	Feast of Tabernacles or Booths
σκηνοποιός, οῦ, ὁ	(1)	tentmaker
σκληρότης, ητος, ἡ	(1)	hardness (of heart), stubbornness
σκληροτράχηλος, ον	(1)	stiff-necked, stubborn
σκόλοψ, οπος, ὁ	(1)	pointed stake, thorn, splinter
σκοπός, οῦ, ὁ	(1)	goal, mark
σκύβαλον, ου, τό	(1)	refuse, garbage, dirt, dung

Σκύθης, ου, ὁ	(1)	a Scythian
σκῦλον, ου, τό	(1)	booty, spoils (pl. in NT)
σκωληκόβρωτος, ον	(1)	eaten by worms
σκώληξ, ηκος, ὁ	(1)	worm
σμαράγδινος, η, ον	(1)	made of emerald
σμάραγδος, ου, ὁ	(1)	emerald
σμυρνίζω	(1)	I treat with myrrh
σορός, οῦ, ἡ	(1)	coffin, bier
Σουσάννα, ης, ἡ	(1)	Susanna
σπεκουλάτωρ, ορος, ὁ	(1)	courier, executioner
σπερμολόγος, ον	(1)	picking up seeds; babbler (subst. in NT)
σπιλάς, άδος, ἡ	(1)	spot, stain, blemish, danger
σπορά, ᾶς, ἡ	(1)	sowing, seed, origin
στάμνος, ου, ἡ	(1)	jar
στασιαστής, οῦ, ὁ	(1)	rebel, revolutionary, insurrectionist
στατήρ, ῆρος, ὁ	(1)	stater (Greek silver coin)
Στάχυς, υος, ὁ	(1)	Stachys
στέμμα. ατος, τό	(1)	wreath or garland (of flowers)
στερέωμα, ατος, τό	(1)	firmness, steadfastness
στηριγμός, οῦ, ὁ	(1)	firmness, firm footing
στιβάς, άδος, ἡ	(1)	leafy branch
στίγμα, ατος, τό	(1)	mark, brand, scar
στιγμή, ῆς, ἡ	(1)	moment
στίλβω	(1)	I shine, am radiant, glisten
Στοϊκός, ή, όν	(1)	Stoic
στόμαχος, ου, ὁ	(1)	stomach
στρατολογέω	(1)	I gather an army, enlist soldiers, enlist
στρατόπεδον, ου, τό	(1)	body of troops, army, legion
στρεβλόω	(1)	I twist, distort
στρῆνος, ους, τό	(1)	sensuality, luxury
στυγητός, ή, όν	(1)	hated, hateful
συγγενίς, ίδος, ἡ	(1)	female relative, kinswoman
συγγνώμη, ης, ἡ	(1)	concession, indulgence, pardon
συγκακουχέομαι	(1)	I suffer with
συγκαλύπτω	(1)	I cover up, conceal
συγκάμπτω	(1)	I (cause to) bend
συγκαταβαίνω	(1)	I go come down with
συγκατάθεσις, εως, ἡ	(1)	agreement, union
συγκατατίθημι	(1)	I agree with, consent to (mid. in NT)
συγκαταψηφίζομαι	(1)	I am chosen together with, am added (pass. in NT)
συγκινέω	(1)	I set in motion, arouse
συγκομίζω	(1)	I bury
συγκύπτω	(1)	I am bent over, bent double
συγκυρία, ας, ἡ	(1)	coincidence, chance
συγχράομαι	(1)	I have dealings with, associate on friendly terms
σύγχυσις, εως, ἡ	(1)	confusion, tumult
συζητητής, οῦ, ὁ	(1)	disputant, debater
σύζυγος, ου, ὁ	(1)	yoke fellow, fellow worker
συκάμινος, ου, ἡ	(1)	mulberry tree
συκομορέα, ας, ἡ	(1)	fig-mulberry tree, sycamore tree

συλαγωγέω	(1)	I carry off as a captive
συλάω	(1)	I rob
συλλογίζομαι	(1)	I reason, discuss, debate
συλλυπέω	(1)	I grieve with; am deeply grieved (pass. in NT)
σύμβουλος, ου, ὁ	(1)	advisor, counselor
συμμαθητής, οῦ, ὁ	(1)	fellow pupil, fellow disciple
συμμερίζω	(1)	I share with (mid. in NT)
συμμιμητής, οῦ, ὁ	(1)	fellow imitator
συμμορφίζω	(1)	I take on the same form, am conformed to (pass in NT)
συμπαθής, ές	(1)	sympathetic
συμπαραγίνομαι	(1)	I come together
συμπαρακαλέω	(1)	I receive encouragement together (pass. in NT)
συμπάρειμι	(1)	I am present with
συμπεριλαμβάνω	(1)	I embrace, throw my arms around
συμπίνω	(1)	I drink with
συμπίπτω	(1)	I fall in, collapse
συμπολίτης, ου, ὁ	(1)	fellow citizen
συμπρεσβύτερος, ου, ὁ	(1)	fellow elder, fellow presbyter
σύμφημι	(1)	I agree with
συμφυλέτης, ου, ὁ	(1)	fellow countryman, compatriot
σύμφυτος, ον	(1)	grown together, united with
συμφύω	(1)	I grow up with (pass. in NT)
συμφώνησις, εως, ἡ	(1)	agreement
συμφωνία, ας, ἡ	(1)	music
σύμφωνος, ον	(1)	agreeing; agreement (subst.)
συμψηφίζω	(1)	I count up, compute
σύμψυχος, ον	(1)	harmonious, united in spirit
συναγωνίζομαι	(1)	I help, assist
συναλίζω	(1)	I eat with, assemble
συναλλάσσω	(1)	I reconcile
συναναπαύομαι	(1)	I rest with
συναπόλλυμι	(1)	I am destroyed or perish with (mid. in NT)
συναποστέλλω	(1)	I send with
συναυξάνω	(1)	I grew together, grow side by side (pass. in NT)
συνδέω	(1)	I bind with; am in prison with (pass. in NT)
συνδοξάζω	(1)	I am glorified with, share in the glory (pass. in NT)
συνδρομή, ῆς, ἡ	(1)	running together, forming of a mob
σύνειμι	(1)	I come together
συνεκλεκτός, ή, όν	(1)	chosen together with; one also chosen (fem. subst. in NT)
συνεπιμαρτυρέω	(1)	I testify at the same time
συνεπιτίθημι	(1)	I join in an attack (mid. in NT)
συνέπομαι	(1)	I accompany
συνεφίστημι	(1)	I rise up together, join in an attack
συνήδομαι	(1)	I rejoice in
συνηλικιώτης, ου, ὁ	(1)	contemporary person
συνθρύπτω	(1)	I break
συνοδεύω	(1)	I travel with
συνοδία, ας, ἡ	(1)	caravan, group of travelers
συνοικέω	(1)	I live with
συνοικοδομέω	(1)	I build together; am built up together (pass. in NT)

συνομιλέω	(1)	I talk or converse with
συνομορέω	(1)	I border on, am next door to
συντέμνω	(1)	I cut short, shorten, limit
σύντριμμα, ατος, τό	(1)	destruction, ruin
σύντροφος, ον	(1)	raised with; foster brother, close friend (subst. in NT)
συντυγχάνω	(1)	I come together with, meet, join
Συντύχη, ης, ἡ	(1)	Syntyche
συνυποκρίνομαι	(1)	I join in pretending, join in playing the hypocrite
συνυπουργέω	(1)	I join in helping, cooperate with
συνωδίνω	(1)	I suffer agony together
συνωμοσία, ας, ἡ	(1)	conspiracy, plot
Συράκουσαι, ῶν, αἱ	(1)	Syracuse
Σύρος, ου, ὁ	(1)	a Syrian
Συροφοινίκισσα, ης, ἡ	(1)	a Syrophoenician woman
Σύρτις, εως, ἡ	(1)	the Syrtis
σύσσημον, ου, τό	(1)	signal, sign, token
σύσσωμος, ον	(1)	belonging to the same body
συστατικός, ή, όν	(1)	commendatory
συστενάζω	(1)	I lament or groan together
συστοιχέω	(1)	I correspond to
Συχάρ, ἡ	(1)	Sychor
σφάγιον, ου, τό	(1)	(sacrificial) victim, offering
σφοδρῶς	(1)	greatly, violently
σφυδρόν, οῦ, τό	(1)	ankle
σχολή, ῆς, ἡ	(1)	school, lecture hall
σωματικῶς	(1)	bodily, in reality
Σώπατρος, ου, ὁ	(1)	Sopater
Σωσίπατρος, ου, ὁ	(1)	Sosipater
σωφρονίζω	(1)	I encourage, advise, urge
σωφρονισμός, οῦ, ὁ	(1)	good judgment, moderation, advice
σωφρόνως	(1)	soberly, moderately, showing self-control
τάγμα, ατος, τό	(1)	order, class, group
τακτός, ή, όν	(1)	fixed, appointed
ταλαιπωρέω	(1)	I lament, complain
ταλαντιαῖος, α, ον	(1)	weighing a talent
ταλιθα	(1)	girl, little girl
ταπεινόφρων, ον	(1)	humble
ταρταρόω	(1)	I hold captive in Tartarus, cast into hell
ταφή, ῆς, ἡ	(1)	burial place
τεκμήριον, ου, τό	(1)	proof
τεκνογονέω	(1)	I bear children
τεκνογονία, ας, ἡ	(1)	bearing of children
τεκνοτροφέω	(1)	I bring up children
τελείως	(1)	fully, perfectly, completely, altogether
τελειωτής, οῦ, ὁ	(1)	perfecter
τελεσφορέω	(1)	I bear fruit to maturity, produce ripe fruit
τελευτή, ῆς, ἡ	(1)	end, death
Τέρτιος, ου, ὁ	(1)	Tertius
τεταρταῖος, α, ον	(1)	happening on the fourth day
τετράγωνος, ον	(1)	square

τετράδιον, ου, τό	(1)	detachment of four soldiers
τετράμηνος, ον	(1)	lasting four months; period of four months (subst. in NT)
τετραπλοῦς, ῆ, οῦν	(1)	four times (as much), fourfold
τεφρόω	(1)	I reduce to ashes
τήκω	(1)	I melt; am melted, dissolve (pass. in NT)
τηλαυγῶς	(1)	plainly, clearly
Τιβέριος, ου, ὁ	(1)	Tiberius
Τιμαῖος, ου, ὁ	(1)	Timaeus
τιμιότης, ητος, ἡ	(1)	costliness, abundance, wealth
Τίμων, ωνος, ὁ	(1)	Timon
τιμωρία, ας, ἡ	(1)	punishment
τίνω	(1)	I pay, undergo
Τίτιος, ου, ὁ	(1)	Titius
τοιόσδε, άδε, όνδε	(1)	such as this, of this kind
τοίχος, ου, ὁ	(1)	wall
τολμηρότερον	(1)	rather boldly
τολμητής, οῦ, ὁ	(1)	bold, audacious person
τομός, ή, όν	(1)	cutting, sharp
τόξον, ου, τό	(1)	bow (of an archer)
τοπάζιον, ου, τό	(1)	topaz
τοὔνομα	(1)	named, by name (= τὸ ὄνομα)
τραπεζίτης, ου, ὁ	(1)	money changer, banker
τραῦμα, ατος, τό	(1)	wound
τραχηλίζω	(1)	I am laid bare, am exposed (pass. in NT)
Τραχωνῖτις, ιδος, ἡ	(1)	Trachonitis
Τρεῖς Ταβέρναι	(1)	Three Taverns
τρῆμα, ατος, τό	(1)	eye (of a needle)
τριετία, ας, ἡ	(1)	period of three years
τρίζω	(1)	I gnash, grind
τρίμηνος, ον	(1)	of three months; three months (subst.)
τρίστεγον, ου, τό	(1)	third story or floor
τρισχίλιοι, αι, α	(1)	three thousand
τρίχινος, η, ον	(1)	made of hair
τροπή, ῆς, ἡ	(1)	turning, variation, change
τροποφορέω	(1)	I put up with (another's conduct)
τροφός, οῦ, ἡ	(1)	nurse
τροχιά, ᾶς, ἡ	(1)	course, way, path
τροχός, οῦ, ὁ	(1)	wheel, course
τρυγών, όνος, ἡ	(1)	turtledove
τρυμαλιά, ᾶς, ἡ	(1)	hole, eye (of a needle)
τρύπημα, ατος, τό	(1)	hole, eye (of a needle)
Τρύφαινα, ης, ἡ	(1)	Tryphaena
τρυφάω	(1)	I lead a life of luxury or self-indulgence, revel, carouse
Τρυφῶσα, ης, ἡ	(1)	Tryphosa
τυμπανίζω	(1)	I torment, torture; am tortured (pass. in NT)
τυπικῶς	(1)	typologically, as an example
Τύραννος, ου, ὁ	(1)	Tyrannus
Τύριος, ου, ὁ	(1)	a Tyrian
τύφω	(1)	I give off smoke; smoke, smolder (pass. in NT)
τυφωνικός, ή, όν	(1)	like a whirlwind

ὑακίνθινος, η, ον	(1)	hyacinth-colored
ὑάκινθος, ου, ὁ	(1)	jacinth, hyacinth
ὑγρός, ά, όν	(1)	moist, green (of wood)
ὑδροποτέω	(1)	I drink water
ὑδρωπικός, ή, όν	(1)	suffering from dropsy
ὕλη, ης, ἡ	(1)	forest, firewood
ὕπανδρος, ον	(1)	married (of a woman)
ὑπείκω	(1)	I yield, submit
ὑπέρακμος, ον	(1)	past one's prime
ὑπεραυξάνω	(1)	I grow wonderfully, increase abundantly
ὑπερβαίνω	(1)	I overstep, transgress, sin
ὑπερβαλλόντως	(1)	exceedingly, immeasurably
ὑπερέκεινα	(1)	beyond (impr. prep. in NT)
ὑπερεκτείνω	(1)	I stretch out beyond, overextend
ὑπερεκχύννω	(1)	I overflow (pass. in NT)
ὑπερεντυγχάνω	(1)	I plead, intercede
ὑπερηφανία, ας, ἡ	(1)	arrogance, haughtiness, pride
ὑπερνικάω	(1)	I am completely victorious
ὑπεροράω	(1)	I overlook, disregard
ὑπερπερισσῶς	(1)	beyond all measure
ὑπερπλεονάζω	(1)	I am present in great abundance
ὑπερυψόω	(1)	I raise to the loftiest height or the highest position
ὑπερφρονέω	(1)	I think too highly of myself, am haughty
ὑπέχω	(1)	I undergo or suffer (punishment)
ὑποβάλλω	(1)	I instigate (secretly)
ὑπογραμμός, οῦ, ὁ	(1)	example
ὑπόδικος, ον	(1)	liable to judgment or punishment, accountable
ὑποζώννυμι	(1)	I undergird, brace
ὑποκρίνομαι	(1)	I pretend
ὑπόλειμμα, ατος, τό	(1)	remnant
ὑπολείπω	(1)	I leave remaining; am left behind (pass. in NT)
ὑπολήνιον, ου, τό	(1)	wine trough
ὑπολιμπάνω	(1)	I leave (behind)
ὑπόνοια, ας, ἡ	(1)	suspicion, conjecture
ὑποπνέω	(1)	I blow gently
ὑποστολή, ῆς, ἡ	(1)	shrinking, timidity
ὑποστρωννύω	(1)	I spread out underneath
ὑποτρέχω	(1)	I run or sail under the shelter of
ὗς, ὑός, ἡ	(1)	sow
ὑφαντός, ή, όν	(1)	woven
ὑψηλοφρονέω	(1)	I am proud or haughty
φαιλόνης, ου, ὁ	(1)	cloak
Φάλεκ, ὁ	(1)	Peleg
φανός, οῦ, ὁ	(1)	lamp, torch, lantern
Φανουήλ, ὁ	(1)	Phanuel
φαντάζω	(1)	I make visible; appear, become visible (pass. in NT)
φαντασία, ας, ἡ	(1)	pomp, pageantry
φάραγξ, αγγος, ἡ	(1)	ravine, valley
φάρμακον, ου, τό	(1)	magic potion, charm
φάσις, εως, ἡ	(1)	information, report, announcement, news

φθινοπωρινός, ή, όν	(1)	belonging to late autumn
φθονέω	(1)	I envy, am jealous
φιλάγαθος, ον	(1)	loving what is good
φιλάδελφος, ον	(1)	loving one's brother or sister
φίλανδρος, ον	(1)	loving one's husband
φιλανθρώπως	(1)	benevolently, kindly
φιλαργυρία, ας, ή	(1)	love of money, miserliness, avarice
φίλαυτος, ον	(1)	loving oneself, selfish
φιλήδονος, ον	(1)	loving pleasure, given over to pleasure
Φιλήμων, ονος, ὁ	(1)	Philemon
Φίλητος, ου, ὁ	(1)	Philetus
φιλία, ας, ή	(1)	friendship, love
Φιλιππήσιος, ου, ὁ	(1)	a Philippian
φιλόθεος, ον	(1)	loving God, devout
Φιλόλογος, ου, ὁ	(1)	Philologus
φιλονεικία, ας, ή	(1)	dispute, strife
φιλόνεικος, ον	(1)	quarrelsome, contentious
φιλοπρωτεύω	(1)	I wish to be first, like to be leader
φιλοσοφία, ας, ή	(1)	philosophy
φιλόσοφος, ου, ὁ	(1)	philosopher
φιλόστοργος, ον	(1)	loving dearly, devoted
φιλότεκνος, ον	(1)	loving one's children
φιλοφρόνως	(1)	friendly, hospitably
Φλέγων, οντος, ὁ	(1)	Phlegon
φλυαρέω	(1)	I talk nonsense about, charge unjustly against
φλύαρος, ον	(1)	gossipy, foolish
φόβητρον, ου, τό	(1)	terrible sight or event, horror
Φοίβη, ης, ή	(1)	Phoebe
Φοῖνιξ, ικος, ὁ	(1)	Phoenix
Φορτουνᾶτος, ου, ὁ	(1)	Fortunatus
φραγέλλιον, ου, τό	(1)	whip, lash
φράζω	(1)	I explain, interpret
φρεναπατάω	(1)	I deceive
φρεναπάτης, ου, ὁ	(1)	deceiver, one who misleads
φρίσσω	(1)	I shudder (from fear)
φρονίμως	(1)	wisely, shrewdly
φροντίζω	(1)	I think of, am intent on, am concerned about
φρυάσσω	(1)	I am arrogant, rage
φρύγανον, ου, τό	(1)	dry wood, firewood (pl. in NT)
Φύγελος, ου, ὁ	(1)	Phygelus
φυγή, ῆς, ή	(1)	flight
φυλακίζω	(1)	I imprison
φυλακτήριον, ου, τό	(1)	amulet, phylactery
φυσικῶς	(1)	naturally, by instinct
φυσίωσις, εως, ή	(1)	pride, conceit
φυτεία, ας, ή	(1)	plant
φωσφόρος, ον	(1)	bearing light; morning star (subst. in NT)
Χαλδαῖος, ου, ὁ	(1)	a Chaldean
χαλκεύς, έως, ὁ	(1)	coppersmith, metal worker
χαλκηδών, όνος, ὁ	(1)	chalcedony, agate

χαλκίον, ου, τό	(1)	(copper) vessel, kettle
χαλκοῦς, ῆ, οῦν	(1)	made of copper, brass, or bronze
Χαναναῖος, α, ον	(1)	Canaanite
χαρακτήρ, ῆρος, ὁ	(1)	reproduction, representation
χάραξ, ακος, ὁ	(1)	palisade, barricade
χάρτης, ου, ὁ	(1)	sheet of papyrus, papyrus roll
χάσμα, ατος, τό	(1)	chasm
χειμάζω	(1)	I toss in a storm; undergo bad weather (pass. in NT)
χειμάρρους, ου, ὁ	(1)	winter stream or torrent, ravine, wadi, valley
χειραγωγός, οῦ, ὁ	(1)	one who leads another by the hand, leader
χειρόγραφον, ου, τό	(1)	handwritten document, document of indebtedness, bond
Χερούβ, τό	(1)	cherub, winged creature
Χίος, ου, ἡ	(1)	Chios
χλευάζω	(1)	I mock, sneer, scoff
χλιαρός, ά, όν	(1)	lukewarm
Χλόη, ης, ἡ	(1)	Chloe
χολάω	(1)	I am angry
χορός, οῦ, ὁ	(1)	dance, dancing
χόρτασμα, ατος, τό	(1)	food
Χουζᾶς, ᾶ, ὁ	(1)	Chuza
χρή	(1)	it is necessary, it ought (impers.)
χρηματισμός, οῦ, ὁ	(1)	divine statement or answer
χρήσιμος, η, ον	(1)	useful, beneficial, advantageous
χρηστεύομαι	(1)	I am kind, loving, merciful
χρηστολογία, ας, ἡ	(1)	smooth talk, plausible speech
χρονοτριβέω	(1)	I spend, lose, or waste time
χρυσοδακτύλιος, ον	(1)	wearing a gold ring
χρυσόλιθος, ου, ὁ	(1)	chrysolite
χρυσόπρασος, ου, ὁ	(1)	chrysoprase
χρώς, χρωτός, ὁ	(1)	skin, surface of the body
χῶρος, ου, ὁ	(1)	northwest
ψευδαπόστολος, ου, ὁ	(1)	false apostle
ψευδοδιδάσκαλος, ου, ὁ	(1)	false teacher, one who teaches falsehoods
ψευδολόγος, ον	(1)	speaking falsely; liar (subst. in NT)
ψευδώνυμος, ον	(1)	falsely called or named
ψεῦσμα, ατος, τό	(1)	lie, falsehood, lying, untruthfulness
ψιθυρισμός, οῦ, ὁ	(1)	whispering, gossip
ψιθυριστής, οῦ, ὁ	(1)	whisperer, gossiper
ψύχω	(1)	I make cool; become cold, am extinguished (pass. in NT)
ψώχω	(1)	I rub (grain)
ὠνέομαι	(1)	I buy
ᾠόν, οῦ, τό	(1)	egg
ὠρύομαι	(1)	I roar (of lions)
Ὡσηέ, ὁ	(1)	Hosea
ὡσπερεί	(1)	like, as though, as it were

Section Three

Principal Parts of Verbs

Section Three contains a list of all the verbs used in the NT, along with their principal parts that are actually found in the text.

The six principal parts represent the forms of the verb which contain the verbal stems used to build all the tense constructions. The first part (Present), the dictionary form, is used by the present and imperfect. The second part (Future) is used by the future active and middle. The third part (Aorist) is used by the aorist active and middle. The fourth part (Perfect) is used by the perfect and pluperfect active. The fifth part (Perfect Passive) is used by the perfect and pluperfect middle and passive. The sixth part (Aorist Passive) is used by the aorist and future passive.

The dictionary form is given in the active, unless the verb is deponent. This is true even if the only forms represented in the NT are middle or passive. Likewise, the other principal parts are listed as middle or passive only if the verb is deponent for those parts. The major exception to this approach is πορεύομαι, which is not truly a deponent. However, the word is exclusively found in this form throughout all the early Christian literature including the NT.

Two verbs require special mention. Because the forms ἐρῶ, εἶπον, εἴρηκα, εἴρημαι, and ἐρρέθην are always used for λέγω outside the present and imperfect, they are listed among the principal parts of λέγω. Likewise, εἶδον is listed as the predominant Aorist principal part of ὁράω.

Some verbs appear in more than one form among their principal parts. In this section, the alternate forms that occur in the second through sixth principal parts are listed below the regular forms. The following contains information about alternate forms and other matters that pertain to the first principal part or dictionary form of certain verbs.

ἀναλίσκω	The aor. act. and pass. for ἀναλίσκω and προσαναλίσκω derives from the alternate form ἀναλόω.
ἀποκαθίστημι	The only form of the pres. used is ἀποκαθιστάνω.
ἀποκτείνω	Alternate form of pres: ἀποκτέννω.
ἀπόλλυμι	Certain -μι verbs and their compounds use the 1 aor. for the ind. act. and the 2 aor. for other moods and the mid. Some other examples include δίδωμι, τίθημι, ὀνίνημι, and the compounds of ἵημι.
αὐξάνω	Alternate form of pres: αὔξω.
βλαστάνω	The only form of the pres. used is βλαστάω.
διαρρήγνυμι	Alternate form of pres: διαρρήσσω.
ἐκχέω	The form ἐκχύννω is the predominant one used in the pres. It

	also gives rise to the perf. and aor. pass.
ἐλλογέω	Alternate form of pres: ἐλλογάω.
ἐμπίμπλημι	Alternate form of pres: ἐμπιπλάω.
ἐσθίω	Alternate form of pres: ἔσθω.
ζώννυμι	The alternate form ζωννύω is not found in the pres. The impf. ἐζώννυες could come from either form.
ἵστημι	The only form of the pres. used is ἱστάνω. This is also true of παριστάνω and συνιστάνω.
καθίστημι	Alternate form of pres: καθιστάνω.
ὁμνύω	Alternate form of pres: ὄμνυμι.
περιρήγνυμι	The only form of the pres. used is περιρήσσω.
ῥίπτω	The only form of the pres. used is ῥιπτέω.
στρωννύω	The impf. ἐστρώννυον could come from either στρωννύω or στρώννυμι.
συγχέω	The only form of the pres. used is συγχύννω.
συνίημι	The form συνίω is the predominant one used in the pres.

In the following list, the asterisk (*) indicates that the dictionary form of the verb is not used in the NT. The symbol for "greater than" (>) identifies any verb whose form is perfect, but whose use is present.

Present	Future	Aorist	Perfect	Perfect Passive	Aorist Passive
ἀγαθοεργέω					
ἀγαθοποιέω		ἠγαθαποίησα			
ἀγαθουργέω					
ἀγαλλιάω		ἠγαλλίασα			ἠγαλλιάθην
ἀγανακτέω		ἠγανάκτησα			
ἀγαπάω	ἀγαπήσω	ἠγάπησα	ἠγάπηκα	ἠγάπημαι	ἠγαπήθην
ἀγγαρεύω	ἀγγαρεύσω	ἠγγάρευσα			
ἀγγέλλω					
ἁγιάζω		ἡγίασα		ἡγίασμαι	ἡγιάσθην
ἁγνίζω		ἥγνισα	ἥγνικα	ἥγνισμαι	ἡγνίσθην
ἀγνοέω		ἠγνόησα			
ἀγοράζω		ἠγόρασα		ἠγόρασμαι	ἠγοράσθην
ἀγραυλέω					
* ἀγρεύω		ἤγρευσα			
ἀγρυπνέω					
ἄγω	ἄξω	ἤγαγον			ἤχθην
ἀγωνίζομαι				ἠγώνισμαι	
ἀδημονέω					
ἀδικέω	ἀδικήσω	ἠδίκησα			ἠδικήθην
* ἀδυνατέω	ἀδυνατήσω				
ᾄδω					
ἀθετέω	ἀθετήσω	ἠθέτησα			
ἀθλέω		ἤθλησα			
* ἀθροίζω				ἤθροισμαι	
ἀθυμέω					
αἱμορροέω					
αἰνέω					

* αἱρετίζω		ἡρέτισα			
* αἱρέω	αἱρήσω	εἷλα			
		εἷλον			
αἴρω	ἀρῶ	ἦρα	ἦρκα	ἦρμαι	ἤρθην
* αἰσθάνομαι		ἠσθόμην			
αἰσχύνω					ἠσχύνθην
αἰτέω	αἰτήσω	ᾔτησα	ᾔτηκα		
* αἰχμαλωτεύω		ᾐχμαλώτευσα			
αἰχμαλωτίζω					ᾐχμαλωτίσθην
ἀκαιρέομαι					
* ἀκμάζω		ἤκμασα			
ἀκολουθέω	ἀκολουθήσω	ἠκολούθησα	ἠκολούθηκα		
ἀκούω	ἀκούσω	ἤκουσα	ἀκήκοα		ἠκούσθην
	ἀκούσομαι				
* ἀκριβόω		ἠκρίβωσα			
ἀκυρόω		ἠκύρωσα			
ἀλαλάζω					
ἀλείφω		ἤλειψα			
ἀληθεύω					
ἀλήθω					
ἀλιεύω					
* ἁλίζω					ἡλίσθην
* ἀλλάσσω	ἀλλάξω	ἤλλαξα			ἠλλάγην
ἀλληγορέω					
ἅλλομαι		ἡλάμην			
ἀλοάω					
ἁμαρτάνω	ἁμαρτήσω	ἡμάρτησα	ἡμάρτηκα		
		ἥμαρτον			
* ἀμάω		ἤμησα			
ἀμελέω		ἠμέλησα			
* ἀμύνομαι		ἠμυνάμην			
ἀμφιβάλλω					
ἀμφιέζω					
ἀμφιέννυμι				ἠμφίεσμαι	
ἀναβαίνω	ἀναβήσομαι	ἀνέβην	ἀναβέβηκα		
* ἀναβάλλω		ἀνέβαλον			
* ἀναβιβάζω		ἀνεβίβασα			
ἀναβλέπω		ἀνέβλεψα			
* ἀναβοάω		ἀνεβόησα			
ἀναγγέλλω	ἀναγγελῶ	ἀνήγγειλα			ἀνηγγέλην
* ἀναγεννάω		ἀνεγέννησα		ἀναγεγέννημαι	
ἀναγινώσκω		ἀνέγνων			ἀνεγνώσθην
ἀναγκάζω		ἠνάγκασα			ἠναγκάσθην
* ἀναγνωρίζω					ἀνεγνωρίσθην
ἀνάγω		ἀνήγαγον			ἀνήχθην
* ἀναδείκνυμι		ἀνέδειξα			
* ἀναδέχομαι		ἀνεδεξάμην			
* ἀναδίδωμι		ἀνέδωκα			
* ἀναζάω		ἀνέζησα			
ἀναζητέω		ἀνεζήτησα			
* ἀναζώννυμι		ἀνέζωσα			
ἀναζωπυρέω					
* ἀναθάλλω		ἀνέθαλον			
ἀναθεματίζω		ἀνεθεμάτισα			
ἀναθεωρέω					

ἀναιρέω	ἀνελῶ	ἀνεῖλον		ἀνῃρέθην
		ἀνεῖλα		
* ἀνακαθίζω		ἀνεκάθισα		
ἀνακαινίζω				
ἀνακαινόω				
ἀνακαλύπτω			ἀνακεκάλυμμαι	
* ἀνακάμπτω	ἀνακάμψω	ἀνέκαμψα		
ἀνάκειμαι				
ἀνακεφαλαιόω		ἀνεκεφαλαίωσα		
* ἀνακλίνω	ἀνακλινῶ	ἀνέκλινα		ἀνεκλίθην
* ἀνακράζω		ἀνέκραξα		
		ἀνέκραγον		
ἀνακρίνω		ἀνέκρινα		ἀνεκρίθην
* ἀνακύπτω		ἀνέκυψα		
ἀναλαμβάνω		ἀνέλαβον		ἀνελήμφθην
* ἀναλίσκω		ἀνήλωσα		ἀνηλώθην
* ἀναλογίζομαι		ἀνελογισάμην		
* ἀναλύω		ἀνέλυσα		
ἀναμένω				
ἀναμιμνῄσκω	ἀναμνήσω			ἀνεμνήσθην
ἀνανεόω				
* ἀνανήφω		ἀνένηψα		
ἀναπαύω	ἀναπαύσω	ἀνέπαυσα	ἀναπέπαυμαι	ἀνεπάην
ἀναπείθω				
* ἀναπέμπω	ἀναπέμψω	ἀνέπεμψα		
* ἀναπηδάω		ἀνεπήδησα		
* ἀναπίπτω		ἀνέπεσον		
		ἀνέπεσα		
ἀναπληρόω	ἀναπληρώσω	ἀνεπλήρωσα		
* ἀναπτύσσω		ἀνέπτυξα		
ἀνάπτω				ἀνήφθην
ἀνασείω		ἀνέσεισα		
ἀνασκευάζω				
* ἀνασπάω	ἀνασπάσω			ἀνεσπάσθην
ἀναστατόω		ἀνεστάτωσα		
ἀνασταυρόω				
* ἀναστενάζω		ἀνεστέναξα		
ἀναστρέφω	ἀναστρέψω	ἀνέστρεψα		ἀνεστράφην
* ἀνατάσσομαι		ἀνεταξάμην		
ἀνατέλλω		ἀνέτειλα	ἀνατέταλκα	
* ἀνατίθημι		ἔθηκα		
ἀνατρέπω		ἀνέτρεψα		
* ἀνατρέφω		ἀνέθρεψα	ἀνατέθραμμαι	ἀνετράφην
ἀναφαίνω		ἀνέφανα		
ἀναφέρω		ἀνήνεγκα		
		ἀνήνεγκον		
* ἀναφωνέω		ἀνεφώνησα		
ἀναχωρέω		ἀνεχώρησα		
* ἀναψύχω		ἀνέψυξα		
ἀνδρίζομαι				
ἀνεμίζω				
* ἀνέρχομαι		ἀνῆλθον		
ἀνετάζω				
ἀνευρίσκω		ἀνεῦρα		
		ἀνεῦρον		

ἀνέχω	ἀνέξω	ἀνέσχον			
ἀνήκω					
ἀνθίστημι		ἀντέστην	ἀνθέστηκα		
ἀνθομολογέομαι					
ἀνίημι		ἀνῆκα			ἀνέθην
ἀνίστημι	ἀναστήσω	ἀνέστησα			
		ἀνέστην			
ἀνοίγω	ἀνοίξω	ἤνοιξα	ἀνέῳγα	ἀνέῳγμαι	ἠνοίχθην
		ἀνέῳξα		ἠνέῳγμαι	ἀνεῴχθην
		ἠνέῳξα			ἠνεῴχθην
* ἀνοικοδομέω	ἀνοικοδομήσω				
* ἀνορθόω	ἀνορθώσω	ἀνώρθωσα			ἀνωρθώθην
ἀνταγωνίζομαι					
ἀνταναπληρόω					
* ἀνταποδίδωμι	ἀνταποδώσω	ἀνταπέδωκα			ἀνταπεδόθην
ἀνταποκρίνομαι					ἀνταπεκρίθην
ἀντέχω	ἀνθέξω				
ἀντιβάλλω					
ἀντιδιατίθημι					
* ἀντικαθίστημι		ἀντικατέστην			
* ἀντικαλέω		ἀντεκάλεσα			
ἀντίκειμαι					
ἀντιλαμβάνω		ἀντέλαβον			
ἀντιλέγω		ἀντεῖπον			
ἀντιλοιδορέω					
* ἀντιμετρέω					ἀντεμετρήθην
* ἀντιπαρέρχομαι		ἀντιπαρῆλθον			
ἀντιπίπτω					
ἀντιστρατεύομαι					
ἀντιτάσσω					
ἀντλέω		ἤντλησα	ἤντληκα		
ἀντοφθαλμέω					
ἀξιόω		ἠξίωσα		ἠξίωμαι	ἠξιώθην
ἀπαγγέλλω	ἀπαγγελῶ	ἀπήγγειλα			ἀπηγγέλην
* ἀπάγχω		ἀπῆγξα			
ἀπάγω		ἀπήγαγον			ἀπήχθην
* ἀπαίρω					ἀπήρθην
ἀπαιτέω					
* ἀπαλγέω			ἀπήλγηκα		
ἀπαλλάσσω		ἀπήλλαξα		ἀπήλλαγμαι	
* ἀπαλλοτριόω				ἀπηλλοτρίωμαι	
* ἀπαντάω	ἀπαντήσω	ἀπήντησα			
* ἀπαρνέομαι	ἀπαρνήσομαι	ἀπηρνησάμην			ἀπηρνήθην
* ἀπασπάζομαι		ἀπησπασάμην			
ἀπατάω					ἠπατήθην
ἀπειθέω		ἠπείθησα			
ἀπειλέω		ἠπείλησα			
ἄπειμι					
ἄπειμι					
ἀπεκδέχομαι					
* ἀπεκδύομαι		ἀπεξεδυσάμην			
* ἀπελαύνω		ἀπήλασα			
ἀπελπίζω					
ἀπέρχομαι	ἀπελεύσομαι	ἀπῆλθον	ἀπελήλυθα		
ἀπέχω					

ἀπιστέω		ἠπίστησα			
* ἀποβαίνω	ἀποβήσομαι	ἀπέβην			
* ἀποβάλλω		ἀπέβαλον			
ἀποβλέπω					
* ἀπογίνομαι		ἀπεγένομην			
ἀπογράφω		ἀπέγραψα		ἀπογέγραμμαι	
ἀποδείκνυμι		ἀπέδειξα		ἀποδέδειγμαι	
ἀποδεκατόω					
ἀποδέχομαι		ἀπεδεξάμην			
ἀποδημέω		ἀπεδήμησα			
ἀποδίδωμι	ἀποδώσω	ἀπέδωκα			ἀπεδόθην
ἀποδιορίζω					
* ἀποδοκιμάζω		ἀπεδοκίμασα		ἀποδεδοκίμασμαι	ἀπεδοκιμάσθην
ἀποθησαυρίζω					
ἀποθλίβω					
ἀποθνῄσκω	ἀποθανοῦμαι	ἀπέθανον			
ἀποκαθίστημι	ἀποκαταστήσω	ἀπεκατέστην			ἀπεκατεστάθην
ἀποκαλύπτω	ἀποκαλύψω	ἀπεκάλυψα			ἀπεκαλύφθην
* ἀποκαταλλάσσω		ἀποκατήλλαξα			
ἀπόκειμαι					
* ἀποκεφαλίζω		ἀπεκεφάλισα			
* ἀποκλείω		ἀπέκλεισα			
* ἀποκόπτω	ἀποκόψω	ἀπέκοψα			
ἀποκρίνομαι		ἀπεκρινάμην			ἀπεκρίθην
* ἀποκρύπτω		ἀπέκρυψα		ἀποκέκρυμμαι	
ἀποκτείνω	ἀποκτενῶ	ἀπέκτεινα			ἀπεκτάνθην
ἀποκυέω		ἀπεκύησα			
* ἀποκυλίω	ἀποκυλίσω	ἀπεκύλισα		ἀποκεκύλισμαι	
ἀπολαμβάνω	ἀπολήμψομαι	ἀπέλαβον			
* ἀπολέγω		ἀπεῖπον			
ἀπολείπω		ἀπέλιπον			
ἀπόλλυμι	ἀπολέσω ἀπολῶ	ἀπώλεσα	ἀπολώλεκα ἀπόλωλα		
ἀπολογέομαι		ἀπελογησάμην			ἀπελογήθην
* ἀπολούω		ἀπέλουσα			
ἀπολύω	ἀπολύσω	ἀπέλυσα		ἀπολέλυμαι	ἀπελύθην
ἀπομάσσω					
ἀπονέμω					
* ἀπονίπτω		ἀπένιψα			
* ἀποπίπτω		ἀπέπεσα			
ἀποπλανάω					ἀπεπλανήθην
ἀποπλέω		ἀπέπλευσα			
* ἀποπνίγω		ἀπέπνιξα			ἀπεπνίγην
ἀπορέω					
* ἀπορίπτω		ἀπέριψα			
* ἀπορφανίζω					ἀπωρφανίσθην
ἀποσπάω		ἀπέσπασα			ἀπεστάσθην
* ἀποστεγάζω		ἀπεστέγασα			
ἀποστέλλω	ἀποστελῶ	ἀπέστειλα	ἀπέσταλκα	ἀπέσταλμαι	ἀπεστάλην
ἀποστερέω		ἀπεστέρησα		ἀπετέρημαι	
ἀποστοματίζω					
ἀποστρέφω	ἀποστρέψω	ἀπέστρεψα			ἀπεστράφην
ἀποστυγέω					
ἀποτάσσω		ἀπέταξα			
ἀποτελέω					ἀπετελέσθην

* ἀποτίθημι		ἀπέθηκα		
ἀποτινάσσω		ἀπετίναξα		
* ἀποτίνω	ἀποτίσω			
ἀποτολμάω				
ἀποτρέπω				
ἀποφέρω		ἀπήνεγκα		ἀπηνέχθην
ἀποφεύγω		ἀπέφυγον		
ἀποφθέγγομαι		ἀπεφθεγξάμην		
ἀποφορτίζομαι				
ἀποχωρέω		ἀπεχώρησα		
* ἀποχωρίζω				ἀπεχωρίσθην
ἀποψύχω				
ἅπτω		ἧψα		
ἀπωθέω		ἀπῶσα		
ἀργέω				
ἀρέσκω		ἤρεσα		
* ἀριθμέω		ἠρίθμησα	ἠρίθμημαι	
* ἀριστάω		ἠρίστησα		
ἀρκέω		ἤρκεσα		ἠρκέσθην
* ἁρμόζω		ἥρμοσα		
ἀρνέομαι	ἀρνήσομαι	ἠρνησάμην	ἤρνημαι	
ἀροτριάω				
ἁρπάζω	ἁρπάυω	ἥρπασα		ἡρπάγην
				ἡρπάσθην
* ἀρτύω	ἀρτύσω		ἤρτυμαι	ἠρτύθην
ἄρχω	ἄρξω	ἦρξα		
* ἀσεβέω		ἠσέβησα		
ἀσθενέω		ἠσθένησα	ἠσθένηκα	
ἀσκέω				
ἀσπάζομαι		ἠσπασάμην		
ἀστατέω				
* ἀστοχέω		ἠστόχησα		
ἀστράπτω				
* ἀσφαλίζω		ἠσφάλισα		ἠσφαλίσθην
ἀσχημονέω				
* ἀτακτέω		ἠτάκτησα		
ἀτενίζω		ἠτένισα		
ἀτιμάζω		ἠτίμασα		ἠτιμάσθην
* αὐγάζω		ηὔγασα		
αὐθεντέω				
αὐλέω		ηὔλησα		
αὐλίζομαι				ηὐλίσθην
αὐξάνω	αὐξήσω	ηὔξησα		ηὐξήθην
αὐχέω				
ἀφαιρέω	ἀφελῶ	ἀφεῖλον		ἀφῃρέθην
ἀφανίζω				ἠφανίσθην
ἀφίημι	ἀφήσω	ἀφῆκα	ἀφέωμαι	ἀφέθην
* ἀφικνέομαι		ἀφικόμην		
ἀφίστημι	ἀποστήσω	ἀπέστησα		
		ἀπέστην		
* ἀφομοιόω			ἀφωμοίωμαι	
ἀφοράω		ἀπεῖδον		
ἀφορίζω	ἀφορίσω	ἀφώρισα	ἀφώρισμαι	ἀφωρίσθην
	ἀφοριῶ			
ἀφρίζω				

* ἀφυπνόω		ἀφύπνωσα			
* ἀχρειόω					ἠχρεώθην
βαθύνω					
βάλλω	βαλῶ	ἔβαλον	βέβληκα	βέβλημαι	ἐβλήθην
		ἔβαλα			
βαπτίζω	βαπτίσω	ἐβάπτισα		βεβάπτισμαι	ἐβαπτίσθην
* βάπτω	βάψω	ἔβαψα		βέβαμμαι	
βαρέω				βεβάρημαι	ἐβαρήθην
βασανίζω		ἐβασάνισα			ἐβασανίσθην
βασιλεύω	βασιλεύσω	ἐβασίλευσα			
* βασκαίνω		ἐβάσκανα			
βαστάζω	βαστάσω	ἐβάστασα			
* βατταλογέω		ἐβατταλόγησα			
βδελύσσομαι				ἐβδέλυγμαι	
βεβαιόω	βεβαιώσω	ἐβεβαίωσα			ἐβεβαιώθην
βεβηλόω		ἐβεβήλωσα			
βιάζομαι					
* βιβρώσκω			βέβρωκα		
* βιόω		ἐβίωσα			
* βλάπτω		ἔβλαψα			
βλαστάνω		ἐβλάστησα			
βλασφημέω		ἐβλασφήμησα			ἐβλασφημήθην
βλέπω	βλέψω	ἔβλεψα			
βοάω		ἐβόησα			
βοηθέω		ἐβοήθησα			
* βολίζω		ἐβόλισα			
βόσκω					
βουλεύω	βουλεύσω	ἐβούλευσα			
βούλομαι					ἐβουλήθην
βραβεύω					
βραδύνω					
βραδυπλοέω					
βρέχω		ἔβρεξα			
βρύχω					
βρύω					
βυθίζω					
γαμέω		ἐγάμησα	γεγάμηκα		ἐγαμήθην
		ἔγημα			
γαμίζω					
γαμίσκω					
γελάω	γελάσω				
γεμίζω		ἐγέμισα			ἐγεμίσθην
γέμω					
γενεαλογέω					
γεννάω	γεννήσω	ἐγέννησα	γεγέννηκα	γεγέννημαι	ἐγεννήθην
* γεύομαι	γεύσομαι	ἐγευσάμην			
γεωργέω					
γηράσκω		ἐγήρασα			
γίνομαι	γενήσομαι	ἐγενόμην	γέγονα	γεγένημαι	ἐγενήθην
γινώσκω	γνώσομαι	ἔγνων	ἔγνωκα	ἔγνωσμαι	ἐγνώσθην
γνωρίζω	γνωρίσω	ἐγνώρισα			ἐγνωρίσθην
γογγύζω		ἐγόγγυσα			
γονυπετέω		ἐγονυπέτησα			
γράφω	γράψω	ἔγραψα	γέγραφα	γέγραμμαι	ἐγράφην
γρηγορέω		ἐγρηγόρησα			

γυμνάζω				γεγύμνασμαι	
γυμνιτεύω					
δαιμονίζομαι					ἐδαιμονίσθην
δάκνω					
* δακρύω		ἐδάκρυσα			
δαμάζω		ἐδάμασα		δεδάμασμαι	
δανίζω		ἐδάνισα			
* δαπανάω	δαπανήσω	ἐδαπάνησα			
δεῖ					
* δειγματίζω		ἐδειγμάτισα			
δείκνυμι	δείξω	ἔδειξα	δέδειχα		ἐδείχθην
δειλιάω					
* δειπνέω	δειπνήσω	ἐδείπνησα			
* δεκατόω			δεδεκάτωκα	δεδεκάτωμαι	
δελεάζω					
δέομαι					ἐδεήθην
δέρω		ἔδειρα			ἐδάρην
δεσμεύω					
δέχομαι		ἐδεξάμην		δέδεγμαι	ἐδέχθην
δέω		ἔδησα	δέδεκα	δέδεμαι	ἐδέθην
δηλόω	δηλώσω	ἐδήλωσα			ἐδηλώθην
δημηγορέω					
* διαβαίνω		διέβην			
* διαβάλλω					διεβλήθην
διαβεβαιόομαι					
* διαβλέπω	διαβλέψω	διέβλεψα			
διαγγέλλω					διηγγέλην
* διαγίνομαι		διεγενόμην			
διαγινώσκω	διαγνώσομαι				
διαγογγύζω					
* διαγρηγορέω		διεγρηγόρησα			
διάγω					
* διαδέχομαι		διεδεξάμην			
διαδίδωμι		διέδωκα			
* διαζώννυμι		διέζωσα		διέζωσμαι	
διαιρέω		διεῖλον			
* διακαθαίρω		διεκάθαρα			
* διακαθαρίζω	διακαθαριῶ				
διακατελέγχομαι					
διακονέω	διακονήσω	διηκόνησα			διηκονήθην
* διακούω	διακούσομαι				
διακρίνω		διέκρινα			διεκρίθην
διακωλύω					
διαλαλέω					
διαλέγομαι		διελεξάμην			διελέχθην
* διαλείπω		διέλιπον			
* διαλλάσσομαι					διηλλάγην
διαλογίζομαι					
* διαλύω					διελύθην
διαμαρτύρομαι		διεμαρτυράμην			
διαμάχομαι					
* διαμένω		διέμεινα	διαμεμένηκα		
διαμερίζω		διεμέρισα		διαμεμέρισμαι	διεμερίσθην
διανέμω					διενεμήθην
διανεύω					

διανοίγω	διήνοιξα	διήνοιγμαι	διηνοίχθην
διανυκτερεύω			
* διανύω	διήνυσα		
διαπεράω	διεπέρασα		
* διαπλέω	διέπλευσα		
διαπονέομαι			διεπονήθην
διαπορεύομαι			
διαπορέω			
* διαπραγματεύομαι	διεπραγματευσάμην		
διαπρίω			
* διαρπάζω	διαρπάσω	διήρπασα	
διαρρήγνυμι	διέρρηξα		
* διασαφέω	διεσάφησα		
* διασείω	διέσεισα		
διασκορπίζω	διεσκόρπισα	διεσκόρπισμαι	διεσκορπίσθην
* διασπάω		διέσπασμαι	διεσπάσθην
* διασπείρω			διεστάρην
διαστέλλω	διέστειλα		
διαστρέφω	διέστρεψα	διέστραμμαι	
* διασῴζω	διέσωσα		διεσώθην
* διαταράσσω			διεταράχθην
διατάσσω	διατάξω	διέταξα	διατέταχα	διατέταγμαι	διετάχθην
					διετάγην
διατελέω			
διατηρέω			
διατίθημι	διαθήσω	διέθηκα	
διατρίβω	διέτριψα		
* διαυγάζω	διαυγάψα		
διαφέρω	διήνεγκα		
* διαφεύγω	διέφυγον		
διαφημίζω	διεφήμισα		διεφημίσθην
διαφθείρω	διέφθειρα	διέφθαρμαι	διεφθάρην
* διαφυλάσσω	διεφύλαξα		
* διαχειρίζω	διεχείρισα		
διαχλευάζω			
διαχωρίζω			
διδάσκω	διδάξω	ἐδίδαξα	ἐδιδάχθην
δίδωμι	δώσω	ἔδωκα	δέδωκα	δέδομαι	ἐδόθην
διεγείρω	διήγειρα		διηγέρθην
διενθυμέομαι			
διερμηνεύω	διερμήνευσα		
διέρχομαι	διελεύσομαι	διῆλθον	διελήλυθα	
* διερωτάω	διηρώτησα		
διηγέομαι	διηγήσομαι	διηγησάμην	
διϊκνέομαι			
* διΐστημι	διέστησα		
	διέστην		
διϊσχυρίζομαι			
δικαιόω	δικαιώσω	ἐδικαίωσα	δεδικαίωμαι	ἐδικαιώθην
διοδεύω	διώδευσα		
διορύσσω			διωρύχθην
* διπλόω	ἐδίπλωσα		
* διστάζω	ἐδίστασα		
διϋλίζω			
* διχάζω	ἐδίχασα		

* διχοτομέω	διχοτομήσω				
διψάω	διψήσω	ἐδίψησα			
διώκω	διώξω	ἐδίωξα		δεδίωγμαι	ἐδιώχθην
δογματίζω					
δοκέω	δόξω	ἔδοξα			
δοκιμάζω	δοκιμάσω	ἐδοκίμασα		δεδοκίμασμαι	
δολιόω					
δολόω					
δοξάζω	δοξάσω	ἐδόξασα		δεδόξασμαι	ἐδοξάσθην
δουλαγωγέω					
δουλεύω	δουλεύσω	ἐδούλευσα	δεδούλευκα		
* δουλόω	δουλώσω	ἐδούλωσα		δεδούλωμαι	ἐδουλώθην
δράσσομαι					
δύναμαι	δυνήσομαι				ἠδυνήθην
δυναμόω					ἐδυναμώθην
δυνατέω					
δύνω		ἔδυν			
δυσφημέω					
* δωρέομαι		ἐδωρησάμην		δεδώρημαι	
ἐάω	ἐάσω	εἴασα			
ἐγγίζω	ἐγγιῶ	ἤγγισα	ἤγγικα		
* ἐγγράφω				ἐγγέγραμμαι	
ἐγείρω	ἐγερῶ	ἤγειρα		ἐγήγερμαι	ἠγέρθην
* ἐγκαινίζω		ἐνεκαίνισα		ἐγκεκαίνισμαι	
ἐγκακέω		ἐνεκάκησα			
ἐγκαλέω	ἐγκαλέσω				
ἐγκαταλείπω	ἐγκαταλείψω	ἐγκατέλιπον			ἐγκατελείφθην
ἐγκατοικέω					
ἐγκαυχάομαι					
* ἐγκεντρίζω		ἐνεκέντρισα			ἐνεκεντρίσθην
* ἐγκομβόομαι		ἐνεκομβωσάμην			
ἐγκόπτω		ἐνέκοψα			
ἐγκρατεύομαι					
* ἐγκρίνω		ἐνέκρινα			
* ἐγκρύπτω		ἐνέκρυψα			
* ἐγχρίω		ἐνέχρισα			
* ἐδαφίζω	ἐδαφιῶ				
* ἐθίζω				εἴθισμαι	
* εἴκω		εἶξα			
εἰμί	ἔσομαι				
εἰρηνεύω					
* εἰρηνοποιέω		εἰρηνοποίησα			
εἰσάγω		εἰσήγαγον			
* εἰσακούω	εἰσακούσομαι				εἰσηκούσθην
* εἰσδέχομαι	εἰσδέξομαι				
εἴσειμι					
εἰσέρχομαι	εἰσελεύσομαι	εἰσῆλθον	εἰσελήλυθα		
* εἰσκαλέομαι		εἰσεκαλησάμην			
* εἰσπηδάω		εἰσεπήδησα			
εἰσπορεύομαι					
* εἰστρέχω		εἰσέδραμον			
εἰσφέρω		εἰσήνεγκα			
		εἰσήνεγκον			
>εἴωθα		εἴωθα			
* ἐκβαίνω		ἐξέβην			

ἐκβάλλω	ἐκβαλῶ	ἐξέβαλον	ἐκβέβληκα	ἐξεβλήθην
* ἐκδαπανάω				ἐξεδαπανήθην
ἐκδέχομαι				
ἐκδημέω		ἐξεδήμησα		
* ἐκδίδωμι	ἐκδώσω	ἐξέδωκα		
ἐκδιηγέομαι				
ἐκδικέω	ἐκδικήσω	ἐξεδίκησα		
* ἐκδιώκω		ἐξεδίωξα		
* ἐκδύω		ἐξέδυσα		
ἐκζητέω		ἐξεζήτησα		ἐξεζητήθην
ἐκθαμβέω				ἐξεθαμβήθην
ἐκθαυμάζω				
* ἐκκαθαίρω		ἐξεκάθαρα		
* ἐκκαίω				ἐξεκαύθην
* ἐκκεντέω		ἐξεκέντησα		
* ἐκκλάω				ἐξεκλάσθην
* ἐκκλείω		ἐξέκλεισα		ἐξεκλείσθην
ἐκκλίνω		ἐξέκλινα		
* ἐκκολυμβάω		ἐξεκολύμβησα		
ἐκκομίζω				
ἐκκόπτω	ἐκκόψω	ἐξέκοψα		ἐξεκόπην
ἐκκρεμάννυμι				
* ἐκλαλέω		ἐξελάλησα		
* ἐκλάμπω	ἐκλάμψω			
* ἐκλανθάνομαι			ἐκλέλησμαι	
ἐκλέγομαι		ἐξελεξάμην	ἐκλέλεγμαι	
* ἐκλείπω	ἐκλείψω	ἐξέλιπον		
ἐκλύω				ἐξελύθην
ἐκμάσσω		ἐξέμαξα		
ἐκμυκτηρίζω				
* ἐκνεύω		ἐξένευσα		
* ἐκνήφω		ἐξένηψα		
ἐκπειράζω	ἐκπειράσω			
* ἐκπέμπω		ἐξέπεμψα		ἐξεπέμφθην
* ἐκπετάννυμι		ἐξεπέτασα		
* ἐκπηδάω		ἐξεπήδησα		
* ἐκπίπτω		ἐξέπεσον	ἐκπέπτωκα	
		ἐξέπεσα		
ἐκπλέω		ἐξέπλευσα		
* ἐκπληρόω			ἐκπεπλήρωκα	
ἐκπλήσσω				ἐξεπλάγην
* ἐκπνέω		ἐξέπνευσα		
ἐκπορεύομαι	ἐκπορεύσομαι			
* ἐκπορνεύω		ἐξεπόρνευσα		
* ἐκπτύω		ἐξέπτυσα		
* ἐκριζόω		ἐξερίζωσα		ἐξεριζώθην
* ἐκστρέφω			ἐξέστραμμαι	
ἐκταράσσω				
ἐκτείνω	ἐκτενῶ	ἐξέτεινα		
* ἐκτελέω		ἐξετέλεσα		
ἐκτίθημι		ἐξέθηκα		ἐξετέθην
* ἐκτινάσσω		ἐξετίναξα		
ἐκτρέπω				ἐξετράπην
ἐκτρέφω				

ἐκφέρω	ἐξοίσω	ἐξήνεγκα			
		ἐξήνεγκον			
* ἐκφεύγω	ἐκφεύξομαι	ἐξέφυγον	ἐκπέφευγα		
ἐκφοβέω					
ἐκφύω					
ἐκχέω	ἐκχεῶ	ἐξέχεα		ἐκκέχυμαι	ἐξεχύθην
ἐκχωρέω					
* ἐκψύχω		ἐξέψυξα			
* ἐλαττονέω		ἠλαττόνησα			
ἐλαττόω		ἠλάττωσα		ἠλάττωμαι	
ἐλαύνω			ἐλήλακα		
ἐλεάω					
ἐλέγχω	ἐλέγξω	ἤλεγξα			ἠλέγχθην
ἐλεέω	ἐλεήσω	ἠλέησα		ἠλέημαι	ἠλεήθην
* ἐλευθερόω	ἐλευθερώσω	ἠλευθέρωσα			ἠλευθερώθην
ἐλίσσω	ἐλίξω				
* ἑλκόω				εἵλκωμαι	
ἕλκω	ἑλκύσω	εἵλκυσα			
ἐλλογέω					
ἐλπίζω	ἐλπιῶ	ἤλπισα	ἤλπικα		
ἐμβαίνω		ἐνέβην			
* ἐμβάλλω		ἐνέβαλον			
ἐμβάπτω		ἐνέβαψα			
ἐμβατεύω					
* ἐμβιβάζω		ἐνεβίβασα			
ἐμβλέπω		ἐνέβλεψα			
ἐμβριμάομαι		ἐνεβριμησάμην			ἐνεβριμήθην
* ἐμέω		ἤμεσα			
ἐμμαίνομαι					
ἐμμένω		ἐνέμεινα			
ἐμπαίζω	ἐμπαίξω	ἐνέπαιξα			ἐνεπαίχθην
* ἐμπεριπατέω	ἐμπεριπατήσω				
* ἐμπίμπλημι		ἐνέπλησα		ἐμπέπλησμαι	ἐνεπλήσθην
* ἐμπίμπρημι		ἐνέπρησα			
ἐμπίπτω	ἐμπεσοῦμαι	ἐνέπεσον			
ἐμπλέκω					ἐνεπλάκην
ἐμπνέω					
* ἐμπορεύομαι	ἐμπορεύσομαι				
ἐμπτύω	ἐμπτύσω	ἐνέπτυσα			ἐνεπτύσθην
ἐμφανίζω	ἐμφανίσω	ἐνεφάνισα			ἐνεφανίσθην
* ἐμφυσάω		ἐνεφύσησα			
* ἐναγκαλίζομαι		ἐνηγκαλίσμην			
* ἐνάρχομαι		ἐνηρξάμην			
ἐνδείκνυμι		ἐνέδειξα			
ἐνδέχομαι					
ἐνδημέω		ἐνεδήμησα			
ἐνδιδύσκω					
* ἐνδοξάζομαι					ἐνεδοξάσθην
ἐνδυναμόω		ἐνεδυνάμωσα			ἐνεδυναμώθην
ἐνδύνω					
* ἐνδύω		ἐνέδυσα		ἐνδέδυμαι	
ἐνεδρεύω					
* ἐνειλέω		ἐνείλησα			
ἔνειμι					
ἐνεργέω		ἐνήργησα			

* ἐνευλογέω				ἐνευλογήθην
ἐνέχω				
ἐνθυμέομαι				ἐνεθυμήθην
ἔνι				
* ἐνίστημι	ἐνστήσω		ἐνέστηκα	
ἐνισχύω		ἐνίσχυσα		
ἐννεύω				
ἐνοικέω	ἐνοικήσω	ἐνῴκησα		
ἐνορκίζω				
ἐνοχλέω				
ἐνταφιάζω		ἐνεταφίασα		
ἐντέλλομαι	ἐντελοῦμαι	ἐνετειλάμην		ἐντέταλμαι
ἐντρέπω				ἐνετράπην
ἐντρέφω				
ἐντρυφάω				
ἐντυγχάνω		ἐνέτυχον		
* ἐντυλίσσω		ἐνετύλιξα		ἐντετύλιγμαι
* ἐντυπόω				ἐντετύπωμαι
* ἐνυβρίζω		ἐνύβρισα		
ἐνυπνιάζομαι				ἐνυπνιάσθην
* ἐνωτίζομαι		ἐνωτισάμην		
* ἐξαγγέλλω		ἐξήγγειλα		
ἐξαγοράζω		ἐξηγόρασα		
ἐξάγω		ἐξήγαγον		
ἐξαιρέω		ἐξεῖλον		
ἐξαίρω				
* ἐξαιτέω		ἐξήτησα		
* ἐξακολουθέω	ἐξακολουθήσω	ἐξηκολούθησα		
* ἐξαλείφω	ἐξαλείψω	ἐξήλειψα		ἐξηλείφθην
ἐξάλλομαι				
* ἐξανατέλλω		ἐξανέτειλα		
* ἐξανίστημι		ἐξανέστησα		
		ἐξανέστην		
ἐξαπατάω		ἐξηπάτησα		
ἐξαπορέομαι				ἐξηπορήθην
* ἐξαποστέλλω	ἐξαποστελῶ	ἐξαπέστειλα		
* ἐξαρτίζω		ἐξήτισα		ἐξήρτισμαι
ἐξαστράπτω				
* ἐξεγείρω	ἐξεγερῶ	ἐξήγειρα		
ἔξειμι				
ἐξέλκω				
* ἐξεραυνάω		ἐξηραύνησα		
ἐξέρχομαι	ἐξελεύσομαι	ἐξῆλθον	ἐξελήλυθα	
ἔξεστι				
* ἐξετάζω		ἐξήτασα		
ἐξηγέομαι		ἐξηγησάμην		
* ἐξηχέω				ἐξήχημαι
ἐξίστημι		ἐξέστησα	ἐξέστηκα	
		ἐξέστην		
* ἐξισχύω		ἐξίσχυσα		
* ἐξολεθρεύω				ἐξωλεθρεύθην
ἐξομολογέω	ἐξομολογήσω	ἐξωμολόγησα		
ἐξορκίζω				
* ἐξορύσσω		ἐξώρυξα		
* ἐξουδενέω				ἐξουδενήθην

ἐξουθενέω		ἐξουθένησα	ἐξουθένημαι ἐξουθενήθην
ἐξουσιάζω			ἐξουσιάσθην
* ἐξυπνίζω	ἐξυπνίσω		
* ἐξωθέω		ἐξῶσα	
>ἔοικα			ἔοικα
ἑορτάζω			
ἐπαγγέλλομαι		ἐπηγγειλάμην	ἐπήγγελμαι
ἐπάγω		ἐπήγαγον	
		ἔπηξα	
ἐπαγωνίζομαι			
ἐπαθροίζω			
ἐπαινέω	ἐπαινέσω	ἐπήνεσα	
ἐπαίρω		ἐπῆρα	ἐπήρθην
ἐπαισχύνομαι			ἐπαισχύνθην
ἐπαιτέω			
ἐπακολουθέω		ἐπηκολούθησα	
* ἐπακούω		ἐπήκουσα	
ἐπακροάομαι			
ἐπανάγω		ἐπανήγαγον	
ἐπαναμιμνήσκω			
ἐπαναπαύομαι			ἐπαναπάην
ἐπανέρχομαι		ἐπανῆλθον	
* ἐπανίστημι	ἐπαναστήσω		
ἐπαρκέω		ἐπήρκεσα	
ἐπαφρίζω			
* ἐπεγείρω		ἐπήγειρα	
ἔπειμι			
* ἐπεισέρχομαι	ἐπεισελεύσομαι		
ἐπεκτείνομαι			
* ἐπενδύομαι		ἐπενεδυσάμην	
ἐπέρχομαι	ἐπελεύσομαι	ἐπῆλθον	
ἐπερωτάω	ἐπερωτήσω	ἐπηρώτησα	ἐπηρωτήθην
ἐπέχω		ἐπέσχον	
ἐπηρεάζω			
ἐπιβαίνω		ἐπέβην	ἐπιβέβηκα
ἐπιβάλλω	ἐπιβαλῶ	ἐπέβαλον	
ἐπιβαρέω		ἐπεβάρησα	
* ἐπιβιβάζω		ἐπεβίβασα	
* ἐπιβλέπω		ἐπέβλεψα	
* ἐπιγαμβρεύω	ἐπιγαμβρεύσω		
* ἐπιγίνομαι		ἐπεγενόμην	
ἐπιγινώσκω	ἐπιγνώσομαι	ἐπέγνων	ἐπέγνωκα ἐπεγνώσθην
ἐπιγράφω			ἐπιγέγραμμαι
ἐπιδείκνυμι		ἐπέδειξα	
ἐπιδέχομαι			
ἐπιδημέω			
ἐπιδιατάσσομαι			
ἐπιδίδωμι	ἐπιδώσω		ἐπεδέδωκα ἐπεδόθην
* ἐπιδιορθόω		ἐπεδιόρθωσα	
ἐπιδύω			
ἐπιζητέω		ἐπεζήτησα	
ἐπιθυμέω	ἐπιθυμήσω	ἐπεθύμησα	
* ἐπικαθίζω		ἐπεκάθισα	
ἐπικαλέω		ἐπεκάλεσα	ἐπικέκλημαι ἐπεκλήθην
* ἐπικαλύπτω			ἐπεκαλύφθην

ἐπίκειμαι				
* *ἐπικέλλω*		*ἐπέκειλα*		
* *ἐπικρίνω*		*ἐπέκρινα*		
ἐπιλαμβάνομαι		*ἐπελαβόμην*		
ἐπιλανθάνομαι		*ἐπελαθόμην*	*ἐπιλέλησμαι*	
ἐπιλέγω		*ἐπέλεξα*		
* *ἐπιλείπω*	*ἐπιλείψω*			
ἐπιλείχω				
ἐπιλύω				*ἐπελύθην*
ἐπιμαρτυρέω				
ἐπιμελέομαι	*ἐπιμελήσομαι*			*ἐπεμελήθην*
ἐπιμένω	*ἐπιμενῶ*	*ἐπέμεινα*		
* *ἐπινεύω*		*ἐπένευσα*		
* *ἐπιορκέω*	*ἐπιορκήσω*			
ἐπιπίπτω		*ἐπέπεσον*	*ἐπιπέπτωκα*	
* *ἐπιπλήσσω*		*ἐπέπληξα*		
ἐπιποθέω		*ἐπεπόθησα*		
ἐπιπορεύομαι				
ἐπιράπτω				
* *ἐπιρίπτω*		*ἐπέριψα*		
ἐπισκέπτομαι	*ἐπισκέψομαι*	*ἐπεσκεψάμην*		
* *ἐπισκευάζομαι*		*ἐπεσκευασάμην*		
* *ἐπισκηνόω*		*ἐπεσκήνωσα*		
ἐπισκιάζω	*ἐπισκιάσω*	*ἐπεσκίασα*		
ἐπισκοπέω				
ἐπισπάομαι				
ἐπισπείρω				
ἐπίσταμαι				
* *ἐπιστέλλω*		*ἐπέστειλα*		
ἐπιστηρίζω		*ἐπεστήριξα*		
ἐπιστομίζω				
ἐπιστρέφω	*ἐπιστρέψω*	*ἐπέστρεψα*		*ἐπεστράφην*
* *ἐπισυνάγω*	*ἐπισυνάξω*	*ἐπισυνήγαγον*	*ἐπισύνηγμαι*	*ἐπισυνήχθην*
		ἐπισυνῆξα		
ἐπισυντρέχω				
ἐπισχύω				
* *ἐπισωρεύω*	*ἐπισωρεύσω*			
ἐπιτάσσω		*ἐπέταξα*		
ἐπιτελέω		*ἐπετέλεσα*		
ἐπιτίθημι	*ἐπιθήσω*	*ἐπέθηκα*		
		ἐπέθην		
ἐπιτιμάω		*ἐπετίμησα*		
ἐπιτρέπω		*ἐπέτρεψα*		*ἐπετράπην*
* *ἐπιτυγχάνω*		*ἐπέτυχον*		
ἐπιφαίνω		*ἐπέφανα*		*ἐπεφάνην*
* *ἐπιφαύσκω*	*ἐπιφαύσω*			
ἐπιφέρω		*ἐπήνεγκον*		
ἐπιφωνέω				
ἐπιφώσκω				
ἐπιχειρέω		*ἐπεχείρησα*		
ἐπιχέω				
ἐπιχορηγέω		*ἐπεχορήγησα*		*ἐπεχορηγήθην*
* *ἐπιχρίω*		*ἐπέχρισα*		
ἐποικοδομέω		*ἐποικοδόμησα*		*ἐποικοδομήθην*
ἐπονομάζω				

ἐποπτεύω		ἐπώπτευσα			
ἐραυνάω		ἠραύνησα			
ἐργάζομαι		ἠργασάμην		εἴργασμαι	
		εἰργασάμην			
ἐρεθίζω		ἠρέθισα			
* ἐρείδω		ἤρεισα			
* ἐρεύγομαι	ἐρεύξομαι				
ἐρημόω				ἠρήμωμαι	ἠρημώθην
* ἐρίζω	ἐρίσω				
ἑρμηνεύω					
ἔρχομαι	ἐλεύσομαι	ἦλθον	ἐλήλυθα		
		ἦλθα			
ἐρωτάω	ἐρωτήσω	ἠρώτησα			
ἐσθίω	φάγομαι	ἔφαγον			
* ἑσσόομαι					ἡσσώθην
ἑτεροδιδασκαλέω					
ἑτεροζυγέω					
ἑτοιμάζω		ἡτοίμασα	ἡτοίμακα	ἡτοίμασμαι	ἡτοιμάσθην
εὐαγγελίζω		εὐηγγέλισα		εὐηγγέλισμαι	εὐηγγελίσθην
εὐαρεστέω		εὐηρέστησα	εὐηρέστηκα		
εὐδοκέω		εὐδόκησα			
εὐεργετέω					
* εὐθυδρομέω		εὐθυδρόμησα			
εὐθυμέω					
εὐθύνω		εὔθυνα			
εὐκαιρέω		εὐκαίρησα			
* εὐλαβέομαι					ηὐλαβήθην
εὐλογέω	εὐλογήσω	εὐλόγησα	εὐλόγηκα	εὐλόγημαι	
εὐνοέω					
* εὐνουχίζω		εὐνούχισα			εὐνουχίσθην
εὐοδόω					εὐοδώθην
εὐπορέω					
* εὐπροσωπέω		εὐπροσώπησα			
εὑρίσκω	εὑρήσω	εὗρον	εὕρηκα		εὑρέθην
		εὗρα			
εὐσεβέω					
* εὐφορέω		εὐφόρησα			
εὐφραίνω					ηὐφράνθην
εὐχαριστέω		εὐχαρίστησα			εὐχαριστήθην
εὔχομαι		εὐξάμην			
εὐψυχέω					
ἐφάλλομαι					
ἐφικνέομαι		ἐφικόμην			
ἐφίστημι		ἐπέστην	ἐφέστηκα		
* ἐφοράω		ἐπεῖδον			
ἔχω	ἕξω	ἔσχον	ἔσχηκα		
ζάω	ζήσομαι	ἔζησα			
	ζήσω				
ζέω					
ζηλεύω					
ζηλόω		ἐζήλωσα			
* ζημιόω					ἐζημιώθην
ζητέω	ζητήσω	ἐζήτησα			ἐζητήθην
ζυμόω					ἐζυμώθην
ζωγρέω				ἐζώγρημαι	

ζώννυμι	ζώσω	ἔζωσα		
ζῳογονέω	ζῳογονήσω			
ζῳοποιέω	ζῳοποιήσω	ἐζῳοποίησα		ἐζῳοποιήθην
ἡγεμονεύω				
ἡγέομαι		ἡγησάμην	ἥγημαι	
ἥκω	ἥξω	ἧξα		
ἡσυχάζω		ἡσύχασα		
ἡττάομαι			ἥττημαι	
ἠχέω				
θάλπω				
θαμβέω				ἐθαμβήθην
θανατόω	θανατώσω	ἐθανάτωσα		ἐθανατώθην
* θάπτω		ἔθαψα		ἐτάφην
θαρρέω		ἐθάρρησα		
θαρσέω				
θαυμάζω		ἐθαύμασα		ἐθαυμάσθην
* θεάομαι		ἐθεασάμην	τεθέαμαι	ἐθεάθην
θεατρίζω				
θέλω		ἠθέλησα		
* θεμελιόω	θεμελιώσω	ἐθεμελίωσα	τεθεμελίωμαι	
θεραπεύω	θεραπεύσω	ἐθεράπευσα	τεθεράπευμαι	ἐθεραπεύθην
θερίζω	θερίσω	ἐθέρισα		ἐθερίσθην
θερμαίνω				
θεωρέω	θεώρησω	ἐθεώρησα		
θηλάζω		ἐθήλασα		
* θηρεύω		ἐθήρευσα		
* θηριομαχέω		ἐθηριομάχησα		
θησαυρίζω		ἐθησαύρισα	τεθησαύρισμαι	
* θιγγάνω		ἔθιγον		
θλίβω			τέθλιμμαι	
* θνήσκω		τέθνηκα		
θορυβάζω				
θορυβέω				
* θραύω			τέθραυσμαι	
θρηνέω	θρηνήσω	ἐθρήνησα		
θριαμβεύω		ἐθριάμβευσα		
θροέω				
* θυμιάω		ἐθυμίασα		
θυμομαχέω				
* θυμόω				ἐθυμώθην
θύω		ἔθυσα	τέθυμαι	ἐτύθην
ἰάομαι	ἰάσομαι	ἰασάμην	ἴαμαι	ἰάθην
ἱερατεύω				
ἱεροσυλέω				
ἱερουργέω				
* ἱκανόω		ἱκάνωσα		
ἱλάσκομαι				ἱλάσθην
* ἱματίζω			ἱμάτισμαι	
ἰουδαΐζω				
ἵστημι	στήσω	ἔστησα / ἔστην	ἔστηκα	ἐστάθην
* ἱστορέω		ἱστόρησα		
ἰσχύω	ἰσχύσω	ἴσχυσα		
καθαιρέω	καθελῶ	καθεῖλον		
καθαίρω				

* καθάπτω		καθῆψα			
καθαρίζω	καθαριῶ	ἐκαθάρισα			
καθέζομαι					
καθεύδω					
καθήκω					
κάθημαι	καθήσομαι				
καθίζω	καθίσω	ἐκάθισα	κεκάθικα		
καθίημι		καθῆκα			
καθίστημι	καταστήσω	κατέστησα			κατεστάθην
* καθοπλίζω				καθώπλισμαι	
καθοράω					
καίω				κεκαύμαι	
κακολογέω		ἐκακολόγησα			
κακοπαθέω		ἐκακοπάθησα			
κακοποιέω		ἐκακοποίησα			
κακουχέω					
κακόω	κακώσω	ἐκάκωσα			
καλέω	καλέσω	ἐκάλεσα	κέκληκα	κέκλημαι	ἐκλήθην
καλοποιέω					
καλύπτω	καλύψω	ἐκάλυψα		κεκάλυμμαι	
* καμμύω		ἐκάμμυσα			
κάμνω		ἔκαμον			
κάμπτω	κάμψω	ἔκαμψα			
καπηλεύω					
καρποφορέω	καρποφορήσω	ἐκαρποφόρησα			
* καρτερέω		ἐκαρτέρησα			
καταβαίνω	καταβήσομαι	κατέβην	καταβέβηκα		
καταβάλλω					
* καταβαρέω		κατεβάρησα			
καταβαρύνω					
καταβραβεύω					
καταγγέλλω		κατήγγειλα			κατηγγέλην
καταγελάω					
καταγινώσκω					
* κατάγνυμι	κατεάξω	κατέαξα			κατεάγην
καταγράφω					
* κατάγω		κατήγαγον			κατήχθην
* καταγωνίζομαι		κατηγωνισάμην			
* καταδέω		κατέδησα			
καταδικάζω		κατεδίκασα			
* καταδιώκω		κατεδίωξα			
καταδουλόω	καταδουλώσω				
καταδυναστεύω					
καταθεματίζω					
καταισχύνω					κατῃσχύνθην
κατακαίω	κατακαύσω	κατέκαυσα			κατεκαύθην
κατακαλύπτω					
κατακαυχάομαι					
κατάκειμαι					
* κατακλάω		κατέκλασα			
* κατακλείω		κατέκλεισα			
* κατακληρονομέω		κατεκληρονόμησα			
* κατακλίνω		κατέκλινα			κατεκλίθην
* κατακλύζω					κατεκλύσθην
* κατακολουθέω		κατηκολούθησα			

κατακόπτω					
*κατακρημνίζω		κατεκρήμνισα			
κατακρίνω	κατακρινῶ	κατέκρινα		κατακέκριμαι	κατεκρίθην
*κατακύπτω		κατέκυψα			
κατακυριεύω		κατεκυρίευσα			
καταλαλέω					
καταλαμβάνω		κατέλαβον	κατείληφα	κατείλημμαι	κατελήμφθην
καταλέγω					
καταλείπω	καταλείψω	κατέλιπον		καταλέλειμμαι	κατελείφθην
*καταλιθάζω	καταλιθάσω				
καταλλάσσω		κατήλλαξα			κατηλλάγην
καταλύω	καταλύσω	κατέλυσα			κατελύθην
*καταμανθάνω		κατέμαθον			
καταμαρτυρέω					
καταμένω					
καταναλίσκω					
*καταναρκάω	καταναρκήσω	κατενάρκησα			
*κατανεύω		κατένευσα			
κατανοέω		κατενόησα			
*καταντάω		κατήντησα	κατήντηκα		
*κατανύσσομαι					κατενύγην
*καταξιόω					κατηξιώθην
καταπατέω	καταπατήσω	κατεπάτησα			κατεπατήθην
*καταπαύω		κατέπαυσα			
καταπίνω					κατεπόθην
καταπίπτω		κατέπεσον			
*καταπλέω		κατέπλευσα			
καταπονέω					
καταποντίζω					
κατεποντίσθην					
καταράομαι		κατηρασάμην		κατήραμαι	
καταργέω	καταργήσω	κατήργησα	κατήργηκα	κατήργημαι	κατηργήθην
*καταριθμέω				κατηρίθμημαι	
καταρτίζω	καταρτίσω	κατήρτισα		κατήρτισμαι	
*κατασείω		κατέσεισα			
*κατασκάπτω		κατέσκαψα		κατέσκαμμαι	
κατασκευάζω	κατασκευάσω	κατεσκεύασα		κατεσκεύασμαι	κατεσκευάσθην
κατασκηνόω	κατασκηνώσω	κατεσκήνωσα			
κατασκιάζω					
*κατασκοπέω		κατεσκόπησα			
*κατασοφίζομαι		κατεσοφισάμην			
*καταστέλλω		κατέστειλα		κατέσταλμαι	
*καταστρέφω		κατέστρεψα			
*καταστρηνιάω		κατεστρηνίασα			
*καταστρώννυμι					κατεστρώθην
κατασύρω					
*κατασφάζω		κατέσφαξα			
*κατασφραγίζω				κατεσφράγισμαι	
*κατατίθημι		κατέθηκα			
*κατατρέχω		κατέδραμον			
καταφέρω		κατήνεγκα			κατηνέχθην
*καταφεύγω		κατέφυγον			
*καταφθείρω				κατέφθαρμαι	
καταφιλέω		κατεφίλησα			
καταφρονέω	καταφρονήσω	κατεφρόνησα			

* καταχέω		κατέχεα		
καταχράομαι		κατεχρησάμην		
* καταψύχω		κατέψυξα		
κατεξουσιάζω				
κατεργάζομαι		κατειργασάμην	κατείργασμαι	κατειργάσθην
κατέρχομαι		κατῆλθον		
κατεσθίω	καταφάγομαι	κατέφαγον		
* κατευθύνω		κατεύθυνα		
κατευλογέω				
* κατεφίσταμαι		κατεπέστην		
κατέχω		κατέσχον		
κατηγορέω	κατηγορήσω	κατηγόρησα		
κατηχέω		κατήχησα	κατήχημαι	κατηχήθην
* κατιόω			κατίωμαι	
κατισχύω	κατισχύσω	κατίσχυσα		
κατοικέω		κατῴκησα		
* κατοικίζω		κατῴκισα		
κατοπτρίζω				
* καυματίζω		ἐκαυμάτισα		ἐκαυματίσθην
καυσόω				
* καυστηριάζω			κεκαυστηρίασμαι	
καυχάομαι	καυχήσομαι	ἐκαυχησάμην	κεκαύχημαι	
κεῖμαι				
* κείρω		ἔκειρα		
κελεύω		ἐκέλευσα		
* κενόω	κενώσω	ἐκένωσα	κεκένωμαι	ἐκενώθην
* κεράννυμι		ἐκέρασα	κεκέρασμαι	
* κερδαίνω	κερδήσω	ἐκέρδησα		ἐκερδήθην
* κεφαλιόω		ἐκεφαλίωσα		
* κημόω	κημώσω			
κηρύσσω		ἐκήρυξα		ἐκηρύχθην
κιθαρίζω				
κινδυνεύω				
κινέω	κινήσω	ἐκίνησα		ἐκινήθην
* κίχρημι		ἔχρησα		
κλαίω	κλαύσω	ἔκλαυσα		
κλάω		ἔκλασα		
κλείω	κλείσω	ἔκλεισα	κέκλεισμαι	ἐκλείσθην
κλέπτω	κλέψω	ἔκλεψα		
κληρονομέω	κληρονομήσω	ἐκληρονόμησα	κεκληρονόμηκα	
* κληρόω				ἐκληρώθην
κλίνω		ἔκλινα	κέκλικα	
κλυδωνίζομαι				
κνήθω				
κοιμάω			κεκοίμημαι	ἐκοιμήθην
κοινόω		ἐκοίνωσα	κεκοίνωκα	κεκοίνωμαι
κοινωνέω		ἐκοινώνησα		
κολάζω		ἐκόλασα		
κολαφίζω		ἐκολάφισα		
κολλάω				ἐκολλήθην
* κολοβόω		ἐκολόβωσα		ἐκολοβώθην
κολυμβάω				
κομάω				
κομίζω	κομίσω κομιῶ	ἐκόμισα		

* κονιάω				κεκονίαμαι	
* κοπάζω		ἐκόπασα			
κοπιάω		ἐκοπίασα	κεκοπίακα		
κόπτω	κόψω	ἔκοψα			
* κορέννυμι				κεκόρεσμαι	ἐκορέσθην
κοσμέω		ἐκόσμησα		κεκόσμημαι	
κουφίζω					
κράζω	κράξω	ἔκραξα	κέκραγα		
		ἐκέκραξα			
κραταιόω					ἐκραταιώθην
κρατέω	κρατήσω	ἐκράτησα	κεκράτηκα	κεκράτημαι	
κραυγάζω	κραυγάσω	ἐκραύγασα			
κρεμάννυμι		ἐκρέμασα			ἐκρεμάσθην
κρίνω	κρινῶ	ἔκρινα	κέκρικα	κέκριμαι	ἐκρίθην
κρούω		ἔκρουσα			
κρύπτω		ἔκρυψα		κέκρυμμαι	ἐκρύβην
κρυσταλλίζω					
κτάομαι		ἐκτησάμην			
* κτίζω		ἔκτισα		ἔκτισμαι	ἐκτίσθην
* κυκλεύω		ἐκύκλευσα			
κυκλόω		ἐκύκλωσα			ἐκυκλώθην
κυλίω					
* κύπτω		ἔκυψα			
κυριεύω	κυριεύσω	ἐκυρίευσα			
* κυρόω		ἐκύρωσα		κεκύρωμαι	
κωλύω		ἐκώλυσα			ἐκωλύθην
* λαγχάνω		ἔλαχον			
* λακάω		ἐλάκησα			
λακτίζω					
λαλέω	λαλήσω	ἐλάλησα	λελάληκα	λελάλημαι	ἐλαλήθην
λαμβάνω	λήμψομαι	ἔλαβον	εἴληφα		
λάμπω	λάμψω	ἔλαμψα			
λανθάνω		ἔλαθον			
* λατομέω		ἐλατόμησα		λελατόμημαι	
λατρεύω	λατρεύσω	ἐλάτρευσα			
λέγω	ἐρῶ	εἶπον	εἴρηκα	εἴρημαι	ἐρρέθην
		εἶπα			
λείπω					
λειτουργέω		ἐλειτούργησα			
* λευκαίνω		ἐλεύκανα			
λιθάζω		ἐλίθασα			ἐλιθάσθην
λιθοβολέω		ἐλιθοβόλησα			ἐλιθοβολήθην
* λικμάω	λικμήσω				
λογίζομαι		ἐλογισάμην			ἐλογίσθην
λογομαχέω					
λοιδορέω		ἐλοιδόρησα			
* λούω		ἔλουσα		λέλουμαι	
				λέλουσμαι	
λυμαίνομαι					
λυπέω		ἐλύπησα	λελύπηκα		ἐλυπήθην
λυσιτελέω					
λυτρόω					ἐλυτρώθην
λύω		ἔλυσα		λέλυμαι	ἐλύθην
μαγεύω					
* μαθητεύω		ἐμαθήτευσα			ἐμαθητεύθην

μαίνομαι					
μακαρίζω					
μακροθυμέω		ἐμακροθύμησα			
μανθάνω		ἔμαθον	μεμάθηκα		
μαντεύομαι					
* μαραίνω					ἐμαράνθην
μαρτυρέω	μαρτυρήσω	ἐμαρτύρησα	μεμαρτύρηκα	μεμαρτύρημαι	ἐμαρτυρήθην
μαρτύρομαι					
μασάομαι					
μαστιγόω	μαστιγώσω	ἐμαστίγωσα			
μαστίζω					
* ματαιόω					ἐματαιώθην
μάχομαι					
μεγαλύνω					ἐμεγαλύνθην
μεθερμηνεύω					
μεθίστημι		μετέστησα			μετεστάθην
μεθύσκω					ἐμεθύσθην
μεθύω					
μέλει					
μελετάω		ἐμελέτησα			
μέλλω	μελλήσω				
μέμφομαι					
μένω	μενῶ	ἔμεινα	μεμένηκα		
* μερίζω		ἐμέρισα		μεμέρισμαι	ἐμερίσθην
μεριμνάω	μεριμνήσω	ἐμερίμνησα			
* μεσιτεύω		ἐμεσίτευσα			
μεσόω					
* μεστόω				μεμέστωμαι	
μεταβαίνω	μεταβήσομαι	μετέβην	μεταβέβηκα		
μεταβάλλω					
μετάγω					
μεταδίδωμι		μετέδωκα			
* μεταίρω		μετῆρα			
* μετακαλέω	μετακαλέσω	μετεκάλεσα			
μετακινέω					
μεταλαμβάνω		μετέλαβον			
* μεταλλάσσω		μετήλλαξα			
μεταμέλομαι					μετεμελήθην
μεταμορφόω					μετεμορφώθην
μετανοέω	μετανοήσω	μετενόησα			
μεταπέμπω		μετέπεμψα			μετεπέμφθην
* μεταστρέφω		μετέστρεψα			μετεστράφην
μετασχηματίζω	μετασχηματίσω	μετεσχημάτισα			
μετατίθημι		μετέθηκα			μετετέθην
* μετατρέπω					μετετράπην
μετέχω		μετέσχον	μετέσχηκα		
μετεωρίζομαι					
* μετοικίζω	μετοικιῶ	μετῴκισα			
μετρέω		ἐμέτρησα			ἐμετρήθην
μετριοπαθέω					
μηκύνω					
* μηνύω		ἐμήνυσα			ἐμηνύθην
μιαίνω				μεμίαμμαι	ἐμιάνθην
* μίγνυμι		ἔμιξα		μέμιγμαι	
μιμέομαι					

μιμνήσκομαι				μέμνημαι	ἐμνήσθην
μισέω	μισήσω	ἐμίσησα	μεμίσηκα	μεμίσημαι	
* μισθόω		ἐμίσθωσα			
μνημονεύω		ἐμνημόνευσα			
* μνηστεύω				ἐμνήστευμαι	ἐμνηστεύθην
μοιχάω					
μοιχεύω	μοιχεύσω	ἐμοίχευσα			ἐμοιχεύθην
μολύνω		ἐμόλυνα			ἐμολύνθην
* μονόω				μεμόνωμαι	
* μορφόω					ἐμορφώθην
* μοσχοποιέω		ἐμοσχοποίησα			
* μυέω				μεμύημαι	
μυκάομαι					
μυκτηρίζω					
* μυρίζω		ἐμύρισα			
μυωπάζω					
* μωμάομαι		ἐμωμησάμην			ἐμωμήθην
* μωραίνω		ἐμώρανα			ἐμωράνθην
* ναυαγέω		ἐναυάγησα			
* νεκρόω		ἐνέκρωσα		νενέκρωμαι	
νεύω		ἔνευσα			
νήθω					
νηπιάζω					
νηστεύω	νηστεύσω	ἐνήστευσα			
νήφω		ἔνηψα			
νικάω	νικήσω	ἐνίκησα	νενίκηκα		
νίπτω		ἔνιψα			
νοέω		ἐνόησα			
νομίζω		ἐνόμισα			
* νομοθετέω				νενομοθέτημαι	
νοσέω					
νοσφίζω		ἐνόσφισα			
νουθετέω					
* νύσσω		ἔνυξα			
νυστάζω		ἐνύσταξα			
ξενίζω		ἐξένισα			ἐξενίσθην
* ξενοδοχέω		ἐξενοδόχησα			
ξηραίνω		ἐξήρανα		ἐξήραμμαι	ἐξηράνθην
ξυράω	ξυρήσω			ἐξύρημαι	
ὁδεύω					
ὁδηγέω	ὁδηγήσω				
ὁδοιπορέω					
ὀδυνάω					
ὄζω					
>οἶδα	εἰδήσω		οἶδα		
οἰκέω					
οἰκοδεσποτέω					
οἰκοδομέω	οἰκοδομήσω	ᾠκοδόμησα		οἰκοδόμημαι	οἰκοδομήθην
οἰκονομέω					
οἰκτίρω	οἰκτιρήσω				
οἴομαι					
* ὀκνέω		ὤκνησα			
ὀλιγωρέω					
ὀλοθρεύω					
ὀλολύζω					

ὁμείρομαι					
ὁμιλέω		ὡμίλησα			
ὀμνύω		ὤμοσα			
* ὁμοιόω	ὁμοιώσω	ὡμοίωσα			ὡμοιώθην
ὁμολογέω	ὁμολογήσω	ὡμολόγησα			
ὀνειδίζω		ὠνείδισα			
* ὀνίνημι		ὤνησα			
ὀνομάζω		ὠνόμασα			ὠνομάσθην
* ὁπλίζω		ὥπλισα			
ὀπτάνομαι					
ὁράω	ὄψομαι	εἶδον	ἑώρακα		ὤφθην
		εἶδα	ἑόρακα		
		ὤψησα			
ὀργίζω					ὠργίσθην
ὀρέγω					
ὀρθοποδέω					
ὀρθοτομέω					
ὀρθρίζω					
ὁρίζω		ὥρισα		ὥρισμαι	ὡρίσθην
ὀρκίζω					
* ὁρμάω		ὥρμησα			
* ὀρύσσω		ὤρυξα			
* ὀρχέομαι		ὠρχησάμην			
ὀφείλω					
ὀχλέω					
* ὀχλοποιέω		ὠχλοποίησα			
* παγιδεύω		ἐπαγίδευσα			
παιδεύω		ἐπαίδευσα		πεπαίδευμαι	ἐπαιδεύθην
παίζω					
* παίω		ἔπαισα			
παλαιόω			πεπαλαίωκα		ἐπαλαιώθην
παραβαίνω		παρέβην			
* παραβάλλω		παρέβαλον			
* παραβιάζομαι		παρεβιασάμην			
* παραβολεύομαι		παρεβολευσάμην			
παραγγέλλω		παρήγγειλα		παρήγγελμαι	
παραγίνομαι		παρεγενόμην			
παράγω					
παραδειγματίζω					
παραδέχομαι	παραδέξομαι				παρεδέχθην
παραδίδωμι	παραδώσω	παρέδωκα	παραδέδωκα	παραδέδομαι	παρεδόθην
παραζηλόω	παραζηλώσω	παρεζήλωσα			
παραθεωρεώ					
παραινέω					
παραιτέομαι		παρῃτησάμην		παρῄτημαι	
* παρακαθέζομαι					παρεκαθέσθην
παρακαλέω		παρεκάλεσα		παρακέκλημαι	παρεκλήθην
* παρακαλύπτω				παρακεκάλυμμαι	
παράκειμαι					
* παρακολουθέω	παρακολουθήσω	παρηκολούθησα	παρηκολούθηκα		
* παρακούω		παρήκουσα			
* παρακύπτω		παρέκυψα			
παραλαμβάνω	παραλήμψομαι	παρέλαβον			παρελήμφθην
παραλέγομαι					
παραλογίζομαι					

* παραλύω				παραλέλυμαι	
παραμένω	παραμενῶ	παρέμεινα			
παραμυθέομαι		παρεμυθησάμην			
παρανομέω					
* παραπικραίνω		παρεπίκρανα			
* παραπίπτω		παρέπεσον			
* παραπλέω		παρέπλευσα			
παραπορεύομαι					
* παραρρέω					παρερρύην
παρασκευάζω	παρασκευάσω			παρεσκεύασμαι	
* παρατείνω		παρέτεινα			
παρατηρέω		παρετήρησα			
παρατίθημι	παραθήσω	παρέθηκα			
παρατυγχάνω					
παραφέρω		παρήνεγκον			
παραφρονέω					
* παραχειμάζω	παραχειμάσω	παρεχείμασα	παρακεχείμακα		
παρεδρεύω					
πάρειμι	παρέσομαι				
* παρεισάγω	παρεισάξω				
* παρεισδύω		παρεισέδυσα			
* παρεισέρχομαι		παρεισῆλθον			
* παρεισφέρω		παρεισήνεγκα			
* παρεμβάλλω	παρεμβαλῶ				
παρενοχλέω					
παρέρχομαι	παρελεύσομαι	παρῆλθον	παρελήλυθα		
παρέχω	παρέξω	παρέσχον			
* παρίημι		παρῆκα		παρεῖμαι	
παρίστημι	παραστήσω	παρέστησα	παρέστηκα		
		παρέστην			
παροικέω		παρῴκησα			
* παροίχομαι				παρῴχημαι	
παρομοιάζω					
παροξύνω					
παροργίζω	παροργιῶ				
* παροτρύνω		παρώτρυνα			
παρρησιάζομαι		ἐπαρρησιασάμην			
πάσχω		ἔπαθον	πέπονθα		
* πατάσσω	πατάξω	ἐπάταξα			
πατέω	πατήσω				ἐπατήθην
παύω	παύσω	ἔπαυσα		πέπαυμαι	
* παχύνω					ἐπαχύνθην
πεζεύω					
πειθαρχέω		ἐπειθάρχησα			
πείθω	πείσω	ἔπεισα	πέποιθα	πέπεισμαι	ἐπείσθην
πεινάω	πεινάσω	ἐπείνασα			
πειράζω		ἐπείρασα		πεπείρασμαι	ἐπειράσθην
πειράομαι					
* πελεκίζω				πεπελέκισμαι	
πέμπω	πέμψω	ἔπεμψα			ἐπέμφθην
πενθέω	πενθήσω	ἐπένθησα			
περιάγω					
περιαιρέω		περιεῖλον			
* περιάπτω		περιῆψα			
* περιαστράπτω		περιήστραψα			

* περιβάλλω	περιβαλῶ	περιέβαλον		περιβέβλημαι	
περιβλέπω		περιέβλεψα			
* περιδέω				περιδέδεμαι	
περιεργάζομαι					
περιέρχομαι		περιῆλθον			
περιέχω		περιέσχον			
* περιζώννυμι	περιζώσω	περιέζωσα		περιέζωσμαι	
περιΐστημι		περιέστην	περιέστηκα		
περικαλύπτω		περιεκάλυψα		περικεκάλυμμαι	
περίκειμαι					
περικρύβω					
* περικυκλόω	περικυκλώσω				
* περιλάμπω		περιέλαμψα			
περιλείπομαι					
περιμένω					
περιοικέω					
περιπατέω	περιπατήσω	περιεπάτησα			
* περιπείρω		περιέπειρα			
* περιπίπτω		περιέπεσον			
περιποιέω		περιεποίησα			
* περιρήγνυμι		περιέρρηξα			
περισπάω					
περισσεύω		ἐπερίσσευσα			ἐπερισσεύθην
περιτέμνω		περιέτεμον		περιτέτμημαι	περιετμήθην
περιτίθημι		περιέθηκα			
περιτρέπω					
* περιτρέχω		περιέδραμον			
περιφέρω					
περιφρονέω					
περπερεύομαι					
πέτομαι					
* πήγνυμι		ἔπηξα			
* πιάζω		ἐπίασα			ἐπιάσθην
* πιέζω				πεπίεσμαι	
πικραίνω	πικρανῶ				ἐπικράνθην
* πίμπλημι		ἔπλησα			ἐπλήσθην
πίμπρημι					
πίνω	πίομαι	ἔπιον	πέπωκα		
πιπράσκω			πέπρακα	πέπραμαι	ἐπράθην
πίπτω	πεσοῦμαι	ἔπεσον	πέπτωκα		
		ἔπεσα			
πιστεύω	πιστεύσω	ἐπίστευσα	πεπίστευκα	πεπίστευμαι	ἐπιστεύθην
* πιστόω					ἐπιστώθην
πλανάω	πλανήσω	ἐπλάνησα		πεπλάνημαι	ἐπλανήθην
* πλάσσω		ἔπλασα			ἐπλάσθην
πλατύνω				πεπλάτυμμαι	ἐπλατύνθην
* πλέκω		ἔπλεξα			
πλεονάζω		ἐπλεόνασα			
πλεονεκτέω		ἐπλεονέκτησα			ἐπλεονεκτήθην
πλέω					
πληθύνω	πληθυνῶ				ἐπληθύνθην
πληροφορέω		ἐπληροφόρησα		πεπληροφόρημαι	ἐπληροφορήθην
πληρόω	πληρώσω	ἐπλήρωσα		πεπλήρωμαι	ἐπληρώθην
* πλήσσω					ἐπλήγην
πλουτέω		ἐπλούτησα	πεπλούτηκα		

πλουτίζω					ἐπλουτίσθην
πλύνω		ἔπλυνα			
πνέω		ἔπνευσα			
πνίγω		ἔπνιξα			
ποιέω	ποιήσω	ἐποίησα	πεποίηκα	πεποίημαι	
ποιμαίνω	ποιμανῶ	ἐποίμανα			
πολεμέω	πολεμήσω	ἐπολέμησα			
πολιτεύομαι				πεπολίτευμαι	
πορεύομαι	πορεύσομαι			πεπόρευμαι	ἐπορεύθην
πορθέω		ἐπόρθησα			
πορνεύω		ἐπόρνευσα			
ποτίζω		ἐπότισα	πεπότικα		ἐποτίσθην
* πραγματεύομαι		ἐπραγματευσάμην			
πράσσω	πράξω	ἔπραξα	πέπραχα	πέπραγμαι	
πρέπω					
πρεσβεύω					
* πρίζω					ἐπρίσθην
προάγω	πρόαξω	προήγαγον			
* προαιρέω				προῄρημαι	
* προαιτιάομαι		προῃτιασάμην			
* προακούω		προήκουσα			
* προαμαρτάνω			προημάρτηκα		
* προβαίνω		προέβην	προβέβηκα		
* προβάλλω		προέβαλον			
* προβιβάζω					προεβιβάσθην
* προβλέπω		προέβλεψα			
* προγίνομαι			προγέγονα		
προγινώσκω		προέγνων		προέγνωσμαι	
* προγράφω		προέγραψα		προγέγραμμαι	προεγράφην
* προδίδωμι		προέδωκα			
* προελπίζω			προήλπικα		
* προενάρχομαι		προενηρξάμην			
* προεπαγγέλλω		προεπηγγειλάμην		προεπήγγελμαι	
προέρχομαι	προελεύσομαι	προῆλθον			
* προετοιμάζω		προητοίμασα			
* προευαγγελίζομαι		προευηγγελισάμην			
προέχω					
προηγέομαι					
προΐστημι		προέστησα	προέστηκα		
προκαλέω					
* προκαταγγέλλω		προκατήγγειλα			
* προκαταρτίζω		προκατήρτισα			
πρόκειμαι					
* προκηρύσσω		προεκήρυξα			
προκόπτω	προκόψω	προέκοψα			
* προκυρόω				προκεκύρωμαι	
προλαμβάνω		προέλαβον			προελήμφθην
προλέγω		προεῖπον	προείρηκα	προείρημαι	
		προεῖπα			
προμαρτύρομαι					
προμελετάω					
προμεριμνάω					
προνοέω					
προοράω		προεῖδον	προεώρακα		
* προορίζω		προώρισα			προωρίσθην

* προπάσχω		προέπαθον	
προπέμπω		προέπεμψα	προεπέμφθην
* προπορεύομαι	προπορεύσομαι		
* προσαγορεύω			προσηγορεύθην
προσάγω		προσήγαγον	
προσαιτέω			
* προσαναβαίνω		προσανέβην	
* προσαναλίσκω		προσανέλωσα	
προσαναπληρόω		προσανεπλήρωσα	
* προσανατίθημι		προσανέθηκα	
* προσαπειλέω		προσαπείλησα	
* προσδαπανάω		προσεδαπάνησα	
προσδέομαι			
προσδέχομαι		προσεδεξάμην	
προσδοκάω			
προσεάω			
* προσεργάζομαι		προσηργασάμην	
προσέρχομαι		προσῆλθον	προσελήλυθα
προσεύχομαι	προσεύξομαι	προσηυξάμην	
προσέχω			προσέσχηκα
* προσηλόω		προσήλωσα	
προσκαλέω		προσεκάλεσα	προσκέκλημαι
προσκαρτερέω	προσκαρτερήσω		
* προσκληρόω			προσεκληρώθην
* προσκλίνω			προσεκλίθην
* προσκολλάω			προσεκολλήθην
προσκόπτω		προσέκοψα	
* προσκυλίω		προσεκύλισα	
προσκυνέω	προσκυνήσω	προσεκύνησα	
προσλαλέω		προσελάλησα	
προσλαμβάνω		προσέλαβον	
προσμένω		προσέμεινα	
* προσορμίζω			προσωρμίσθην
προσοφείλω			
* προσοχθίζω		προσώχθισα	
* προσπήγνυμι		προσέπηξα	
προσπίπτω		προσέπεσον	
		προσέπεσα	
* προσποιέω		προσεποίησα	
προσπορεύομαι			
* προσρήγνυμι		προσέρηξα	
* προστάσσω		προσέταξα	προστέταγμαι
προστίθημι		προσέθηκα	προσετέθην
προστρέχω		προσέδραμον	
προσφέρω		προσήνεγκα	προσενήνοχα	προσηνέχθην
		προσήνεγκον	
προσφωνέω		προσεφώνησα	
προσψαύω			
προσωπολημπτέω			
* προτείνω		προέτεινα	
* προτίθημι		προέθηκα	
* προτρέπω		προέτρεψα	
* προτρέχω		προέδραμον	
προϋπάρχω			
προφέρω			

προφητεύω	προφηρεύσω	ἐπροφήτευσα		
* προφθάνω		προέφθασα		
* προχειρίζομαι		προεχειρισάμην	προκέχειρσμαι	
* προχειροτονέω			προκεχειροτόνημαι	
πρωτεύω				
πταίω		ἔπταισα		
* πτοέω				ἐπτοήθην
πτύρω				
* πτύσσω		ἔπτυξα		
* πτύω		ἔπτυσα		
* πτωχεύω		ἐπτώχευσα		
πυκτεύω				
πυνθάνομαι		ἐπυθόμην		
πυρέσσω				
πυρόω			πεπύρωμαι	ἐπυρώθην
πυρράζω				
πωλέω		ἐπώλησα		
* πωρόω		ἐπώρωσα	πεπώρωμαι	ἐπωρώθην
ῥαβδίζω				ἐραβδίσθην
ῥαντίζω		ἐράντισα	ῥεράντισμαι	
ῥαπίζω		ἐράπισα		
* ῥέω	ῥεύσω			
ῥήγνυμι	ῥήξω	ἔρρηξα		
* ῥιζόω			ἐρρίζωμαι	
ῥιπίζω				
ῥίπτω		ἔρριψα	ἔρριμμαι	
ῥύομαι	ῥύσομαι	ἐρρυσάμην		ἐρρύσθην
* ῥυπαίνω				ἐρρυπάνθην
* ῥώννυμι			ἔρρωμαι	
σαίνω				
σαλεύω		ἐσάλευσα	σεσάλευμαι	ἐσαλεύθην
σαλπίζω	σαλπίσω	ἐσάλπισα		
σαρόω			σεσάρωμαι	
σβέννυμι	σβέσω	ἔσβεσα		
* σεβάζομαι				ἐσεβάσθην
σέβω				
σείω	σείσω			ἐσείσθην
σεληνιάζομαι				
σημαίνω		ἐσήμανα		
σημειόω				
* σήπω			σέσηπα	
* σθενόω	σθενώσω			
σιγάω		ἐσίγησα	σεσίμημαι	
* σινιάζω		ἐσινίασα		
σιωπάω	σιωπήσω	ἐσιώπησα		
σκανδαλίζω		ἐσκανδάλισα		ἐσκανδαλίσθην
σκάπτω	σκάψω	ἔσκαψα		
σκηνόω	σκηνώσω	ἐσκήνωσα		
* σκιρτάω		ἐσκίρτησα		
σκληρύνω		ἐσκλήρυνα		ἐσκληρύνθην
σκοπέω				
σκορπίζω		ἐσκόρπισα		ἐσκορπίσθην
* σκοτίζω				ἐσκοτίσθην
* σκοτόω			ἐσκότωμαι	ἐσκοτώθην
σκύλλω			ἔσκυλμαι	

* σμυρνίζω		ἐσμύρνισμαι	
* σοφίζω	ἐσόφισα	σεσόφισμαι	
σπαράσσω	ἐσπάραξα		
* σπαργανόω	ἐσπαργάνωσα	ἐσπαργάνωμαι	
σπαταλάω	ἐσπατάλησα		
* σπάω	ἔσπασα		
σπείρω	ἔσπειρα	ἔσπαρμαι	ἐσπάρην
σπένδω			
σπεύδω	ἔσπευσα		
σπιλόω		ἐσπίλωμαι	
σπλαγχνίζομαι			ἐσπλαγχνίσθην
σπουδάζω	σπουδάσω	ἐσπούδασα	
σταυρόω	σταυρώσω	ἐσταύρωσα	ἐσταύρωμαι	ἐσταυρώθην
στέγω			
στέλλω			
στενάζω	ἐστέναξα		
στενοχωρέω			
στερεόω	ἐστερέωσα		ἐστερεώθην
στεφανόω	ἐστεφάνωσα	ἐστεφάνωμαι	
στήκω	ἔστηκα		
* στηρίζω	στηρίξω	ἐστήριξα	ἐστήριγμαι	ἐστηρίχθην
		ἐστήρισα		
στίλβω			
στοιχέω	στοιχήσω		
στρατεύομαι			
* στρατολογέω	ἐστρατολόγησα		
στρεβλόω			
στρέφω	ἔστρεψα		ἐστράφην
* στρηνιάω	ἐστρηνίασα		
στρωννύω	ἔστρωσα	ἔστρωμαι	
στυγνάζω	ἐστύγνασα		
συγκάθημαι			
* συγκαθίζω	συνεκάθισα		
* συγκακοπαθέω	συνεκακοπάθησα		
συγκακουχέομαι			
συγκαλέω	συνεκάλεσα		
* συγκαλύπτω		συγκεκάλυμμαι	
* συγκάμπτω	συνέκαμψα		
* συγκαταβαίνω	συγκατέβην		
συγκατατίθημι			
* συγκαταψηφίζομαι			συγκατεψηφίσθην
* συγκεράννυμι	συνεκέρασα	συγκεκέρασμαι	
* συγκινέω	συνεκίνησα		
* συγκλείω	συνέκλεισα		
συγκοινωνέω	συνεκοινώνησα		
* συγκομίζω	συνεκόμισα		
συγκρίνω	συνέκρινα		
συγκύπτω			
συγχαίρω			συνεχάρην
συγχέω		συγκέχυμαι	συνεχύθην
συγχράομαι			
συζάω	συζήσω		
* συζεύγνυμι	συνέζευξα		
συζητέω			
* συζωοποιέω	συνεζωοποίησα		

* συκοφαντέω		ἐσυκοφάντησα		
συλαγωγέω				
* συλάω		ἐσύλησα		
συλλαλέω		συνελάλησα		
συλλαμβάνω	συλλήμψομαι	συνέλαβον	συνείληφα	συνελήμφθην
συλλέγω	συλλέξω	συνέλεξα		
* συλλογίζομαι		συνελογισάμην		
συλλυπέω				
συμβαίνω		συνέβην	συμβέβηκα	
συμβάλλω		συνέβαλον		
* συμβασιλεύω	συμβασιλεύσω	συνεβασίλευσα		
συμβιβάζω	συμβιβάσω	συνεβίβασα		συνεβιβάσθην
συμβουλεύω		συνεβούλευσα		
συμμαρτυρέω				
συμμερίζω				
συμμορφίζω				
* συμπαθέω		συνεπάθησα		
* συμπαραγίνομαι		συμπαρεγενόμην		
* συμπαρακαλέω				συμπαρεκλήθην
συμπαραλαμβάνω		συμπαρέλαβον		
συμπάρειμι				
συμπάσχω				
* συμπέμπω		συνέπεμψα		
* συμπεριλαμβάνω		συμπεριέλαβον		
* συμπίνω		συνέπιον		
* συμπίπτω		συνέπεσον		
συμπληρόω				
συμπνίγω		συνέπνιξα		
συμπορεύομαι				
συμφέρω		συνήνεγκα		
σύμφημι				
* συμφύω				συνεφύην
συμφωνέω	συμφωνήσω	συνεφώνησα		συνεφωνήθην
* συμψηφίζω		συνεψήφισα		
συνάγω	συνάξω	συνήγαγον	συνῆγμαι	συνήχθην
* συναγωνίζομαι		συνηγωνισάμην		
συναθλέω		συνήθλησα		
* συναθροίζω		συνήθροισα	συνήθροισμαι	
συναίρω		συνῆρα		
συνακολουθέω		συνηκολούθησα		
συναλίζω				
συναλλάσσω				
* συναναβαίνω		συνανέβην		
συνανάκειμαι				
συναναμίγνυμι				
* συναναπαύομαι		συνανεπαυσάμην		
* συναντάω	συναντήσω	συνήντησα		
συναντιλαμβάνομαι		συναντελαβόμην		
συναπάγω				συναπήχθην
* συναποθνήσκω		συναπέθανον		
* συναπόλλυμι		συναπώλεσα		
* συναποστέλλω		συναπέστειλα		
συναρμολογέω				
* συναρπάζω		συνήρπασα	συνήρπακα	συνηρπάσθην
συναυξάνω				

* συνδέω			συνδέδεμαι	
* συνδοξάζω				συνεδοξάσθην
* συνεγείρω		συνήγειρα		συνηγέρθην
σύνειμι				
σύνειμι				
* συνεισέρχομαι		συνεισῆλθον		
συνεπιμαρτυρέω				
* συνεπιτίθημι		συνεπέθηκα		
συνέπομαι				
συνεργέω				
συνέρχομαι		συνῆλθον	συνελήλυθα	
συνεσθίω		συνέφαγον		
συνευδοκέω				
συνευωχέομαι				
* συνεφίστημι		συνεπέστην		
συνέχω	συνέξω	συνέσχον		
συνήδομαι				
* συνθάπτω				συνετάφην
* συνθλάω				συνεθλάσθην
συνθλίβω				
συνθρύπτω				
συνίημι	συνήσω	συνῆκα		
συνίστημι		συνέστησα	συνέστηκα	
συνοδεύω				
>σύνοιδα			σύνοιδα	
συνοικέω				
συνοικοδομέω				
συνομιλέω				
συνομορέω				
* συνοράω		συνεῖδον		
* συντάσσω		συνέταξα		
συντελέω	συντελέσω	συνετέλεσα		συνετελέσθην
συντέμνω				
συντηρέω				
* συντίθημι		συνέθηκα		συντέθειμαι
συντρέχω		συνέδραμον		
συντρίβω	συντρίψω	συνέτριψα		συντέτριμμαι	συνετρίβην
* συντυγχάνω		συνέτυχον		
* συνυποκρίνομαι				συνυπεκρίθην
συνυπουργέω				
συνωδίνω				
σύρω				
* συσπαράσσω		συνεσπάραξα		
* συσταυρόω			συνεσταύρωμαι	συνεσταυρώθην
* συστέλλω		συνέστειλα		συνέσταλμαι
συστενάζω				
συστοιχέω				
συστρέφω		συνέστρεψα		
συσχηματίζω				
* σφάζω	σφάξω	ἔσφαξα		ἔσφαγμαι	ἐσφάγην
* σφραγίζω		ἐσφράγισα		ἐσφράγισμαι	ἐσφραγίσθην
σχίζω	σχίσω	ἔσχισα			ἐσχίσθην
σχολάζω		ἐσχόλασα		
σῴζω	σώσω	ἔσωσα	σέσωκα	σέσωσμαι	ἐσώθην
				σέσωμαι	

* σωρεύω	σωρεύσω			σεσώρευμαι	
σωφρονέω		ἐσωφρόνησα			
σωφρονίζω					
* ταλαιπωρέω		ἐταλαιπώρησα			
ταπεινόω	ταπεινώσω	ἐταπείνωσα			ἐταπεινώθην
ταράσσω		ἐτάραξα		τετάραγμαι	ἐταράχθην
* ταρταρόω		ἐταρτάρωσα			
τάσσω		ἔταξα		τέταγμαι	
τεκνογονέω					
* τεκνοτροφέω		ἐτεκνοτρόφησα			
τελειόω		ἐτελείωσα	τετελείωκα	τετελείωμαι	ἐτελειώθην
τελεσφορέω					
τελευτάω		ἐτελεύτησα	τετελεύτηκα		
τελέω		ἐτέλεσα	τετέλεκα	τετέλεσμαι	ἐτελέσθην
τετρααρχέω					
* τεφρόω		ἐτέφρωσα			
τήκω					
τηρέω	τηρήσω	ἐτήρησα	τετήρηκα	τετήρημαι	ἐτηρήθην
τίθημι	θήσω	ἔθηκα	τέθεικα	τέθειμαι	ἐτέθην
τίκτω	τέξομαι	ἔτεκον			ἐτέχθην
τίλλω					
τιμάω	τιμήσω	ἐτίμησα		τετίμημαι	
τιμωρέω					ἐτιμωρήθην
* τίνω	τίσω				
τολμάω	τολμήσω	ἐτόλμησα			
* τραυματίζω		ἐτραυμάτισα		τετραυμάτισμαι	
* τραχηλίζω				τετραχήλισμαι	
τρέμω					
τρέφω		ἔθρεψα		τέθραμμαι	
τρέχω		ἔδραμον			
τρίζω					
* τροποφορέω		ἐτροποφόρησα			
* τρυγάω		ἐτρύγησα			
τρυφάω		ἐτρύφησα			
τρώγω					
τυγχάνω		ἔτυχον	τέτυχα		
* τυμπανίζω					ἐτυμπανίσθην
τύπτω					
* τυφλόω		ἐτύφλωσα	τετύφλωκα		
* τυφόω				τετύφωμαι	ἐτυφώθην
τύφω					
ὑβρίζω		ὕβρισα			ὑβρίσθην
ὑγιαίνω					
ὑδροποτέω					
ὑμνέω	ὑμνήσω	ὕμνησα			
ὑπάγω					
ὑπακούω		ὑπήκουσα			
* ὑπαντάω		ὑπήντησα			
ὑπάρχω					
ὑπείκω					
ὑπεραίρω					
ὑπεραυξάνω					
ὑπερβαίνω					
ὑπερβάλλω					
ὑπερεκτείνω					

ὑπερεκχύννω				
ὑπερεντυγχάνω				
ὑπερέχω				
ὑπερνικάω				
* *ὑπεροράω*		*ὑπερεῖδον*		
ὑπερπερισσεύω		*ὑπερεπερίσσευσα*		
* *ὑπερπλεονάζω*		*ὑπερεπλεόνασα*		
* *ὑπερυψόω*		*ὑπερύψωσα*		
ὑπερφρονέω				
ὑπέχω				
ὑπηρετέω		*ὑπηρέτησα*		
* *ὑποβάλλω*		*ὑπέβαλον*		
* *ὑποδείκνυμι*	*ὑποδείξω*	*ὑπέδειξα*		
* *ὑποδέχομαι*		*ὑπεδεξάμην*	*ὑποδέδεγμαι*	
* *ὑποδέω*		*ὑπέδησα*	*ὑποδέδεμαι*	
ὑποζώννυμι				
ὑποκρίνομαι				
ὑπολαμβάνω		*ὑπέλαβον*		
* *ὑπολείπω*				*ὑπελείφθην*
ὑπολιμπάνω				
ὑπομένω	*ὑπομενῶ*	*ὑπέμεινα*	*ὑπομεμένηκα*	
ὑπομιμνῄσκω	*ὑπομνήσω*	*ὑπέμνησα*		*ὑπεμνήσθην*
ὑπονοέω				
* *ὑποπλέω*		*ὑπέπλευσα*		
* *ὑποπνέω*		*ὑπέπνευσα*		
ὑποστέλλω		*ὑπέστειλα*		
ὑποστρέφω	*ὑποστρέψω*	*ὑπέστρεψα*		
ὑποστρωννύω				
ὑποτάσσω		*ὑπέταξα*	*ὑποτέταγμαι*	*ὑπετάγην*
ὑποτίθημι		*ὑπέθηκα*		
* *ὑποτρέχω*		*ὑπέδραμον*		
ὑποφέρω		*ὑπήνεγκα*		
ὑποχωρέω		*ὑπεχώρησα*		
ὑπωπιάζω				
ὑστερέω		*ὑστέρησα*	*ὑστέρηκα*	*ὑστερήθην*
ὑψηλοφρονέω				
ὑψόω	*ὑψώσω*	*ὕψωσα*		*ὑψώθην*
φαίνω	*ἐφανῶ*	*ἔφανα*		*ἐφάνην*
φανερόω	*φανερώσω*	*ἐφανέρωσα*	*πεφανέρωμαι*	*ἐφανερώθην*
φαντάζω				
φάσκω				
φείδομαι	*φείσομαι*	*ἐφεισάμην*		
φέρω	*οἴσω*	*ἤνεγκα*		*ἠνέχθην*
φεύγω	*φεύξομαι*	*ἔφυγον*		
φημί				
* *φθάνω*		*ἔφθασα*		
φθέγγομαι		*ἐφθεγξάμην*		
φθείρω		*ἔφθειρα*		*ἐφθάρην*
φθονέω				
φιλέω		*ἐφίλησα*	*πεφίληκα*	
φιλοπρωτεύω				
φιλοτιμέομαι				
φιμόω	*φιμώσω*	*ἐφίμωσα*	*πεφίμωμαι*	*ἐφιμώθην*
φλογίζω				
φλυαρέω				

φοβέω				ἐφοβήθην
φονεύω	φονεύσω	ἐφόνευσα		
φορέω	φορέσω	ἐφόρεσα		
φορτίζω			πεφόρτισμαι	
* φραγελλόω		ἐφραγέλλωσα		
* φράζω		ἔφρασα		
* φράσσω		ἔφραξα		ἐφράγην
φρεναπατάω				
φρίσσω				
φρονέω	φρονήσω			
φροντίζω				
φρουρέω	φρουρήσω			
* φρυάσσω		ἐφρύαξα		
φυλακίζω				
φυλάσσω	φυλάξω	ἐφύλαξα		
φυσιόω			πεφυσίωμαι	ἐφυσιώθην
φυτεύω		ἐφύτευσα	πεφύτευμαι	ἐφυτεύθην
φύω				ἐφύην
φωνέω	φωνήσω	ἐφώνησα		ἐφωνήθην
φωτίζω	φωτίσω	ἐφώτισα	πεφώτισμαι	ἐφωτίσθην
χαίρω	χαρήσομαι			ἐχάρην
χαλάω	χαλάσω	ἐχάλασα		ἐχαλάσθην
χαλιναγωγέω		ἐχαλιναγώγησα		
χαρίζομαι	χαρίσομαι	ἐχαρισάμην	κεχάρισμαι	ἐχαρίσθην
* χαριτόω		ἐχαρίτωσα	κεχαρίτωμαι	
χειμάζω				
χειραγωγέω				
* χειροτονέω		ἐχειροτόνησα		ἐχειροτονήθην
χλευάζω				
χολάω				
χορηγέω	χορηγήσω			
χορτάζω		ἐχόρτασα		ἐχορτάσθην
χράομαι		ἐχρησάμην	κέχρημαι	
χρή				
χρήζω				
χρηματίζω	χρηματίσω	ἐχρημάτισα	κεχρημάτισμαι	ἐχρηματίσθην
χρηστεύομαι				
* χρίω		ἔχρισα		
χρονίζω	χρονίσω			
* χρονοτριβέω		ἐχρονοτρίβησα		
* χρυσόω			κεχρύσωμαι	
χωρέω		ἐχώρησα		
χωρίζω	χωρίσω	ἐχώρισα	κεχώρισμαι	ἐχωρίσθην
ψάλλω	ψαλῶ			
ψεύδομαι		ἐψευσάμην		
ψευδομαρτυρέω	ψευδομαρτυρήσω	ἐψευδομαρτύρησα		
ψηλαφάω		ἐψηλάφησα		
ψηφίζω		ἐψήφισα		
* ψύχω				ἐψύγην
ψωμίζω		ἐψώμισα		
ψώχω				
ὠδίνω				
* ὠνέομαι		ὠνησάμην		
ὠρύομαι				
ὠφελέω	ὠφελήσω	ὠφέλησα		ὠφελήθην

Section Four

Proper Words

The vocabulary list in this section contains all the proper words used in the NT. Because of the complex nature of these words, the organization of such a list requires some arbitrary decisions. Most proper words fall naturally into the categories of persons, places, and things. However, others are more difficult to classify.

The subsection entitled "Names of Persons" includes the names of human persons, deities, and the titles associated with each., e.g., Φαραώ, Χριστός, Μεσσίας, and Σαβαώθ. The place names that form part of the names of persons, e.g., Μαγδαληνή, appear in this subsection. Also found here are the names of the twelve sons of Jacob, even though in a few instances they are used to identify places.

The second subsection, "Names of Places," contains the names of countries, regions, cities, towns, geographical features and phenomena, and buildings. It also includes the proper words for languages and the inhabitants of particular places, as well as the corresponding proper adjectives and adverbs. The words that relate to Ἰουδαία, i.e., Ἰουδαϊκός, Ἰουδαϊκῶς, and Ἰουδαῖος, are found in this part of the list. However, the word Ἰουδαισμός, the name of a religion, is included in the next part.

The final subsection, "Other Proper Words," includes the names of religious, philosophical, political, and social groups and the words used to describe their members. This part also contains some miscellaneous proper words, such as Ἀσιάρχης and Χερούβ.

The following contains information about alternate forms of certain proper words.

Γόμορρα, ων, τά	The form Γόμορρα, ας, ἡ also occurs.
Πέργαμος	The form Πέργαμον, ου, τό is also possible.
Σολομών	The form Σολομῶν, ῶντος, ὁ also occurs.

Names of Persons

Ἀαρών, ὁ	(5)	Aaron
Ἀβαδδών, ὁ	(1)	Abaddon
Ἄβελ, ὁ	(4)	Abel
Ἀβιά, ὁ	(3)	Abijah
Ἀβιαθάρ, ὁ	(1)	Abiathar
Ἀβιούδ, ὁ	(2)	Abiud
Ἀβραάμ, ὁ	(73)	Abraham
Ἄγαβος, ου, ὁ	(2)	Agabus
Ἀγάρ, ἡ	(2)	Hagar
Ἀγρίππας, α, ὁ	(11)	Agrippa

Ἀδάμ, ὁ	(9)	Adam
Ἀδδί, ὁ	(1)	Addi
Ἀδμίν, ὁ	(1)	Admin
Ἀζώρ, ὁ	(2)	Azor
Αἰνέας, ου, ὁ	(2)	Aeneas
Ἀκύλας, ὁ	(6)	Aquila
Ἀλέξανδρος, ου, ὁ	(6)	Alexander
Ἀλφαῖος, ου, ὁ	(5)	Alphaeus
Ἀμιναδάβ, ὁ	(3)	Amminadab
Ἀμπλιᾶτος, ου, ὁ	(1)	Ampliatus
Ἀμώς, ὁ	(3)	Amos
Ἀνανίας, ου, ὁ	(11)	Ananias
Ἀνδρέας, ου, ὁ	(13)	Andrew
Ἀνδρόνικος, ου, ὁ	(1)	Andronicus
Ἄννα, ας, ἡ	(1)	Anna
Ἄννας, α, ὁ	(4)	Annas
Ἀντιπᾶς, ᾶ, ὁ	(1)	Antipas
Ἀπελλῆς, οῦ, ὁ	(1)	Apelles
Ἀπολλύων, ονος, ὁ	(1)	Apollyon, Destroyer
Ἀπολλῶς, ῶ, ὁ	(10)	Apollos
Ἀπφία, ας, ἡ	(1)	Apphia
Ἀράμ, ὁ	(2)	Aram
Ἀρέτας, α, ὁ	(1)	Aretas
Ἀρίσταρχος, ου, ὁ	(5)	Aristarchus
Ἀριστόβουλος, ου, ὁ	(1)	Aristobulus
Ἀρνί, ὁ	(1)	Arni
Ἀρτεμᾶς, ᾶ, ὁ	(1)	Artemas
Ἄρτεμις, ιδος, ἡ	(5)	Artemis
Ἀρφαξάδ, ὁ	(1)	Arphaxad
Ἀρχέλαος, ου, ὁ	(1)	Archelaus
Ἄρχιππος, ου, ὁ	(2)	Archippus
Ἀσάφ	(2)	Asaph
Ἀσήρ, ὁ	(2)	Asher
Ἀσύγκριτος, ου, ὁ	(1)	Asyncritus
Αὐγοῦστος, ου, ὁ	(1)	Augustus
Ἀχάζ, ὁ	(2)	Ahaz
Ἀχαϊκός, οῦ, ὁ	(1)	Achaicus
Ἀχίμ, ὁ	(2)	Achim
Βάαλ, ὁ	(1)	Baal
Βαλαάμ, ὁ	(3)	Balaam
Βαλάκ, ὁ	(1)	Balak
Βαραββᾶς, ᾶ, ὁ	(11)	Barabbas
Βαράκ, ὁ	(1)	Barak
Βαραχίας, ου, ὁ	(1)	Barachiah
Βαρθολομαῖος, ου, ὁ	(4)	Bartholomew
Βαριησοῦς, οῦ, ὁ	(1)	Bar-Jesus
Βαριωνᾶ, ὁ	(1)	Bar-Jona
Βαρναβᾶς, ᾶ, ὁ	(28)	Barnabas
Βαρσαββᾶς, ᾶ, ὁ	(2)	Barsabbas
Βαρτιμαῖος, ου, ὁ	(1)	Bartimaeus

Βεελζεβούλ, ὁ	(7)	Beelzebub
Βελιάρ, ὁ	(1)	Belial
Βενιαμίν, ὁ	(4)	Benjamin
Βερνίκη, ης, ἡ	(3)	Bernice
Βλάστος, ου, ὁ	(1)	Blastus
Βοανηργές	(1)	Boanerges
Βόες, ὁ	(2)	Boaz
Βόος, ὁ	(1)	Boaz
Βοσόρ, ὁ	(1)	Bosor
Γαβριήλ, ὁ	(2)	Gabriel
Γάδ, ὁ	(1)	Gad
Γάϊος, ου, ὁ	(5)	Gaius
Γαλλίων, ωνος, ὁ	(3)	Gallio
Γαμαλιήλ, ὁ	(2)	Gamaliel
Γεδεών, ὁ	(1)	Gidcon
Γώγ, ὁ	(1)	Gog
Δάμαρις, ιδος, ἡ	(1)	Damaris
Δανιήλ, ὁ	(1)	Daniel
Δαυίδ, ὁ	(59)	David
Δημᾶς, ᾶ, ὁ	(3)	Demas
Δημήτριος, ου ὁ	(3)	Demetrius
Δίδυμος, ου, ὁ	(3)	Didymus
Διονύσιος, ου, ὁ	(1)	Dionysius
Διόσκουροι, ων, οἱ	(1)	the Dioscuri (twin sons of Zeus)
Διοτρέφης, ους, ὁ	(1)	Diotrephes
Δορκάς, άδος, ἡ	(2)	Dorcas
Δρούσιλλα, ης, ἡ	(1)	Drusilla
Ἔβερ, ὁ	(1)	Eber
Ἐζεκίας, ου, ὁ	(2)	Hezekiah
Ἐλεάζαρ, ὁ	(2)	Eleazar
Ἐλιακίμ, ὁ	(3)	Eliakim
Ἐλιέζερ, ὁ	(1)	Eliezer
Ἐλιούδ, ὁ	(2)	Eliud
Ἐλισάβετ, ἡ	(9)	Elizabeth
Ἐλισαῖος, ου, ὁ	(1)	Elisha
Ἐλμαδάμ, ὁ	(1)	Elmadam
Ἐλύμας, α, ὁ	(1)	Elymas
Ἐμμανουήλ, ὁ	(1)	Emmanuel
Ἐμμώρ, ὁ	(1)	Hamor
Ἐνώς, ὁ	(1)	Enos
Ἐνώχ, ὁ	(3)	Enoch
Ἐπαίνετος, ου, ὁ	(1)	Epaenetus
Ἐπαφρᾶς, ᾶ, ὁ	(3)	Epaphras
Ἐπαφρόδιτος, ου, ὁ	(2)	Epaphraditus
Ἔραστος, ου, ὁ	(3)	Erastus
Ἑρμᾶς, ᾶ, ὁ	(1)	Hermas
Ἑρμῆς, οῦ, ὁ	(2)	Hermes
Ἑρμογένης, ους, ὁ	(1)	Hermogenes
Ἐσλί, ὁ	(1)	Esli
Ἑσρώμ, ὁ	(3)	Hezron

Εὔα, ας, ἡ	(2)	Eve
Εὔβουλος, ου, ὁ	(1)	Eubulus
Εὐνίκη, ης, ἡ	(1)	Eunice
Εὐοδία, ας, ἡ	(1)	Euodia
Εὔτυχος, ου, ὁ	(1)	Eutychus
Ζαβουλών, ὁ	(3)	Zebulun
Ζακχαῖος, ου, ὁ	(3)	Zacchaeus
Ζάρα, ὁ	(1)	Zerah
Ζαχαρίας, ου, ὁ	(11)	Zechariah
Ζεβεδαῖος, ου, ὁ	(12)	Zebedee
Ζεύς, Διός, ὁ	(2)	Zeus
Ζηνᾶς, ὁ	(1)	Zenas
Ζοροβαβέλ, ὁ	(3)	Zerubbabel
Ἠλί, ὁ	(1)	Heli
Ἠλίας, ου, ὁ	(29)	Elijah
Ἤρ, ὁ	(1)	Er
Ἡρῴδης, ου, ὁ	(43)	Herod
Ἡρῳδιάς, άδος, ἡ	(6)	Herodias
Ἡρῳδίων, ωνος, ὁ	(1)	Herodion
Ἠσαΐας, ου, ὁ	(22)	Isaiah
Ἠσαῦ, ὁ	(3)	Esau
Θαδδαῖος, ου, ὁ	(2)	Thaddaeus
Θαμάρ, ἡ	(1)	Tamar
Θάρα, ὁ	(1)	Terah
Θεόφιλος, ου, ὁ	(2)	Theophilus
Θευδᾶς, ᾶ, ὁ	(1)	Theudas
Θωμᾶς, ᾶ, ὁ	(11)	Thomas
Ἰάϊρος, ου, ὁ	(2)	Jairus
Ἰακώβ, ὁ	(27)	Jacob
Ἰάκωβος, ου, ὁ	(42)	James
Ἰαμβρῆς, ὁ	(1)	Jambres
Ἰανναί, ὁ	(1)	Jannai
Ἰάννης, ὁ	(1)	Jannes
Ἰάρετ, ὁ	(1)	Jared
Ἰάσων, ονος, ὁ	(5)	Jason
Ἰεζάβελ, ἡ	(1)	Jezebel
Ἰερεμίας, ου, ὁ	(3)	Jeremiah
Ἰεσσαί, ὁ	(5)	Jesse
Ἰεφθάε, ὁ	(1)	Jephthah
Ἰεχονίας, ου, ὁ	(2)	Jechoniah
Ἰησοῦς, οῦ, ὁ	(917)	Jesus, Joshua
Ἰούδας, α, ὁ	(44)	Judah, Judas
Ἰουλία, ας, ἡ	(1)	Julia
Ἰούλιος, ου, ὁ	(2)	Julius
Ἰουνιᾶς, ᾶ, ὁ	(1)	Junias
Ἰοῦστος, ου, ὁ	(3)	Justus
Ἰσαάκ, ὁ	(20)	Isaac
Ἰσκαριώθ, ὁ	(3)	Iscariot
Ἰσκαριώτης, ου, ὁ	(8)	Iscariot
Ἰσσαχάρ, ὁ	(1)	Issachar

Ἰωαθάμ, ὁ	(2)	Jotham
Ἰωανάν, ὁ	(1)	Joanan
Ἰωάννα, ας, ἡ	(2)	Joanna
Ἰωάννης, ου, ὁ	(135)	John
Ἰώβ, ὁ	(1)	Job
Ἰωβήδ, ὁ	(3)	Obed
Ἰωδά, ὁ	(1)	Joda
Ἰωήλ, ὁ	(1)	Joel
Ἰωνάμ, ὁ	(1)	Jonam
Ἰωνᾶς, ᾶ, ὁ	(9)	Jonah
Ἰωράμ, ὁ	(2)	Joram
Ἰωρίμ, ὁ	(1)	Jorim
Ἰωσαφάτ, ὁ	(2)	Jehoshaphat
Ἰωσῆς, ῆτος, ὁ	(3)	Joses
Ἰωσήφ, ὁ	(35)	Joseph
Ἰωσήχ, ὁ	(1)	Josech
Ἰωσίας, ου, ὁ	(2)	Josiah
Καϊάφας, α, ὁ	(9)	Caiaphas
Κάϊν, ὁ	(3)	Cain
Καϊνάμ, ὁ	(2)	Cainan
Καῖσαρ, αρος, ὁ	(29)	Caesar, emperor
Κανδάκη, ης, ἡ	(1)	Candace
Κάρπος, ου, ὁ	(1)	Carpus
Κηφᾶς, ᾶ, ὁ	(9)	Cephas
Κίς, ὁ	(1)	Kish
Κλαυδία, ας, ἡ	(1)	Claudia
Κλαύδιος, ου, ὁ	(3)	Claudius
Κλεοπᾶς, ᾶ, ὁ	(1)	Cleopas
Κλήμης, εντος, ὁ	(1)	Clement
Κλωπᾶς, ᾶ, ὁ	(1)	Clopas
Κόρε, ὁ	(1)	Korah
Κορνήλιος, ου, ὁ	(8)	Cornelius
Κούαρτος, ου, ὁ	(1)	Quartus
Κρήσκης, εντος, ὁ	(1)	Crescens
Κρίσπος, ου, ὁ	(2)	Crispus
Κυρήνιος, ου, ὁ	(1)	Quirinius
Κωσάμ, ὁ	(1)	Cosam
Λάζαρος, ου, ὁ	(15)	Lazarus
Λάμεχ, ὁ	(1)	Lamech
Λευί, ὁ	(2)	Levi
Λευίς, Λευί, ὁ	(6)	Levi
Λίνος, ου, ὁ	(1)	Linus
Λουκᾶς, ᾶ, ὁ	(3)	Luke
Λούκιος, ου, ὁ	(2)	Lucius
Λυδία, ας, ἡ	(2)	Lydia
Λυσανίας, ου, ὁ	(1)	Lysanias
Λυσίας, ου, ὁ	(2)	Lysias
Λωΐς, ΐδος, ἡ	(1)	Lois
Λώτ, ὁ	(4)	Lot
Μάαθ, ὁ	(1)	Maath

Μαγδαληνή, ῆς, ἡ	(12)	Magdalene
Μαγώγ, ὁ	(1)	Magog
Μαθθαῖος, ου, ὁ	(5)	Matthew
Μαθθάτ, ὁ	(2)	Matthat
Μαθθίας, ου, ὁ	(2)	Matthias
Μαθουσαλά, ὁ	(1)	Methuselah
Μαλελεήλ, ὁ	(1)	Maleleel
Μάλχος, ου, ὁ	(1)	Malchus
Μαναήν, ὁ	(1)	Manaen
Μανασσῆς, ῆ, ὁ	(3)	Manasseh
Μάρθα, ας, ἡ	(13)	Martha
Μαρία, ας, ἡ	(27)	Mary
Μαριάμ, ἡ	(27)	Mary
Μᾶρκος, ου, ὁ	(8)	Mark
Ματθάν, ὁ	(2)	Matthan
Ματταθά, ὁ	(1)	Mattatha
Ματταθίας, ου, ὁ	(2)	Mattathias
Μελεά, ὁ	(1)	Melea
Μελχί, ὁ	(2)	Melchi
Μελχισέδεκ, ὁ	(8)	Melchizedek
Μεννά, ὁ	(1)	Menna
Μεσσίας, ου, ὁ	(2)	Messiah
Μιχαήλ, ὁ	(2)	Michael
Μνάσων, ωνος, ὁ	(1)	Mnason
Μολόχ, ὁ	(1)	Moloch
Μωϋσῆς, έως, ὁ	(80)	Moses
Ναασσών, ὁ	(3)	Nahshon
Ναγγαί, ὁ	(1)	Naggai
Ναθάμ, ὁ	(1)	Nathan
Ναθαναήλ, ὁ	(6)	Nathanael
Ναιμάν, ὁ	(1)	Naaman
Ναούμ, ὁ	(1)	Nahum
Νάρκισσος, ου, ὁ	(1)	Narcissus
Ναχώρ, ὁ	(1)	Nahor
Νεφθαλίμ, ὁ	(3)	Naphtali
Νηρεύς, εως, ὁ	(1)	Nereus
Νηρί, ὁ	(1)	Neri
Νίγερ, ὁ	(1)	Niger
Νικάνωρ, ορος, ὁ	(1)	Nicanor
Νικόδημος, ου, ὁ	(5)	Nicodemus
Νικόλαος, ου, ὁ	(1)	Nicolaus
Νύμφα, ας, ἡ	(1)	Nympha
Νῶε, ὁ	(8)	Noah
Ὀζίας, ου, ὁ	(2)	Uzziah
Ὀλυμπᾶς, ᾶ, ὁ	(1)	Olympas
Ὀνήσιμος, ου, ὁ	(2)	Onesimus
Ὀνησίφορος, ου, ὁ	(2)	Onesiphorus
Οὐρβανός, οῦ, ὁ	(1)	Urbanus
Οὐρίας, ου, ὁ	(1)	Uriah
Παρμενᾶς, ᾶ, ὁ	(1)	Parmenas

Πατροβᾶς, ᾶ, ὁ	(1)	Patrobas
Παῦλος, ου, ὁ	(158)	Paul
Περσίς, ίδος, ἡ	(1)	Persis
Πέτρος, ου, ὁ	(156)	Peter
Πιλᾶτος, ου, ὁ	(55)	Pilate
Πόντιος, ου, ὁ	(3)	Pontius
Πόπλιος, ου, ὁ	(2)	Publius
Πόρκιος, ου, ὁ	(1)	Porcius
Πούδης, εντος, ὁ	(1)	Pudens
Πρίσκα, ης, ἡ	(3)	Prisca
Πρίσκιλλα, ης, ἡ	(3)	Priscilla
Πρόχορος, ου, ὁ	(1)	Prochorus
Πύρρος, ου, ὁ	(1)	Pyrrhus
Ῥαάβ, ἡ	(2)	Rahab
Ῥαγαύ, ὁ	(1)	Reu
Ῥαιφάν, ὁ	(1)	Rephan
Ῥαχάβ, ἡ	(1)	Rahab
Ῥαχήλ, ἡ	(1)	Rachel
Ῥεβέκκα, ας, ἡ	(1)	Rebecca
Ῥησά, ὁ	(1)	Rhesa
Ῥοβοάμ, ὁ	(2)	Rehoboam
Ῥόδη, ης, ἡ	(1)	Rhoda
Ῥουβήν, ὁ	(1)	Reuben
Ῥούθ, ἡ	(1)	Ruth
Ῥοῦφος, ου, ὁ	(2)	Rufus
Σαβαώθ	(2)	Sabaoth, Almighty
Σαδώκ, ὁ	(2)	Zadok
Σαλά, ὁ	(2)	Shelah
Σαλαθιήλ, ὁ	(3)	Shealtiel, Salathiel
Σαλμών, ὁ	(2)	Salmon
Σαλώμη, ης, ἡ	(2)	Salome
Σαμουήλ, ὁ	(3)	Samuel
Σαμψών, ὁ	(1)	Samson
Σαούλ, ὁ	(9)	Saul
Σάπφιρα, ης, ἡ	(1)	Sapphira
Σάρρα, ας, ἡ	(4)	Sarah
Σατανᾶς, ᾶ, ὁ	(36)	Satan, the Adversary
Σαῦλος, ου, ὁ	(15)	Saul
Σεκοῦνδος, ου, ὁ	(1)	Secundus
Σεμεΐν, ὁ	(1)	Semein
Σέργιος, ου, ὁ	(1)	Sergius
Σερούχ, ὁ	(1)	Serug
Σήθ, ἡ	(1)	Seth
Σήμ, ὁ	(1)	Shem
Σιλᾶς, ᾶ, ὁ	(12)	Silas
Σιλουανός, οῦ, ὁ	(4)	Silvanus
Σίμων, ωνος, ὁ	(75)	Simon
Σκευᾶς, ᾶ, ὁ	(1)	Sceva
Σολομών, ῶνος, ὁ	(12)	Solomon
Σουσάννα, ης, ἡ	(1)	Susanna

Στάχυς, υος, ὁ	(1)	Stachys
Στεφανᾶς, ᾶ, ὁ	(3)	Stephanas
Στέφανος, ου, ὁ	(7)	Stephen
Συμεών, ὁ	(7)	Symeon, Simeon
Συντύχη, ης, ἡ	(1)	Syntyche
Σώπατρος, ου, ὁ	(1)	Sopater
Σωσθένης, ους, ὁ	(2)	Sosthenes
Σωσίπατρος, ου, ὁ	(1)	Sosipater
Ταβιθά, ἡ	(2)	Tabitha
Τέρτιος, ου, ὁ	(1)	Tertius

Τέρτυλλος, ου, ὁ	(2)	Tertullus
Τιβέριος, ου, ὁ	(1)	Tiberius
Τιμαῖος, ου, ὁ	(1)	Timaeus
Τιμόθεος, ου, ὁ	(24)	Timothy
Τίμων, ωνος, ὁ	(1)	Timon
Τίτιος, ου, ὁ	(1)	Titius
Τίτος, ου, ὁ	(13)	Titus
Τρόφιμος, ου, ὁ	(3)	Trophimus
Τρύφαινα, ης, ἡ	(1)	Tryphaena
Τρυφῶσα, ης, ἡ	(1)	Tryphosa

Τύραννος, ου, ὁ	(1)	Tyrannus
Τυχικός, οῦ, ὁ	(5)	Tychicus
Ὑμέναιος, ου, ὁ	(2)	Hymenaeus
Φάλεκ, ὁ	(1)	Peleg
Φανουήλ, ὁ	(1)	Phanuel
Φαραώ, ὁ	(5)	Pharaoh
Φάρες, ὁ	(3)	Perez
Φῆλιξ, ικος, ὁ	(9)	Felix
Φῆστος, ου, ὁ	(13)	Festus
Φιλήμων, ονος, ὁ	(1)	Philemon

Φίλητος, ου, ὁ	(1)	Philetus
Φίλιππος, ου, ὁ	(36)	Philip
Φιλόλογος, ου, ὁ	(1)	Philologus
Φλέγων, οντος, ὁ	(1)	Phlegon
Φοίβη, ης, ἡ	(1)	Phoebe
Φορτουνᾶτος, ου, ὁ	(1)	Fortunatus
Φύγελος, ου, ὁ	(1)	Phygelus
Χλόη, ης, ἡ	(1)	Chloe
Χουζᾶς, ᾶ, ὁ	(1)	Chuza
Χριστός, οῦ, ὁ	(529)	Christ, Anointed One, Messiah

Ὡσηέ, ὁ	(1)	Hosea

Names of Places

Ἀβιληνή, ῆς, ἡ	(1)	Abilene
Ἀδραμυττηνός, ή, όν	(1)	of Adramyttium
Ἀδρίας, ου, ὁ	(1)	Adriatic Sea
Ἄζωτος, ου, ἡ	(1)	Azotus
Ἀθῆναι, ῶν, αἱ	(4)	Athens

Ἀθηναῖος, α, ον	(2)	Athenian; an Athenian (subst.)
Αἰγύπτιος, α, ον	(5)	Egyptian; an Egyptian (subst.)
Αἴγυπτος, ου, ἡ	(25)	Egypt
Αἰθίοψ, οπος, ὁ	(2)	an Ethiopian
Αἰνών, ἡ	(1)	Aenon
Ἀκελδαμάχ	(1)	Akeldama, Field of Blood
Ἀλεξανδρεύς, έως, ὁ	(2)	an Alexandrian
Ἀλεξανδρῖνος, η, ον	(2)	Alexandrian
Ἀμφίπολις, εως, ἡ	(1)	Amphipolis
Ἀντιόχεια, ας, ἡ	(18)	Antioch
Ἀντιοχεύς, έως, ὁ	(1)	an Antiochean
Ἀντιπατρίς, ίδος, ἡ	(1)	Antipatris
Ἀπολλωνία, ας, ἡ	(1)	Apollonia
Ἀππίου Φόρον	(1)	Appii Forum, Forum of Appius
Ἀραβία, ας, ἡ	(2)	Arabia
Ἄραψ, βος, ὁ	(1)	an Arab
Ἄρειος Πάγος, ὁ	(2)	Areopagus, Hill of Ares
Ἀρεοπαγίτης, ου, ὁ	(1)	an Areopagite
Ἀριμαθαία, ας, ἡ	(4)	Arimathea
Ἀρμαγεδών	(1)	Armageddon
Ἀσία, ας, ἡ	(18)	Asia
Ἀσιανός, οῦ, ὁ	(1)	an Asian
Ἄσσος, ου, ἡ	(2)	Assos
Ἀττάλεια, ας, ἡ	(1)	Attalia
Ἀχαΐα, ας, ἡ	(10)	Achaia
Βαβυλών, ῶνος, ἡ	(12)	Babylon
Βέροια, ας, ἡ	(2)	Beroea
Βεροιαῖος, α, ον	(1)	Beroean; a Beroean (subst. in NT)
Βηθανία, ας, ἡ	(12)	Bethany
Βηθζαθά, ἡ	(1)	Bethzatha
Βηθλέεμ, ἡ	(8)	Bethlehem
Βηθσαϊδά, ἡ	(7)	Bethsaida
Βηθφαγή, ἡ	(3)	Bethphage
Βιθυνία, ας, ἡ	(2)	Bithynia
Γαββαθᾶ	(1)	Gabbatha
Γαδαρηνός, ή, όν	(1)	Gadarene; a Gadarene (subst. in NT)
Γάζα, ης, ἡ	(1)	Gaza
Γαλάτης, ου, ὁ	(1)	a Galatian
Γαλατία, ας, ἡ	(4)	Galatia
Γαλατικός, ή, όν	(2)	Galatian
Γαλιλαία, ας, ἡ	(61)	Galilee
Γαλιλαῖος, α, ον	(11)	Galilean; a Galilean (subst.)
Γεθσημανί	(2)	Gethsemane
Γεννησαρέτ, ἡ	(3)	Gennesaret
Γερασηνός, ή, όν	(3)	Gerasene; a Gerasene (subst.)
Γολγοθᾶ, ἡ	(3)	Golgotha
Γόμορρα, ων, τά; ας, ἡ	(4)	Gomorrah
Δαλμανουθά, ἡ	(1)	Dalmanutha
Δαλματία, ας, ἡ	(1)	Dalmatia
Δαμασκηνός, ή, όν	(1)	Damascene; a Damascene (subst. in NT)

Δαμασκός, οῦ, ἡ	(15)	Damascus
Δεκάπολις, εως, ἡ	(3)	Decapolis
Δερβαῖος, α, ον	(1)	Derbean; a Derbean (subst. in NT)
Δέρβη, ης, ἡ	(3)	Derbe
Ἐλαμίτης, ου, ὁ	(1)	an Elamite
Ἑλλάς, άδος, ἡ	(1)	Greece
Ἕλλην, ηνος, ὁ	(25)	a Greek, Gentile, pagan, heathen
Ἑλληνικός, ή, όν	(1)	Greek
Ἑλληνίς, ίδος, ἡ	(2)	Greek or Gentile woman
Ἑλληνιστής, οῦ, ὁ	(3)	a Hellenist, Greek-speaking Jew
Ἑλληνιστί	(2)	in the Greek language
Ἐμμαοῦς, ἡ	(1)	Emmaus
Εὐρακύλων, ωνος, ὁ	(1)	Euraquilo, northeast wind
Εὐφράτης, ου, ὁ	(2)	Euphrates
Ἐφέσιος, α, ον	(5)	Ephesian; an Ephesian (subst.)
Ἔφεσος, ου, ἡ	(16)	Ephesus
Ἐφραίμ, ὁ	(1)	Ephraim
Θεσσαλονικεύς, έως, ὁ	(4)	a Thessalonian
Θεσσαλονίκη, ης, ἡ	(5)	Thessalonica
Θυάτειρα, ων, τά	(4)	Thyatira
Ἰδουμαία, ας, ἡ	(1)	Idumea
Ἱεράπολις, εως, ἡ	(1)	Hierapolis
Ἱεριχώ, ἡ	(7)	Jericho
Ἱεροσόλυμα, τά, ἡ	(62)	Jerusalem
Ἱεροσολυμίτης, ου, ὁ	(2)	inhabitant of Jerusalem
Ἱερουσαλήμ, ἡ	(77)	Jerusalem
Ἰκόνιον, ου, τό	(6)	Iconium
Ἰλλυρικόν, οῦ, τό	(1)	Illyricum
Ἰόππη, ης, ἡ	(10)	Joppa
Ἰορδάνης, ου, ὁ	(15)	Jordan
Ἰουδαία, ας, ἡ	(43)	Judea
Ἰουδαϊκός, ή, όν	(1)	Jewish
Ἰουδαϊκῶς	(1)	in a Jewish manner, like a Jew
Ἰουδαῖος, α, ον	(195)	Jewish; a Jew, Jewess (subst.)
Ἰσραήλ, ὁ	(68)	Israel
Ἰσραηλίτης, ου, ὁ	(9)	an Israelite
Ἰταλία, ας, ἡ	(4)	Italy
Ἰταλικός, ή, όν	(1)	Italian
Ἰτουραῖος, α, ον	(1)	Ituraea
Καισάρεια, ας, ἡ	(17)	Caesarea
Καλοὶ Λιμένες, οἱ	(1)	Fair Havens
Κανά, ἡ	(4)	Cana
Καναναῖος, ου, ὁ	(2)	a Cananaean, enthusiast, zealot
Καππαδοκία, ας, ἡ	(2)	Cappadocia
Καῦδα	(1)	Cauda
Καφαρναούμ, ἡ	(16)	Capernaum
Κεγχρεαί, ῶν, αἱ	(2)	Cenchreae
Κεδρών, ὁ	(1)	Kidron
Κιλικία, ας, ἡ	(8)	Cilicia
Κνίδος, ου, ἡ	(1)	Cnidus

Κολοσσαί, ῶν, αἱ	(1)	Colossae
Κορίνθιος, ου, ὁ	(2)	a Corinthian
Κόρινθος, ου, ἡ	(6)	Corinth
Κρής, ητός, ὁ	(2)	a Cretan
Κρήτη, ης, ἡ	(5)	Crete
Κύπριος, ου, ὁ	(3)	a Cyprian
Κύπρος, ου, ἡ	(5)	Cyprus
Κυρηναῖος, ου, ὁ	(6)	a Cyrenian
Κυρήνη, ης, ἡ	(1)	Cyrene
Κώς, Κῶ, ἡ	(1)	Cos
Λαοδίκεια, ας, ἡ	(6)	Laodicea
Λαοδικεύς, έως, ὁ	(1)	a Laodicean
Λασαία, ας, ἡ	(1)	Lasea
Λιβύη, ης, ἡ	(1)	Libya
Λύδδα, ας, ἡ	(3)	Lydda
Λυκαονία, ας, ἡ	(1)	Lycaonia
Λυκαονιστί	(1)	in the Lycaonian language
Λυκία, ας, ἡ	(1)	Lycia
Λύστρα, ἡ, τά	(6)	Lystra
Μαγαδάν, ἡ	(1)	Magadan
Μαδιάμ, ὁ	(1)	Midian
Μακεδονία, ας, ἡ	(22)	Macedonia
Μακεδών, όνος, ὁ	(5)	a Macedonian
Μελίτη, ης, ἡ	(1)	Malta
Μεσοποταμία, ας, ἡ	(2)	Mesopotamia
Μῆδος, ου, ὁ	(1)	a Mede
Μίλητος, ου, ἡ	(3)	Miletus
Μιτυλήνη, ης, ἡ	(1)	Mitylene
Μύρα, ων, τά	(1)	Myra
Μυσία, ας, ἡ	(2)	Mysia
Ναζαρά, ἡ	(2)	Nazareth
Ναζαρέθ, ἡ	(6)	Nazareth
Ναζαρέτ, ἡ	(4)	Nazareth
Ναζαρηνός, ή, όν	(6)	Nazarene; inhabitant of Nazareth, a Nazarene (subst.)
Ναζωραῖος, ου, ὁ	(13)	inhabitant of Nazareth, a Nazarene
Ναΐν, ἡ	(1)	Nain
Νέα Πόλις, ἡ	(1)	Neapolis
Νικόπολις, εως, ἡ	(1)	Nicopolis
Νινευίτης, ου, ὁ	(3)	a Ninevite
Παμφυλία, ας, ἡ	(5)	Pamphylia
Πάρθοι, ων, οἱ	(1)	Parthians
Πάταρα, ων, τά	(1)	Patara
Πάτμος, ου, ὁ	(1)	Patmos
Πάφος, ου, ἡ	(2)	Paphos
Πέργαμος, ου, ἡ	(2)	Pergamum
Πέργη, ης, ἡ	(3)	Perga
Πισιδία, ας, ἡ	(1)	Pisidia
Πισίδιος, α, ον	(1)	Pisidian
Ποντικός, ή, όν	(1)	Pontian; a Pontian (subst. in NT)
Πόντος, ου, ὁ	(2)	Pontus

Ποτίολοι, ων, οἱ	(1)	Puteoli
Πτολεμαΐς, ίδος, ἡ	(1)	Ptolemais
Ῥαμά, ἡ	(1)	Rama
Ῥήγιον, ου, τό	(1)	Rhegium
Ῥόδος, ου, ἡ	(1)	Rhodes
Ῥωμαῖος, α, ον	(12)	Roman; Roman person or citizen (subst. in NT)
Ῥωμαϊστί	(1)	in the Latin language
Ῥώμη, ης, ἡ	(8)	Rome
Σαλαμίς, ῖνος, ἡ	(1)	Salamis
Σαλείμ, τό	(1)	Salim
Σαλήμ, ἡ	(2)	Salem
Σαλμώνη, ης, ἡ	(1)	Salmone
Σαμάρεια, ας, ἡ	(11)	Samaria
Σαμαρίτης, ου, ὁ	(9)	a Samaritan
Σαμαρῖτις, ιδος, ἡ	(2)	a Samaritan woman
Σαμοθράκη, ης, ἡ	(1)	Samothrace
Σάμος, ου, ἡ	(1)	Samos
Σάρδεις, εων, αἱ	(3)	Sardis
Σάρεπτα, ων, τά	(1)	Zarephath
Σαρών, ῶνος, ὁ	(1)	Sharon
Σελεύκεια, ας, ἡ	(1)	Seleucia
Σιδών, ῶνος, ἡ	(9)	Sidon
Σιδώνιος, α, ον	(2)	Sidonian; country around Sidon, a Sidonian (subst.)
Σιλωάμ, ὁ	(3)	Siloam
Σινά	(4)	Sinai
Σιών, ἡ	(7)	Zion
Σκύθης, ου, ὁ	(1)	a Scythian
Σμύρνα, ης, ἡ	(2)	Smyrna
Σόδομα, ων, τά	(9)	Sodom
Σπανία, ας, ἡ	(2)	Spain
Συράκουσαι, ῶν, αἱ	(1)	Syracuse
Συρία, ας, ἡ	(8)	Syria
Σύρος, ου, ὁ	(1)	a Syrian
Συροφοινίκισσα, ης, ἡ	(1)	a Syrophoenician woman
Σύρτις, εως, ἡ	(1)	the Syrtis
Συχάρ, ἡ	(1)	Sychor
Συχέμ, ἡ	(2)	Shechem
Ταρσεύς, έως, ὁ	(2)	person from Tarsus
Ταρσός, οῦ, ἡ	(3)	Tarsus
Τιβεριάς, άδος, ἡ	(3)	Tiberias
Τραχωνῖτις, ιδος, ἡ	(1)	Trachonitis
Τρεῖς Ταβέρναι	(1)	Three Taverns
Τρῳάς, άδος, ἡ	(6)	Troas
Τύριος, ου, ὁ	(1)	a Tyrian
Τύρος, ου, ἡ	(11)	Tyre
Φιλαδέλφεια, ας, ἡ	(2)	Philadelphia
Φιλιππήσιος, ου, ὁ	(1)	a Philippian
Φίλιπποι, ων, οἱ	(4)	Philippi
Φοινίκη, ης, ἡ	(3)	Phoenicia
Φοῖνιξ, ικος, ὁ	(1)	Phoenix

Φρυγία, ας, ἡ	(3)	Phrygia
Χαλδαῖος, ου, ὁ	(1)	a Chaldean
Χανάαν, ἡ	(2)	Canaan
Χαναναῖος, α, ον	(1)	Canaanite
Χαρράν, ἡ	(2)	Haran
Χίος, ου, ἡ	(1)	Chios
Χοραζίν, ἡ	(2)	Chorazin

Other Proper Words

Ἀσιάρχης, ου, ὁ	(1)	Asiarch
Ἑβραῖος, ου, ὁ	(4)	a Hebrew
Ἑβραΐς, ίδος, ἡ	(3)	Hebrew language (Aramaic)
Ἑβραϊστί	(7)	in Hebrew or Aramaic
Ἐπικούρειος, ου, ὁ	(1)	Epicurean
Ἡρῳδιανοί, ῶν, οἱ	(3)	Herodians
Ἰουδαϊσμός, οῦ, ὁ	(2)	Judaism
Λευίτης, ου, ὁ	(3)	Levite
Λευιτικός, ή, όν	(1)	Levitical
Λιβερτῖνος, ου, ὁ	(1)	Freedman
Νικολαΐτης, ου, ὁ	(2)	Nicolaitan
Σαδδουκαῖος, ου, ὁ	(14)	Sadducee
Στοϊκός, ή, όν	(1)	Stoic
Φαρισαῖος, ου, ὁ	(98)	Pharisee
Χερούβ, τό	(1)	cherub, winged creature
Χριστιανός, οῦ, ὁ	(3)	a Christian

Section Five

Other Lists

The vocabulary of the Greek NT exhibits several phenomena of nonstandard word construction, accentuation, and word order. These are represented in this section by the lists of crasis and elision forms, proclitics, enclitics, and postpositives.

Crasis is the combination of two words into one, the first usually involving the word καί, e.g., κἀγώ, which is a blending of καὶ ἐγώ. The crasis form has a diacritical mark that looks like a smooth breathing mark in the middle of the word, indicating the point of crasis.

Elision is the shortening of a word for purposes of creating easier pronunciation or euphony. The change, which involves the removal of a vowel at the end of certain words, is made to avoid such a vowel coming immediately before a word that begins with a vowel. Elision is indicated by an apostrophe. Further changes sometimes occur to the resultant final consonants if the following word has a rough breathing mark. The preposition κατά becomes κατ' before a word that starts with a vowel having a smooth breathing mark and καθ' if the vowel has a rough breathing mark. Elision before vowels is not entirely consistent in the NT.

A proclitic is an unaccented word that depends on the following word for its accent. Proclitics are accented only when they occur directly before an enclitic.

On the other hand, an enclitic, which is generally unaccented, depends on the preceding word for its accent. The word before an enclitic may undergo a change in its accent and may even have two accents. Enclitics are accented when they begin a clause, directly follow another enclitic, or receive emphasis. An enclitic with two syllables may also retain its accent, depending on the accent of the preceding word. The enclitic forms of εἰμί are accented when they directly follow certain words.

Postpositives are words that logically begin a clause or phrase but actually occur in the second or a later position. Most are enclitics or conjunctions, e.g., δέ. A few are improper prepositions, e.g., χάριν.

This section also contains lists of regular propositions with their elision forms and other words that function as prepositions. Most of the latter, called improper prepositions, are actually adverbs.

Also included is a list of all the cardinal and ordinal number words and related forms that appear in the NT.

The first and second declensions contain predominantly feminine and masculine words respectively. However, many words of the first declension are masculine, and some words of the second declension are feminine. Furthermore, some other words of the second declension are both masculine and feminine. One word of the second declension is both masculine and neuter, three words of the third declension are both masculine and feminine, and one word of the third declension exhibits all three genders. All these declensional gender anomalies are included in the lists of this section.

The final group of lists contains the non-Greek words used in the NT, as well as the Greek words that derived directly from another language. These include words from Aramaic, Coptic, Hebrew, Latin, and Persian. One list has the few words that are given the general classification of Semitic.

In addition to these non-Greek words, the NT uses two words of unknown origin, κολλούριον and κράβαττος. Greek words that derived from original loanwords are usually not included, e.g., the derivatives of βύσσινος. The lists contain some words that are disputed, e.g., ζιζάνιον, νάρδος, and ῥακά. Some words that came into Greek very early are not included, e.g., συκάμινος and χιτών.

Crasis Forms

κἀγώ	(76)	= καὶ ἐγώ (and I, but I, I also, I myself, I in turn)
κἀκεῖ	(10)	= καὶ ἐκεῖ (and there, there also)
κἀκεῖθεν	(10)	= καὶ ἐκεῖθεν (and from there, and then)
κἀκεῖνα	(4)	= καὶ ἐκεῖνα (neut. nom./acc. pl. of ἐκεῖνος)
κἀκεῖνοι	(7)	= καὶ ἐκεῖνοι (masc. nom. pl. of ἐκεῖνος)
κἀκεῖνον	(3)	= καὶ ἐκεῖνον (masc. acc. sing. of ἐκεῖνος)
κἀκεῖνος, η, ο	(7)	= καὶ ἐκεῖνος (and that one or he, that one or he also)
κἀκείνους	(1)	= καὶ ἐκείνους (masc. acc. pl. of ἐκεῖνος)
κἀμέ	(3)	= καὶ ἐμέ (acc. of ἐγώ)
κἀμοί	(5)	= καὶ ἐμοί (dat. of ἐγώ)
κἄν	(17)	= καὶ ἐάν (and if, even if, if only)
τοὐναντίον	(3)	= τὸ ἐναντίον (on the other hand, rather)
τοὔνομα	(1)	= τὸ ὄνομα (named, by name)

Elision Forms

ἀλλ'	(= ἀλλά before vowels)
ἀν'	(= ἀνά before vowels)
ἀνθ'	(= ἀντί before rough breathing)
ἀντ'	(= ἀντί before smooth breathing)
ἀπ'	(= ἀπό before smooth breathing)
ἀφ'	(= ἀπό before rough breathing)
δ'	(= δέ before vowels)
δι'	(= διά before vowels)
ἐπ'	(= ἐπί before smooth breathing)
ἐφ'	(= ἐπί before rough breathing)
καθ'	(= κατά before rough breathing)
κατ'	(= κατά before smooth breathing)
μεθ'	(= μετά before rough breathing)
μετ'	(= μετά before smooth breathing)
οὐδ'	(= οὐδέ before vowels)
παρ'	(= παρά before vowels)
τοῦτ'	(= τοῦτο before ἐστί[ν])

ὑπ᾽   (= ὑπό before smooth breathing)
ὑφ᾽   (= ὑπό before rough breathing)

Proclitics

αἱ		(fem. nom. pl. of ὁ)
εἰ	(503)	if, that, whether
εἰς	(1768)	into, in, toward, to, among, near, on, for, against, as, at
ἐκ	(914)	from, out of, away from, by, of, because of
ἐν	(2752)	in, on, at, near, to, by, before, among, with, within, when
ἐξ		(= ἐκ before vowels)
ἡ		(fem. nom. sing. of ὁ)
ὁ, ἡ, τό	(19870)	the
οἱ		(masc. nom. pl. of ὁ)
οὐ	(1606)	not (gener. used w. ind. verbs and pos. answer questions)
οὐκ		(= οὐ before smooth breathing)
οὐχ		(= οὐ before rough breathing)
ὡς	(504)	as, like, because, when, while, in order that, that, about

Enclitics

γέ	(25)	indeed, even, at least
εἰμί	(2460)	I am, exist, occur, mean, live, stay, am present
εἰσί(ν)		(pres. ind. act. 3 pl. of εἰμί)
ἐσμέν		(pres. ind. act. 1 pl. of εἰμί)
ἐστέ		(pres. ind. act. 2 pl. of εἰμί)
ἐστί(ν)		(pres. ind. act. 3 sing. of εἰμί)
μέ		(acc. of ἐγώ)
μοί		(dat. of ἐγώ)
μοῦ		(gen. of ἐγώ)
ποτέ	(29)	at some time, once, formerly, ever
πού	(4)	somewhere, about, approximately
πώς	(15)	somehow, in some way, perhaps
σέ		(acc. of σύ)
σοί		(dat. of σύ)
σοῦ		(gen. of σύ)
τέ	(215)	and, and so, so
τί		(neut. nom./acc. sing. of τίς)
τίνα		(masc./fem. acc. sing. and neut. nom./acc. pl. of τίς)
τινάς		(masc./fem. acc. pl. of τίς)
τινές		(masc./fem. nom. pl. of τίς)
τίνι		(masc./fem./neut. dat. sing. of τίς)
τίνος		(masc./fem./neut. gen. sing. of τίς)
τινῶν		(masc./fem./neut. gen. pl. of τίς)
τίς, τί	(525)	someone, anyone, something, anything; some, any (adj.)
τισί(ν)		(masc./fem./neut. dat. pl. of τίς)
φημί	(66)	I say, affirm, mean
φησί(ν)		(pres. ind. act. 3 sing. of φημί)

Postpositives

ἄν	(167)	conditional part., part. of contingency (untrans.)
ἄρα	(49)	so, then, consequently, perhaps
γάρ	(1041)	for, so, then
γέ	(25)	indeed, even, at least
δέ	(2792)	but, and, rather, now, then, so
εἰμί	(2460)	I am, exist, occur, mean, live, stay, am present
εἰσί(ν)		(pres. ind. act. 3 pl. of εἰμί)
ἕνεκα	(26)	because of, on account of, for the sake of (impr. prep.)
ἐσμέν		(pres. ind. act. 1 pl. of εἰμί)
ἐστέ		(pres. ind. act. 2 pl. of εἰμί)
ἐστί(ν)		(pres. ind. act. 3 sing. of εἰμί)
μέ		(acc. of ἐγώ)
μέν	(179)	on the one hand, to be sure, indeed
μενοῦνγε	(3)	rather, on the contrary, indeed
μέντοι	(8)	really, actually, though, to be sure, indeed, but
μοί		(dat. of ἐγώ)
μοῦ		(gen. of ἐγώ)
οὖν	(499)	so, therefore, consequently, accordingly, then
ποτέ	(29)	at some time, once, formerly, ever
πού	(4)	somewhere, about, approximately
πώς	(15)	somehow, in some way, perhaps
σέ		(acc. of σύ)
σοί		(dat. of σύ)
σοῦ		(gen. of σύ)
τέ	(215)	and, and so, so
τί		(neut. nom./acc. sing. of τίς)
τίνα		(masc./fem. acc. sing. and neut. nom./acc. pl. of τίς)
τινάς		(masc./fem. acc. pl. of τίς)
τινές		(masc./fem. nom. pl. of τίς)
τίνι		(masc./fem./neut. dat. sing. of τίς)
τίνος		(masc./fem./neut. gen. sing. of τίς)
τινῶν		(masc./fem./neut. gen. pl. of τίς)
τίς, τί	(525)	someone, anyone, something, anything; some, any (adj.)
τισί(ν)		(masc./fem./neut. dat. pl. of τίς)
τοιγαροῦν	(2)	then, therefore, for that very reason
τοίνυν	(3)	hence, so, indeed, therefore, then
φημί	(66)	I say, affirm, mean
φησί(ν)		(pres. ind. act. 3 sing. of φημί)
χάριν	(9)	for the sake of, because of, by reason of (impr. prep.)
χωρίς	(41)	separately; without, apart from, besides (impr. prep.)

Prepositions

ἀμφί	(0)	about, around, on both sides (only in compounds in NT)
ἀνά	(13)	upwards, up, each; among, between (w. μέσον)
ἀν'		(= ἀνά before vowels)
ἀντί	(22)	instead of, for, in behalf of
ἀντ'		(= ἀντί before smooth breathing)
ἀνθ'		(= ἀντί before rough breathing)

ἀπό	(646)	from, away from, because of, with, for, of, by
ἀπ'		(= ἀπό before smooth breathing)
ἀφ'		(= ἀπό before rough breathing)
διά	(667)	through, during, with, at, by (gen.); because of (acc.)
δι'		(= διά before vowels)
εἰς	(1768)	into, in, toward, to, among, near, on, for, against, as, at
ἐκ	(914)	from, out of, away from, by, of, because of
ἐξ		(= ἐκ before vowels)
ἐν	(2752)	in, on, at, near, to, by, before, among, with, within, when
ἐπί	(890)	on, over, when (gen.); on, at, in (dat.); on, to, for (acc.)
ἐπ'		(= ἐπί before smooth breathing)
ἐφ'		(= ἐπί before rough breathing)
κατά	(473)	down from, against (gen.); along, to, according to (acc.)
κατ'		(= κατά before smooth breathing)
καθ'		(= κατά before rough breathing)
μετά	(469)	with, among, against (gen.); after, behind (acc.)
μετ'		(= μετά before smooth breathing)
μεθ'		(= μετά before rough breathing)
παρά	(194)	from (gen); beside, with (dat.); at, on, more than (acc.)
παρ'		(= παρά before vowels)
περί	(333)	about, concerning, for (gen.); around, near (acc.)
πρό	(47)	before, in front of, at, above
πρός	(700)	for (gen.); at (dat.); to, for, against, with, at, by (acc.)
σύν	(128)	with, together with, accompany, besides
ὑπέρ	(150)	for, in behalf of, about (gen.); above, beyond, than (acc.)
ὑπό	(220)	by, at the hands of (gen.); under, below (acc.)
ὑπ'		(= ὑπό before smooth breathing)
ὑφ'		(= ὑπό before rough breathing)

Improper Prepositions

ἅμα	(10)	at the same time, together; together with (impr. prep.)
ἄνευ	(3)	without (impr. prep.)
ἄντικρυς	(1)	opposite (impr. prep. in NT)
ἀντιπέρα	(1)	opposite (impr. prep. in NT)
ἀπέναντι	(5)	opposite, against, contrary to (impr. prep. in NT)
ἄτερ	(2)	without, apart from (impr. prep.)
ἄχρι	(49)	until, to, as far as (impr. prep.); until (conj.)
ἐγγύς	(31)	near, close to; near, close to (impr. prep.)
ἐκτός	(8)	outside; outside, except (impr. prep.)
ἔμπροσθεν	(48)	in front, ahead; in front of, before (impr. prep.)
ἔναντι	(2)	opposite, before, in the judgment of (impr. prep. in NT)
ἐναντίον	(8)	before, in the judgment of (impr. prep. in NT)
ἕνεκα	(26)	because of, on account of, for the sake of (impr. prep.)
ἐντός	(2)	inside, within, among (impr. prep. in NT)
ἐνώπιον	(94)	before, in the presence of, in the opinion of (impr. prep.)
ἔξω	(63)	outside, outer, out; outside, out of (impr. prep.)
ἔξωθεν	(13)	from the outside, outside; (from) outside (impr. prep)
ἐπάνω	(19)	above, over, more than; over, above, on (impr. prep.)
ἐπέκεινα	(1)	farther on, beyond (impr. prep. in NT)
ἔσω	(9)	in, inside; inside, into (impr. prep.); insider (subst.)
ἐσώτερος, α, ον	(2)	inner; inside (adv. as impr. prep.)

ἕως	(146)	until, while (conj.); until, as far as (impr. prep.)
κατέναντι	(8)	opposite; opposite, in the sight of, before (impr. prep.)
κατενώπιον	(3)	before, in the presence of (impr. prep. in NT)
κυκλόθεν	(3)	all around, from all sides; around (impr. prep.)
κύκλῳ	(8)	around, all around; nearby (adj.); around (impr. prep.)
μέσος, η, ον	(58)	middle; the middle (subst.); in the middle of (impr. prep.)
μεταξύ	(9)	meanwhile, after; between, in the middle (impr. prep.)
μέχρι	(17)	until (conj.); until, as far as, to the point of (impr. prep.)
ὄπισθεν	(7)	from behind, on the back; behind, after (impr. prep.)
ὀπίσω	(35)	behind, back; behind, after (impr. prep.)
ὀψέ	(3)	late in the day, in the evening; after (impr. prep.)
παραπλήσιος, α, ον	(1)	similar; nearly, almost (neut. as impr. prep. in NT)
παρεκτός	(3)	besides, outside; apart from, except for (impr. prep.)
πέραν	(23)	on the other side; other side (subst.); across (impr. prep.)
πλήν	(31)	but, yet, only, however (conj.); except (impr. prep.)
πλησίον	(17)	neighbor, fellow (subst.); near, close to (impr. prep.)
ὑπεράνω	(3)	(high) above (impr. prep. in NT)
ὑπερέκεινα	(1)	beyond (impr. prep. in NT)
ὑπερεκπερισσοῦ	(3)	beyond all measure; infinitely more than (impr. prep.)
ὑποκάτω	(11)	under, below (impr. prep. in NT)
χάριν	(9)	for the sake of, because of, by reason of (impr. prep.)
χωρίς	(41)	separately; without, apart from, besides (impr. prep.)

Number Words

ἥμισυς, εια, υ	(5)	half; one half (neut. subst.)
εἷς, μία, ἕν	(344)	one, a, single, someone, anyone
πρῶτος, η, ον	(155)	first, earlier, foremost; first, before (neut. as adv.)
δύο	(135)	two
δεύτερος, α, ον	(43)	second, secondly; second time (subst.)
διπλοῦς, ῆ, οῦν	(4)	double, two-fold
δίς	(6)	twice
τρεῖς, τρία	(68)	three
τρίς	(12)	three times
τρίτος, η, ον	(56)	third; third part, a third (neut. subst.); third time (adv.)
τέσσαρες, α	(41)	four
τέταρτος, η, ον	(10)	fourth
τετραπλοῦς, ῆ, οῦν	(1)	four times (as much), fourfold
πέντε	(38)	five
πέμπτος, η, ον	(4)	fifth
πεντάκις	(1)	five times
ἕξ	(13)	six
ἕκτος, η, ον	(14)	sixth
ἑπτά	(88)	seven
ἕβδομος, η, ον	(9)	seventh; the seventh (subst.)
ἑπτάκις	(4)	seven times
ὀκτώ	(8)	eight
ὄγδοος, η, ον	(5)	eighth
ἐννέα	(5)	nine
ἔνατος, η, ον	(10)	ninth
δέκα	(25)	ten
δέκατος, η, ον	(7)	tenth; tithe, tenth part, tithe (subst.)

ἔνδεκα	(6)	eleven
ἑνδέκατος, η, ον	(3)	eleventh
δώδεκα	(75)	twelve
δωδέκατος, η, ον	(1)	twelfth
δεκατέσσαρες	(5)	fourteen
τεσσαρεσκαιδέκατος, η, ον	(2)	fourteenth
δεκαπέντε	(3)	fifteen
πεντεκαιδέκατος, η, ον	(1)	fifteenth
δεκαοκτώ	(2)	eighteen
εἴκοσι	(11)	twenty
τριάκοντα	(11)	thirty
τεσσεράκοντα	(22)	forty
πεντήκοντα	(7)	fifty
ἑξήκοντα	(9)	sixty
ἑβδομήκοντα	(5)	seventy
ἑβδομηκοντάκις	(1)	seventy times
ὀγδοήκοντα	(2)	eighty
ἐνενήκοντα	(4)	ninety
ἑκατόν	(17)	one hundred
ἑκατονταπλασίων, ον	(3)	a hundred fold
διακόσιοι, αι, α	(8)	two hundred
τριακόσιοι, αι, α	(2)	three hundred
τετρακόσιοι, αι, α	(4)	four hundred
πεντακόσιοι, αι, α	(2)	five hundred
ἑξακόσιοι, αι, α	(2)	six hundred
χίλιοι, αι, α	(11)	thousand
δισχίλιοι, αι, α	(1)	two thousand
τρισχίλιοι, αι, α	(1)	three thousand
τετρακισχίλιοι, αι, α	(5)	four thousand
πεντακισχίλιοι, αι, α	(6)	five thousand
ἑπτακισχίλιοι, αι, α	(1)	seven thousand
μύριοι, αι, α	(2)	ten thousand
μυριάς, άδος, ἡ	(8)	myriad, ten thousand
δισμυριάς, άδος, ἡ	(1)	double myriad, twenty thousand

Masculine Nouns of the First Declension

ᾅδης, ου, ὁ	(10)	Hades, underworld, death
ἀκροατής, οῦ, ὁ	(4)	hearer
ἀνδραποδιστής, οῦ, ὁ	(1)	slave dealer, kidnapper
ἀρσενοκοίτης, ου, ὁ	(2)	male homosexual
ἀρχιτελώνης, ου, ὁ	(1)	chief tax collector
αὐλητής, οῦ, ὁ	(?)	flute player
αὐτόπτης, ου, ὁ	(1)	eyewitness
βαπτιστής, οῦ, ὁ	(12)	Baptist, Baptizer
βασανιστής, οῦ, ὁ	(1)	torturer, jailer
βιαστής, οῦ, ὁ	(1)	violent person
βορρᾶς, ᾶ, ὁ	(2)	north
βουλευτής, οῦ, ὁ	(2)	council member
γνώστης, ου, ὁ	(1)	one acquainted, expert
γογγυστής, οῦ, ὁ	(1)	grumbler
δανιστής, οῦ, ὁ	(1)	money lender, creditor

δεσμώτης, ου, ὁ	(2)	prisoner
δεσπότης, ου, ὁ	(10)	lord, master, owner
διερμηνευτής, οῦ, ὁ	(1)	interpreter, translator
δικαστής, οῦ, ὁ	(2)	judge
διώκτης, ου, ὁ	(1)	persecutor
δότης, ου, ὁ	(1)	giver
δυνάστης, ου, ὁ	(3)	ruler, sovereign, court official
ἐθνάρχης, ου, ὁ	(1)	ethnarch, governor, official
εἰδωλολάτρης, ου, ὁ	(7)	idolater
ἑκατοντάρχης, ου, ὁ	(20)	centurion, captain, officer
ἐμπαίκτης, ου, ὁ	(2)	mocker
ἐξορκιστής, οῦ, ὁ	(1)	exorcist
ἐπενδύτης, ου, ὁ	(1)	outer garment, coat
ἐπιθυμητής, οῦ, ὁ	(1)	one who desires
ἐπιστάτης, ου, ὁ	(7)	master
ἐπόπτης, ου, ὁ	(1)	eyewitness
ἐργάτης, ου, ὁ	(16)	workman, laborer, doer
εὐαγγελιστής, οῦ, ὁ	(3)	one who proclaims good news, evangelist
εὐεργέτης, ου, ὁ	(1)	benefactor
ἐφευρετής, οῦ, ὁ	(1)	inventor, contriver
ζηλωτής, οῦ, ὁ	(8)	zealot, enthusiast, fanatic
θεριστής, οῦ, ὁ	(2)	reaper, harvester
ἰδιώτης, ου, ὁ	(5)	layman, amateur, untrained, ungifted
καθηγητής, οῦ, ὁ	(2)	teacher
καρδιογνώστης, ου, ὁ	(2)	knower of hearts
καταφρονητής, οῦ, ὁ	(1)	despiser, scoffer
κερματιστής, οῦ, ὁ	(1)	money-changer
κλέπτης, ου, ὁ	(16)	thief
κοδράντης, ου, ὁ	(2)	quadrans, penny (Roman copper coin)
κολλυβιστής, οῦ, ὁ	(3)	money-changer
κριτής, οῦ, ὁ	(19)	judge
κτίστης, ου, ὁ	(1)	Creator
κυβερνήτης, ου, ὁ	(2)	captain, steersman, pilot
λῃστής, οῦ, ὁ	(15)	bandit, robber, revolutionary, insurrectionist
λυτρωτής, οῦ, ὁ	(1)	redeemer
μαθητής, οῦ, ὁ	(261)	disciple, learner, pupil, follower
μαργαρίτης, ου, ὁ	(9)	pearl
μεριστής, οῦ, ὁ	(1)	divider, arbitrator
μεσίτης, ου, ὁ	(6)	mediator, arbitrator, intermediary
μετρητής, οῦ, ὁ	(1)	measure (liquid)
μητρολῴας, ου, ὁ	(1)	one who murders one's mother
μιμητής, οῦ, ὁ	(6)	imitator
μισθαποδότης, ου, ὁ	(1)	rewarder
ναύτης, ου, ὁ	(3)	sailor
νεανίας, ου, ὁ	(3)	youth, young man, servant
νομοθέτης, ου, ὁ	(1)	lawgiver
ξέστης, ου, ὁ	(1)	pitcher, jug
οἰκέτης, ου, ὁ	(4)	house slave, domestic, servant
οἰκοδεσπότης, ου, ὁ	(12)	master of the house
οἰνοπότης, ου, ὁ	(2)	wine drinker, drunkard
ὀλοθρευτής, οῦ, ὁ	(1)	destroyer (angel)
ὀφειλέτης, ου, ὁ	(7)	debtor, one who is obligated or guilty, sinner
παιδευτής, οῦ, ὁ	(2)	instructor, teacher, one who disciplines
παραβάτης, ου, ὁ	(5)	transgressor, sinner

πατριάρχης, ου, ὁ	(4)	patriarch, father of a nation
πατρολῴας, ου, ὁ	(1)	one who murders one's father
πλανήτης, ου, ὁ	(1)	wanderer, roamer; wandering (adj.)
πλεονέκτης, ου, ὁ	(4)	greedy or covetous person
πλήκτης, ου, ὁ	(2)	combative person, bully
ποιητής, οῦ, ὁ	(6)	doer, maker
πολιτάρχης, ου, ὁ	(2)	civic magistrate, politarch
πολίτης, ου, ὁ	(4)	citizen, fellow citizen
πρεσβύτης, ου, ὁ	(3)	old or elderly man
προδότης, ου, ὁ	(3)	traitor, betrayer
προσαίτης, ου, ὁ	(2)	beggar
προσκυνητής, οῦ, ὁ	(1)	worshiper
προσωπολήμπτης, ου, ὁ	(1)	one who shows partiality
προφήτης, ου, ὁ	(144)	prophet; prophets (pl. as a division of scripture)
πρωτοστάτης, ου, ὁ	(1)	leader, ringleader
σαλπιστής, οῦ, ὁ	(1)	trumpeter
στασιαστής, οῦ, ὁ	(1)	rebel, revolutionary, insurrectionist
στρατιώτης, ου, ὁ	(26)	soldier
συζητητής, οῦ, ὁ	(1)	disputant, debater
συμμαθητής, οῦ, ὁ	(1)	fellow pupil, fellow disciple
συμμιμητής, οῦ, ὁ	(1)	fellow imitator
συμπολίτης, ου, ὁ	(1)	fellow citizen
συμφυλέτης, ου, ὁ	(1)	fellow countryman, compatriot
συνηλικιώτης, ου, ὁ	(1)	contemporary person
συστρατιώτης, ου, ὁ	(2)	fellow soldier, comrade in arms
τελειωτής, οῦ, ὁ	(1)	perfecter
τελώνης, ου, ὁ	(21)	tax collector, revenue officer
τετραάρχης, ου, ὁ	(4)	tetrarch
τεχνίτης, ου, ὁ	(4)	craftsman, artisan, designer
τολμητής, οῦ, ὁ	(1)	bold, audacious person
τραπεζίτης, ου, ὁ	(1)	money changer, banker
ὑβριστής, οῦ, ὁ	(2)	violent or insolent person
ὑπηρέτης, ου, ὁ	(20)	servant, helper, assistant
ὑποκριτής, οῦ, ὁ	(17)	hypocrite, pretender
φαιλόνης, ου, ὁ	(1)	cloak
φρεναπάτης, ου, ὁ	(1)	deceiver, one who misleads
χάρτης, ου, ὁ	(1)	sheet of papyrus, papyrus roll
χρεοφειλέτης, ου, ὁ	(2)	debtor
ψευδοπροφήτης, ου, ὁ	(11)	false prophet
ψεύστης, ου, ὁ	(10)	liar
ψιθυριστής, οῦ, ὁ	(1)	whisperer, gossiper

Feminine Nouns of the Second Declension

ἄβυσσος, ου, ἡ	(9)	abyss, depth, underworld
ἀγριέλαιος, ου, ἡ	(2)	wild olive tree
ἀμέθυστος, ου, ἡ	(1)	amethyst
ἄμμος, ου, ἡ	(5)	sand, seashore
ἄμπελος, ου, ἡ	(9)	vine, grapevine
βάσανος, ου, ἡ	(3)	torture, torment, severe pain
βίβλος, ου, ἡ	(10)	book, sacred book, record
βύσσος, ου, ἡ	(1)	fine linen

διάλεκτος, ου, ἡ	(6)	language
διέξοδος, ου, ἡ	(1)	outlet (used of streets)
δοκός, οῦ, ἡ	(6)	beam of wood
εἴσοδος, ου, ἡ	(5)	entrance, access, coming
ἔξοδος, ου, ἡ	(3)	the Exodus, departure, death
καλλιέλαιος, ου, ἡ	(1)	cultivated olive tree
κάμινος, ου, ἡ	(4)	oven, furnace
κιβωτός, οῦ, ἡ	(6)	ark (ship), ark (covenant box)
ληνός, οῦ, ἡ	(5)	wine press
νάρδος, ου, ἡ	(2)	nard, oil of nard
νῆσος, ου, ἡ	(9)	island
νόσος, ου, ἡ	(11)	disease, illness
ὁδός, οῦ, ἡ	(101)	way, road, journey, way of life, conduct, Way, teaching
πάροδος, ου, ἡ	(1)	passage, passing by
πυρετός, οῦ, ἡ	(6)	fever
ῥάβδος, ου, ἡ	(12)	rod, staff, stick, scepter
σάπφιρος, ου, ἡ	(1)	sapphire
σορός, οῦ, ἡ	(1)	coffin, bier
σποδός, οῦ, ἡ	(3)	ashes
στάμνος, ου, ἡ	(1)	jar
συκάμινος, ου, ἡ	(1)	mulberry tree
τρίβος, ου, ἡ	(3)	path
τροφός, οῦ, ἡ	(1)	nurse
ὕαλος, ου, ἡ	(2)	glass, crystal
ψῆφος, ου, ἡ	(3)	pebble, vote, stone

Masculine and Feminine Nouns of the Second Declension

ἄρκος, ου, ὁ, ἡ	(1)	bear
ἄψινθος, ου, ὁ, ἡ	(2)	wormwood
βάτος, ου, ὁ, ἡ	(5)	thorn bush
βήρυλλος, ου, ὁ, ἡ	(1)	beryl
γείτων, ονος, ὁ, ἡ	(4)	neighbor
διάκονος, ου, ὁ, ἡ	(29)	servant, helper, deacon (masc.); helper, deaconess (fem.)
θεός, οῦ, ὁ, ἡ	(1317)	God, god; goddess (fem.)
θυρωρός, οῦ, ὁ, ἡ	(4)	doorkeeper
κάμηλος, ου, ὁ, ἡ	(6)	camel
κοινωνός, οῦ, ὁ, ἡ	(10)	companion, partner, sharer
λιμός, οῦ, ὁ, ἡ	(12)	hunger, famine
ὄνος, ου, ὁ, ἡ	(5)	donkey
παῖς, παιδός, ὁ, ἡ	(24)	boy, son, child, servant, slave; girl, child (fem.)
παρθένος, ου, ἡ, ὁ	(15)	virgin (female or male)
ὕσσωπος, ου, ὁ, ἡ	(2)	hyssop

Masculine and Neuter Noun of the Second Declension

πλοῦτος, ου, ὁ, τό	(22)	wealth, riches, abundance

Masculine and Feminine Nouns of the Third Declension

βοῦς, βοός, ὁ, ἡ	(8)	head of cattle, ox, cow
νῆστις, ιδος, ὁ, ἡ	(2)	not eating, hungry
ὄρνις, ιθος, ὁ, ἡ	(2)	bird, cock or hen

Masculine, Feminine, and Neuter Noun of the Third Declension

δεῖνα, ὁ, ἡ, τό	(1)	so-and-so, a certain person, somebody (masc. in NT)

Aramaic Words

αββα	(3)	father, abba
γέεννα, ης, ἡ	(12)	Gehenna, valley of the sons of Hinnom, hell
ελωι	(2)	my God!
εφφαθα	(1)	be opened
κορβανᾶς, ᾶ, ὁ	(1)	temple treasury
κουμ	(1)	stand up
λεμα	(2)	why?
μαμωνᾶς, ᾶ, ὁ	(4)	wealth, property
μαρανα θα	(1)	our Lord, come!
πάσχα, τό	(29)	Passover, Passover meal, Passover lamb
ραββουνι	(2)	my master, my teacher
ῥακά	(1)	fool, empty head
σαβαχθανι	(2)	you have forsaken me
σίκερα, τό	(1)	strong drink
ταλιθα	(1)	girl, little girl
ὡσαννά	(6)	hosanna

Coptic Word

βάϊον, ου, τό	(1)	palm branch

Hebrew Words

ἁλληλουϊά	(4)	hallelujah, praise Yahweh
ἀμήν	(129)	amen, so let it be, truly
ἀρραβών, ῶνος, ὁ	(3)	first installment, deposit, down payment
βάτος, ου, ὁ	(1)	bath (Hebrew liquid measure)
βύσσος, ου, ἡ	(1)	fine linen
ηλι	(2)	my God
κορβᾶν	(1)	corban, gift
κόρος, ου, ὁ	(1)	cor, kor (Hebrew dry measure)
μάννα, τό	(4)	manna
ῥαββί	(15)	rabbi, master, teacher
σάββατον, ου, τό	(68)	Sabbath (seventh day of the week)
σάπφιρος, ου, ἡ	(1)	sapphire

ὕσσωπος, ου, ὁ, ἡ   (2)   hyssop

Latin Words

ἀσσάριον, ου, τό	(2)	assarion (Roman copper coin)
δηνάριον, ου, τό	(16)	denarius (Roman silver coin)
κεντυρίων, ωνος, ὁ	(3)	centurion
κῆνσος, ου, ὁ	(4)	tax
κοδράντης, ου, ὁ	(2)	quadrans, penny (Roman copper coin)
κολωνία, ας, ἡ	(1)	colony
κουστωδία, ας, ἡ	(3)	guard
λεγιών, ῶνος, ἡ	(4)	legion
λέντιον, ου, τό	(2)	towel
λίτρα, ας, ἡ	(2)	Roman pound
μεμβράνα, ης, ἡ	(1)	parchment
μίλιον, ου, τό	(1)	mile (Roman)
μόδιος, ίου, ὁ	(3)	basket, container (for measuring grain)
ξέστης, ου, ὁ	(1)	pitcher, jug
πραιτώριον, ου, τό	(8)	praetorium, imperial guard
ῥέδη, ης, ἡ	(1)	(four-wheeled) carriage
σικάριος, ου, ὁ	(1)	sicarius, assassin, terrorist
σιμικίνθιον, ου, τό	(1)	apron
σουδάριον, ου, τό	(4)	face cloth, handkerchief
σπεκουλάτωρ, ορος, ὁ	(1)	courier, executioner
τίτλος, ου, ὁ	(2)	inscription, notice
φαιλόνης, ου, ὁ	(1)	cloak
φραγέλλιον, ου, τό	(1)	whip, lash
φραγελλόω	(2)	I flog, scourge, beat with a whip
χῶρος, ου, ὁ	(1)	northwest

Persian Words

ἀγγαρεύω	(3)	I press into service, force, compel
γάζα, ης, ἡ	(1)	treasury, treasure
γαζοφυλάκιον, ου, τό	(5)	treasure room, treasury, contribution box
παράδεισος, ου, ὁ	(3)	paradise

Semitic Words

ζιζάνιον, ου, τό	(8)	darnel, weed
κιννάμωμον, ου, τό	(1)	cinnamon
κύμινον, ου, τό	(1)	cummin
μνᾶ, μνᾶς, ἡ	(9)	mina (Greek monetary unit)
νάρδος, ου, ἡ	(2)	nard, oil of nard
σεμίδαλις, εως, ἡ	(1)	fine wheat flour

Index of Words